Rhetoric in Popular Culture

Fifth Edition

For Elizabeth Duncan Windler
and Katharine Duncan Brummett

Rhetoric in Popular Culture

Fifth Edition

Barry Brummett
The University of Texas at Austin

Los Angeles | London | New Delhi
Singapore | Washington DC | Melbourne

FOR INFORMATION:

SAGE Publications, Inc.
2455 Teller Road
Thousand Oaks, California 91320
E-mail: order@sagepub.com

SAGE Publications Ltd.
1 Oliver's Yard
55 City Road
London, EC1Y 1SP
United Kingdom

SAGE Publications India Pvt. Ltd.
B 1/I 1 Mohan Cooperative Industrial Area
Mathura Road, New Delhi 110 044
India

SAGE Publications Asia-Pacific Pte. Ltd.
3 Church Street
#10-04 Samsung Hub
Singapore 049483

Printed in the United States of America

Library of Congress Cataloging-in-Publication Data

Names: Brummett, Barry, 1951- author.

Title: Rhetoric in popular culture / Barry Brummett, The University of Texas at Austin, USA.

Description: Fifth edition. | Thousand Oaks, California : Sage, [2017] | Includes bibliographical references and index.

Identifiers: LCCN 2017021693 | ISBN 9781506315638 (pbk. : alk. paper)

Subjects: LCSH: Rhetoric. | Popular culture. | Rhetorical criticism.

Classification: LCC P301 .B67 2017 | DDC 808—dc23 LC record available at https://lccn.loc.gov/2017021693

Acquisitions Editors:
  Karen Omer, Terri Accomazzo
Editorial Assistants:
  Sarah Dillard, Erik Helton
Content Development Editor:
  Jennifer Jovin
Production Editor: Tracy Buyan
Copy Editor: Rachel Keith
Typesetter: Hurix Systems Pvt. Ltd.
Proofreader: Theresa Kay
Indexer: Maria Sosnowski
Cover Designer: Candice Harman
Marketing Manager: Jenna Retana

This book is printed on acid-free paper.

SUSTAINABLE FORESTRY INITIATIVE
Certified Chain of Custody
Promoting Sustainable Forestry
www.sfiprogram.org
SFI-01268

SFI label applies to text stock

17 18 19 20 21 10 9 8 7 6 5 4 3 2 1

BRIEF CONTENTS

DETAILED CONTENTS

PART 2 · APPLICATION   217

6. Paradoxes of Personalization: Race Relations in Milwaukee 218

PREFACE

Welcome to the fifth edition of *Rhetoric in Popular Culture*. Here I want to address instructors who may be considering adopting this volume for their courses. This book brings together two vital scholarly traditions: rhetorical criticism and critical studies. There are several good textbooks, either well established or new, that cover rhetorical criticism from a fairly traditional perspective. They focus on the analysis of discursive, reason-giving texts, such as public speeches. On the other hand, there are several good books of critical studies available. Some of the newer textbooks of critical studies are much improved over their predecessors in covering techniques of Marxist, feminist, and other critical approaches in ways that are accessible to students. But there is a need to apply the growing and cutting-edge methods of critical studies to the study of rhetoric and to link these new approaches to the rhetorical tradition. That is what this book tries to do. It sees critical studies as rhetorical criticism, and it argues that the most exciting form of rhetorical criticism today is found in methods of critical studies.

There have been some changes between the fourth and fifth editions, primarily in Part II, the Application sections. Of course, the entire book has been updated in regard to examples, which must be done in every edition. Regrettably, even these updates may be a little out of date by the time you see the fifth edition! Beyond that, these major changes deserve note: Applications in Chapters 7, 9, and 10 are changed from the fourth edition. Chapter 7, *Notes from a Texas Gun Show*, uses a culture-centered approach to study an aspect of gun culture in America: the gun show. In doing so, it also studies a central aspect of Texas—especially rural and working-class—culture. Because the gun show is such a visual experience, the chapter also uses a visual rhetoric approach.

Chapter 9, *Jumping Scale in Steampunk: One Gear Makes You Larger, One Duct Makes You Small*, studies the recently popular cultural and aesthetic movement of steampunk. It primarily uses the media-centered and visual rhetoric approach, also giving some attention to dramatistic/narrative criticism. Both Chapters 7 and 9 are reprints of studies published by the author elsewhere and are used in this book for the first time. Chapter 10, *The Bad Resurrection in American Life and Culture*, is a newly written essay published here for the first time. It uses the dramatistic/narrative approach and media-centered approach to trace the recurrence of a narrative theme in a homology that crosses many experiences and texts.

I have consistently refused to "dumb down" this textbook despite the occasional appeal to do so, having faith in the ability of today's undergraduates to wrestle with challenging ideas that are (I hope) clearly explained. I also have faith in you, the instructor, to carry them through it. Theory and method need not be scary, and they must not be something distinct from the lives of ordinary people. If our students do not understand challenging ideas, then we have failed them—or possibly they have failed themselves by not trying. I have also not attempted to exhaust any topic I have brought up, but instead I have faith that my teaching colleagues will ably fill in whatever gaps I have left. Any textbook should be the beginning of a discussion, not the whole of the discussion, and surely not the end of it.

ACKNOWLEDGMENTS

I am grateful to the editorial staff of SAGE, especially Karen Omer, who has been instrumental in bringing this fifth edition of *Rhetoric in Popular Culture* to fruition. I also want to thank Rachel Keith for a masterful, helpful, and thoroughly professional job of editing the manuscript.

Reviewers for all five editions of the book have been more than helpful, and I want to acknowledge their assistance here.

In preparation of the **fifth** edition:

    Cori Brewster (Eastern Oregon University)

    Ken Corbit (University of Alabama)

    Mindy Fenske (University of South Carolina)

    Leslie Hahner (Baylor University)

    Matthew Meier (West Chester University)

    Matthew Petrunia (Fashion Institute of Technology, SUNY)

    Patrick Richey Middle (Tennessee State University)

    Anne Marie Todd (San Jose State University)

In preparation of the **fourth** edition:

    Mary Elizabeth Bezanson (University of Minnesota, Morris)

    Michael L. Butterworth (Bowling Green State University)

    Peter Ehrenhaus (Pacific Lutheran University)

    Trischa Goodnow (Oregon State University)

    Christine Horton (University of Waterloo)

    Kristy Maddux (University of Maryland)

    Peter Marston (California State University, Northridge)

    Theresa Russell-Loretz (Millersville University)

In preparation of the **third** edition:

    Donathan L. Brown (Texas A&M University)

    John Fritch (University of Northern Iowa)

    Yvonne Prather (Austin Peay State University)

    Roy Schwartzman (University of North Carolina at Greensboro)

    Joseph Zompetti (Illinois State University)

In preparation of the **second** edition:

Paul E. Bender (Ohio Northern University)

Christy Friend (University of South Carolina)

Donna M. Kowal (The College at Brockport, SUNY)

Michael W. McFarland (Stetson University)

Ronald B. Scott (Miami University)

Deanna D. Sellnow (University of Kentucky)

Donna Strickland (University of Missouri–Columbia)

In preparation of the **first** edition:

Bruce Herzberg (Bentley University)

Tom Hollihan (University of Southern California)

James F. Klummp (University of Maryland, College Park)

John Llewellyn (Wake Forest University)

Skip Rutledge (Point Loma Nazarene University)

Helen Sterk (Calvin College)

Barbie Zelizer (University of Pennsylvania)

I am grateful to all who have profited from reading previous editions of this book and used it in their own work. Finding references to this textbook elsewhere is always a nice reminder that one's efforts are making a difference. I am grateful to the many students who have used this book in my classes and in classes taught by others. Taking the principles explained here, they have taught me through their insights about popular culture. I hear often that readers of this book see the world differently; I could ask for no higher thanks or praise.

THEORY

In Part I, we learn about the history of the practice and theory of persuasion, which is called *rhetoric*. We will see why the rhetoric of popular culture is so important today.

1

RHETORIC AND THE
RHETORICAL TRADITION

Do you know what your blue jeans are doing to you? What kind of person do you turn into when you go to shopping malls? After a day of hard knocks at work or at school, do you use social media to "fight back" or to escape?

If you are like most people, you are probably not in the habit of asking yourself questions like these. We may think of our clothing, favorite kinds of music, favorite websites, or preferred forms of recreation as ways to express ourselves or to have fun. But we may think it a little far-fetched to believe that there is any serious meaning in TMZ, or Jimmy Fallon, or that our personalities and values are involved in checking out this spring's new swimsuits.

Although most of us realize that clickbait ads or political commercials are designed to influence us, it may not be clear to us how the regular programming outside and between the advertisements has the same function. A lot of us may feel that we wear our hair in certain styles for aesthetic reasons—because we like it that way. We may not often think that those styles also express certain positions in important social and political battles. We may feel that we consistently shop at Abercrombie & Fitch rather than at Old Navy only for reasons of taste; we might be surprised to hear that our choice has the potential to turn us into different kinds of people.

This book asks you to think about how everyday actions, objects, and experiences affect you and others. You are probably already familiar with some of the more serious and newsworthy consequences of music, television, or films, such as the association of country-and-western music with conservative patriotism or the criticism of certain hip-hop musicians for their use of particular words and images. This book will expand on things you may already be aware of, leading you to see how *all* of popular culture works to influence the public. You will have noticed that the book has two key terms: *rhetoric* and *popular culture*. In this chapter, we will focus on *rhetoric* and its traditions.

There are some well-developed theories available for studying how messages influence people. These are theories of *rhetoric*, or persuasion. The word *rhetoric* has many meanings, and we will examine many of them in this chapter. Many people understand rhetoric to mean the ways in which words influence people. "That's just a lot of rhetoric," we say, and by that we mean that it's just so many empty but persuasive words. In this book, we will work from a different, expanded understanding of what rhetoric means: *the ways in which signs influence people.*

Let's pause for some quick definitions. The term *signs* refers to the countless meaningful items, images, and so on that surround us; it will be explained more fully in the next chapter, beginning on page 41). A sign is something that induces you to think about something other than itself—and everything has that potential. The clearest example of a sign is a word; you read the word *hat*, and you think of something other than— something beyond—the marks on the page that are that sign. There can be nonverbal signs also, such as the American flag, which encourages you to think of something—the United States—beyond the colored cloth that is the sign. There will be more on signs in the next chapter. In this chapter, we will also use the word *text*, which will also be discussed in more detail in the next chapter, but for now we can think of a text as a message, as a collection of verbal and/or nonverbal signs that create meaning. This book is a text composed of many signs in the form of words and pictures.

Has popular culture always been an important site of rhetoric? Not necessarily. To understand why the conjunction of rhetoric and popular culture is especially potent today, we first need to understand the history of rhetorical theory. We will begin with the ancient Greeks and how they thought about and practiced rhetoric. As we move toward our own time, we will come to realize why the focus of rhetorical practice has shifted from great oratory in public speaking in ancient times to music, film, television, and the Internet in our time. The historical review in this chapter will help you to understand why, if you want to influence people far and wide today, you start a viral video rather than preparing a public speech.

Rhetoric has been around for centuries, both as something that people do and as a subject that people study. One thing that is particularly striking about rhetoric is the many different ways in which it has been defined, today and throughout history. In this chapter, we will explore some of those definitions. Students of rhetoric are often frustrated with so many definitions for a term; "Why can't people just settle on a meaning?" they sometimes ask. To anticipate that frustration, let us first think about what a *definition* is and about defining as a strategy.

DEFINITIONS AND THE MANAGEMENT OF POWER

You may have taken courses that were a little frustrating because you learned that key terms have been defined by different authors and in different eras in different ways. You may also have noticed that the ways in which you define certain terms can make a lot of difference; in fact, definitions can be a way of securing power. If you define *culture*, for instance, as high culture—as ballet and oil paintings and symphony orchestras—that lets you reduce to second-class status everything else, including baseball games, cheeseburgers, reggae music, and hip-hop. This arrangement makes a pretty nice setup for the wealthy and talented people who already control "high culture," doesn't it? If "culture" is something that people think of as generally a good thing, then being able to define some things and not others as "culture" is a source of power.

If you study history, you find that certain terms have been defined in many different ways. Throughout history there have been varying definitions of what it means to be human. Some societies defined humanity by way of race; such a definition empowered people of one race to enslave whole groups of people who did not look like them on the theory that they were not really enslaving humans. In the twentieth century, Adolf Hitler and the Nazis in Germany attempted to define humanity along ethnic lines, portraying German Aryans as the only authentic humans. Through that definition, the Nazis denied that Jews, Gypsies, and others were fully human. Women have been defined in different ways throughout history, generally in ways that were disempowering (as incomplete or imperfect copies of men, as inferior versions of humanity, as essentially assistants or helpers for men, and so forth).

There are many terms that can have different definitions, such as terms used in describing families or sexual orientation. But there are also many terms that do not have varying definitions. There are not widely different definitions for *carrots*, *cats*, *dogs*, *umbrellas*, or *walking*, for instance. What is the difference? What makes one term have lots of different definitions while other terms seem relatively straightforward? Some words have little to do with power; you will find that these terms do not get defined in very many ways. When power and influence are at stake, the words in which power and influence (or disempowerment) are expressed or embodied will come to have lots of definitions. Settling the definition of *carrots* will not affect who has control over others, who has freedom to do as they will, who will have to accommodate others, and so forth.

EXERCISE 1.1

The following exercise, which you can do on your own or in class with the instructions of your teacher, will help you understand what is at stake in the general strategies of definition.

One of the most important ways in which people are defined is in terms of race. Consider these questions:

1. What are the major terms for human races?
2. Are there any disagreements over what to call certain racial groups? Is there lack of agreement over what to call other groups?

3. What does it mean that certain racial groups seem to be called by only one term, with little struggle over what to call them?
4. Do different terms of races imply different definitions of people? If so, what does that have to do with power? Why are those terms struggled over? For example, in the last sixty years, one group of people has "officially" been called Negroes, Blacks, Afro-Americans, and African-Americans (and other, "unofficial" terms). Why so many terms? What does each term have to do with empowerment and disempowerment?

People struggle over power; therefore, they struggle over the words that express power. We may take it as a general rule that terms that have several different definitions—definitions that are controversial or argued over—are usually terms about important dimensions of human life. Such terms will have something to do with how power is created, shared, or denied. To control words is to control the world.

We have seen how there are disagreements and struggles for power over how the word *culture* is defined. Now we will see that an even greater disagreement exists over how to define *rhetoric*. Struggles over how to define rhetoric run through history. It seems, therefore, that there must be some connection between rhetoric and power. This connection was clear from the very beginning of thinking about rhetoric in Western civilization. We are about to take a detour of some length through ancient Greece. The reason for this is that the ways we—both the general public and rhetorical scholars— think about and define rhetoric are grounded in the ways the ancient Greeks thought about rhetoric. When we do rhetoric differently today, we do it differently from Greek practices. The Greek legacy to us includes ideas about the relationship between power and rhetoric as well as about the ways in which popular culture is related to both. Let us see what the Greeks thought rhetoric was all about.

THE RHETORICAL TRADITION: ANCIENT GREECE

Rhetoric has been studied for centuries throughout the world, although, in this country, we are most influenced by Western traditions of rhetoric that originated in the Mediterranean world. Western civilization has historically thought that the formal study

Hutton Archive/Stringer/Hutton Archive/Getty Images

of rhetoric began in about the sixth and fifth centuries B.C.E. in the ancient city-states of Greece and their colonies. To understand what rhetoric meant to these people, how they practiced it, and what they studied, we will make a quick (and therefore somewhat simplified) survey of their history.

The Rise of the City-States: How Democracy Grew Up with Rhetoric

Greece used to be a considerably more fertile, prosperous, and even more populous land than it is now; some scholars think poor farming and land use techniques eroded the soil. At any rate, at one time the Greek land supported a large population that was organized largely around city-states—relatively small political entities, each anchored in a capital city such as Sparta, Athens, or Mycenae. In the sixth and fifth centuries B.C.E., several important developments took place. The Greek city-states had joined together to subdue their common enemy to the east, Persia, and thus they enjoyed a period of relative peace and safety from outside dangers. Many of these city-states were on or near the sea, and they developed navies and advanced techniques of navigation. Many of them became great trading powers and began to prosper economically as a result. As is so often the case, trade brought with it new ideas about science, government, philosophy, and technology, especially from Asia and Africa. Another important development was political; many, though not all, of the city-states developed strong democratic forms of government.

A democracy requires that people govern themselves, and to the extent that people are self-governing, they must talk about common problems and devise procedures for shared decision-making. When new ideas are coming quickly into a place, the people will want to talk about them, weigh them to determine their usefulness for themselves, and debate their applications. Peace gives people the freedom and leisure to participate fully in public discussions. And as economic prosperity grows, the consequences of public discussions also grow; what was decided in a prosperous city-state could have an effect on half the Mediterranean world. Do you notice the common theme in this paragraph? The ancient Greek world was an especially fertile context for the growth and development of rhetorical communication, particularly public speaking, as an important human activity.

Nowhere was that more true than in Athens, the largest and most prosperous of the city-states. This time period was known as the Golden Age of Athens; under leaders such as Pericles, it prospered and came to dominate many of the other city-states culturally, economically, and militarily. To understand some important assumptions that people make even today about rhetoric, we must understand how rhetoric was practiced in this important city-state.

Rhetoric in Athens

The Athenians had no lawyers, no legislators, and no public relations or advertising professionals. All public decisions were made by an assembly of the citizens of Athens. We often hear of Athens as a perfect example of a democracy. In fact, it was not; only the free, native-born, property-holding, adult males of Athens were counted as citizens. In such a cosmopolitan and rapidly changing population, that number came to only about 15 percent of the total. Still, given a population of about 150,000 for the entire city-state during this period, it made for a sizable group of people who participated in public decisions.

From time to time, these citizens would gather at a place outside the city, and any and all issues of important public business would be raised then. When an issue was raised, it was dealt with through debate and discussion. Because such gatherings required that large groups of people be addressed at once, the discussion took the form of public speaking. That meant that every citizen needed to be able to speak in public at a moment's notice and on any topic that might come up. If you were an olive grower and someone proposed a new law that would regulate olive growing, you had to be able to speak on that issue immediately to protect your livelihood. If you were a young man of the proper age for the military and someone proposed sending an army or navy on some action, you might need to speak on that issue. If you wanted some public works constructed in town, there were no city council representatives to call; you had to stand up yourself and suggest that a bridge or dam be built. If you thought your neighbor was violating the law, there were no police or district attorneys to call; you had to stand up and accuse the rascal yourself. On the other hand, someone might accuse you of some form of wrongdoing, and you would be called upon to defend yourself in an impromptu speech.

In sum, an ability to speak, clearly and forcefully, on any subject that might come up was a vital skill for these Athenian citizens, crucial for their business and personal affairs. Today, nobody would think of starting a business without some training in accounting, business mathematics, administration, business law, and so forth. For many Athenians, the sine qua non—the most essential component—of successful business was public speaking.

Public speaking was also vital for the Athenians' political affairs. Athenians took participation in political discussion to be both a duty and an entertainment. Unlike the situation for most of us today, political decisions would be carried out by those who made them; if you voted to repair the city wall, you had to help with the planning, construction, and financing. Politics also required well-honed public speaking skills.

This need to be able to speak in public created a market for those who could teach such skills. (An analogous need today would be the great demand for training in computer competence, a demand created in just the last few decades around the world.) A class of traveling teachers of public speaking, known as the Sophists, arose to meet this need in ancient Greece. You may be familiar with the term *sophist* or *sophistry*; today, such terms are used to refer to those who argue for the sake of arguing, who devise empty arguments that sound good but are not solid. A sophist is, in this sense, one who is more concerned with winning an argument than with establishing the truth. But the Sophists of ancient Greece would not have defined themselves that way. These definitions of sophistry actually arose from the viewpoint of another philosopher of ancient Greece, Plato. Let us see why.

Plato's Complaints against the Sophists

Two complaints were lodged against the Sophists. The first is that they claimed to have knowledge about public speaking but really did not. It would not be surprising if this complaint was true of some of them. After all, there have been quacks and charlatans in every profession throughout history. In ancient Greece, there were no accrediting agencies that could certify whether a given Sophist was a qualified teacher. So, certainly, some Sophists claimed to be able to teach something they really knew little about, though this was not true of all Sophists.

A second complaint is more substantial and was the primary reason for Plato's objection to the Sophists. This complaint centers on the idea that public speaking is not an art of anything in particular, because a person can speak about everything. If public speaking is not an art of anything in particular, Plato argued, then it ought not to be taught at all; instead, speakers should learn more about the things they spoke about. Certainly, given the way that public decisions were made in ancient Athens, people needed to be able to speak on any subject at a moment's notice. They might have to speak about shipbuilding if Athens was trying to decide whether to construct a navy; about wheat farming if Athens was trying to decide what sort of agricultural laws to have; about rules of evidence under the criminal statutes if an accusation of lawbreaking was made. The problem was, as a person took a course and learned about public speaking, that person did not, through those studies, learn about shipbuilding, agriculture, or law. Instead, a student of public speaking learned about introductions and conclusions, arguments, and verbal embellishments that could be applied to any topic.

Plato objected to this state of affairs because he thought it made more sense to learn the subjects about which you would speak than to learn techniques of speaking itself (Plato discusses this idea in the dialogue called *Gorgias*). Pursuing that logic to its conclusion, Plato argued that because true democracies refer all issues to all the people and because nobody can be an expert on every issue, democracy itself was flawed because it asked people to discuss problems and issues on which they were not experts. Plato instead preferred to refer problems to experts in the appropriate subject rather than to democratic decision-making (see his *Republic*). He feared that democratic gatherings would be too swayed by rhetoric itself, by technique rather than substance. He therefore defined rhetoric as "pandering," as an art of appearances rather than reality (see the *Gorgias*). Only later in his thinking did he allow some room for rhetoric as a tool or servant of those who were already knowledgeable in a subject matter for better instructing their audiences (see Plato's later dialogue, *Phaedrus*).

Thus, at the very birth of thinking about rhetoric, we find disagreements over definitions. And once again we see that the struggle over different definitions has a lot to do with power. For the Sophists, rhetoric was the art of persuasion carried out through public speaking, the art of determining how to speak to popular audiences on the wide range of subjects that might come before them for review and decision. For Plato, rhetoric was an art of fooling people, of flattering them, of getting the public to make decisions based on oratorical technique rather than on knowledge or a grasp of the truth. These definitional disagreements arose precisely because power was at stake: the power to make public decisions about important public business. If the Sophists were correct in their definition, then all citizens should share in the power to speak about important decisions, to influence others, to sway the judgments of others. If Plato's definition was correct, then decisions should be made by a small group of experts in whatever subject came up, and persuasive speaking should not at all be a factor in what was decided.

So, what is rhetoric, really? Bear in mind that any answer this book might give would have its author's own arguments for rhetoric—in other words, its author's own power issues—embedded within it. But the impulse behind asking such a question is understandable; it would indeed be useful to have some "core idea" of what rhetoric is, a basic notion underlying all the definitions rhetoric has accumulated over the centuries. Such a single summing up is probably not possible, but we might return to a general sense of rhetoric that we have already examined. Earlier, we used an extremely broad definition of rhetoric that could underlie at least most of these other definitions: the ways in which signs influence people. A public speech, like an essay or article, consists of lots of signs (words) working together in what we will call a text; rhetoric is, very generally, the ways in which these texts influence people. We will learn more about what a text is and the different forms it can take in the next chapter, but for now, think of it as a message, as an attempt to influence someone. Certainly, the Athenians had to use the public speaking form of communication in their assemblies to influence others. But what were they doing when they used those texts to influence others? What are we doing today when we use signs with rhetorical influence upon other people, or when signs influence us? How that influence is carried out, and ideas about whether that is a good thing or a bad thing to do, will be expressed more clearly in the narrower definitions that different thinkers offer.

Two Legacies We Have Inherited from the Greek Rhetorical Tradition

The ancient Greeks were extremely influential in the development of rhetorical theory. The Sophists and Plato initiated arguments over rhetorical theory, and Plato's pupil Aristotle wrote the most famous work on this subject, the *Rhetoric*, which in one way or another influenced all subsequent rhetorical theory. Many of the assumptions, theories, and practices of ancient Athens have had an extraordinary effect on how people have thought about rhetoric ever since. We need to evaluate what the Greeks taught us, and whether the rhetorical tradition they began is relevant to rhetoric today. Let's examine two important legacies from that rhetorical tradition: (1) Rhetoric is conventionally equated with traditional texts, and (2) Traditional rhetoric is paradoxically linked to power management.

Rhetoric Is Conventionally Equated with Traditional Texts

When the ancient Greeks spoke of rhetoric, they were referring to a particular kind of text. The Greek rhetorical legacy encourages people to assume that only the texts of public speaking had rhetorical functions. In exploring this idea further, it is useful to draw a distinction between rhetoric as a *function* and rhetoric as a certain kind of *manifestation*.

Rhetoric does certain things; it has certain functions. In its broadest sense, rhetoric refers to the ways in which signs influence people, and through that influence, rhetoric makes things happen. When people speak, when they make television advertisements, when they write essays, they are attempting to carry out some function. What that function specifically is, whether it is good or bad, will vary with one's definition. The Sophists would say that the function of rhetoric is to persuade others while participating in a democratic society, while Plato would say that the function of rhetoric is to flatter or mislead people. But the general function—that of influence—remains the same.

On the other hand, whatever rhetoric is doing, whatever functions it is performing, it must take on some physical form that can be seen or heard. The signs that influence people come together as texts in certain forms or manifestations. In ancient Greece, the manifestation that was almost universally called "rhetoric" was public speaking. There are, of course, many different kinds of public speeches. But, for the Greeks, public speeches shared four important characteristics as a form of text. These four characteristics describe what we might call traditional rhetorical texts. The Greek ideal of public speaking called for a traditional text that was (1) *verbal*, (2) *expositional*, (3) *discrete*, and (4) *hierarchical*.

Public speaking is a primarily verbal text: its main tool is language. Certainly, nonverbal dimensions of the experience, such as gestures or vocal expression, are important, but the words in public speaking are of primary concern. When we study the great speeches of the past, for instance, we look primarily at what was said; there is rarely any record of how the speakers moved or used their voice to emphasize certain points, how they dressed or combed their hair for maximum effect.

Public speaking is also a largely expositional text: its main purpose is to argue and explain. Here we will draw on critic Neil Postman's usage of the term *expositional* in 1985. Postman's broad definition refers to the sort of speeches that make several claims, then defend or develop those claims by providing evidence, clarification, examples, and elaboration in carefully organized structures. Such speeches rely on evidence—especially technical, scientific, historical, or other knowledge—to make and defend points. In other words, traditional texts are based on argument, not in the sense of being disputatious but in the sense of advancing and defending propositions. Expositional speaking entails lengthy development. By way of contrast, President Donald Trump took the themes of "change" and "draining the swamp" among several campaign slogans, often without specific explanation of what changes he meant or what he felt he could do. These expressions were not expositional in that the challenge was not developed, explained, or elaborated upon.

Public speaking is also a discrete text. By *discrete*, we mean clearly distinct and separate in time and space, surrounded by clear boundaries. A snail mail letter in an envelope is discrete: it is all contained in one place and usually read at once, at one time. Text messages, although they may respond to previous texts and may prompt new ones, are usually discrete messages: you hear the familiar jingling of your cell phone, you call up that particular text, you read it, you either reply or ignore it, and you are done.

A discrete text is a unified series of signs that are perceived to be separate and distinct from other signs. Elevator music is not usually perceived to be a discrete text, because it blends into other texts. It is heard as its producers mean it to be heard: as a background noise that merges with whatever else you happen to be doing. Traditional speeches are usually perceived as discrete texts. They begin when the speaker begins to speak, and they end as the speaker is finished. The words of a speech form the text for the most part; coughs and clearings of the throat by the speaker are not considered part of the text. Similarly, reactions by the audience—what they said and did in response to the speaker (even during the speech)—are not part of the discrete text that is the speech.

Traditional speeches are especially discrete texts in that they occur in special times and places. You go to a certain place at a certain hour to hear a speech. Speeches are not likely to be found breaking out unexpectedly in your living room. In that sense, traditional speeches are the epitome of discrete texts, texts that are bounded in time and space.

Finally, traditional public speeches are hierarchical texts. By that we mean that a structure of relationships is imposed on the process of using signs, of sending and receiving a message. In traditional public speaking, the structure of relationship calls for one person to speak while many people listen. One person is, therefore, put in a position of advantage over others, at least for the moment. The audience may heckle or shout approval; they may violently disagree; others may stand up to speak in agreement or opposition afterward—but as long as a speech remains a speech (rather than turning into a riot, for instance), the roles of speaker and audience are relatively different. It is very clear in public speaking who is the source of the message. The speech is identified with an individual, and that individual is, during the moment of speaking, put in a relatively privileged position. After all, that individual gets to claim the attention of an audience for the duration of his or her speech. In contrast, think of how often during the day you get to command the attention of thirty, one hundred, or more people all at once.

An example of a nonhierarchical message would be graffiti. Any of us can place a message on a public wall, and any of us may choose to read or not to read it. There is no structure prescribed or imposed for how we are to relate to either writers or readers of graffiti. Another example would be a highly informal, animated discussion among friends: people talk over, around, and through one another, paying little attention to anybody having more status or more of a right to speak.

The Greek legacy tells us, then, that rhetoric occurs in traditional texts (verbal, expositional, discrete, and hierarchical). While the mainstay of Greek rhetoric was public speaking, other kinds of texts (such as newspaper editorials) can also be traditional in form. But rhetoric occurs in many different manifestations. If rhetoric is using signs to influence others, then editorials, letters to the editor, advertisements, and public speeches as well as your lunch, your blue jeans, Beyoncé's latest recording, and so forth, are ways in which that influence is materialized, or made manifest, in the texts found in real life. The Greeks, however, did not share that understanding, nor did later theorists who wrote under their influence. Theorists of rhetoric throughout history have mostly assumed that rhetoric is found in traditional forms and manifestations. In sum, the first Athenian legacy that we have inherited is an assumption that whatever is called *rhetoric* must have most or all of the four characteristics of traditional texts.

Rhetoric Is Paradoxically Linked to Power Management

The second part of the legacy that the Greek rhetorical tradition has given us is a paradox. A paradox is an apparent contradiction. The paradox we inherit from the Greek legacy is that traditional texts both include and exclude people from the management of public business and thus from positions of power. To understand this paradox, we must first clarify the idea of power management, or of managing important public business.

When we manage power, we make use of our ability to control events and meanings. Our ability to manage the decisions we face or that influence us varies with the amount of power we have. Imagine an invalid, unable to rise from a hospital bed. Although largely helpless and subject to the routines of hospital staff, this person will still manage what happens to him or her as well as possible through the means at his or her disposal, such as using the call button or granting and withholding cooperation. At work, others of us might be invited to help manage decisions concerning who gets to take vacations during prime months. Other decisions, however, are managed without our involvement, such as whether to sell the company we work for to a foreign investor. An ability to participate in the management of decisions is empowering. Public business must similarly be managed. To the extent that we are excluded from or included in decisions to pave streets, finance welfare programs, or go to war, we are correspondingly empowered or disempowered.

We often manage power in one more important way. Note that power has been defined as the ability to control both events and meaning. Sometimes, as in the case of our imaginary invalid, the ability to control events may be sharply limited. But a kind of power can be gained by controlling the meanings of what happens; it makes a difference whether the invalid sees his situation as "recovery" or as "hopelessness," for instance. Similarly, the president has the power to send troops at a moment's notice into action in the Korean peninsula, a decision very few might participate in managing, but the press and public have a different kind of power insofar as they manage what the military action means: Is it a noble gesture, an act of self-defense, or the last gasp of imperialism? Given how responsive many public officials are to opinion polls, management of the meaning that results in public opinion can be a form of empowerment.

This second "paradoxical" legacy from the Greek rhetorical tradition can best be understood by considering two aspects of the way in which rhetoric is defined. First, the more favorably rhetoric is defined, the more people it involves in managing public business. This is because rhetoric and democracy fit together naturally. When the public are officially entrusted with managing public business, they make those decisions through arguing about them together. The more decisions are made by involving people in the rhetorical exchange of open discussion, the more democracy occurs. Therefore, if rhetoric is something people are able to do and feel that they should do, and if rhetoric is the way important public business is managed, then rhetoric is a form of communication that distributes power widely.

If, on the other hand, rhetoric is defined unfavorably as something that not everyone should do because not everyone should be persuasive, have a voice, or be influential, then public business will be managed by people who have some special status, some special claim to decision-making other than being persuasive. These people will be the experts—those who are already powerful, the highly born or the specially chosen few.

We have learned that within the Greek rhetorical legacy, a favorable definition of rhetoric enhances the democratic management of society's important business. But, paradoxically, the specific Greek understanding of rhetoric as pertaining to traditional texts—texts that are verbal, expositional, discrete, and hierarchical—is not as democratic as it might be.

There is a reason for this paradox. When people assume that democracy occurs with rhetorical discussions but then go on to define rhetoric as referring only to verbal, expositional, discrete, and hierarchical texts, they are unable to see the democratic participation in public decision-making that can occur through different, nontraditional kinds of texts. In ancient Greece, democracy was officially conducted within the assemblies. But after the assembly, citizens returned to the marketplace and conversed informally there. All the while, women instructed and nurtured children. Slaves and

EXERCISE 1.2

This choice between defining rhetoric (a) in order to democratize power and defining it (b) in order to concentrate power among a few is one that we continue to face today. Let's leap over several centuries and think for a minute about how this choice confronts you. For each decision listed below, think about how you would prefer that the decision be made and by whom.

Decisions	Should this decision be made democratically or by an expert few?	If democratically, who will be involved in the decision?	If by an expert few, who will the experts be?
1. How should city officials organize their office filing system?			
2. Should your state permit construction of a new nuclear power plant?			
3. What should you do about a lump that you have discovered in your body?			
4. Is the president doing a good job?			

foreigners talked among themselves within their own groups. People were, of course, exposed to nonverbal signs of all sorts, and there was surely the ancient Greek version of today's blue jeans that all the younger people wore. But in the thinking and writing about rhetoric at that time, there is no mention at all of these everyday communications. There is no awareness of what is rhetorical about everyday texts, or of how they might also be involved in the management of important public business.

Some classical theorists such as Plato were concerned about the effects of certain kinds of texts—such as music, poetry, or drama—on the public. These kinds of texts may appear to be just the sort of popular culture texts we are studying in this book. But there are actually some important differences. First, the forms of ancient Greek music, poetry, and drama were closer to traditional texts than they would be to today's texts. A Greek drama, for instance, was highly verbal, with frequent expositional passages and not much in the way of the kinds of special effects you find in *Red Dead Redemption*. Second, part of what was traditional about those texts was that they were experienced less in the moment-to-moment flow of everyday life than today's popular culture is. They tended to be presented as special, and thus discrete, moments of high culture, very much under the auspices of established power structures. And, finally, nobody ever thought of calling those entertainments rhetoric.

To refer back to our very general definition of rhetoric, there was no attempt among the ancient Greeks to theorize how any and all signs might have been influencing people. Instead, we find in Greek rhetoric an assumption that the important business of the society would be conducted largely in traditional rhetorical texts. However, many everyday, moment-to-moment decisions are not made by reasoning them out through the knowledge associated with traditional rhetorical texts. We arrange dates, figure out how to get along with the new family next door, and decide which television program to watch, all using something other than traditional texts. But within the Greek legacy, experiences and decisions that people face in everyday, mundane contexts, and the ways in which those decisions are made, are all assumed to be of little consequence.

The chief result of this paradox within the Greek legacy for the study of popular culture is that traditional thinking does not recognize any important rhetoric of everyday life. If any important business of society is being conducted through the texts of everyday experience—through nonverbal signs or informal conversation, for example—then any thinking grounded in the Greek legacy will not recognize a rhetorical dimension in the management of that business. This is because Greek rhetorical theory views rhetoric as sharing the four characteristics described on page 10, and everyday conversation, nonverbal signs, and ordinary social practices will probably not be verbal, discrete, expositional, and hierarchical. In the traditional view, texts that do not share those four characteristics have been seen as not fully rhetorical and as not fully performing rhetoric's important functions. But students of popular culture take issue with the idea that texts that do not have those four characteristics are less important and not concerned with a society's serious business.

In talking about different kinds of texts, we should not make any absolute distinctions. Clearly, many kinds of communication will have some but not all of the four characteristics of the traditional texts of public speaking. There is no sudden cutoff at which everyday, mundane business becomes public (and therefore important) business. Also, societies have a full continuum of business, from the vitally important to the trivial; the majority of a society's business probably falls somewhere in the middle. But historically, traditional rhetorical theorists have assumed that the closer a communication is to having all four characteristics of the traditional texts of public speaking, the more clearly it deserves to be called rhetoric.

In sum, the ancient Greek rhetorical legacy assumes that rhetoric means verbal, expositional, discrete, and hierarchical—that is to say, traditional—texts. This legacy links rhetoric and democracy: the more public business is decided rhetorically, the more people will be involved in managing that business. But, paradoxically, the Greek conception of a traditional text places limits on the widespread management of public business. The Greek legacy does not allow for the rhetorical management of public business within popular culture. That inability to see the rhetoric of the everyday lasted for centuries beyond the time of the Greeks.

EXERCISE 1.3

To understand the assumptions that are sometimes made about what is rhetoric and what is not, write down your reactions to the following exercise. In this exercise, you will indicate whether the texts listed below share the four characteristics of public speaking.

Is this text verbal? expositional? discrete? hierarchical?

a. A speech by the president of the United States

b. This book

c. A website

d. An Internet-based video game

e. A mother's routine for getting children ready for school

f. Your favorite song

g. A city bus going along its route

You probably answered yes to more of the four characteristics of traditional rhetorical texts for the first two or perhaps three items on the list than for the later ones. Not coincidentally, most people would have no trouble identifying a speech by the president or perhaps even this book as rhetoric— but the ways in which a city bus is a rhetorical text may not be at all clear to most people.

Now look over that list of texts again, this time asking yourself which ones are most often involved in the management of society's serious business. Which texts are composed of signs that influence people in important ways? We are likely to think that the more traditionally rhetorical texts fit that description. A list of other traditionally rhetorical texts—texts that would be likely to share all four characteristics of the texts of public speaking— would probably include most essays and articles in periodicals and to some extent the literature of novels, poems, plays, and so forth.

DEFINITIONS OF RHETORIC AFTER PLATO

In the centuries between Plato and the present, many thinkers and writers have devised their own understandings of what rhetoric is, what functions it performs, what manifestations it takes on, and whether and how it manages important public business. This book is not meant to be a history of rhetorical theory, but it would be useful to review very briefly some of the ways in which some of these later thinkers and writers thought about rhetoric. We will see that the Greek legacy has remained strong; though there are differences, these people's ideas are fundamentally similar to those of the Greeks. However, we will also see that as cultures have changed through history, definitions of rhetoric have moved more toward an understanding of popular culture as also rhetorical.

We noted earlier that Plato's student, the philosopher Aristotle, diverged from his teacher's views to write a comprehensive treatise, the *Rhetoric*. This book is a system for studying as well as doing rhetoric, and since Aristotle's time, *rhetoric* has been a term that can be applied both to what people do and to systems of knowledge or explanation about what people do. Thus, we might say that someone delivering a speech is "doing" rhetoric. At the same time, however, there is likely to be a systematic explanation of how the introduction and conclusion to the speech are constructed, how the arguments are devised, how emotional appeals are used, and so forth; we would refer to this system of rules and practical advice as a rhetoric. You could also call a systematic set of rules a rhetorical theory.

Aristotle broke with Plato over the subject of rhetoric because Aristotle viewed it more consistently as an activity worth doing, a subject worth studying. In Chapter 2 of Book 1 of the *Rhetoric*, Aristotle defined rhetoric as "the faculty of observing in any given case the available means of persuasion." In further defining his subject, he made it clear that he viewed rhetoric as public speaking in legal, political, and ceremonial contexts; it was in those contexts that he saw much of the important business of his society being managed. Aristotle did not include within his definition everyday conversation, bargaining in the marketplace, entertainment, religion, or other experiences of communication. His treatise is concerned with the construction of public speeches, which are clearly discrete and verbal texts. His focus is on expositional texts as well; how to discover and express argument is a major focus of his theory. And, for Aristotle, rhetoric is also hierarchical: He envisions the classic relationship of a speaker holding the floor before an audience that has gathered to listen.

In the first century B.C.E., the Roman statesman and philosopher Marcus Tullius Cicero wrote extensively on the subject of rhetoric, most notably in *Of Oratory*. Cicero exemplified the Roman ideal at that time, which maintained that life is lived most fully when one is actively involved in public life—that is, in public debate and discussion and in public decision-making. Romans considered it both a duty and the very rationale behind life to be involved in public life, discussing the important business of their society. One of the most important ways in which that involvement occurred was through oratory, or eloquent public speaking, which is how Cicero defined rhetoric.

Cicero was a Roman senator, and at that time the senate made many of the most important decisions for the Roman Republic. It made those decisions through inspired public speaking, many examples of which are still studied as model speeches today. Cicero also valued lively and learned discussions among his fellow patricians as a profitable way to pass the time and to acquire knowledge. But he would assign the management of most of his society's public problems to rhetoric in the form of public speaking; the involvement of every citizen in public affairs, rather than the assignment of problems to experts, was his ideal. And, clearly, when rhetoric was used to manage public problems, it did so through forms of public speaking that were verbal, expositional, discrete, and hierarchical.

Cicero died, the Roman Republic came to an end, and the age of the Caesars was ushered in. Within the Roman Empire, public business was managed largely by the emperor and by officials appointed by him. Although Plato would probably have disapproved of many of the people who were in charge of imperial Rome, the Roman Empire did follow Plato's model, which called for the removal of the management of public business from the hands of the people and, consequently, from rhetoric in the form of public speaking. Consistent with Greek assumptions, as democracy faded, theorists began writing as if rhetoric were also reduced in scope and importance. In the first century C.E., the Roman teacher and rhetorician Marcus Fabius Quintilianus, or Quintilian, wrote a long rhetoric called the *Institutes of Oratory* that both prescribed a course of study for training in rhetoric and gave practical advice for its use. But Quintilian was forced to define rhetoric primarily in terms of public speaking in the courts because that was the only important arena left in Rome in which public speaking could be exercised meaningfully. It is interesting that Quintilian did not look for rhetoric—for the ways in which signs influence people—in manifestations other than speaking; clearly, the Greek tradition was influencing him as well. This shrunken definition of rhetoric as legal public speaking reflects the relationship between rhetoric and power: As power was denied to the public and as rhetoric (public speaking) was restricted in terms of what it could control, so was the sense of what counted as "rhetoric" more narrowly defined. For Quintilian, rhetoric continued to be defined as the manifestation that is traditional public speaking, with its four key characteristics.

An important rhetorician after Quintilian was Saint Augustine, Bishop of Hippo, in Africa, who lived around 400 C.E. St. Augustine took on one of the most pressing problems for the early Christian Church: what to retain and what to discard among the artifacts of the polytheistic culture that the Christians were replacing. Rhetoric especially came under suspicion, as many in the Church thought that the faithful had no business seeking to gain advantage over others through any means, including public speaking. In *On Christian Doctrine*, especially in Book IV, St. Augustine argued that rhetoric should be used by Christians—that, in fact, it had the high calling of inducing belief and stimulating faith in people. St. Augustine shows the influence of the Greek legacy as well, for his view of rhetoric is embodied in the written texts of the Bible and the form of public speaking that is the sermon or homily, traditional texts that embody the four characteristics very clearly (particularly the verbal and hierarchical traits). It is significant that St. Augustine does not have much to say about person-to-person witnessing or testimony, rituals and ceremonies, or nonverbal signs such as pictures, icons, and costumes, as elements of rhetoric. His writings instead reflect a sense of traditional rhetorical texts as managing the important business of the Church.

Widespread participation in public decision-making was scarce in Europe for centuries after the collapse of the Roman Republic. Various forms of powerful, centralized political control succeeded one another: the Roman Empire, the Catholic Church, the feudal system with its absolute monarchies and principalities, and so forth. The important business of societies was officially being managed by priests and princes in their abbeys and castles, not by peasants and merchants. Certainly, people talked and went about their business as they had for centuries, but we can find little evidence that any thinkers thought that those everyday experiences were important in shaping society or managing its business. Significantly, because what was considered the important business of society was being managed by an elite few and not through public speaking, rhetoric came to be defined in increasingly narrow and restrictive ways.

Between St. Augustine's time and the eighteenth century, the Greek legacy continued to hold sway. The most interesting developments in rhetorical theory were the ways in which the definition of rhetoric became limited, paralleling the highly centralized and nondemocratic forms of government and social control of the times. One way in which rhetoric was limited was its restriction to certain kinds of texts and not others. For instance, the province of letter writing was assigned to rhetoric. In the centuries after Cicero, letter writing was not unimportant; it was a major means of communication over long distances. But letter writing certainly represented a restricted scope of subject matter and contexts compared to the days when rhetoric involved thousands of people in political, legal, and ceremonial speaking.

Another means of restricting rhetoric had to do with the kinds of strategies or techniques it used. Peter Ramus, a sixteenth-century thinker, defined rhetoric so as not to include logic or reason; those strategies he set apart as a separate field of study. Instead, he defined rhetoric more narrowly as the study and art of verbal style. Because logic was undergoing systematic development and was seen as an important tool of thought and decision-making (especially in the Church and in academia), restricting the definition of rhetoric to style alone, apart from logic, was a disempowering move on the part of Ramus and his colleagues.

RHETORIC IN THE EIGHTEENTH CENTURY

We often think of the eighteenth century as the Age of Reason, as a time when nondemocratic forms of social control were rejected. It was during that century that the American and French Revolutions both took place, for instance. Significantly, the eighteenth century also saw renewed interest in rhetorical theory, especially in Great Britain. Many thinkers returned to the ancient Greek and Roman rhetoricians and reestablished that legacy. Richard Whately, for instance, extended Greek and Roman ideas of argument to include the concepts of presumption and burden of proof. In argument, presumption means you do not have the primary responsibility to develop a detailed argument, since it is presumed that your position is correct. Tradition, custom, and power usually create a sense of presumption. If a parent tells a child to go to bed, the parent enjoys presumption. The parent does not have to give reasons why the child should go. On the contrary, it is the child who has what is called the burden of proof. If the child has an argument for going to bed at a different time than usual, an argument for overturning parental authority, it is the child who must devise the argument, not the parent.

But alternatives to the Greek legacy were also developed at this time. It would be inaccurate to say that any eighteenth-century rhetorician proposed a theory of rhetoric in popular culture, but a number of thinkers did propose ideas that suggest ways of going beyond the Greek legacy, thereby planting the seeds of alternative ways of thinking. Let us briefly review just a few of the people who proposed such alternatives.

Giambattista Vico was a professor in Italy during the late seventeenth and early eighteenth centuries. Vico directly confronted the restrictive definitions of rhetoric that had limited it to style and verbal embellishment while the more substantive areas of reason and logic were assumed to be something other than rhetoric. Rhetoric, he proposed, should be seen as the ways in which we think about probabilities and make decisions about issues that we cannot be totally certain of. Contrary to the pretensions of philosophers such as René Descartes of France, who thought that many if not most decisions could be made through formal reason rather than rhetoric, Vico argued that most, if not all, decisions were based on thinking about probabilities and thus had a rhetorical dimension. He claimed that for humans, reality is a matter of what we perceive—that we create our own realities out of signs. Since reality is human-made, it must be understood by using human faculties, and rhetoric is a primary human faculty. By carefully defining both human reality and rhetoric, Vico created a possibility for thinking about our experiences of reality (including public events as well as everyday experiences) as places where rhetoric is at work, influencing us to create our realities by seeing the world in one way or another. Vico's perspective is very close to the ideas that we will explore in Chapter 2 when we think about the world of culture as both one that is made by humans and one that has a great deal of influence bound up in the artifacts (signs) of which it is composed.

Another important departure from the Greek legacy during the eighteenth century had to do with the development of the idea of taste as a basis for making decisions and for constructing and judging communication. Rhetorical theorists such as Joseph Addison and Hugh Blair began suggesting that taste, an aesthetic way of thinking and perceiving, is and should be a factor in how people communicate and in how people make decisions on the basis of that communication. Blair and other rhetoricians were primarily concerned with taste as found in traditional texts, including oratory, letters, essays, and so forth. But whereas a concern for argument, for instance, entails a restricted focus on traditional texts, a concern for taste and aesthetics enables extension of those concepts beyond rhetorical texts. If taste is acknowledged to be a reason why people might do certain things, why decisions might be made, that acknowledgment sets up ways of thinking about how taste in clothing, in grooming products, in interior decoration—in popular culture overall—might be rhetorical. If you look for rhetoric only in terms of how evidence can be mustered in support of a point, then you cannot see both a speech and a country-and-western star's cowboy hat as rhetorical. But if rhetoric can be defined to include aesthetic judgment, or taste, then that hat, too, becomes rhetorical.

The development of interest in psychology, and the application of that new human science to rhetoric, also created possibilities for envisioning the rhetoric of popular culture. British theorists such as John Locke, David Hartley, Joseph Priestley, and George Campbell began to probe into how people think, how the mind operates, during the full range of experience. Campbell developed a rhetorical theory that explained how human understanding and imagination were addressed by others. Although Campbell also restricted his focus in practice to traditional texts, he and his colleagues opened up the possibility of thinking about ways in which people might be influenced through things other than verbal, expositional, and discrete texts. Because they were concerned with the whole operation of the human mind, these rhetorical psychologists introduced the possibility of thinking about how the mind might be influenced by signs and artifacts found throughout everyday experience, not just during moments of reading essays or listening to speeches.

One consequence of a concern for psychology was the development of methods of criticism. By criticism, we mean critiquing or analyzing, not just being contentious. Rhetorical thinkers had always been concerned with how audiences received messages and thought about them. Plato urged rhetoricians to study the different "souls" that could be found in an audience, for example, and Aristotle discussed the ways in which messages would be received and understood. But their concern was largely with offering advice for speakers, for those who would produce signs and texts, rather than for those who would see or hear them. In the eighteenth century, rhetorical thinkers such as Lord Kames and Blair began to expand their understanding of the different kinds of reactions that people might have to signs and texts and to identify specific techniques for analyzing, or critiquing, messages, audiences, and the connections between the two.

This concern for criticism also created a possibility for thinking about the rhetoric of popular culture, because it is as critics, or as consumers, that most people confront the artifacts of popular culture. We will see later how the rhetoric of popular culture is concerned mainly with how people encounter and then use, rather than originally produce, the texts of popular culture. To begin thinking about criticism is a step in that direction.

The eighteenth century was an age of powdered wigs, of candlelit salons, Mozart and Haydn, and Voltaire. It was the dawn of modern science and industry. The eighteenth century would not seem to have much to do with Toby Keith or Lady Gaga, but developments in rhetorical theory during that period laid the groundwork for understanding the rhetoric of popular culture. So far we have considered four specific developments:

1. With Vico came an understanding that rhetoric runs throughout the experiences of human reality.
2. With Blair came a concern for taste and aesthetics as a basis for decision-making.
3. With Campbell came a widening understanding of the human mind and how it works in response to signs and symbols.
4. With several thinkers, including Blair, came a concern for refined methods of criticism, particularly in relation to the reception of communication.

NEW THEORIES (AND NEW REALITIES) EMERGE IN THE TWENTIETH CENTURY

During all these centuries in which rhetoric was defined primarily in terms of traditional texts, people were still experiencing signs and texts that were not in that traditional form. Informal conversation, architecture, clothing styles, common entertainments, food—in short, the whole range of cultural artifacts other than traditional rhetorical texts—were being experienced by people as influential and moving, while rhetorical theorists continued to call only the traditional texts rhetoric. One purpose of this book is to demonstrate that many of today's rhetorical theorists now understand the rhetorical dimension of that wider range of cultural artifacts. In other words, many theorists today would choose not to limit rhetoric to those traditional texts (although some still would, however; see Leff and Kauffeld for an excellent review of scholarship grounded in traditional texts). That shift in understanding raises the question of what changed, rhetorically, between the eighteenth century and the present. Are people being influenced by signs in different ways now, such that we must now call the texts of everyday experience rhetorical but did not need to call them that two hundred years ago? Have rhetorical theorists awakened to truths that were always there but went unrecognized until recently? In other words, does a change in thinking about what rhetoric is follow from a change in the world or a change in theory?

The answer to that final question is both. The world and our experience of the world have changed. The main locus of that change was the twentieth century, although it continues today at an even faster pace. People do things differently, new technologies alter the realities of life, environmental and political changes occur, wars come and go, and so forth. Theories, or our ways of understanding the world, also change. Often, theories change because it is felt that the old theories no longer describe experience, which has changed, accurately. But theories sometimes change for the reasons we discovered at the beginning of this chapter. A theory is a complicated way of defining something as well as explaining it, and so one important reason why rhetorical theories change is because people may have reason to define and explain the world differently. In short, changes in theory may be part of changes in power.

A sampling of just a few definitions of rhetoric from rhetorical theorists within the last hundred years will show that the seeds of the eighteenth century have grown into conceptions of rhetoric that are markedly different from that of the Greeks. In 1936, I. A. Richards defined rhetoric as "a study of misunderstanding and its remedies" (3). Richards's concern is almost exclusively with verbal texts, but his definition is important in that it places rhetoric within the contexts of everyday communication and interaction. Misunderstanding is at least as likely to occur in the give-and-take of conversation as in the more carefully prepared traditional texts of essays or speeches. A concern for misunderstanding also emphasizes the role of audiences or receivers of communication and the question of how they understand and interpret texts in their everyday experience.

Perhaps the most famous definition of rhetoric in the twentieth century was that of Kenneth Burke, who defined it as "the use of language as a symbolic means of inducing cooperation in beings that by nature respond to symbols" (*Rhetoric of Motives*, 43). Like Richards, Burke tends to restrict his focus to language, although he also finds rhetoric in art forms such as music. But his definition is widely applicable. Many kinds of signs, in many forms and contexts, can induce cooperation. Although it does not focus mainly on popular culture, Burke's definition tells us to look for how people are induced to cooperate with others, potentially in any texts, whether that be to their benefit (their empowerment) or not. Similarly, Donald C. Bryant sees rhetoric's function as "adjusting ideas to people and people to ideas" (413). Although Bryant restricts his focus to "the rationale of informative and suasory discourse" (404), the wider idea of adjusting ideas and people to one another is descriptive of a process that can and does occur outside traditional texts.

Although James L. Kinneavy objects to those who would define rhetoric too broadly, he himself prefers anchoring its definition in "persuasion," which encourages us to consider the ways in which many kinds of texts persuade. Kinneavy's definition is geared to the function of rhetoric rather than to a particular kind of manifestation (216–18). Similarly, in his definition of rhetoric, Stephen Toulmin proposes a model of argument, which would seem to be largely an expositional type of text (*Uses of Argument*). But he develops his definition from actual arguments used in court decisions and other "real-life" situations. Toulmin's model has been widely used to explore the ways in which the arguments of everyday life are persuasive.

What Changed in the Twentieth Century and Beyond

What prompted these changes in theory and definitions of rhetoric in the twentieth century? What has led to today's explosion of rhetoric in popular culture? To begin to answer these questions, let us examine some important ways in which the world changed in the twentieth century. That century was, of course, significantly different from the past in a number of ways that continue to be true in the twenty-first century. Our concern here is with differences in how signs influence people. Some of these differences are radical, or extreme. Most, however, are relative, or matters of degree (though still significant). In each instance, the difference has to do with a change that the Greek rhetorical legacy and its assumptions cannot fully account for; thus, these are "real-life" changes that have prompted changes in theory. Furthermore, these are changes that situate rhetoric squarely within popular culture. We will review changes in these interrelated areas: population, technology, pluralism, and knowledge.

Population

Little argument should be needed to establish that in the twentieth century and beyond, the world's population exploded. Populations grew at the greatest rate in the poorer countries of the Third World, but nearly every industrialized nation experienced the same phenomenon. Of particular interest in industrialized countries was the pattern of population growth: populations first became more urbanized, then suburbanized

and exurbanized as the century progressed. That is to say, the experience of living with only limited contact with others, or even of living on farms or in rural areas, became increasingly rare. Farm populations shifted to the cities during the first half of the century. During the second half, city populations began spreading out into suburbs and smaller towns on the outskirts of larger cities. The main result of these developments has been that today, in the twenty-first century, more people are being exposed to more people, and more different kinds of people, than ever before.

This difference in population patterns is to some extent a matter of degree. It was rare for people to be completely isolated or in touch with only a few others centuries ago. Nor is it the case that no one is ever alone today. But, relatively speaking, more people are living and working near more other people today than ever before. That is an important difference, because it means that more people are exposed to a wider variety of cultural artifacts than before. We must note that the issue is one of greater exposure to cultural artifacts, a concept we will study in the next chapter; briefly, a cultural artifact is some kind of action, object, or event that particularly represents a group of people. Artifacts are highly charged with meanings *of* people. Certainly, people are no more conscious today than they ever were, nor do people have more things to perceive today than they did in the past. A person's experience is no fuller today than it was three thousand years ago. But today, a person's day is relatively more full of signs that are artifacts, signs that are charged with meaning and that bespeak the presence of others. This is especially true of those who live in the population- and message-dense urban areas. Ian Chambers pictures the city dweller as "caught up in the communication membrane of the metropolis, with your head in front of a cinema, TV, video or computer screen, between the headphones by the radio, among the record releases and magazines" (11).

Two hypothetical cases might help to make this relative difference clear. Imagine a farm family living on the Great Plains 125 years ago. What would they see and hear during the course of the day? Many of their experiences would be of nature, of signs that were not necessarily produced by humans and that did not bespeak human groups. That is not to say that their culture was impoverished but rather that, relatively speaking, their exposure to cultural artifacts that represented others was limited. Compare that family with a family living in a city today. Certainly, the urban family encounters natural signs, but many of those might take on the status of artifacts to the extent that they were put in place by other people, such as urban landscape architects. Of more importance is that as this family goes about its business during the day, it is bombarded by artifacts of every sort, by a pressure cooker of signs that bespeak other people, certainly to a greater extent than was the farm family. Most of us live somewhere in between these two extremes, but the point to remember is that, in general, people today are exposed to more artifacts.

As an expanding population puts more of us in touch with more people and with the artifacts they have produced, more of us are influenced by more signs coming to us, not only in our surroundings but also by way of new technologies. Some have described this process as the development of a new kind of culture—mass culture—that is significantly different from the more localized and physically centered cultures of earlier times. People have, obviously, had their everyday experiences in all times and places, but today's everyday experiences are, relatively speaking, more filled with human voices than in the past. Those voices call to us from the objects and events of everyday experience. What are they saying to us? How are they influencing us? Such rhetorical questions about popular culture are more pressing today.

Exposure to artifacts produced during daily living with many more people also means that we are exposed to more artifacts and texts that are not verbal, expositional, discrete, or hierarchical. When we are surrounded by more people and thus by more signs that they have produced, artifacts come to us in a hodgepodge. We are exposed to signs that come and go quickly, without time for expositional development; to signs that are nonverbal rather than

EXERCISE 1.4

A quick exercise will illustrate the extent to which you are surrounded by other people and by their artifacts. Consider, either on your own or in class discussion, the following questions:

1. From where you are right now, physically, how far would you have to go to be able to see or hear any three things that were not designed, produced, or placed where they are by other people?

2. When was the last time that you were more than one minute away from the sight or sound of another person?

3. Of all the sights and sounds you have experienced in the last twenty-four hours, what percentage would you say took the form of verbal, expositional, discrete, and hierarchical texts?

verbal; and to signs that are mixed in with other signs rather than discrete. And the clear imposition of a hierarchical relationship that is present in the experience of public speaking is much less apparent in today's signs. Instead, we, as consumers of signs and artifacts, become more instrumental in structuring how those signs and artifacts are experienced and understood. How we do so, and how that influences the effects those signs and artifacts have upon us, are also rhetorical questions that are relatively more important today.

Technology

A second development within real life in the last hundred years has been expanding technology. This development has been both quantitative (we are exposed to more technologies, more often, in more different experiences than people used to be) and qualitative (we are exposed to technologies that are wholly different and unprecedented in human history). Of particular interest for the rhetoric of popular culture are the technologies of communication.

In the centuries following the ancient Greeks, technologies for distributing the written word were gradually developed, most notably the printing press. Although print technologies can certainly distribute other kinds of texts, think about how well suited these technologies are for the distribution of traditional rhetorical texts (see Boggs). Clearly, print is verbal; it presents words "as good as they can get," so to speak, whereas nonverbal or pictorial images in print are "still" and thus able to represent far less, proportionally, of the visual dimension of experience than words in print can of the verbal dimension. The long and careful development of arguments is very well suited to print, for print allows readers to go over difficult proofs and arguments repeatedly if they need to. Most printed texts (such as this book, for instance) are perceived as discrete texts. And printed texts establish a clear, one-way hierarchy of communication; readers cannot talk back while using that medium.

But radical differences in communication began in the twentieth century. These differences are the products of developments of technology for the distribution and transfer of other kinds of signs and texts. As we progress through the twenty-first century, the pace of these changes increases continually.

Today, the individual with an iPod and headphones can go through the entire day literally attached to a technology of communication. There is not a single moment of that person's day, no place of retreat at all, where technology cannot

©iStockphoto.com/Geber86

carry a message. If the person is listening to SiriusXM satellite radio, that person can be reached by messages and other texts generated only an instant before anywhere in the world. Smartphones in the home, office, car, or in the mall allow a person to be in visual or voice communication with others at all times.

Elaborate messages for distribution to others can be prepared on tiny computers that can be carried anywhere. The Internet is accessible now through devices combining many functions into instruments that used to be only telephones, and through the Internet one can be in touch with anybody anywhere instantly. Television has given people easy access to a wide range of sights and sounds that they used to have to travel to theaters to experience, and tiny portable televisions now also allow battery-powered mobility. Cable and video recording technologies have expanded this particular form of access to messages even more; a person in possession of cable television and a digital recorder has access every hour to more information and entertainment, to a greater volume of artifacts tumbling across the screen, than someone living a hundred years ago could have experienced in a year. Could a person one hundred years ago have sat surrounded by more books than he or she could read in a lifetime? Of course, but today a person has instant access, by way of computer networks, to an exponentially larger number of artifacts even than that.

Not only does technology expose the individual to more messages; it also exposes more of us to the same global or mass culture of messages. Hip-hop, for instance, is now heard all over the world. People in distant parts of the world see recycled American television shows. People are connected technologically at a cultural level in ways we were not before.

One important result of a vastly increased number of advanced technologies in everyday life has been a vastly increased exposure to artifacts. Technologies like satellite radio or smartphones with ever-expanding networks allow us to fill our every moment with artifacts should we choose to do so. More exposure to information technologies means exposure to more artifacts and thus to more rhetorical influences in our everyday lives.

EXERCISE 1.5

To understand the extent to which new information technologies are a fact of everyday life, consider the following questions on your own or in class discussion:

1. Name at least four information or communication technologies that you could have access to within a two-minute walk from where you are now (extra points for naming three such technologies that you can see or hear without moving from your chair).

2. Name the last complete public speech, or similar traditional text, that you gained access to by using one of the electronic information technologies of information (the Internet, television, radio, and so on). If you are not able to think of many, draw some conclusions about the sorts of texts that today's technologies seem best suited for.

3. Draw up a list of important activities in your personal or work life that you simply could not do without some of the technologies of communication that we have discussed here. Now draw up a list of such activities that do not need such technologies at all. What picture surfaces of how your life is shaped by technologies of communication?

A less obvious result of the increase in information technologies has been an increase in people's reception of texts that are not verbal, expositional, discrete, and hierarchical. Much of our communication today is visual. Other messages are verbal but in different forms. The lyrics of the latest country-and-western hit coming to us through our headphones may be verbal, but they are not likely to be expositional. The quick scrolling of numbers across a personal computer screen is not verbal, nor is much of the content of the videos on YouTube. A person who switches constantly from one station to another while watching television is paying little attention to discrete texts. Instead of merely facilitating the more hierarchical relationship of public speaking, today's information technologies can place receivers of communications in a much more coequal relationship with the producers of communications. For example, when using instant messaging on a computer, a person can respond instantly online to the author of a message that appears on his or her screen. Bloggers can post their thoughts about what is happening where they are and receive very fast responses from readers all around the world.

When people have more exposure to and control over a wide range of technologies in their everyday experiences, they acquire more control over how and when they experience signs and artifacts. Ultimately, the Greek rhetorical tradition is inadequate when it comes to understanding how people use and understand the wide range of signs and artifacts available to them through contemporary technologies.

Pluralism

A third significant development in the twentieth century and beyond is the growth of pluralism. This term can mean many things. Here, by *pluralism*, we mean the awareness of many perspectives, philosophies, points of view, codes of ethics, aesthetic sensibilities, and so forth, and the awareness of a legitimate grounding for all of these.

The growth of pluralism is directly related to the growth of population and to the spread of information technologies. If you are not directly exposed to very many people during the day, chances are the people to whom you are exposed are people who are just like you. The Great Plains farm family used as an example before would probably have experienced other people who were largely like them—of similar values, religion, ethnic background, and so on. They would surely have been aware of Indian people living near them, but they would probably not have had much accurate information about them. Limited contact with people who are different limits people's awareness of the beliefs, values, practices, and experiences of those different others.

However, increased contact with different groups of people will not necessarily increase understanding, particularly if people remain ethnocentric, judging different others only by the standards and perspectives of their own group. Thus, the Great Plains family might have known people who traded frequently with the Indians, traders who were aware of what these people thought and felt and did yet nevertheless dismissed their whole way of life as second-rate and degraded. This Great Plains family was not likely to be pluralistic, in the first case because they were not aware of a wide range of different points of view; they were not exposed to the variety of human thought and experience that there is in the world. In the second case, neither the Great Plains family nor their trader friends were pluralistic because, whatever the differences of which they were aware, they probably would have seen no legitimacy for those different ideas and experiences.

But expanding population and information technologies have made for a change. As more and more people come to live in proximity to one another, they become more aware of their differences. The experience of immigrants clustering in American cities in the first part of the twentieth century is a good example. In this case, people from Ireland, Italy, Germany, and other countries were suddenly forced to live in relatively close proximity to each other, and thus to learn about each other. Information technologies serve the same function, allowing us to find out more about people who live even on the other side of the world, as if we were neighbors, through things like the National Geographic Channel on television. Today, it is hard not to be aware of many other groups of people—of their habits, customs, and beliefs. (See Klotz for a discussion of the extent to which technologies of communication, especially on the Internet, are responsible for revealing and connecting groups of people to each other today.)

An even more important dimension of pluralism, however, is a growing recognition that the beliefs and customs of other, different people have some sort of legitimacy or grounding. This is not to say that we must agree with those who are different (nor that people often do so), but rather that we are aware that others feel that they have good reasons for thinking and doing the things they do. People are becoming increasingly aware that other people have philosophical, social, religious, or other reasons for their thoughts and behavior, just as "we" do.

In the nineteenth century, for instance, people might have marveled at stories, brought back by explorers of faraway societies, of people who put their elderly onto ice floes and cast them off into the sea; "civilized" people might have shuddered and condemned the members of such societies as hopeless "savages." Today, however, although we might consider such a practice wrong, we would be relatively more willing to seek to understand the reason for it; we would expect such a practice to have legitimacy for that particular society, even if we would be appalled at the thought of doing anything of the sort ourselves. This sort of understanding of difference is relatively new; such understanding has always been held by some but is held more widely today. There is no doubt that prejudice and ethnocentrism still exist, but they exist in a curious mixture with increased knowledge of other people and of why others are different.

One important result of pluralism—that is, of an awareness and acknowledgment of the legitimacy of others who are different—has been a democratization of status. Prejudice, bigotry, racism, classism, and sexism do still exist, of course. Nevertheless, there has been a relative increase in such pluralistic awareness in many countries over the last few decades, with the result being that many different groups have been granted legal and political power, or status, that they did not have before.

At the beginning of the twentieth century, for instance, only white males could vote throughout much the United States. Women and members of other races did not have as much of a voice as they do today; laws and the Fifteenth Amendment to the Constitution that guaranteed rights were often not enforced. Certainly, biases against these groups still exist, but today's intentional pursuit of rights and prerogatives for all sorts of groups is practically unprecedented in history. Whereas second-class status was common for many groups in nearly all earlier times and nations, many democratic nations today try not to place any of their citizens in second-class positions. Of a different kind of importance than traditional power (such as the right to vote) is the power that comes from increased presence in the shared texts of a culture. Pick up most newspapers and turn on most television shows, and you will see, hear, and learn from and about whole groups of people who might have been, in African-American novelist Ralph Ellison's terms, "invisible" people only a few decades before.

Pluralism challenges the Greek legacy in a number of ways, two of which we will explore here. First, it legitimizes signs and texts that are not verbal, expositional, discrete, and hierarchical in the ways that traditional public speaking is. The Greek legacy is predominantly a European legacy, since European culture was strongly influenced by Greece. That European culture has been dominant in the West for centuries, of course. But people from non-European (for example, African, Asian, or Latin American) backgrounds who came to industrialized democracies such as the United States have developed other ways of communicating, through texts that do not share the same discrete, verbal, expositional, and hierarchical characteristics.

In his book *The Afrocentric Idea*, for example, Molefi Kete Asante shows how the "Afrocentric" pattern of communicating features unity, wholeness, dialogue, and aesthetics in ways that are distinct from the structure and argumentative patterns of traditional European-based public speaking. Women from all backgrounds, who historically had relatively less access to the forums of public speaking than did men, developed more interactional and dialogic forms of communication geared to the patterns of everyday conversation (Kramer; Rakow and Wackwitz; Treichler and Kramarae). Other ethnic and cultural groups have patterns of communicating rhetorically that are specific to their own heritages and that do not follow the Greek model. Pluralism demands, in other words, that we consider alternative rhetorics, other ways in which people use signs to influence others and are influenced by signs in their turn.

A second way in which pluralism challenges the Greek legacy is by creating the possibility of shifting the locus of where and when the important business of a society is conducted. In the Greek legacy, important business is conducted only by those who are officially empowered to conduct it, either members of the public, using traditional texts, or the expert few. These, of course, will be the people who are empowered generally, who are in charge within a society. If important business is conducted only by those officially empowered to do so, then only in specifically designated places and times will you find business that is considered important or valuable going on. So, for the Greeks, important business happened in their assemblies more than in their homes. In the Roman Empire, important business was done in the legal and imperial courts more than in the baths.

When certain groups and classes in complex societies are not empowered or are suppressed, they become marginalized. Their actions, thoughts, voices, feelings, practices, and so forth are assumed not to have any part in the management of important business. Instead, these groups are moved to the "margins" of power; whatever they do, it is assumed that their actions are not part of the exercise of power taking place at the official "center" of society. In other words, society allows such groups to live and communicate only within the times and places in which that important, official business is not being conducted.

Of course, all of us step into the margins from time to time; for instance, if you go fishing, play cards, or watch television with your family, the Greek legacy would hold that you are not doing anything of much importance. But people who are often and repeatedly disempowered are made to occupy the margin for the long term. One outcome of such marginalizing is the assumption that whatever the group in question does must perforce be marginal or of less value; such an assumption is the very essence of racism and sexism, for instance. This point is illustrated by the Greeks themselves: Official business was conducted by the citizens in their assembly, while women, slaves, foreigners, and so forth continued to talk and do their business within the "margins" of society: homes, taverns, farms, and so forth. What women, slaves, foreigners, and so on did was not considered the important business of society.

But in a more pluralistic society (which nearly all industrialized democracies are now or are increasingly becoming), awareness of different groups and of the legitimacy of those groups' practices and beliefs brings an increase in the status of those practices and beliefs. And this means that what marginalized people say and do assumes more importance in terms of what happens generally in a society. Thus, the margin shrinks. People who were ignored a century ago are now publicly noticed and heard. The margin is still there and probably always will be, but pluralism shrinks it.

The challenge a shrinking margin poses to the Greek legacy has to do with the fact that traditional texts have not usually been found in that margin. Many of the signs and texts found in society's margins are not verbal, expositional, discrete, or hierarchical. As noted before, people who have previously been disempowered have developed texts that differ from traditional forms. The growth of pluralism has given rise to texts that cannot be accounted for in the Greek legacy.

Knowledge

A fourth development in the twentieth century and beyond that has worked against the Greek legacy is the incredible expansion of knowledge, specifically technical and scientific knowledge. It can hardly be denied that what there is to know increased exponentially in the twentieth century. Science especially, aided by the information technologies (such as the computer) that we discussed earlier in this chapter, has amassed enormous amounts of information. So much information has been gathered and is being gathered even as you read this book that the ability to organize, understand, and gain access to that information has become a major problem, one as complicated as that of discovering new information.

Knowledge is becoming increasingly specialized. Whereas one hundred years ago one might simply be a physician, today even a specialization like internal medicine is rather broad; subspecialties such as gastroenterology exist, and even the knowledge covered within that subspecialty is vast. New scholarly journals and books are being churned out

©iStockphoto.com/Nikada

by the hundreds at this very moment. The explosion of knowledge is obvious and simply stated; the impact of that explosion upon the Greek legacy is significant and complex.

One effect of the knowledge explosion has to do with the relationship between knowledge and how decisions are made—that is, with the specialization of decision-making. Of course, you need knowledge to make decisions. Historically, technical or scientific knowledge has been used in the decision-making associated with traditional texts. By "technical or scientific knowledge," we mean knowledge based on research, public knowledge acquired through scientific methods rather than simply through personal experience. For example, when we argue expositionally, we consult facts and figures, examples, history, expert testimony, and so forth. Such knowledge has traditionally been considered more valuable than knowledge acquired simply through everyday experience or through other means. But the available technical and scientific knowledge is becoming more and more specialized as it increases in sheer volume. As such specialization happens, the location of decision-making also tends to become more specialized.

The problem is that there is a limit to what decision-makers can understand. As total knowledge grows, the amount that decision-makers can understand stays about the same; thus, decision-makers' knowledge must become more specialized, since the amount that a person can understand and control shrinks as a percentage of what is known overall. The result is that decisions based on technical or scientific knowledge are increasingly being referred to specialists and experts. The general public cannot possess enough technical and scientific knowledge to argue expositionally and to make judgments about many issues that depend upon that knowledge.

Today, for instance, public decisions must be made about the issue of pharmaceuticals: how to regulate them, when to approve or disapprove them, how to finance the cost of prescription drugs, and so forth. To make these decisions, knowledge is needed. But who can know enough about the pharmaceutical industry to make a decision that is informed by technical knowledge? It is unlikely that ordinary people know very much about that subject, nor do our representatives in government. Increasingly, it is scientists in governmental or industrialized bureaucracies who are specialized enough in their knowledge to be able to make decisions about what sort of tolerance there should be for side effects, how much profit margin is reasonable for the drug companies, how to evaluate experiments to test new drugs, and so on.

But suppose you take it to be your duty to read up on pharmaceuticals. The next issue to come along, however, is whether the state should control stem cell research. Do you know all the medical and legal facts you need to know to participate in making that decision? After stem cell research, we need to decide what to do about international trade—are you knowledgeable about that? And so it goes.

The problem that this situation poses for the Greek legacy is rooted in the fact that the ideal of that legacy is popular participation in public decision-making through public speaking. The Greek legacy is built upon the model of citizens who know enough about the issues that confront them to be able to form and develop expositional arguments about such issues, to understand the issues well enough to debate them. Traditional rhetorical texts, with their four characteristics, are designed for a rational, well-informed, step-by-step consideration of issues. The problem is that the public can no longer confront most of the issues faced today in that way. Today's issues and problems are too vast for people to debate them rationally and expositionally in the way envisioned by the ancient Greeks.

A number of thinkers have complained that the public is no longer able to argue expositionally and rationally (for examples, see Boggs; Postman). The problem is actually a result of the knowledge explosion: people cannot possibly know all they need to know, and gather that knowledge into rational arguments, in order to debate public issues expositionally. It would take hours simply to recite all the studies, facts and figures, statistics, and so forth that one would need to know to be able to make a decision about most public issues. A further problem is that there are so many public issues for which there is an overabundance of specialized knowledge that the chances of an audience understanding and being able to follow a knowledgeable speaker on a technical topic are not great. This problem is true for all traditional rhetorical texts, essays, and articles as well as speeches. Information has outgrown the ability of this type of text to handle it.

The explosion of knowledge confronts us with this choice: Either the public will become increasingly excluded from important decision-making as those decisions are referred to experts with specialized technical and scientific knowledge, or people will find ways to understand public problems through other means besides traditional texts that rely upon scientific and technical knowledge. It may be that important public business is already being managed in ways that are not limited to texts that depend upon scientific and technical knowledge. And, if that is true, then important public business is being conducted through texts other than traditional texts that are verbal, expositional, discrete, and hierarchical.

Managing Power Today in Traditional Texts: Neo-Aristotelian Criticism

We have learned so far that the shapes taken by rhetoric are changing as more and more of our social business is managed in the rhetoric of popular culture. The verbal, expositional, discrete, and hierarchical forms of traditional texts are giving way to the new texts of television, films, and popular music. But it would be a mistake to assume that traditional texts have vanished, or that no important business is ever done using those tools. Think for a moment of times when the rhetorical conditions of ancient Greece still occur today, when empowered speakers still present reasoned, verbal arguments in carefully crafted addresses to attentive audiences. Those moments would certainly include nearly the whole of our legal system, much of the communication in places of worship, educational and technical instruction—in fact, you can likely

©iStockphoto.com/GreenPimp

find traditional texts offered up by your instructors in your college classrooms on a daily basis! This very book you are holding is a traditional text.

Since traditional texts have not gone away, it would be useful to understand a method that has been devised over the course of centuries for analyzing those texts. It is known as neo-Aristotelian criticism. It is based on the rhetorical principles explained by Aristotle but is "neo" because that great theorist himself did not set out a specific method for the critique of traditional texts. More recent scholars have developed this scheme. Let us take a look at the main principles of neo-Aristotelian criticism and how to use them in analyzing traditional texts. These principles may be summarized in this scheme:

The Situation

- Context
- Exigency
- Audience

The Speaker

- Background
- Intentions

The Speech

- Invention: logos, ethos, pathos
- Arrangement
- Style
- Delivery
- Memory (technology)

Evaluation

- Effects and effectiveness
- Ethical assessment

Neo-Aristotelian critics think of texts as tools that persuaders use to address specific problems. They want to know what prompted the speaker to craft a message, what the speaker hoped to accomplish in speaking, and whether the message met the speaker's expectations and addressed the problem that generated the whole process. So, neo-Aristotelian criticism begins with considering the situation, by which we mean the event, problem, issue, or difficulty that called forth the message—we call this the exigency—and the context in which the exigency occurred.

Sometimes the exigency, the event that sets the rhetorical process in motion, is a happy one (a high school class is graduating), sometimes it is sad (a funeral), sometimes it is dangerous (there has been a terrorist attack), but in all cases the exigency is the kind of problem that can be addressed through rhetorical communication. Nobody thinks of addressing the exigency that is a sprained ankle by giving a speech; that's not the sort of problem that gives itself up to rhetorical manipulation. But there are problems that need to be addressed by someone talking, and those problems are the exigencies that the neo-Aristotelian critic identifies as having occupied a speaker.

Of course, problems do not occur in a vacuum. There is a context for them. If there has been a terrorist attack, is this something new or part of a long, dismal pattern? Is it in a friendly or unfriendly part of the world? On our soil or in another country? From enemies we know or enemies we don't? The context into which the exigency enters will affect how the event is understood and will establish limits and possibilities for response. The neo-Aristotelian critic always places the exigency into the context as understood by the speaker and audience.

This brings us to the third part of the situation, and that is the audience. To whom did the speaker present this message in hopes of addressing the exigency? What did the audience know about and think about the speaker before the speech? The speaker assumes that the audience addressed was in a position to resolve the exigency, so the neo-Aristotelian critic studies the audience to identify who they were, what they knew and felt about the exigency and the speaker, what their strengths and weaknesses were, and what role they could play in addressing the exigency.

There is some reason why this particular speaker stepped up to offer a rhetorical response to the exigency for that particular audience, so the speaker is the next major category of analysis. The neo-Aristotelian critic should identify the speaker's background— who that person is, what her reputation was before the speech; if possible identify what the audience thought of her; and explain the speaker's qualifications, training, and experience that would be relevant in addressing the exigency. The critic wants to say why this particular speaker was put in the position of solving the exigency rhetorically.

The speaker's intentions are a key part of analysis. If we are to assess the success of a speech as a tool, we need to know the purpose for which it was intended. The neo-Aristotelian determines as much as possible what the speaker planned to do. Since few critics are mind readers, identifying intentions can be difficult. Fortunately, many speakers leave a record of what they intended to do in speeches, and the more important the occasion, the more likely there is to be a record. A president discussing with top aides how to respond to a crisis will leave a record of notes, sometimes tape-recorded conversations, and press releases. Often those aides themselves will write books recalling what the president meant to do. From these historical records, the critic can reconstruct the goals the speaker was trying to achieve. An understanding of the speaker's intentions then becomes a benchmark for evaluating the success of the speech.

The speech is the most complicated category of neo-Aristotelian analysis and the one on which the critic spends the most time. We should be clear that we are referring to "the speech" as the exemplar of traditional texts, just as we refer to "the speaker," but the techniques of this neo-Aristotelian method apply equally well to other forms of traditional texts. The first and most complicated unit within this category is invention.

Invention means the inventing of what to say. Here the critic identifies the substance of the speech and does so on three dimensions. First, the critic explains the logos, or logical (expositional) appeals of the speech. Second, the critic explains the ways in which the speaker built up an appeal based on his own character, trustworthiness, goodwill toward the audience, expertise, and qualifications. These appeals based on the speaker himself are called ethos. Finally, the critic explains the emotional appeals, or pathos, used by the speaker. For each of these subcategories of invention, the critic always relates the analysis back to what the speaker intended to do and what the audience needed or expected to hear in confronting the exigency, for those are the standards against which the rhetorical effort is judged.

Another category for analyzing the speech itself is arrangement: How did the ordering of different appeals in the speech affect the audience? How did the speech begin; how did it end? Were there issues the speaker delayed in raising; were there some issues that were addressed first, before other issues could be tackled? The next category is style, or language choice. The neo-Aristotelian critic studies key terms in the speech and the ideas that those terms bring to the foreground. The critic studies stylistic devices or figures of speech such as metaphor, irony, metonymy, and so forth to identify ways in which the speech was made both pleasing and effective.

Delivery is a category of analysis of the speech concerned with nonverbal rhetoric. This category will be immediately recognizable as a major concern of many political commentators today who remark on the physical expressions, tone of voice, regional accents, animated or wooden gestures, and odd pronunciations of so many political leaders and candidates. This category reminds us that a concern for the physical presentation and appeal of messages is ancient, predating today's popular culture of images and impressions.

Neo-Aristotelian critics do not pay much attention to the category that is sometimes called the "lost canon" of rhetoric: memory. In the early days of Greek oratory, an ability to memorize lengthy speeches was crucial, and several schemes were available for speakers to do so. In an age of teleprompters and PowerPoint, such a concern seems irrelevant. I propose that the category be updated rather than discarded, however. People had to memorize speeches because of the condition of technology in ancient Greece: there were no teleprompters! But the condition of technology in our times can dramatically affect the impact of even traditional texts. In place of memory, neo-Aristotelian critics should study the speaker's use of technology: Were visual aids to the speech used, and how were they presented? Was video or music incorporated into the speech at all? If the speech was broadcast on television, how were camera angles used? When did the camera move in for a tight focus on the speaker's face, when did it pull back, and to what effect?

The final major category of analysis in neo-Aristotelian criticism is evaluation. The critic must assess whether the speech worked as a tool to do the job for which it was intended. The first subcategory of analysis here is effects and effectiveness. Studying the effects of any persuasive effort can be notoriously difficult. The critic can examine public opinion polls taken after the speech to see whether audience attitudes changed. The critic can examine historical records of what actually happened after a speech to see whether actions called for by the speaker took place. The critic can examine other, later rhetorical documents to see whether key phrases or ideas introduced by the speech were taken up by others as a sign that the speech was influential.

However, there are some difficulties in determining effects. There is the question of time frames: A speech may have very little effect when it is given but come to gain greater attention and respect as time goes on. On the other hand, an initially successful speech may come to seem unwise or dated as time marches on. There is also the question of intervening causes: Other rhetorical efforts as well as events may occur that contribute to whatever effects may be observed, so that knowing how much to attribute to a particular speech is difficult. Finally, there is the question of very difficult rhetorical challenges: A speech may be effective even though it created few practical effects because it did the best it could under difficult circumstances. The case of Abraham Lincoln's first inaugural address is often given as an example of these difficulties. It was intended to keep the Union together, but the Civil War took place nevertheless. There were simply too many pressures for war for it to overcome, and too many intervening causes that negated any positive effect it might have. But over time it came to be understood as a powerful argument for unity that guided the nation's path even after Lincoln's death, and for these reasons it is judged more in terms of effectiveness than effect, as a speech that did the best that it could against overwhelming odds.

Finally, the neo-Aristotelian critic is allowed to make ethical evaluations of the speech. Whether a speech succeeded in practical terms may not be the only criterion for judgment. Many dictators and despots have been rhetorically successful in persuading people to follow them in their questionable policies, and so they would have to be judged practically successful. But those same speakers may also be judged on ethical grounds as having defended policies or points of view that were reprehensible.

In sum, the methods of neo-Aristotelian criticism can help us to understand how traditional texts work today. That is true whether the traditional text is in the form of a public speech, an editorial in a newspaper, or a sermon. Neo-Aristotelian criticism is a tool that is appropriate for studying traditional texts in just the same way as tools that we will learn about in later chapters are appropriate for studying the texts of popular culture.

Summary and Review

We began this chapter by posing the question of how everyday objects, actions, and events influence people. The idea that these everyday experiences of popular culture have an important effect on people should already seem more plausible to you. Rhetoric was defined initially as the ways in which signs influence people, and in this chapter we began to understand some basic concepts that will help us to see how popular culture is rhetorical in just that way. We also briefly noted that influencing other people is a way of securing power. And we noted that power often creates privilege, which may exist outside the conscious awareness of those who enjoy it.

This chapter has covered many ideas and more than two thousand years. First, we discussed the idea that definitions in general are a means of empowerment and disempowerment; how you define a term is an act of power. Some terms that have a lot to do with power have therefore been defined in many different ways throughout history; rhetoric is such a term.

We learned a quick definition of signs and of texts, although these will be developed further in the next chapter. We learned a little about the history of ancient Greece, and about how public speaking was the public's way of rhetorically managing important business. In subsequent years, this experience of the Greeks would create a legacy that strongly affected the development of rhetorical

theory. This legacy comprises what we might call traditional rhetoric. Traditional rhetoric assumes, first, that rhetoric means a particular kind of text, the kind that is most clearly exemplified in public speaking—that is, a text that is verbal, expositional, discrete, and hierarchical. The second part of the Greek legacy for traditional rhetoric is a paradox. We learned here that the more favorably rhetoric is defined, the more it democratizes power, because widespread participation in public decisions is conducted through rhetorical discussion. But, paradoxically, we also learned that because rhetoric meant traditional texts for the Greeks, the rhetorical tradition fails to see how important business might be conducted by texts that are not verbal, expositional, discrete, and hierarchical. A useful idea in connection to these issues is the distinction between the functions of rhetoric—what it does—and its manifestations, the form it takes. The Greeks had a narrower understanding of how rhetoric might be manifested, which was restricted to traditional texts.

We saw how this Greek legacy, embodied in traditional rhetorical theory, influenced writers and thinkers for centuries. It is still important today, and we learned techniques of neo-Aristotelian criticism designed to help us understand how traditional texts work. We learned how a neo-Aristotelian critique based on the categories of the situation, the speaker, the speech, and evaluation can guide the critic in understanding the rhetorical effectiveness of traditional texts even today.

From the eighteenth through the twentieth centuries, the germs of new ideas were planted, new ideas that would eventually allow for the development of a rhetoric of popular culture that is becoming fully developed in the twenty-first century. We also learned that "real-life" developments in the twentieth and now the twenty-first century have increasingly challenged the rhetorical tradition. We explored the specific developments of (1) an expanding population, (2) new technologies (especially of information), (3) pluralism, and (4) an explosion of knowledge.

Because of these developments, we concluded that much of the important business of a society might not be conducted in traditional texts as exclusively as the Greek legacy would have us believe. Instead of seeking only verbal texts, we will look for texts that also include nonverbal elements. Instead of seeking only expositional texts, we will look for metonymy and narrative as well. Instead of seeking only discrete texts, we will also look for diffuse texts. And instead of using only hierarchical texts, we will also look for democratic texts. In the next two chapters, then, we will deal more specifically with how the rhetoric of popular culture works and how to study it.

Looking Ahead

At this point, you may very well have several questions left unanswered. Let us consider some questions that *should* arise from this chapter. You might think about these questions, discuss them in class, or use them to prepare for later chapters.

1. We have talked about rhetoric but not so much about culture; what do we mean by *culture*, especially popular culture?

2. We have not said much about the different forms that texts can take and how they participate in creating meaning.

3. We have not yet explored the idea of *struggle* over power very thoroughly. Are there ways in which you would say that popular culture is a site of struggle? For instance:

   • What happens when actions, object, and events mean several things, or mean contradictory things? Who decides what meanings they will have?
   • How do actions, objects, and events come to have several meanings?
   • Can the assignment of meaning lead to power and disempowerment? How does that happen?
   • How can people resist the meanings that others try to impose on them?
   • How is struggle over meaning conducted? What are the tools or strategies that people use?

4. We have learned about the characteristics of traditional rhetoric and its texts. What do the texts of popular culture look like, the texts that carry so much weight in everyday experience?

2

RHETORIC AND
POPULAR CULTURE

Now we turn to the second important set of concepts in this book. Following our introduction to rhetoric, let's learn about what we mean when we say popular culture and thus the rhetoric of popular culture. In comparison to traditional rhetoric, when we think about how rhetoric works in popular culture, we are concerned with the rhetoric of everyday life. How can we understand the persuasive influences that are all around us? In this chapter, we will examine the rhetorical dimension of those everyday objects, actions, and events to which we are constantly exposed. We will also see in Chapter 2 what it means to refer to these everyday objects, actions, and events as popular culture.

We will learn that many, even most, of the ways in which we are influenced through signs can be observed on this everyday, minute-by-minute level of popular culture. As we go through life experiencing and enjoying music, clothing, architecture, food, and so forth, we are also participating in rhetorical struggles over what kind of society we will live in and what sort of people we will be. This book will empower you to see those struggles as well, so that you will be able to find the rhetoric in Rihanna, the motivations on Facebook, and the arguments in RVs.

THE RHETORIC OF EVERYDAY LIFE

To begin seeing everyday experience as alive with persuasive influences, let us begin by considering power. Power is the ability to control events and meanings. We are used to thinking that certain people, groups, or classes of people have power and that others do not. We say that the Bush and Clinton families, Bill Gates, Barack Obama, Donald Trump, and so forth all have power. Perhaps you have worked in offices or on committees with individuals whom you could clearly identify as powerful. Perhaps there have been other individuals whom you thought were relatively lacking in power. Certainly, we might all agree that, compared with adults, children are relatively powerless for several reasons. But did you ever stop to wonder specifically when and where all this empowerment and disempowerment comes about?

Many people believe that, compared to men, women in some fields are relatively disempowered in some societies: women sometimes earn lower salaries for the same jobs; fewer women have high-ranking jobs and positions of prestige (e.g., U.S. presidents or senators); there are not as many female judges, physicians, police officers, college professors, and so forth. How does this relative empowerment of men and disempowerment of women occur? It is almost as if young males were all taken aside at a certain age and initiated into certain mysteries of dominance; it would seem as if all the men working at certain companies met in secret once a month to plan dastardly deeds of disempowerment against women. But this management of power does not really happen during isolated moments of conspiracy. Instead, the relative disempowerment of women and empowerment of men at the workplace occurs from moment to moment during everyday experiences—in short, in popular culture. For example:

- In fashion, where women often have available to them largely uncomfortable shoes and clothing designed to accentuate their bodies rather than to create ease of movement and repose.
- Around the office coffee pot, where the preferred topics of conversation among men are often things like sports or sexual innuendo (and when the boss is a male sports nut, guess which sort of knowledge revealed in conversation is more empowering when it comes to impressing superiors?).
- In social expectations, as when a male who leaves work early to pick up a sick child at school is considered responsible and sensitive, whereas a woman who does the same thing is often perceived as compromising her professional "commitment" to her career.

Of course, many women do not take these moments of disempowerment quietly. Women devise strategies of resistance, refusing the disempowerment that everyday experience often offers to them and seeking alternative means of empowerment. These actions have paid off on a societal level, and there is greater equality among men and women now than ever before. How this progress has occurred may also be studied in terms of popular, everyday sites. Everyday actions, objects, and experiences are really

EXERCISE 2.1

This exercise is designed to help you see how some commonly held, even fundamental, notions are born and maintained in your everyday experiences. Pick, from among the following statements, the one that you agree with most strongly:

- American workers are suffering from unfair foreign outsourcing.
- In this country, urban problems are mainly economic problems.
- It is important to look nice and to smell nice.
- Pornography is a serious problem on the Internet.
- The United States is threatened by terrorists.
- Most politicians are dishonest, self-serving, or incompetent.

Now, do some thinking and reflecting on this question: Specifically when and where did you come to have that belief? Another way to ask this question would be, can you remember specific experiences that influenced you to hold that belief? To help you in your thinking, you might want to write down some specific experiences that fall under these categories:

a. Television commercials

b. Social media (Twitter, Facebook, etc.)

c. Movies

d. Faith communities

e. Popular music

f. Television news

g. Television drama or comedy

h. Teachers

i. Talking with friends

j. Family discussions

k. Internet blogs

l. Other

The earlier statements are widely held ideas; they are a sort of "party line" for many people living in the United States today. They seem for many of us to be "common sense"—statements that "grease the wheels" of everyday social interaction, allowing it to function smoothly. Perhaps not coincidentally, these statements are also what most people who are in positions of authority or established power would want the public to believe. That is because in general, these statements maintain present arrangements of power and privilege. If it is important to smell nice, then consumers will run out and buy lots of deodorant, perfumed soap, and so on that will keep the manufacturers of such products wealthy and powerful. If we are afraid of terrorists, we will tend to stick with political leaders who we believe have protected us so far. It is equally important to understand that we do not always accept what established and powerful interests want us to believe. We don't always "go with the flow" with those beliefs that seem to be most common or easiest to hold. Which of the above statements do you disagree with? If you do disagree with any of them, do you do so with the distinct feeling that you are in a minority, or bucking the tide of public opinion, in doing so? If so, use the preceding list of commercials, articles, movies, and so forth to identify how you developed your ability to resist a popular idea or ideas. In other words, how did you learn to struggle against some widely held ideas?

battlefields, sites of struggle among political and social forces. We will talk more about that struggle later in this book. Many kinds of social and political influence—empowerment and disempowerment—happen in the same way: from one moment to the next, in everyday experiences. A quick exercise will emphasize this point.

There may be an opportunity for you to discuss with your class or with friends how you acquired the beliefs that you examined in the exercise above. If you are like most people, you will realize that most of what you think did not come to you in one big moment of revelation. Instead, many of your ideas were acquired through the influence of lots of transitory, everyday experiences of the kind you listed in doing this exercise.

Power arrangements that have been around for a while and that are not often questioned may foster a sense of privilege in those who benefit from them. Although this may be changing, for centuries people of European heritage have had privilege in the United States: they have been empowered in many ways that are not often questioned. Our example of gender above reminds us that men have enjoyed privilege, and in some parts of the world they do so to an extreme extent. Paradoxically, those who benefit from privilege are usually those least aware of it, and especially least aware of how power and privilege are maintained. When our experiences in popular culture are important sources of maintaining power and privilege, being able to understand and analyze them is especially important. People who benefit from privilege need to be able to see that empowerment and its sources so they can live more ethical lives. People who are not privileged need to see precisely the sources of their lack of privilege so they may struggle against it.

For instance, heterosexual people still enjoy the privilege of relative empowerment in the United States. Heterosexuals will hardly ever be denigrated or attacked for their sexual identity. Yet very few heterosexuals go around being aware of that privilege; it simply seems natural. What are the sources of this privilege? Chief among them are the messages in popular culture, such as advertisements that consistently show heterosexual rather than gay or lesbian couples or movies in which romantic storylines are far more likely to be heterosexual. These ever-present but unseen (by the privileged) voices prop up structures of power. On the other hand, popular movies and shows depicting nonheterosexuals in positive ways are increasing and may be a resource in the struggle against repressive attitudes. In this book, we will come to perceive the complex network of those experiences as popular culture, and we will study ways to grasp the rhetoric embodied in popular culture. To comprehend how culture influences us, we need to develop an understanding of what popular culture is—what it is made of, and how we live in and through it.

THE BUILDING BLOCKS OF CULTURE: SIGNS

If we are going to think about the ways in which the things and events we encounter in everyday experience influence us, then we need to start by thinking about how those things and events come to have meaning. That is because influence occurs through the management of meaning. If a bigot is persuaded to treat people of all races equally, it is because the meaning of racial difference is changed for that individual. If you are influenced to vote for Senator Smith, it is because the senator (his or her ideas, positions, and so on) has taken on a positive meaning for you. Commercials are rather explicit about the link between influence and meaning; we are urged to attach meanings of glamour and mystery to a certain perfume, for example, in hopes that we will be influenced to buy the perfume.

Let's return to the idea with which we began Chapter 1, the concept of a sign (here we will follow a very sensible scheme proposed by the American philosopher Charles Sanders Peirce). Everything is a sign. That's because a sign is something that induces you to think about something other than itself—and everything has that potential.

Take the book you are holding. When you see it, you do not think only about the book itself; you think about the class in which you are enrolled, about the ideas you have been reading, about the attractive person next to you in class, about how much the book costs, and so forth. Now lift your eyes from your book and look around you. For each thing you see, other thoughts associated with that thing will arise: the iPod on the desk will remind you of the previous one you owned, the picture on the wall will lead you to think of the shopping trip on which you bought it, and so on.

Every sight and sound, every touch, smell, and taste you experience, prompts you to think about things other than, or in addition to, itself. Therefore, everything is a sign of something else. We might also say that everything is a signifier, that everything signifies something else, or that everything has signification. And signification—or the other thing that is signified—is just another way of referring to meaning. If I say the word *professor*, and the thought of that learned individual who is teaching you pops into your head, then that thought is the meaning of the sign "professor."

If you think about it, signification is a pretty strange fact. We hear words coming out of a friend's mouth, and ideas (meanings) start jumping into our heads; we see a cap lying on a table, and the sight makes us think of the soccer game we recently wore it to. How does it happen that when we see and hear things, ideas that are not the things themselves pop into our heads? Things act as signs in one or a combination of the three following ways:

1. Indexically (from the word *index*, referring to indexical meaning)
2. Iconically (from the word *icon*, referring to iconic meaning)
3. Symbolically (from the word *symbol*, referring to symbolic meaning)

Indexical Meaning

First, some things get you to think about something else because the "thing" (sign) and the "something else" (meaning) are linked by way of cause or association. One thing is always or often found with another thing, and so one gets you to think of the other. This kind of meaning is indexical; we say that the sign is an index, or that it is functioning indexically. Smoke is an index of fire; if you see smoke, it causes you to think of fire because you know that one thing is associated with (caused by, in this case) the other. A thermometer is a sign with indexical meaning; a rise in the mercury in the column means a rise in the surrounding environment's temperature. Why? Because the one thing is always associated with the other; in this case, too, the association is causal.

Every character on the television show *Homeland* is an index of every other character because the members of that complex community are associated with (though in this case, not caused by) each other. Some characters are more strongly indexical of certain other characters, however; the lead characters, Carrie Mathison and Nicholas Brody, are more central than characters such as Saul Berenson and Jessica Brody, so they both may make you think of each other but also of Mathison and Nicholas Brody. The same set of indexical meanings is true of other shows with groups of closely connected characters, such as the different franchises of *CSI* or *Law and Order*, or *Modern Family* or *The Big Bang Theory*.

Everyone has played the word-association game in which players are supposed to say which words come into their minds upon hearing a cue word. That game can be an interesting indication of indexical meanings. The word *cat* might prompt someone to think *dog*, for instance. Does that mean that the meaning of cat is a dog? In part—indexically—it does. That linkage reveals the fact that one part of the meaning of cats really is their association, as proverbial enemies, with dogs.

Many indexical meanings are widely shared. Is there a person who has seen any sports news broadcast in the last few years, for example, who will not think about basketball upon seeing a picture of LeBron James? NBA player Jeremy Lin is celebrated by many people but seems to be held in special esteem by those who share his Chinese heritage; he might be said to be an index of that community. Other indexical meanings are less widespread, being limited to particular groups of people, and some indexical meanings are even private. Sand may induce only veterans of our military involvement in Afghanistan to think of Afghanistan; to everyone else, sand may have the indexical meaning of a day at the beach. For your author, the smell of a cigar is an indexical sign of a grandfather who could sometimes be found with one, a more private meaning (an association) unlikely to be widely shared by others outside his particular family.

©iStockphoto.com/pagadesign

Iconic Meaning

If a sign makes you think of something else because the sign resembles that thing, then the sign has iconic meaning. We would also say that the sign is an icon or that it has meaning iconically. The clearest example of an icon is a photograph. You look at the photograph and think, "Aunt Griselda!" Why? Because the patterns of light and dark on the photographic paper resemble her. Computer operating systems such as Apple or Windows use icons to signify the choices available to the user (what resembles a talking mouth is the volume control, for instance). Impressionists such as Key and Peele, Dave Chappelle, and many of the actors on the television show *Saturday Night Live* (especially during the 2016–2017 political election and ensuing administration) make their living producing icons; the combination of an inflection of the voice, a few gestures, and a stance or way of walking prompt the audience to think "Hillary Clinton" or "Donald Trump," because those signs resemble the voice, gestures, and stances of the original people. Halloween is a great iconic holiday; little children, icons themselves, dress up to resemble Rush Limbaugh, Dracula, ghosts, and other horrors. Many words are signs with iconic meaning. Say the words *boom*, *bang*, and *tinkle* out loud. Part of the meaning of those words is that they resemble (by way of sound) the events to which they refer.

As with indexical meaning, signs may vary in terms of how widely their iconic meaning is shared. Your author once wore a set of nose-and-mustache glasses into class and asked the eighteen-year-old students what those glasses meant. "Halloween parties!" they all replied, giving an indexical meaning (nose glasses are found at, or associated with, Halloween parties). But this indexical meaning broke your author's heart. For him, nose glasses will forever mean Groucho Marx, because they resemble Groucho iconically. Evidently, however, the group of people who share that iconic meaning is dwindling as poor Groucho recedes into late-night television movie land. Iconic meanings can also be private; your picture of Aunt Griselda may cause only you to think of her if nobody else knows her. For others, the iconic meaning of the photo may be something more general, such as "an elderly female," because that is what the photo resembles for them.

Symbolic Meaning

Finally, signs can get you to think about something else purely because of agreement or convention, because people are in the habit of connecting a particular sign with a particular meaning. When that happens, a sign is a symbol, has symbolic meaning, or is functioning symbolically. The clearest examples of symbols are words. Why does this mark:

Book

mean the thing that you are holding? Only because everyone who speaks English agrees that it does. People are simply in the habit of thinking of the kind of thing you are holding whenever they see that mark above, and they know that others have agreed to think the same thing. If everyone decided that this mark:

Glorpus

would mean the thing you are holding, that would work just as well. Symbolic meaning comes about purely by way of what people agree to do. In fact, in Spanish-speaking communities, everyone has agreed that the mark *libro* means what you are holding. One way to refer to that agreement is to say that symbolic meaning is conventional—a product of certain conventions, or agreed-upon rules.

©iStockphoto.com/Levente_Naghi

Symbolic meaning is in some ways the most difficult kind of meaning to learn, because it is not natural and because symbolic meanings vary from one group to another. Smoke naturally means fire. The photograph of your aunt naturally refers to her. There is a strong, clear, and necessary connection. Smoke also means fire in Japan, Germany, and Zimbabwe. And once you learn that indexical meaning, it does not change.

But anyone who has struggled through learning a foreign language knows that, as comedian Steve Martin said of the French, "It's like they have a different word for everything!" If you want to speak French, you must learn what certain signs mean for the French and assign the same meanings that they do to the words of their language. The rule for understanding symbolic meaning is to consult the group that is using the symbol to discover what the symbol means. For instance, in some geographically or culturally specific communities, the expression *fall out* means to faint or to pass out. A person not familiar with that usage might assume these words refer to a long drop from a window. A nuclear strategist, on the other hand, might assume that they refer to the radioactive particles produced by a nuclear explosion. And a soldier might assume they are an order to disperse.

Words are not the only things with symbolic meaning. The particular pattern of red, white, and blue stars and stripes that you know as the flag of the United States means this country, symbolically, because the U.S. Congress has ordained it so, and people everywhere are agreed on this signification. In the U.S. Army, the figure of a golden eagle on the shoulder strap, epaulets, or collar of a uniform means a full colonel for no other reason than that everyone in the army agrees that this is what it means; a figure of the sun, or a tiny Washington monument, would do just as well if everyone agreed to it.

We noted above that smoke has the indexical meaning of fire, but it can also have symbolic meaning. Cigarette smoke goes through cycles of meaning in which sometimes it symbolically means "coolness," sometimes it is "low class," sometimes it means "toughness," and so forth. Think about the symbolic meanings given to cigarettes by recent movies and television shows you have seen. When the Roman Catholic Church is in need of a new pope, as in the latest election of Francis I, the College of Cardinals will meet in closed session to cast ballots. Those who wait outside the building for news of the election watch a certain chimney. The ballots are burned in such a way that if a new pontiff has been chosen, the smoke is white; if not, the smoke is black. In this way, too, smoke has been assigned symbolic meaning. The meaning of the colors could easily be reversed, or chemicals could be added to make other colors, as long as everyone understood which color meant which outcome.

Symbolic meaning differs from iconic or indexical meaning in that it can easily be altered. Nobody can decide that smoke does not mean fire (indexically). Nobody can decide that a picture of a horse does not cause you to think of a horse (iconically). With both indexical and iconic meaning, once you learn what a sign means, the meaning simply cannot change. You can discover iconic or indexical meaning, and you can forget it, but you cannot legislate it.

But symbolic meaning changes all the time. Sixty and more years ago, the word *gay* meant happy and carefree. Now it more commonly refers to a particular sexual orientation. Sixty years from now, it may mean something entirely different. That is the nature of symbolic meaning: You can mess with it. You can change it. And, for that reason, symbolic meaning is always slippery. This changeable quality of symbolic signs (principally language) has sometimes been described as the constant "slippage" of the signified (meaning) under the signifier (word). That is, the sign (for example, *gay*) holds still while the meaning, or what it signifies, slips around (from happy and carefree to homosexual and perhaps beyond). What something means is never precise, because there is never complete agreement among everybody as to what symbols mean. We will see that this "slippage" of symbolic meaning creates great possibilities for influence in popular culture.

Complexity of the Three Kinds of Meaning

We learned earlier that signs have meaning in one or more of these three ways: indexically, iconically, and symbolically. You may have noticed that we have already demonstrated how words can carry two kinds of meaning: all words are symbolic, and some words are indexical (as seen in the example of the word *smoke*). The point is worth stressing: Most signs do mean in more than one way; in fact, most signs have very rich meanings. Sometimes those meanings are widely shared, sometimes they are shared by a few groups, and sometimes they are very personal. But it is a mistake to ask what single thing a sign means, or in which of the three ways it has meaning, because signs are typically very complex in their meaning.

Pull out a dollar bill (if you have one after buying this book). This is a sign that has meaning in all three ways. You will see icons on it: some markings that resemble George Washington, other markings that look like a pyramid. You will find indexical meaning: you might think of shopping, of your wallet, or of your next payday, because all those things are associated with the dollar bill. You will certainly find symbolic meanings: the bald eagle clutching arrows and an olive branch in its talons means the United States by convention; moreover, the fact that this piece of paper is worth anything at all is purely conventional and by way of agreement. Congress could pass a law tomorrow saying that pocket handkerchiefs will be the unit of economic trade. If that were to happen and if everyone agreed to it, then you could blow your nose on dollar bills but slave away at your job for handkerchiefs. The fact that a dollar bill can be exchanged for a small candy bar or (at this writing) a third of a gallon of gasoline is only a matter of agreement and, therefore, symbolic meaning.

THE BUILDING BLOCKS OF CULTURE: ARTIFACTS

In this book, we will be concerned with all signs that make up messages. In this section, though, we are going to focus on a subset of particularly powerful signs known as cultural artifacts. An artifact is

1. an action, event, or object perceived as a unified whole,
2. having widely shared meanings, and
3. manifesting group identifications to us.

EXERCISE 2.2

Here is an exercise to help you appreciate how complicated the meanings of signs are. Review the signs listed below and identify whether each has indexical, iconic, or symbolic meaning. Also, determine whether those meanings are shared widely, by smaller groups, or are relatively private for you or perhaps your family.

Sign	Indexical Meanings (How widely shared?)	Iconic Meanings (How widely shared?)	Symbolic Meanings (How widely shared?)
Guitarist Jack White			
Rolex watch			
Diamond ring			
A tattoo			
Statue of Liberty			
Nike shoes			
Star of David			
Halle Berry			

Now, work through some examples that you or your classmates or teacher can suggest. Whenever possible, try to find at least one meaning per category.

Everything in your experience—every object, action, or event—is a sign. But that statement, although correct and important, is so broad that it does not go far enough to help us to understand how the things we experience in everyday life influence us. So we must go on to consider even more specific ways in which signs have meaning.

This definition of an artifact is meant to be rather wide; nevertheless, not everything is an artifact. Let's look more closely at that definition. It will take us a little while to go through it carefully and unpack its meaning.

An Action, Event, or Object Perceived as a Unified Whole

You may have heard the word *artifact* associated with an actual object, something you could hold in your hand. An archaeologist who digs up a pot might claim to have found an artifact of Minoan culture, for instance. That idea of an artifact as something that represents a culture will become important when we discuss the third clause of the definition ("manifesting group identifications to us") later. But in this first clause of the definition, notice that by *artifact*, we mean not only a material object that is tangible but also an event or action that is perceived as a unified whole; in this sense, events and actions occurring in the material world are also material. Nike shoes are artifacts and they are concrete, physical objects. But slam dunks, stealing second base, the latest popular song, and the Fourth of July are also artifacts.

It is also important to notice that the artifact must be some action, event, or object that is perceived as a unified whole. In other words, perceptions of a whole "thing" or "happening" that has some identity or character in itself make an artifact. The bottom stripe on the United States flag is not an artifact because, although you can perceive it all by itself if you make the effort, it is not usually seen as a thing in itself with its own separate meaning. Neither is the field of stars in the flag's upper left-hand corner perceived as a unified whole. Rather, the whole flag is perceived as a unit, and that makes the flag itself an artifact.

This first clause in the definition of an artifact is based on an old, but still controversial, idea that the reality in which humans live and move is one that is fundamentally socially created. The idea here is that people live in a world of perceptions. For instance, the French have more words for different kinds of bread and pastries than do most Americans. Bread is more important to them, and they appreciate subtle differences in the size and texture of loaves. That means that they perceive differences in bread that Americans might not ("It's all baguettes to me!"). That does not mean that we cannot learn to see all those distinctions ourselves (in fact, American tourists must learn to recognize more kinds of bread so that they can order lunch more accurately). On the other hand, people living in the United States today have many different words for vehicles: Fords, Chevys, 4 by 4s, pickups, SUVs, RVs, Jaguars, and on and on. People in a part of the world that does not have so many vehicles may not need to perceive so many different kinds and so may think of all vehicles as being pretty much the same thing.

We see certain things and not others because of the social contexts that we grew up in; the people around us have called our attention to certain things but not others. People organize the world in ways that fit the physical and social environment they are in. That means that perceptions are adaptive mechanisms to help us adjust to the situations in which we live. If you live next door to a snarling Doberman Pinscher, your perception of the dog as dangerous is an adaptive mechanism that causes you to avoid the animal and thus live another day.

Furthermore, groups of people that live and work together try to adapt to their shared situations; thus, perceptions are also socially grounded. And so we grow up organizing the world, perceiving the world, in the ways that our social context encourages us to. For example, an important part of most Americans' situations is the need to recognize different kinds of vehicles. In addition, most Americans have the same, shared need to adapt to an environment in which vehicles are prominent. Football fans can see a bunch of people running around on a field and identify all kinds of things going on: an option play, the pass rush, and so forth. These fans have a recreational need to perceive lots of different plays, and they talk about the plays among themselves, encouraging each other to perceive the plays similarly. People who are not fans do not perceive the world of a football game in the same way because they do not need or want to; for them, a football game may look like just a bunch of people running around on a field.

. . . Having Widely Shared Meanings

To become an artifact, a sign must be more than just a perceived, unified whole. The second clause of the definition tells us that an artifact is a sign that has become charged with widely shared meaning, just like a battery that has been charged with energy.

Take the expression "Not that there's anything wrong with that!" That expression has an ordinary, straightforward meaning. It says that there is nothing wrong with "that," whatever "that" may be. But in the mid-1990s, it was an expression used on a popular episode of the *Seinfeld* television show in which the male characters were trying to put down rumors that they were gay. They were not, in the story, actually gay and did not wish to be perceived as such, but every denial was followed by the expression "Not that there's anything wrong with that!" It was delivered in such a way, with a sweeping gesture of the arms, as if to imply that they were leaning over backward to express liberal, tolerant sensitivities on an issue with which some might indeed still find "something wrong." Soon the expression was picked up and used as a follow-up to all kinds of similar denials. To "work," it depends on people understanding the humorous, ironic intent of the expression. It is remarkable the extent to which this expression, delivered in just the right way, still carries these ironic meanings decades after the fact. People will know how to read such a declaration, given with the right intonation and gesture, even if they have never seen *Seinfeld*. It is now part of the culture.

What happened was that those words, a simple English expression, became charged with widely shared, additional meanings. They meant something beyond the ordinary meaning derived from just combining those words. The phrase "Not that there's anything wrong with that!" has a definite symbolic meaning stemming from the conventions of the English language. But it picked up complicated indexical meanings when it became associated with a cute television episode, eccentric and classic television characters, and an ongoing social issue.

In another example, Kanye West has always meant something to his friends and family, just as you do. But you are not a cultural artifact because you are not charged with the extra meanings that West has picked up as a popular music star, tabloid fodder, and notable rapper. So one necessary condition for an ordinary sign becoming an artifact is that it becomes charged with more meanings than it had before and with more meanings that are widely shared.

Now, it is possible that the "Not that there's anything wrong with that!" example reads like ancient history to some of you. That's because this expression has by now lost some of its status as cultural artifact. As *Seinfeld* fades into syndication obscurity and fans move on to other, newer shows, the impact of that particular phrase (with its accompanying expression and gesture) will at some point fade. Eventually the phrase will not have that unity as a whole and particular thing, nor the widely shared meanings, that once made it a cultural artifact. And, likewise, someday there will arise a generation that knows not Kanye West.

These examples demonstrate that there is a threshold at which objects, events, or actions become artifacts. Furthermore, that threshold can be crossed in either direction; in other words, things, actions, and events are often in the process of either becoming, or declining as, cultural artifacts. Because perceptions change, the artifactual status of any sign must be changeable as well.

In contrast to Kanye West, think about yellow ribbons. Before the 1970s, they had no special unity, no particular meaning in themselves beyond just being yellow ribbons. An early 1970s song by the group Tony Orlando and Dawn proposed the idea of tying a yellow ribbon around a tree to indicate to someone who has been gone a long time that they are still wanted back. Although the song was popular and catchy, the song itself was more of a perceptual unity, more of a cultural artifact, than was the idea of a yellow ribbon.

But when sixty-three Americans were taken hostage at the United States Embassy in Tehran, Iran, in 1979, yellow ribbons came to be used as a gesture of remembrance by the American public. They began to appear everywhere, with the specific meaning of (1) a demonstration of solidarity with those who were absent (the hostages) and (2) a desire to have them back. Since then, foreign political crises involving absent or missing Americans have repeatedly been accompanied by widespread, spontaneous sproutings of yellow ribbons around trees, lampposts, and traffic signs. People wear them as pins on their clothing. They may be seen as tokens of solidarity with troops in the Middle East even now. They have crossed the threshold into the realm of cultural artifacts, and they are being maintained in that status by continuing social customs that encourage people to perceive them as artifacts—as things that have special meanings, as unified whole entities. And other causes have taken up the idea of ribbons as artifacts, as sporting ribbons of different colors is a way to show support for those with different kinds of cancer, AIDS sufferers, and so forth.

One consequence of becoming charged with widely shared meanings is that artifacts can be very complex; sometimes an artifact might even be composed of other artifacts. The Beatles were (in fact, still are, even if half of them are deceased) a cultural artifact as a group, but John Lennon, Paul McCartney, George Harrison, and Ringo Starr are cultural artifacts each in their own right (John Lennon and George Harrison, individually, remain so even after their deaths). The same has been true of the New York Yankees during several periods of their history. The television show *The Tonight Show* is so popular that it is an artifact, but so are some of its more visible characters, such as the host, Jimmy Fallon, as well as his studio band, the venerable The Roots. The New England Patriots are an artifact, but so are quarterback Tom Brady and coach Bill Belichick. Complex artifacts are charged with meaning, and if they comprise artifacts, then those constituent artifacts are also charged with meaning. This creates some very elaborate webs of meaning, and thus of influence.

. . . Manifesting Group Identifications to Us

The third and final clause in the definition of a cultural artifact identifies all artifacts as signs of group identifications. We have noticed that the charged meanings of an artifact must be widely shared; let us turn now to a consideration of how the shared nature of an artifact's meanings relates to group identifications. Here we will learn that artifacts are the material signs of abstract groups.

Part of the meaning of an artifact is its connection with a group. All of us belong to many groups. Some of those groups are ethnic or racial: you might identify yourself as Italian-American, African-American, Polish-American, or Southern white, for example. Some of those groups are geographical: you are an American, a Kansan, a Brooklynite, a resident of your neighborhood. Some groups are social: you might be a member of the Latin Kings, of a bridge club, of a tennis team. Some groups are religious: you might be Catholic, Methodist, Rastafarian. Some groups are economic: you might be wealthy, middle class, working class. Male and female are two large group identifications. Identifications sometimes have emotional or aesthetic bases: allegiances to particular sports teams or to clothing or product brands or designers are very often the grounding for group identifications, as with "Packer Backers" or those who buy only Calvin Klein jeans.

All of us, in other words, have many different group identifications. But, in fact, we very rarely see those groups in total. If you are a member of a local motorcycle club, you might very well see the whole group together at the same time. But most of our other group or social "memberships" are much larger or more abstract.

Perhaps you think of yourself as a Quaker; how, where, and when are you ever in touch with the Quakers? You see particular other Quakers, but never all of them and never at once. Perhaps you think of yourself as an African-American and identify with other African-Americans, but when and where does that identification occur? Another way to put this question would be, when does the "group" of African-Americans touch you? When does it speak to you? How are you reminded of what to do, how to act, and what to believe, so as to identify with that group? Many of us identify ourselves as "American"—a very broad identification—but how does that identification occur? Are you being American as you sit here reading? If you stop for coffee? When does that group, "American," speak to you?

Large or abstract groups of people (and nearly all of the groups with which we identify are large and abstract) connect with us, and influence us, through cultural artifacts. There are objects, actions, and events that manifest those groups to us that make the groups real, particular, and material. Artifacts represent groups to us, they show us what it is like to be part of or to identify with those groups, or they remind us of those groups and of what we are committed to by our identification with them. Artifacts are charged with meaning, but many of those meanings bespeak (that is, speak of or speak for) our identifications with groups. You need not be a member of a given group to understand an artifact that manifests that group identification, but it helps. That is to say, being a member of the group allows you to appreciate more of the meanings and to understand the ways in which the artifact is standing in for the group as a whole. In that way, a cultural artifact is a sort of an "in-joke." Others may understand something of what it means, but it is really the people "in the know," those who identify with the group (or groups) for which the artifact speaks, who find the richest meanings in an artifact.

Artifacts span the continuum from those that are quite obviously associated with a specific group identification to those that do not so clearly bespeak a group. Often, you may see more clearly how an artifact manifests a group identification if you are not part of that group (although then, paradoxically, you probably will not fully understand the meanings that the artifact conveys).

For instance, think about the form that cable television takes in the United States: a widely available opportunity to choose among hundreds of channels, many of them with very narrow, specific purposes. Now, this artifact (cable television) is part of being in that very large and abstract group, "American." Nearly all Americans have access to cable, or if not that, satellite or Internet television. Because so many of the readers of this book are part of that group, because we so rarely step outside of it or confront in any meaningful way the people who do not identify with that group, the artifacts that bespeak "being American" to us may seem natural, universal, or even invisible. Those artifacts may simply seem the only way to be. We do not notice how they create a group for us. It may take going to another country, with different patterns of television broadcast and consumption, to see American cable TV as not universal but a particular way of doing things, as our "American" way of doing things, as our sort of entertainment in-joke. Seeing alternatives to such a distinctive cultural artifact helps us to realize that widespread access to cable TV is peculiarly American.

Americans are defined in many ways, and we have many points of identification with being "American," but one of them is that we are the people with ready access to that kind of cable TV. What is useful about recognizing the ways in which cultural artifacts manifest groups to us is that we can then begin understanding the meanings of the artifact, and at that point we begin to understand our groups as well. To pursue the present example a bit further, think about what all those cable choices mean, especially in terms of what it means to be an American. We can tell from what cable TV means that being American has something to do with an abundance of choices. You might consider other distinctly American experiences that display the same embarrassment of riches (such as large restaurant menus or giant supermarkets)—the availability of more choices than anyone can possibly use.

Cable TV is one of those artifacts not obviously connected to a group, yet, as we have seen, it does manifest the group identification of being "American" to us. Consider a narrower example. I once went into a small-town delicatessen in a Pennsylvania Dutch county and asked for a pound of the salami displayed in the case. The woman behind the counter was dressed (as were all the other clerks) in the traditional long dress and hooded bonnet that the Mennonite or Amish women wear in that part of the country. She looked at me with dark suspicion: "What are you calling salami?" she asked. It turns out that all hard sausage there is called "bologna." What I wanted was "Lebanon bologna" (made near Lebanon, Pennsylvania). For this store clerk, "Lebanon bologna" is an artifact that is a material sign of her group identifications, and manifests that group so strongly and so often that she has ceased to think of that sausage as in any way special to her group. Lebanon bologna now seems natural and universal to her. Now, it's flatlanders like me who ask for artifacts that bespeak our group identifications, artifacts such as "salami."

Certain artifacts very clearly are the material signs of group identifications; they manifest specific groups to all sorts of other people. Take African-based hairstyles, for instance. One such style is dreadlocks, that style of long, twisted skeins that originated in Jamaica and in Africa before that. Plenty of people who are not of African heritage imitate such styles to an extent—and on the other hand, most African-Americans do not wear dreadlocks—but the artifacts of that hairstyle are firmly and unchangeably African-based. It is a style grounded in African heritage: African people have been wearing dreads for centuries. Dreads are even best suited physically to the characteristics of African hair.

Let's summarize what we have covered so far. We have seen that everything is a sign, but that not every sign is a cultural artifact. We have defined an artifact as

1. an action, event, or object perceived as a unified whole,
2. having widely shared meanings, and
3. manifesting group identifications to us.

EXERCISE 2.3

Identify yourself as a member of at least two broad social groups (for example, Hispanic and a union member, American Southerner and a motorcycle club member, male and United Methodist). For each group, identify:

a. An artifact that "belongs" only to the group that only members of the group are likely to see as charged with meanings. Identify some of those meanings. (Example: Only college professors are likely to know about and use the term *curriculum vitae*. Ask your instructor about it.)

b. An artifact that is closely identified with the group but that persons outside the group know about, use, and appreciate. Identify differences in what the artifact means for those inside the group and for the public at large. (Example: What does "Mexican food" mean for members of that ethnic group as well as for the general public? Does what is considered "Mexican food" differ between Mexicans or Mexican-Americans and the public at large?)

In elaborating on this definition, we discovered some important characteristics of artifacts:

1. Artifacts are a socially created reality.
2. Signs become artifacts as they become charged with meaning, thus crossing a threshold into artifact status.
3. An artifact can be very complex, even being made up of other artifacts.
4. Artifacts are the material signs of group identifications.

Now, let's do an exercise designed to familiarize you with the concept of an artifact. Do this exercise on your own or according to the directions of your instructor.

We have learned about signs and about the "supersigns" that are cultural artifacts. Both ordinary signs and cultural artifacts are key components not only because they are components of messages but also because they are also components of culture, and culture is the stuff out of which you and I are made. Let us turn now to the idea of culture.

DEFINITIONS OF CULTURE

In learning about signs and artifacts, we are studying the building blocks of culture. Now we need to turn to the term *culture* itself to understand what that means. Throughout history, culture has been a central concept with a number of definitions. As the scholar Raymond Williams put it, "culture is one of the two or three most complicated words in the English language" (*Keywords* 76).

Elitist Meanings of Culture

Perhaps the most widely known definition of culture has an elitist flavor to it: culture is the very best, the finest, and most refined experiences that a society or nation has to offer. This sense is found in the *Oxford English Dictionary* definition of culture, as "the training, development, and refinement of mind, tastes, and manners; the condition of being thus trained and refined; the intellectual side of civilization." This definition of culture underlies Moe's recurring complaint to Larry and Curly of *The Three Stooges*: "Mind your manners! Ain't ya got no culture? What would Emily Post say?" This idea of culture is often referred to as high culture.

This first, elitist sense of culture sees relatively few artifacts as making up culture. Only those objects or events having meanings associated with the very best, with high intellectual, aesthetic, or spiritual achievement, would be considered cultural artifacts under this definition. By exposing ourselves to them, we "become cultured." Those who are not exposed to those artifacts are not cultured, in this view. Some familiar artifacts that would be subsumed under this sense of culture would include the ballet, the symphony orchestra, public television, music by Bach or Beethoven, paintings by Rembrandt and Van Gogh, and sculptures by Michelangelo and Rodin. Some objects or events that would certainly not be considered cultural artifacts by this first definition would include heavy metal rock, polka bands, cage fighting, Rihanna, and corn dogs.

Often, those who talk about culture with this first definition in mind have what might be called an edifying impulse. In other words, they hope to improve people (which is not necessarily a bad thing) by exposing the public to the right artifacts. For these people, there is a sense that if you listen to Brahms rather than Common, if you see Shakespeare plays rather than *Friday Night Fights*, if you eat gourmet cuisine rather than Ho Hos, you will be a better person for it (and, by extension, our country will be a better place as well). This edifying impulse has been around for centuries and can be found in nearly every instruction from parents or teachers to do certain things because they are good for you. The edifying impulse is not necessarily limited to conservatives or those in power, either. It can also be found among certain Marxist scholars; for example, theorists such as Theodor Adorno and Herbert Marcuse (who were part of the so-called Frankfurt School around the middle of the twentieth century) thought that the pleasures to which the masses of ordinary Americans were addicted (things like television, pro football, and church bingo nights) were contributing to the oppression of those people (Adorno; Alford; Modleski ix; Mukerji and Schudson 56).

On the other hand, there have been radical twists to this first definition of culture. Some people have argued that it is the radical or subversive elements of culture to which people should be exposed. This effort to "turn the Frankfurt School on its head" to celebrate the liberating power of popular culture involves identifying experimental or alternative forms and experiences—such as guerrilla theatre, alternative rock or folk music,

EXERCISE 2.4

Consider the following questions for individual thought or group discussion.

1. If paintings, opera, poetry readings, and so forth are the products of high culture, what is everything else? Have you heard any particular terms (such as *low culture* or *mass culture*) used to refer to everything else?

2. What kind of power is created by calling certain things high culture? Who gets to wield that power?

3. Has anyone ever tried to "improve" you by referring to the idea of culture? Think about the specific ways in which that happened.

performance theatre, and so forth—as the kinds of cultural artifacts that will liberate the common people so as "to achieve dignity and to make life full" (Buhle xx). The particular artifacts identified by this school of thought as desirable, as the right things to do or hear or see, are very different from those included in the concept of high culture. But the edifying impulse is the same. In both of these versions of what culture is, the focus is on a very limited set of artifacts, such as the objects and experiences of art, that deserve to be called culture. In its 1987 supplement, for instance, the *Oxford English Dictionary* updated its old definition of *culture* to emphasize "the civilization, customs, artistic achievements, etc. of a people especially at a certain stage of its development."

Popular Meanings of Culture

There is a second meaning of culture that is also fairly widespread, although perhaps not as well known as the first. Raymond Williams explains this second meaning of "'Culture' . . . as the growth and tending of crops and animals, and by extension the growth and tending of human faculties" (*Marxism and Literature* 11). In other words, culture is that which sustains and nourishes those who live and move within it. We see one aspect of this meaning of culture in biological science: The culture within a petri dish is what allows microorganisms to grow and multiply. It feeds them and supports them; it is by consuming the culture, by living in that culture, that the microorganisms grow.

What would this sense of culture mean for people? We must remember that people do not live by bread alone; unlike microorganisms, we require more than simply physical nourishment to support us. We need to be able to talk to people, to entertain and be entertained, to enjoy all kinds of diversions and distractions, to work at something we find meaningful, to meet with other people. In short, for us, culture is our "whole way of life" (Williams, *Marxism and Literature* 17). Williams defines culture as "a very active world of everyday conversation and exchange. Jokes, idioms, characteristic forms not just of everyday dress but occasional dress, people consciously having a party, making a do, marking an occasion" (Heath and Skirrow 5). Does Williams's definition sound familiar? It should; he is really talking about the artifacts to which we are exposed.

We must be careful in how we understand the relationship among signs, artifacts, and culture, however. If you took a random collection of signs and artifacts from all around the world and piled them in a building, you would not have a culture within the building. When Williams defines cultures as "whole ways of life," he is implying a kind of connectedness among artifacts rather than simply a motley collection of many different artifacts. What turns a group of artifacts into a culture is that they are systemically related: they make up a system of artifacts anchored in group identifications.

Individuals identify with other people and see themselves as parts of groups, as we have already noted. Sometimes those groups are very small and completely present to the individual. More often, however, the groups are large and abstract, extending over wide geographical areas and broad reaches of time. Culture is the integrated set or system of artifacts that is linked to a group. The linkage between artifacts and a group occurs because the artifacts are how the group is manifested to its members. The artifacts are systematically linked to each other as they are linked to culture.

Culture is the system of material manifestations of our group identifications (remember that artifacts are actions and events as well as objects, and that what people do is just as material as are the objects that people can touch or see). Part of the culture of your local motorcycle club is the mangy mutt that is your mascot. Part of the culture of being Norwegian Minnesotans is eating lefse and lutefisk. But the club mascot is also part of a system of artifacts that includes your club insignia, the meeting place, certain eccentric characters who are members, the kind of motorcycles you have, your rituals and practices, and so forth. That system of artifacts, all of which are interrelated through their

EXERCISE 2.5

This exercise is designed to help clarify the idea of culture as a system of artifacts linked to group identifications. When you read the words *sauerbraten* or *Tannenbaum*, what comes to mind? Germany, of course. Not only that group identification, however, but other artifacts that make up the interrelated (and vast) system of German culture: Wagner, schnitzel, beer, lederhosen, Berlin, Munich, and so forth. To think further about culture as systems of artifacts, sort the following group of terms into what you consider the appropriate cultures:

grits	the IRA
corned beef and cabbage	Stone Mountain
shillelagh	the Mississippi
kudzu	the Blarney Stone
Guinness stout	stars and bars
catfish	peat moss
leprechauns	Spanish moss
William Butler Yeats	antebellum mansions
NASCAR	Catholics versus Protestants
rebel yells	y'all

link to the group of the motorcycle club, is the club's culture. Similarly, lutefisk and lefse are part of a system of many other things that bespeak being Norwegian.

Take a look at Exercise 2.5. Most likely, you had no trouble discerning that certain artifacts in this list were part of the system of Irish culture and the rest were part of the system of Southern (United States) culture.

Popular culture refers to those systems or artifacts that most people share and that most people know about. For those who identify with playing for a symphony orchestra, there is an interrelated system of artifacts made up of rehearsals, performances, instruments, and so forth. But that culture is not popular culture because most people neither identify with symphony orchestras nor know about their systems of artifacts. But television is an immensely rich world of popular culture, as nearly everyone watches television, and even if not everyone sees the same shows, they are likely to know in general about the shows they do not see. In speaking of popular culture, then, we are concerned with things, like television, that are part of the everyday experience of most people.

We now need to refine our exploration of meaning to realize that few meanings are truly individual. Instead, meaning usually comes from a cultural context. What a given sign means, especially as an artifact, is determined in large part by the system of signs (the culture, the system of artifacts) in which it is placed. For instance, what a candle means is largely shaped by the system or cultural context in which you find it. It means one thing within the system of signs that make up a movie about a haunted house, where it might flicker and then go out in the night. It means something else within the cultural system of a given religion, as a votive candle or an altar candle, for instance. And it means something else within the system of a dinner for two people in courtship, as it casts a low, warm light over the proceedings. In sum, to understand what a sign means as an artifact, we must consider that sign within the context of the system of artifacts in which it appears.

CHARACTERISTICS OF CULTURES

The idea of a culture as an integrated system of artifacts needs further development and explanation. Let us explore three important characteristics of cultures:

1. Cultures are highly complex and overlapping.
2. Cultures entail consciousness, or ideologies.
3. Cultures are experienced through texts.

Cultures Are Highly Complex and Overlapping

When we say that cultures are highly complex, we mean two things. First, there are a great many things that go into making up the system of artifacts that is a culture. Remember that cultures can be very broad (American) or very small (this particular monastery), but even the small ones will be made up of quite a few interrelated artifacts: the food, clothing styles, ways of walking and sitting, architecture, forms of entertainment, sayings and expressions, moral and ethical norms, religious practices, and other artifacts that are the material manifestations of the group. So when we think about cultures, we are thinking about many different artifacts that are still related to each other through being part of a system.

There is a second, more interesting way of thinking about the complexity and overlapping nature of cultures. Ordinary language usage sometimes causes us to think that we belong to only one culture. But that is not the case; we identify with many different groups through the many different cultures that nurture and support us. We can approach this second point by returning to Williams's definition of a culture as "a whole way of life." This definition is actually problematic; there really isn't a single, whole way of life for most of us today. To understand why, let's take a brief detour through history.

It probably used to be the case, many centuries ago, that any given person lived within one large, overarching culture. Such a culture may have been complex, but it was not multiple. If you had lived in Britain during the Dark Ages, for instance (say, around 900 C.E.), everything around you, everything you encountered during the day, probably even everything you knew about, would have been part of the same system, the same group identification, and thus the same culture. You saw and spoke only to others of your own group. Different aspects of life, such as work, religion, and government, were all closely interrelated; they all manifested the same overarching culture to you. This kind of social situation may still be found in some tribal cultures around the world, where people are primarily enveloped in a small, single group of people and surrounded by the artifacts that represent that single group. Perhaps the clearest modern version of this kind of immersion in a culture would be a cloistered monastery or convent, in which the members encounter, almost exclusively, the experiences having to do with just their own, single culture.

But clearly, few of us live in such an extremely monocultural situation today. Communication and transportation have become much easier and more common, especially over long distances. We are therefore exposed to a bewildering variety of messages and signs, often originating materially in other cultures. People of many different backgrounds live with or near each other. We may now belong to a number of groups rather than one large, overarching group that surrounds us. For instance, you can become deeply involved with simulations such as *Call of Duty*, or with electronic/email "bulletin boards" that are spread out all across the country or even the world, such as the Nextdoor system. Such a group need not have anything to do with the company you work for, which may have very little connection with where you go for recreation, which may have little to do with your ethnic or cultural identification, and so forth. In short, because there are many different groups with which you identify, you belong simultaneously to many different cultures. Because of this abundance of group identifications, many people today feel that their lives are fragmented. Some social observers have called this fragmentation the postmodern condition.

To return to Williams's definition, for nearly all of us in today's postmodern world, there simply are not any "whole ways of life" in which we immerse ourselves exclusively. We stand within a complex structure of ways of life, identifying with many different groups that may have very little in common with each other. This is especially likely to be true for people who travel a great deal, who associate with many different kinds of people, and who hold a variety of jobs. A person who lives in a largely Hispanic neighborhood, attends a local, largely Hispanic Roman Catholic church, works in a local bodega, and hangs out at the nearby community center is much closer to living within a single, overarching culture than is the person who moves out of that neighborhood, works downtown, watches French and German films, eats in Thai and African restaurants, and becomes a Buddhist. It would be a mistake to say that everyone today is one way or another, but increasing numbers of people are becoming like the second person in this example. At any rate, the more you are like that second person—the more you move around, the more you vary your experience and your environment—the more different cultures you will find identifications with. That variety is, increasingly, the condition of most people's lives today.

It is also important to understand that our identifications with different cultures are one important source of contradictions in terms of what artifacts mean. For instance, if your business requires you to go in to work on Sunday while your religion requires you to attend Mass, you will be torn in two directions. What it means to skip Mass will mean one thing to your business and another thing to your religion. Thus, our location in different cultures creates contradictions in what a given sign or artifact means.

Cultures Entail Consciousness, or Ideologies

The second important characteristic of culture is that cultures entail consciousness, or ideologies. Let's start with the second of these terms, ideology, which has traditionally been associated more closely with culture.

Ideology is a widely used term today. There are so many different uses for it that you should expect to find little agreement among scholars as to what it means. For some thinkers, such as Karl Marx, ideology referred to a false set of beliefs and perceptions that the ruling classes attempted to impose upon lower classes in an attempt to make those in lower classes cooperate in perpetuating the power of the rulers. This meaning of the term is explained in one definition given by Raymond Williams, "a system of illusory beliefs—false ideas or false consciousness—which can be contrasted with true scientific knowledge" (*Marxism and Literature* 55). Marx's idea was to get rid of false ideas, of ideology, so that people could see things the way they really are. Then, he thought, oppressed people would see the flimsy premises upon which ruling classes built their power and would rise up and overthrow them. For instance, if the "divine right of kings" could be revealed to be a lot of ideological humbug, then people who had been bowing to kings for centuries could be enabled to see that in reality all people are equal, and they would overthrow their kingly rulers.

That view of ideology as a system of false ideas that hide reality is still held by some, but increasingly the term has come to mean something else. Williams also gives two other definitions of the term that are now more widely used: (1) "a system of beliefs characteristic of a particular class or group," and (2) "the general process of the production of meanings and ideas" (*Marxism and Literature* 55); furthermore, Williams suggests that these two definitions can be combined. This more recent notion of ideology is more consistent with the understanding of culture and artifacts that we have been developing here. To distinguish these senses of ideology from the older sense of false ideas, it may be more useful to think of the term *consciousness*, which is more clearly implied by Williams's last two definitions. To grasp what consciousness (or ideology) should mean, we need to integrate several of the ideas we have covered so far.

First, recall that people live in a world of artifacts that are accessible only by perceptions. That means that people might change their perceptions or trade some perceptions for others, but it is not possible to do away with perceptions to discover some bedrock reality underneath. To think that kings rule by divine right is one perception; to think that they do not is another. There are legitimate social and political reasons to prefer one perception over another, but because we as human beings can be aware of only that which we perceive, it is impossible to identify one set of perceptions as "natural" or "simply the way things are." You will recall our earlier discussion of empowered privilege as being propped up by just such a perception of what is natural.

Second, recall that all signs are meaningful, and that artifacts in particular are signs that are charged with extra meaning. Third, recall that the meaning of an artifact is significantly determined by its link to groups. Finally, recall that culture is a system, or interrelated group, of artifacts. An ideology or consciousness is an interrelated system of meanings that is generated by the system of artifacts that constitute a culture.

The idea of systematicity is key to ideology or consciousness. To return to Williams's definitions of ideology, consciousness is a system: The beliefs that make up consciousness (or ideology) relate to each other; they are part of an interrelated set. Consciousness, or ideology, is a system of beliefs—not the way things "really, truly are," but what people perceive to be true. Consciousness is the production of meanings (through artifacts) that are "characteristic of a particular class or group." Ideology is based on a sense of what ideas go with other ideas. It is the system of meanings linked to a system of artifacts that is a culture.

This last idea needs some further explanation. It points to the fact that cultures, or systems of artifacts, are the locations of meanings (beliefs, values, ideas, perceptions). A sign becomes an artifact as it becomes charged with particular meanings that belong to a system. That meaning relates to the meanings of other artifacts in the cultural system; the whole group or system of those meanings is consciousness or ideology. Let's take a cross as an example. This simple sign made up of two sticks becomes charged with meanings of one sort when it is considered as a Christian artifact, or when one places it or thinks about it within that system of artifacts. The cross has one set of meanings when considered in the context of baptism, grace, communion, Christ's crucifixion, and so forth.

The cross takes on a different set of charged meanings for fans of vampire movies, although those meanings are certainly related to the meanings derived from Christianity. This smaller and less cohesive group is nevertheless a system, for the cross relates to the undead, to magical protection, to Count Dracula, and so forth. Finally, consider the meanings that the cross takes on within the system of fashion accessories. Here the sign becomes an artifact as it is linked to earrings or necklace pendants; meanings having to do with design or material (gold or cast iron, slim or stubby) become more important than they are in religious usage. It is realistic to say that the cross is perceived very differently—that, in fact, it becomes a different artifact—for the different groups that use it within their system of artifacts (Christians, vampire movie fans, fashion-conscious people). We will examine in later chapters how the meaning of an artifact can become quite complex as it shuttles back and forth among these cultural systems. But, for now, it is important to understand that artifacts, such as the cross, mean what they mean according to their placement in a system of artifacts, a culture that is the manifestation of a group.

But those meanings are also often contradictory. We noted previously that contradictions in the meaning of artifacts arise as a result of our identification with different cultures, different groups. We noted how the different meanings read into a sign by different cultures will cause contradictions in what that sign means. But even within single cultures, contradictory meanings arise. When we say that meanings of artifacts arise from groups, we are not saying that those meanings are always simple and straightforward. For instance, the Reverend Martin Luther King, Jr., is surely an American cultural artifact. But within that "American" cultural system, he means several things, some of them contradictory. He stands for racial harmony and understanding but also for a turbulent and violent period of our nation's history. For white Americans, he is a promise that they can get along with blacks as well as a reminder of what whites have done to prevent such getting along. For African-Americans, he is a moral exemplar of nonviolent civil disobedience, as well as a reminder—through his own violent death—of the frustrations that may make violence seem justifiable. Many cultural artifacts are contradictory in similar ways.

Consciousness or ideology is the sum of meanings, or the system of meanings, that is most obvious or most strongly implied by a system of artifacts. We often refer to such meanings as preferred meanings. These are simply the most popular, or the easiest, meanings to attach to signs. There is a Christian consciousness that is the sum of what the artifacts of Christianity mean. The meaning of baptism is linked to the meaning of grace, which is linked to the meaning of the Eucharist or communion, and so on. To become a Christian is to enter into that system of meanings, to know them, to see their relationships.

Preferred meanings also tend to be those meanings that prop up already established interests and powers in any culture—meanings that maintain privilege. If Christianity is empowered in a culture (relative to, say, Hinduism), then the Christian meanings of the cross are more likely to come to mind first when one sees a cross. A key component of power is the ability to control preferred meanings that are widely shared.

That is not to say that Christianity has no contradictions or that every Christian embraces the Christian consciousness wholly and completely. But it does mean that there are preferred meanings that make up the Christian consciousness. Since the meanings of many of the artifacts constituting a culture are contradictory, consciousness or ideology also contains the seeds of potential contradiction and instability. In this book, we will pay special attention to the ways in which signs, artifacts, and whole messages may become sites of struggle because of conflicting, multiple meanings, and we will learn methods that help us to understand how those struggles proceed in the rhetoric of popular culture.

In an earlier exercise, you were asked to identify some group that you are a part of and to name artifacts that materially manifest that group to you. Take a second look at that list of artifacts. Can you identify a consciousness that "fits" with a group that you are part of, a set of meanings that you use to make sense of the world, a set that would probably be different if you were part of another group?

We will see in Chapter 3 that people do not necessarily accept the consciousness of a culture to which they belong totally and uncritically. In fact, several factors that we will examine (such as contradiction) make it necessary for people to struggle over what

EXERCISE 2.6

To understand where you fit into a network of cultures, you might take an inventory of yourself. If you really want to understand how cultural artifacts affect people, you need to understand what your own cultural artifacts are and how they are shaping you. On a sheet of paper, construct the chart below, leaving plenty of space to write in.

Groups	Artifacts		
	Typical Events	Typical Objects	Other Typical Artifacts
Group 1:			
Group 2:			
Group 3:			
Group 4:			

Now, start thinking about some of the groups with which you identify the most—in other words, the cultures to which you belong. If you are like most people, there will probably be more than one. Fill in your names for these groups on the lines in the "Groups" column, and for each group, identify some of the artifacts that most clearly manifest that group for you. For example, if Group 1 for you is Indian, which typical events most clearly make that group real and material for you? Which typical objects? Which other typical artifacts? Make similar lists for several other groups of which you are a part.

Now go back and compare the groups of artifacts within each column. Do the typical events of Group 1 relate to the typical objects of Group 2 in any way? Are the events of Groups 3 and 4 connected with each other in any way? Do you find any examples of the same artifact meaning very different things as defined by different groups? In other words, do you find contradictions? To the extent that you find a lack of connectedness, your cultures are complex, fragmented, and overlapping. Later in this book, we will consider what that complexity, fragmentation, and overlap mean in terms of how power is shared and how social and political struggles are managed today.

artifacts mean, to pit the meanings of one cultural identification against another. For now, however, keep in mind that whether one accepts it wholeheartedly or not, there is a consciousness, or an ideology, implied for most people by the artifacts of a given culture.

Cultures Are Experienced through Texts

The third characteristic of cultures that we need to understand is that they are experienced through texts. We have learned that we hardly ever experience the whole of the groups with which we identify, and that cultural artifacts are the material manifestations of those large, abstract groups. Similarly, we rarely experience the entirety of a culture. While there is a set of artifacts that makes the large and abstract group of Polish-Americans materially present for individuals within that group, the individual Polish-American person is still unlikely to experience that entire set of artifacts, and certainly never all of them at once. Instead, we experience smaller, interrelated sets of signs and artifacts. It will be useful for us to call those sets *texts*.

The term *text* is important to the study of the rhetoric of popular culture. It is probably most familiar to you as a set of words, in the sense of a linguistic text; and, in fact, very many cultural texts are linguistic, since words and expressions can also be cultural artifacts. This textbook is a text. A newspaper article or editorial is a text. A letter is a text. We speak of the text of a poem or of a novel.

But, as we have seen, words are not the only signs, the only entities with meaning. Things other than or in addition to words can be texts as well. A text is a set of signs related to each other insofar as their meanings all contribute to the same set of effects or functions. All the words and parts of this book make a set, because they work together to produce certain effects in you at this moment. But a baseball game is a text, too, because all the signs you see within the game work together to produce several effects: relaxation, exhilaration, allegiance to a team, and so forth. On the other hand, a group comprising your wristwatch, the potted palm on my desk, and Jay Z in all likelihood is not a text, because (unless something very strange is going on) their meanings are not contributing to the same effects or functions.

A text is usually a set or group of signs, as noted above, but that group can be large or small. To the extent that a single artifact is complex, comprising several signs within itself that all contribute to the same effect, a single artifact can sometimes be read as a text. Beyoncé, for instance, is certainly a complex enough artifact to be readable as a text in her own right. More often, larger groups of signs and artifacts, contributing to the same effect, are read as texts; an entire Beyoncé video might be analyzed in that way, for example.

A text is something that people perceive, notice, or unify in their everyday experiences; it is also something that critics or students of popular culture create. A text is something that people put together out of signs, insofar as people unify the meanings of several signs. You might go to the movies and understand the large collection of signs that you see and hear as the text of the latest *Fast and Furious*, because you can see that the meanings of those signs work together to create the same set of effects in you and the rest of the audience. On the other hand, you might not think of the next meeting of a class in which you are enrolled as a text. But suppose a critic were to point out to you how the arrangement of desks, lecture techniques of the instructor, clothing styles of the students, and subject matter somehow all work together as a set of signs with interconnected meanings, all contributing to the same effects or functions. Suppose you had not thought of your class in this way before. In that case, the critic has identified the text, and having had it identified for you, you now can identify it as a text yourself. We will see later in this book that one of the primary reasons for the informed criticism of popular culture is that it can help people to identify texts of which they were not aware.

As we rarely or never experience the whole of a culture (the entire system of artifacts), we can extend our definition of a text by noting that texts are the ways in which we experience culture. Suppose we take the whole of country-and-western to be a culture, a system of artifacts. Music, of course, is an important part of that set of artifacts, but so are certain practices such as dancing, going to concerts, and styles of dress and grooming. In addition, there are several subcultures of country-and-western that are more specialized systems of artifacts within the larger culture; such subcultures might include country gospel, bluegrass, and so forth. Clearly, we might identify ourselves as "country-and-western fans" and yet never experience that entire system of artifacts.

Instead, we might sit down one evening and listen to a new Taylor Swift CD or download some of her songs to our iPods; we experience that album as a text, and that is how we experience the country-and-western culture at that moment. Or we might go to a concert. The whole experience of the concert can function as a text as well, a text made up of the crowd, the security system, dancing in the aisles, whiffs of cigarette smoke floating around, and so on. The country-and-western star Tim McGraw himself might be perceived and studied as a text: what he does, how he dresses, how he moves, his music, his public image, his romantic affairs, and so forth.

There is an important continuum in types of texts between those that are diffuse and those that are discrete. A discrete text is one in which all its signs are together in time and space, relatively tightly bounded. If you get a letter in an envelope in the mail, that text is relatively discrete. You do not expect it to be part of the wallpaper or the tune you are hearing through your earbuds. On the other hand, a Facebook page is a relatively diffuse text. Any Facebook home page that has any degree of complexity is full of links to other texts, comments, websites, photos, and so forth. You begin with one Facebook wall, and pretty soon you are three or four pages away from it. The original Facebook home page is thus a diffuse text in that it bleeds out, chains out, into many other signs, potentially without limit.

For many of the texts of popular culture, it can be difficult to identify the textual boundaries. In the musical concert, for instance, where does the concert begin and end? What is and is not the concert? Some signs—such as the music being played—are clearly constituents of that text. Some signs may be questionable: Is the difficulty in finding a

EXERCISE 2.7

To better understand the idea of a text, think about the following examples (two of them your own) and answer the questions below the examples that can help in identifying something as a text.

a. Your lunch today

b. Latest episode of *Modern Family*

c. Local baseball game, seen live

d. Your own example (#1)

e. Your own example (#2)

Answer the following questions for each example:

1. How is this composed of a set of related signs? How do those signs work together to contribute meanings to the same effects or functions?

2. What are some artifacts that make up this text? In other words, what are its constituent artifacts?

3. How does this text "stand in for" other texts or signs in a larger cultural system? How does it represent other cultural artifacts in the same system?

parking place before the concert, or the ringing in the ears after the concert, part of that concert as a unified experience, as a text? Some signs, such as the bird you see flying on your way home from the concert, may clearly not be part of the text. We will think about how to identify and define texts more carefully at a later point.

EXERCISE 2.8

To understand this point, consider an example of a possible text that you considered earlier in the chapter: your lunch today. Think about two texts, or two lunches, that two people sitting at the same table might have.

Lunch #1	Lunch #2
Double martini	Hot herbal tea
Twelve-ounce T-bone steak	Pita bread sandwich with avocado, alfalfa sprouts, and cheese
French fries	
Corn on the cob	Raw vegetables and yogurt dip
Apple pie à la mode	
Stoneware plate, bone-handled knife and fork, plenty of paper napkins	Simple china plate, stainless steel knife and fork, cloth napkin

Of course, an entire consciousness or ideology would be absorbed only after prolonged and repeated exposure to the meanings of a wide range of artifacts within a cultural system. But each of these lunches nevertheless has a "voice" of its own, and the voice speaks both to and about the diners. Would you say that either lunch shows a consistent set of meanings, beliefs, attitudes, or values? Does either lunch allow you to say something with some measure of assurance about either of the two diners? Could you make an "educated guess" in response to any of the following questions?

1. Which of these diners is more concerned about the environment?
2. Which of these diners is a fan of professional football?
3. Which of these diners is female and which is male?
4. Which diner is a Republican and which is a Democrat?
5. Which diner is over fifty-five and which one is under thirty?

Now stop and think: most of us likely assign meanings rather quickly. Why? Are we rushing to judgment or using unfortunate stereotypes? Why do we feel so sure of our answers, as I suspect most of us do? The purpose of posing these questions is not to perpetuate stereotypes but to demonstrate that you probably felt that you could answer at least some of them. In order for you to have this sense that you could know the answers to such questions, the text of each lunch must mean something (at least approximately); each lunch must somehow fit into larger systems of artifacts and meaning. This is what we mean by stressing the systematic nature of culture, of its artifacts, and of the ideologies that come from cultures.

Of course, if something is a text, then it can be read. What do we do when we read? We examine signs and artifacts and identify their meanings. That is clearly what we do when we read words. We do the same thing when we experience other kinds of artifacts, so it may be useful to retain the term *reading*, even when the texts we are examining include things other than words. A text, in other words, is something that has meaning, a meaning grounded in the culture behind the text, a meaning that can be examined and understood. We will see that those meanings are complex and are often struggled over, since what a text means has a lot to do with power.

Because they cohere around meanings, texts are the ways in which we are exposed to consciousness. A text is the mouthpiece for a culture; it is a representative sampling of the overall system of meanings that constitute an ideology or consciousness that is linked to a group. Texts urge a consciousness on us (and thus they also contain the contradictions that are part of a consciousness). We do not always accept that consciousness in its entirety, but the urging to do so is there nonetheless.

So we have come full circle, back to the question of your blue jeans with which this chapter began. Suppose you see a man of about age seventy, wearing faded blue jeans and a tie-dyed shirt, his long hair pulled back and tied in a ponytail. Furthermore, suppose he is sitting on the hood of an aged Volkswagen Beetle plastered with Grateful Dead stickers, selling homemade jewelry from a battered display tray.

The picture just described is a unified experience—it is a text. Just like the text of an editorial in the newspaper, or the text of a speech by the president, the text of this seventy-year-old man is speaking to us. It has meaning, and it is articulating a certain consciousness for us. That picture has a voice—what is it saying? What do the blue jeans this man is wearing add to that voice that would not be there if he were wearing pleated wool slacks?

These questions have to do with rhetoric, with how the meanings that we would find in or assign to that text are being managed so as to influence people. Rhetoric is an ancient human activity, as well as an ancient discipline that studies that activity. In the next chapter, we will examine that term in more detail and arrive at a better understanding of how to apply the concept of rhetoric to the texts of popular culture.

MANAGING POWER TODAY IN TEXTS OF POPULAR CULTURE

What kind of business is managed through the texts of popular culture? That question raises the whole issue of what popular culture is and why it is worth studying. Earlier we learned that people grow in and are sustained by popular culture, by the artifacts and experiences of everyday life. Furthermore, we considered the idea that empowerment and disempowerment in our society do not occur only in grand, isolated moments but are enacted in the artifacts and experiences of everyday life. Because of the growth in population, technology, pluralism, and knowledge that we have been discussing in this chapter, it is increasingly the case that public business is not being managed, and cannot be managed, in occasional, single moments of rhetoric (the "great speech," the "important essay," the "pivotal book," and so forth). Because of the growth in these four areas, more of the important business of our society is now done from moment to moment in people's experiences of popular culture.

This is a relative difference: there has always been some public business done within the realm of popular culture, even if theorists did not recognize it; and today, there is still some business conducted through the "great speech" and so on. A century ago, the business of managing the problem of racism would have depended primarily on the impact of great, occasional rhetorical efforts by leaders such as Booker T. Washington and W. E. B. DuBois. But today many of the problems of racism are managed in Spike Lee films, with different styles of clothing and grooming, and in moment-to-moment interactions in public schools.

Let us pursue the example of racism further. Earlier in this book (pages 4–5), we discussed the meaning of the management of power. How do the ideas we explored there apply to the public problem of racism as it is managed in popular culture? People must decide what to do and how to behave in relation to people of other races. We must also decide what cultural differences mean: for example, is it threatening or disrespectful when people of another race speak more loudly or softly than we do, walk in a different way, stand too close to or too far from us, or use eye contact differently? Are such decisions managed, or influenced, by stirring speeches or lengthy essays today? Probably not. Instead, the problem of racism is being managed in the plots of television sitcoms and dramas that take racism as an occasional theme and urge certain audience responses to it. Racism is managed in fashion, as shirts and caps with the name or photograph of a popular hip-hop group, or slogans of racial pride (e.g., "La Raza"), are worn in public and seen by people of all races. And racism is managed in athletics, as people of color are elevated to heroic, even mythic, status by their exploits on the field. Racism is being managed and struggled over every time two twelve-year-old white kids debate whether the latest Dirty South rap album is worth spending this week's allowance on. There, in the everyday texts of popular culture, is where racism is increasingly managed today.

The same holds true for the management of many other public issues. Earlier, we discussed the increasing inability of traditional texts to manage the problem of how we develop and market pharmaceuticals. For the public at large, concerns about prescription drugs may be embodied in the plots of movies that champion lawsuits against drug companies or that feature exciting quests to find new antibiotics in the Amazon. Comic books or video games influence young minds with depictions of monsters created by drug company programs gone awry, and many jokes are made

©iStockphoto.com/Alina555

on television comedy shows about drugs, like Viagra, for more "personal" problems. These texts of popular culture shape many of today's arguments over the issue of pharmaceuticals.

If we want to understand how people are influenced on these and other issues, and how public affairs are nudged in one direction or another, we need to look more at what is happening on television than on the Senate floor. The theory of rhetoric today is increasingly recognizing the important business that is done through popular culture, as we will see in upcoming discussions in this book. In short, more important business is being done in the culture of everyday life, and theory has begun to recognize that business more fully than it ever has before.

FOUR CHARACTERISTICS OF THE TEXTS OF POPULAR CULTURE

In the next two chapters, we will look more closely at how the rhetoric of popular culture works, at how to study it and examine it. By way of preparation, though, we need to think very broadly about how the texts of popular culture differ from traditional texts. These differences can be best understood in reference to the four characteristics—*verbal, expository, discrete, and hierarchical*—of traditional texts.

First, in addition to verbal texts, the rhetoric of popular culture will be manifested more often in *nonverbal* texts. People are influenced not only through words but also through the images they see. Furthermore, the struggle over power can be conducted nonverbally as well as verbally. One person flies an American flag proudly while another person wears it on the seat of his or her pants; both are rhetorical attempts to use signs to influence others and to manage what it means to be American. A coal mining company shows pictures of a beautifully restored former strip mining pit, while opponents to mining show pictures of devastation and ruin; here, too, is the use of nonverbal signs, in this case as part of the struggle over how the public business of energy and land use is to be managed.

Second, in addition to *expositional* texts, the rhetoric of popular culture will be manifested more often in texts that are *metonymic* and *narrative.* Metonymy is the name of a classical *trope*, or way of thinking, that means reduction. When you think about something by reducing it to a simpler, smaller, more manageable image that leaves out certain details of the larger whole, you are using metonymy. The president is a metonymy of the whole executive branch of the government, for example. The executive branch is actually many, many offices and officers, aides, and advisers, all hard at work behind the scenes. But when we say, "President Trump decided that . . ." or "President Trump sent to Congress . . . ," we are using metonymy to describe this very complex institution in terms of a person. In reality, President Trump's appropriate Cabinet secretary and a hundred of that person's aides executed the action with the president's approval. The idea of an individual, solitary president is understandable; the web of officials and offices that actually make up the executive branch, however, is much harder to grasp.

Metonymy is a reaction to the problem of the explosion of knowledge, which we have already discussed. The political problems of the Middle East, for instance, are vast and complex. It is unlikely that most of the public could claim to understand the intricacies of those problems or of the relationship of that region to the United States. Therefore, we often find metonymy at work in reducing the Middle East and its problems to images, stories, or quick explanations that allow the public to "get a grasp" of a complex situation. Metonymy is crucial to the aspect of power management that controls meaning. Part of the metonymy of the Middle East will be a focus on American or European hostages; any time one of "our people" is taken prisoner in the Middle East, the event will dominate media attention for a while. That is because our frustrations about dealing with so-called terrorists, with a seemingly unending conflict over which we have little control and with people who do things differently from us, can all be reduced to stories about the abduction of hostages. Through metonymy, American fears about uncontrollable political forces in the Middle East can also be reduced to images of feared leaders of states or organizations that allegedly sponsor terrorism or threaten war; such leaders have included figures such as Kim Jong-un and Bashar al-Assad.

One of the most important ways in which metonymy is used to deal with complex issues is through *narrative*, or the telling of stories. Instead of developing complex arguments and amassing proof, as in expositional texts, many texts of popular culture either tell stories or are storylike, using both words and images. Think about the various complex social issues that have been struggled over through the means of popular films, for instance, such as race relations in *Black or White* and *Friday Night Lights*, or the management of intimate or social relationships in *La La Land* and the *28 Days/Weeks Later* series, or *The Walking Dead* on television. Television shows will often air episodes that deal with complex social issues in thirty-minute installments by turning them into stories (this week will address alcoholism, next week will take on child abuse, and so forth). Through metonymy and narrative, texts in popular culture participate in struggles over power and disempowerment and manage issues that were (and sometimes still are) debated in lengthy, expositional arguments elsewhere.

In addition to discrete texts, the rhetoric of popular culture will be manifested in *diffuse* texts. Several points must be understood here. First, many texts of popular culture do take the form of discrete texts, although they often do not share the other characteristics of traditional texts (they are largely nonverbal or are not expositional, for example). A discrete text, you will recall, is a group of signs that is perceived to be discrete in time and space with clear boundaries and clearly separate from its context. A diffuse text will sometimes not be recognized as a text by those who experience it, and at other times it will be recognized by them as a very complex experience. A diffuse text is a collection of signs working for the same rhetorical influence or related that is not discretely separated from its context. Many of the texts of popular culture occur in diffuse form.

One good example of a diffuse text would be the whole experience of watching televised football. Most people who are fans will watch televised football with other people in small groups. Think about what typically goes on during such an experience: people talk with each other, both about the game and about issues relating to other dimensions of life; the television set is broadcasting both images of the game and an overlay of the commentators' talk about the game; people come and go between where the television is situated and other parts of the house or bar (for refreshments, bathroom breaks, and so forth); people often switch rapidly among several channels to check on other games as well. All of these signs and artifacts, mixed together in an incredible jumble, contribute to the same rhetorical effect of enjoyment, of involvement in football, of being a fan. Yet we would be hard-pressed to identify where this text begins and where it ends, to put boundaries in time and space on this system of signs. Thus, the experience of watching televised football is a diffuse text. Yet it has rhetorical influence, and because so many people are so enthusiastically involved in following football, it even manages what has become some of society's important business. Contrast this kind of text to the relatively more discrete experience of reading a newspaper article about the previous night's football game by yourself over coffee the next morning. That text is more bounded in time and space.

EXERCISE 2.9

In the preceding paragraph, it was suggested that spectator sports manage some of our society's important business. On your own or in class, consider these questions carefully: When people follow their favorite sport on television, in the newspapers, or at the stadium, are some important public problems being addressed? Which problems do today's spectator sports industries help to manage? In other words, when people become sports fans, are they *just* sports fans or are there wider implications to what they are doing?

The following points may help you to think about the questions posed above:

1. Criticism or praise of the performance of some African-American athletes, such as Colin Kaepernick, Richard Sherman, or Venus or Serena Williams, is sometimes read as being based on race. Criticism or praise of white athletes is rarely assumed to be race-based.

2. When sports figures are involved in various scandals such as gambling, steroid use, or sexual abuse, sports commentators often sadly claim that it is especially tragic that sports figures should be involved in such activities.

3. Bicyclist Lance Armstrong has admitted using performance-enhancing drugs. This led to his being stripped of his Tour de France titles, losing endorsements, and so forth. It prompted discussions of drug use and the extreme importance of winning at all costs in American society.

Finally, in addition to texts that are hierarchical, the rhetoric of popular culture is manifested in texts that are *democratic*. In the preceding example of watching televised football, who makes the text? Who puts it all together? Clearly, the fans, the viewers, the audience or receivers of communication do. Of course, a person reading a book or listening to a speech has a choice in how to experience those traditional texts to some extent, but, relatively speaking, the football viewer has more choice and control. The fan is not placed in a situation where time, place, and procedures for experiencing texts are constrained as much as they are in the case of most public speeches. The fan is more actively at work assembling many related signs into a diffuse text. This is how much of the rhetoric of popular culture occurs: people walk through the crowded sea of signs that are available today (down a city street, for instance), assembling diffuse texts to suit their needs and desires in ways over which they have more choice and control.

Because the rhetoric of popular culture is (relatively) democratic, it may be found to be at work in marginalized areas of society where traditional rhetoric is not so likely to reach. Some scholars, such as John Fiske (*Reading the Popular, Understanding Popular Culture*) and Malcolm Barnard (*Fashion as Communication*), even argue that popular culture springs *mainly* from groups of people who have been oppressed and marginalized. It is true that the texts of popular culture often emerge from, and do their work among, the young, the poor, women, racial minorities, and others who have not been officially empowered. This is a relative difference as well, but a real one. The upper classes from Nob Hill watch ballet, while the disempowered from South Boston go bowling.

In general, then, texts of popular culture will be relatively more nonverbal, metonymic and narrative, diffuse, and democratic than are more traditional texts. Increasingly, because of the changes in real-life conditions that we have discussed in this chapter, the important business of society is managed in those texts of popular culture. In this chapter, we have seen what the rhetorical tradition is and why changing conditions are moving us away from it.

Summary and Review

To understand what culture means, we began with its building blocks: signs. Everything can be a sign; a sign is something that has meaning or that gets you to think of something else. Signs have meaning in three ways: indexically, iconically, and symbolically. In discussing symbolic meanings, we noted that because symbols are arbitrary and conventional, their meaning is easily changed. And because they are not naturally or permanently connected to their meanings, symbols are imprecise and changeable in meaning.

We defined an artifact as (1) an action, event, or object perceived as a unified whole, (2) having widely shared meanings, and (3) manifesting group identifications to us. In discussing that definition, we reviewed some important characteristics that contribute to this idea of an artifact:

1. Artifacts are a socially created reality.
2. Signs become artifacts as they become charged with meaning, thus crossing a threshold into artifact status.
3. An artifact can be very complex, even being made up of other artifacts.
4. Artifacts are the material signs of group identifications.

(Continued)

(Continued)

We defined culture as the integrated set or system of artifacts that is linked to a group and noted that culture in this sense is what we grow in, what supports us and sustains us. Popular culture, more specifically, is made up of those systems of artifacts to which most people are exposed. We noted three important characteristics of culture:

1. Cultures are highly complex and overlapping.
2. Cultures entail consciousness, or ideologies.
3. Cultures are experienced through texts.

We learned that a text is defined as a set of signs related to each other insofar as their meanings all contribute to the same set of effects or functions. Furthermore, texts are the ways in which we experience culture.

We learned that relative to traditional texts, texts of popular culture are more nonverbal, metonymic and narrative, diffuse, and democratic. We saw how these characteristics match a state of affairs in which more important rhetorical work is done in popular culture.

Looking Ahead

We have left many questions unanswered. So far, we have only a general idea of the basic characteristics of the texts that enact the rhetoric of popular culture. We need a clearer idea of *what to look for* in texts of popular culture. Thus, one important question in the next chapter will be, what does the critic look for in identifying the texts of popular culture?

Critical analysis of rhetoric is never a lockstep procedure, though. Different critics will be interested in different aspects of a given subject or will want to ask different questions about a text. Thus, a second question for us in the next chapter will be, what choices are available to the critic of popular culture?

We also need a clearer sense of how texts work to manage society's business through popular culture. Thus, an important final question for us will be, what is it about texts that persuades people? And since most texts are complex and exert influence in several different ways, we will also want to know how to analyze texts on several different levels. These and other questions will be taken up in Chapters 3, 4, and 5.

3

RHETORICAL METHODS IN CRITICAL STUDIES

I f you are an alert reader of chapter titles, you may be wondering about the title of this one. You knew that you were going to study rhetoric, but here, apparently, is a chapter that also seems to be about critical studies, whatever that may be.

There are at least two reasons for this chapter's title. First, most of those who study the ways in which popular culture influences people are working within a general approach to scholarship known as *critical studies* (although not all of these people use the term *rhetoric*). We will look at what *critical studies* means in more detail a little later on. Second, what you do when you study the rhetoric of popular culture and then share your findings with others is known as *criticism*; you will end up writing or presenting criticism, or a critique, of the particular aspect of popular culture that you are studying. The last five chapters of this book, for instance, are examples of critical studies—of race relations in Milwaukee, gun shows, the movie *Groundhog Day*, steampunk, and "bad resurrections" in American life and culture.

This chapter is concerned with *how to think about rhetorical criticism*. It should not be taken as a set of instructions for how to march lockstep through a term paper. The different sections of this chapter, for instance, are not a "step 1, step 2" guide to how to write a critical study. Preparing an actual critical study is like writing an essay, and you should proceed as you would for writing any essay or report. What is more important is understanding how to go about critiquing popular culture so that you will have something to say in your critique. That is what this chapter will equip you to do.

Ryan McVay/Photodisc/Getty Images

TEXTS AS SITES OF STRUGGLE

Before we learn more about critiquing the rhetoric of popular culture, we need to clarify two basic principles that will underlie the critical methods explained in the rest of the book. These two principles together create a paradox about the nature of texts. First, we will learn that texts wield rhetorical influence because of the meanings they support. In other words, texts facilitate the creation of meanings that influence those who receive them. Second, we will learn that because texts can mean *different* things, they are often sites of struggle over meaning (and thus, over how and what or whom they will influence). Creation of a text may be the point of rhetorical struggle. The paradox is that a text is both a means to, and an outcome of, rhetorical struggle.

Texts Influence through Meanings

We noted earlier in this book that texts influence people to think and act in certain ways. That influence is the rhetorical dimension of texts. Here we need to be more specific about exactly what motivates or drives that influence: the *meanings* that texts encourage people to accept. We think or act in certain ways in response to texts because of the meanings the texts have for us and the meanings they urge us to attribute to our experience.

In the 2015–2016 National Football League season, it was discovered that footballs used and managed by the New England Patriots were underinflated, which allegedly gave an advantage to a team's offense, and that meant to the Patriots' stellar quarterback, Tom Brady. For months, arguments flew back and forth as to whether New England had intentionally deflated the balls, whether Brady knew about it, and so forth. Some argued that even if the balls were deflated, it didn't matter. Others saw a consistent pattern in conduct by the Patriots and Brady. Eventually Brady was given a temporary suspension from play in the following season (2016–2017), which hardly hampered the Patriots at all. To this day, you can get a good argument started among sports fans by mentioning this incident. Why did all these texts create all these meanings, and why did they urge such meanings upon the public? Because *choices and actions* that the public might adopt *usually depend on meaning.* You will not think that Brady should be suspended unless cheating on football inflation means something criminal or at least wicked to you. And you will be moved to forgive the Patriots and Brady and move on if, to you, deflation simply means something that everybody does now and then.

Texts generate meanings about other things in the world. Texts also have meanings themselves; for example, Tom Brady himself is a text, or at least a complex artifact, with meaning. Whatever influence texts have on people's thoughts and actions arises from what those texts mean to them. Faced with a row of otherwise indistinguishable jugs of motor oil in a hardware store, you will buy the oil that has the most favorable meanings. Of course, advertisers for oil, gasoline, soap, and other largely similar products spend a great deal of money trying to attach certain meanings to their products, since those goods are hard to distinguish on the basis of their own intrinsic values. So if you pick Quaker State over Pennzoil, it is because advertisers have succeeded in causing Quaker State to mean something to you that you prefer over whatever Pennzoil has come to mean.

Texts Are Sites of Struggle over Meaning

We now have to complicate the first principle we have learned by turning to the "struggle" side of the paradox of texts. As we learned in the first chapter, meaning is rarely simple. Instead, what a given text means, what a sign or artifact means as the result of a text's persuasive influence, is often very complicated. That is because, especially in the case of symbolic meaning, meaning itself is rarely simple and straightforward. You can see this complexity in our example of Lance Armstrong. What he and his steroid use mean is being struggled over, even today, in the texts of popular culture. Within the last decade, we have seen a dramatic change in the meaning of Middle Eastern nations in the minds of Americans. These nations have "meant" either friend or foe as governments have come and gone, rebellions and terrorist insurgencies have occurred and been crushed, and relationships to the United States have varied. Until two young men from Chechnya were accused of the Boston Marathon bombing of 2013, most Americans likely had few or no meanings for Chechnya. A string of terrorist bombings in Paris, Brussels, and elsewhere by agents from Morocco, Syria, and elsewhere brought awareness of Middle Eastern countries perhaps not previously often thought of by Americans. Now the meanings many people have are likely to be negative.

The meaning of the popular music favored by young people has always been struggled over. From Bruno Mars to Insane Clown Posse, these artifacts have meant one thing to their fans and another thing to parents, police, and priests. In other words, people struggle over how to construct these different texts in ways that suit their own interests. Making a musical artist into one kind of text or another is therefore one goal of rhetorical struggle.

These meanings are struggled over precisely because of the first principle we discussed: meanings are where the rhetorical power lies. The meaning of a president's decision to send troops into action against a foreign power will have enormous payoff in terms of who runs the government after the next election. Therefore, the president's political friends and enemies will spend a great deal of time and effort urging the public to adopt competing meanings of that action. Furthermore, the meanings of the very texts produced by those friends and enemies are also at stake. The whole business of so-called spin doctors, or public opinion shapers, is to struggle over the meanings of texts themselves so that texts can go on to influence further meanings. Scholars in the field of critical studies describe this state of affairs when they note that meanings, and therefore the texts that generate meanings, are *sites of struggle.* The idea is that struggles over power occur in the creation and reception of texts as much as (or more than) they occur at the ballot box, in the streets, or during revolutions.

Take a look at Image 3.1 toward the end of this chapter. In his 2016 campaign, candidate Donald Trump vowed to "make America great again." Caps, shirts, and signs such as the hat Mr. Trump is wearing in the photo were common. Now, why would such a promise be a site of struggle? His supporters were in full agreement that American power and economic success had slipped during the Obama administration. Trump's opponents thought quite the opposite—that the nation was strong and successful under Obama. Many of these opponents thought the slogan was a coded reference to Obama's race, as in those Trump supporters who wanted to "take back America." Even seemingly simple slogans like this can be struggled over.

The critic of the rhetoric of popular culture (which is what you, as a reader of this book, are training to become) can play an important role in those struggles. Critics are *meaning detectives*; their role is to explain what texts mean. Rarely do good critics claim to explain the only possible meaning that a text could have. Instead, the best and richest analyses show ranges of meanings and may explain the ways in which certain texts are sites of struggle over meaning. Because meaning is the avenue through which texts wield influence, critics work directly to explain how it is that people are empowered or disempowered by the meanings of various texts.

An important tradition in the study of struggle in texts is what is often called the "Birmingham School" because it was originally grounded in the Centre for Contemporary Cultural Studies at the University of Birmingham in England. A major theorist of this school was Stuart Hall. The Birmingham School arose in response to what is sometimes called the "Frankfurt School" and its leading scholars, such as Theodor Adorno or Herbert Marcuse. The Frankfurt School argued that popular culture was a means for empowered interests to control mass populations. The Birmingham School argued, against the Frankfurt School position, that ordinary people in their everyday lives often adapt texts to their own purposes. This may include combining texts in creative ways or appropriating texts for purposes not imagined by those who created the texts. Through

EXERCISE 3.1

To better understand why meaning is the source of the influence exerted by the rhetoric of popular culture, do this quick exercise on your own or in class on the instructions of your teacher.

Think about the last article of clothing that you bought because you really liked it and wanted to own it (that is, not some socks you bought in a rush because your other gray pair had too many holes). Do some self-examination and think about what that article of clothing means to you. Does it mean physical attractiveness? Elegance? Fun in the sun? List your own meanings.

Now back up from that article of clothing and consider the meanings you just listed. Think about other things you might do or items you might buy

because of those meanings. For instance, if you bought a T-shirt because it meant summertime fun to you, what else will you buy or do to produce that same meaning? Sunglasses? An hour in a tanning booth? A Caribbean vacation? If you think about it, it is the *meaning* of these items or experiences that is primary; what you make of the tank top and the shades and the hour in the tanning booth—what these things *mean* to you—is what is going to stick with you.

Finally, think about the paradoxical nature of the various texts in this example. Some texts (such as ads for Caribbean cruises) urge you to accept certain meanings. But an article of clothing is a text that you yourself work over so as to make it support meanings that serve your interests.

such creative adaptation, the rhetorical demands of power may be resisted if not entirely avoided. A consistent theme in the writings of these scholars is that texts are sites of struggle and are rarely taken to mean only what those in power intend them to mean. Critical studies by members of this school, such as Hall, focus on the range and variety of different readings in which audiences engage.

To think about the rhetoric of popular culture, or the ways in which the texts and artifacts of popular culture influence us (along with our own participation in making meaning), we need to think about what popular culture means to people—the ways in which those meanings can be multiple and contradictory and how those meanings are struggled over. Because critics are meaning detectives, a rhetorical criticism is an exercise in showing the influences exerted by signs through their meanings. There are many *methods* (organized, systematic, and reliable ways of thinking) for thinking about popular culture already available to you. Let's begin to consider such methods by examining the wide-ranging, loosely connected set of methods known as *critical studies.*

THREE CHARACTERISTICS OF CRITICAL STUDIES

A large number of people all around the world are studying exactly what you are learning about here (see, for example, S. K. Foss; Storey). Working as university professors, as columnists and commentators, or as independent writers of books and articles, these thinkers and scholars are studying the ways in which experiences of popular culture influence people. Their work follows many different approaches and is based on widely differing assumptions. But taken as a group, they constitute a loosely knit school of thought or way of thinking that has been called *cultural studies* or *critical studies.* For the sake of convenience, we will use the latter term.

Critical studies is not a professional or social club with its own set of rules. It is not a tightly knit, clearly defined, precisely delineated set of principles. Many of the theories and methods used by scholars in the field of critical studies are, in fact, at odds with one another on important issues. Critical studies overlaps considerably with other fields such as literary studies and film studies. But there are also some principles that link these theories and methods together and help to define critical studies as a school of thought. In this chapter, we will examine the principles that different branches of critical studies have in common, the theories and methods they share. In Chapters 4 and 5, we will look more closely at some differences among a few specific branches of critical studies. Now, however, we will learn that all branches of critical studies are (1) *critical* in attitude and in method, (2) *concerned with power,* and (3) *interventionist.*

The Critical Character

One thing that characterizes the different branches of critical studies is that they are all, unsurprisingly enough, *critical.* In this sense, the term *critical* refers to both (1) an attitude and (2) a method.

©iStockphoto.com/Wavebreakmedia

Attitude

The critical attitude is somewhat related to the everyday, colloquial sense of the term *critical*, though without its negative connotations. If you are being critical in this negative sense, you are disagreeing with, or finding fault with, something. In finding fault, you take apart or dissect another's words and actions to show their true (and pernicious) meanings. Now, critical studies is not exclusively negative in this sense, but it does refuse to take things at face value. It adopts an attitude of suspicion, in other words, in which it assumes that things are often other than (or more than) they seem. Again, this attitude is not intended to be hostile or destructive; it simply means that people in critical studies want to know what else is going on besides the obvious.

Critical studies is always looking beneath the surface. For instance, a critical scholar watching an episode of one of the television *Real Housewives* series would assume that besides being a set of interrelated stories about some unfulfilled suburban women, the show has meanings and is influencing people in a number of ways. To give another example, it is *not* being critical to say that vampire shows, such as *Let the Right One In*, *Buffy the Vampire Slayer*, and *From Dusk Till Dawn*, are stories about the undead who go around biting people on the neck. Such a statement has not gone beyond what is obvious, or merely on the surface. It *is* being critical, however, to say that vampire movies help people deal with problems of conformity and industrialization (Brummett, "Burke's Representative Anecdote"). An observation like that is not obvious, but it can be an interesting insight that the critic discovers and shares with readers. So, in sum, the critical scholar must be prepared to dig into texts, to think about the ways that people are being influenced as well as entertained, informed, and so forth by such texts.

Method

Critical studies is also a method, a way of asking certain kinds of questions about whatever is being studied. These questions are about meaning, complexity, and evaluation. A critical method wants to know about meaning. It asks, "What does a text, an experience, an object, an action, and so forth mean to different people?"

Rather than breaking them up into isolated parts, a critical method deals with the *complexity* of texts and experiences as they are actually experienced. Such a method asks, "What are some suggested meanings in the text, what are some of their influences or effects, and how do these influences interrelate with each other?"

Finally, a critical method seeks to *evaluate* that which it studies, to make some judgment about whether that object or experience's meanings and influences are good or bad, desirable or undesirable, and so forth. The methods best suited to answering these kinds of questions are sometimes called *qualitative methods* (in contrast to *quantitative methods* that rely more heavily on experimental or survey research). *Critical* is probably a clearer term than *qualitative*, however, so we will return to that usage after the following discussion of the difference between qualitative and quantitative methods.

EXERCISE 3.2

Turn to the examples of images and ads on pages 116–146. We will refer to these ads often as illustrations of how to use critical methods. Consider Image 3.2, the Play men's fragrance advertisement. We'll think about more specific ways to study this ad later, but for now, try to "work up some suspicions" about it. Consider these questions: What overall meanings are created in this text? The intended purpose is, of course, to persuade people to buy the fragrance, but what widely shared meanings does the text tap into so as to lure people to that purchase, and what widely shared meanings does the text reinforce or contribute to? The following are specific clues that could lead you to become suspicious:

Why is the fragrance presented in a bottle that resembles some sort of portable media player, such as an iPod?

Why is Justin Timberlake pictured in an airplane seat, with an empty seat beside him? Why not in a bus, a train, or in coach class?

Based on the signs you observe in this text, what sort of audience do you think the text is designed to attract? Male or female? How about nationality or race? Does the text either use or contribute to any stereotypes?

Consider the use of images in the text. What meanings are created by the clothing that Timberlake wears? What is that around his neck and what does it mean?

There are no absolutely right or wrong answers to these questions, but there are some better and worse answers! You will need to provide evidence from the text to support your claims. The point is for you to see that for this advertisement, as for most texts, there may be some interesting meanings, or influences, at work beyond the obvious ones. Note that whatever answers you come up with, they require close readings of the texts; you have to dig into them with both hands!

For an example of the difference between qualitative and quantitative approaches, let's go back to the example of a critic studying one of the *Real Housewives* shows. Some questions that might be asked in relation to that show are: (1) Did that aspirin commercial halfway through last night's episode increase sales of that particular product? (2) Does the show as a whole series affect how people understand gender roles? (3) How should we understand the ways in which the show and its characters are viewed in moral or ethical terms in an era when more and more people at least say they are concerned about morality and ethics?

Now think about the best ways to answer those questions. Questions 1 and 2 are not critical questions, by and large. They might best be answered by survey research; you could simply go out and ask people about their aspirin-buying habits or their views on gender. Or they might be answered by experimental manipulation of variables, in which you compare the aspirin-buying habits and gender views of a select group of the show's viewers against a control group that does not view the show. Clearly, survey and experimental research (rather than simply sitting in a chair and musing about the answers) provide better ways to answer such questions. Both survey and experimental research are considered *quantitative* methods because many of their findings will be expressed using numbers (the numbers of those who buy more aspirin will be compared to the numbers of those who do not, and so forth).

Question 3 is a little different; it is more complex and might be answered in more than one way. You could answer it quantitatively, by surveying people as to their reactions, or by experimentally comparing those who saw the show with those who did not. But if you share the assumption with which we began this chapter—that an important dimension of influences and effects is meaning—then it is clear that these quantitative methods will not answer such a question adequately.

Question 3 becomes a critical question when you start to think about what ethics and morality in *Real Housewives*, or in American society as a whole, mean. This is a question that the critic must address. But asking an audience about meaning is usually not sufficient. You can ask people what the morality of the series means to them and get an answer, but that is not a sufficient and efficient way to determine meaning, for three important reasons.

First, meaning is complex. We have already discussed the idea that a given text or artifact means different things as it is considered within different contexts or cultural systems. Even within a single culture, a text will usually have many different meanings. We have noted how contradictions in meaning occur for many artifacts. Opposing meanings might be found in texts that are sites of struggle. All of this means that few people who are not accustomed to thinking about wide ranges of meaning will be able to say, comprehensively, what a text or artifact means. Texts usually have many more meanings than most people are able to see.

Second, people may not be able to articulate meanings. We learned in Chapter 2 that people participate in making meanings, but that does not mean that they can always say how they do so. A meaning detective might consider asking people to say what some text means. But some people are not very good at saying what a text means to them, even though it may mean a lot. This does not mean such people are unintelligent; it means that intelligence, and an ability to detect meanings, comes in many forms. Some meanings may be nonverbal, intuitive, or emotional, and therefore not the kind of thing that can easily be put into words. It may take a critic who is trained in talking about meaning to articulate what certain texts mean.

Third, meaning is sometimes *beyond awareness*; people may not consciously know what a particular text meant to them. They may not even be aware they are being influenced by certain texts. Participation in making meaning need not be done intentionally and with full awareness. Most people do not go through the kind of conscious introspection and probing of meaning that you are becoming acquainted with in reading this book. So, for many people, artifacts may have meanings of which they are unaware, and therefore meanings that they could not report.

Critical studies is qualitative because it is concerned with qualities more than quantities—and that is another way of saying that it is concerned with meanings. The critic's job is to explore what a text or artifact means, including its different or contradictory meanings as well as the ways that meanings are struggled over, forced upon some people and rejected by others. As critics reveal the *meanings* of texts and artifacts, they are simultaneously doing two things:

1. Critics are *explaining the rhetoric* of popular culture, since, as we discussed above, what texts and artifacts mean are the ways in which they influence people.

2. Critics are showing *how to experience life* by demonstrating how texts and artifacts might be understood, the meanings that can be found in them. When we can see a different set of meanings in a conversation, or a film, or some music, we can experience that little part of life in a new way.

We have seen earlier in this book that people make sense of, or find meaning in, signs and artifacts as they experience them. To have an experience is to organize signs and artifacts and make them meaningful. For example, take two people watching a parade go by. One is filled with patriotic fervor at the flags and bands. The other is more cynical and not very patriotic, and every flag and band prompts her to grouse about the nation and its policies. These two people are finding very different meanings in the artifacts that go past them, and it would also be fair to say that they are constructing very different experiences for themselves.

The critic's job is to demonstrate ways of experiencing parades by explaining the different ways that parades (or films, or sporting events) have meaning. But the critic does not have to step into the skins of these two people to show what a given parade definitely meant to a particular person. That would be impossible to do, since nobody can see completely into another's mind. Northrop Frye (63) makes a useful distinction that explains what the critic does instead: The critic shows what people, in general, *do*, not what specific people *did*. The critic does not say, "Here is what that parade meant to Juan on that particular day." Instead the critic says, "Here is one way that this parade might be experienced [might have meaning]." In doing so, the critic shows his or her reader how meanings might be constructed and how life might be experienced.

Concern over Power

The second main characteristic shared by most varieties of critical studies is one that you are already familiar with: a concern for power. Critical studies examines what power is or

---

EXERCISE 3.3

This exercise is designed to help you to understand the kinds of questions that are critical, that look into meaning, as opposed to the kinds of questions asked by other methods such as experimentation or survey research. You will find some questions listed below. For each question, determine (1) what methods, steps, or procedures would allow you to answer that question and (2) whether it (or some aspect of it) can be answered critically.

1. Why do some people think that the world is coming to an end?
2. What caused World War I?
3. What motivates Tyler Perry to make his films?
4. Does my car need a new battery?
5. Does television fairly represent all races in the United States?
6. Is television more violent than movies today?

Note: You may need to break some of these questions up into issues that can be dealt with critically and issues that cannot be. To answer some questions, you may have to count, compare, or observe something as well as apply critical thinking about meaning and evaluation.

what it has been understood to be, and how power is created, maintained, shared, lost, and acquired. Critical studies acknowledges that power is often secured through the more traditional routes of elections or physical force. But within critical studies there is also an awareness, stemming from the characteristic "suspicion" that we discussed earlier in this chapter, that power is seized and maintained in other, less obvious ways: in architecture, in classroom layouts in public schools, in social norms for proper behavior during movies and sporting events—in other words, in all the experiences of popular culture. As noted at the beginning of this book, the empowerment and disempowerment of whole groups of people occurs bit by bit, drop by drop, in the moment-to-moment experiences of popular culture. The rhetoric of popular culture, or the ways in which popular culture wields its influences, therefore has a lot do with power.

In thinking about empowerment and disempowerment, critical studies assumes that although they occur from moment to moment in the experiences of individuals, they follow a pattern set by groups. It is as large classes that people tend to be empowered or disempowered. Of course, individuals do things that empower or disempower them individually. Being elected to the U.S. Senate is personally empowering, immoderate consumption of alcohol is personally disempowering, and so forth. But critical studies assumes that most of the time, people experience power in ways that are similar to the experiences of other members of their groups. If a child is disempowered, according to critical studies, it is because nearly all children are disempowered as a group.

The major demographic categories that have most preoccupied scholars in critical studies have been those of gender, race, and economic class. There are other categories one might consider, including age, religion, sexual/affectional orientation, body type or shape, and degree of physical ability or disability. Actually, the list of such categories is potentially endless and may vary from one time or situation to another.

Critical Interventionism

We have learned that critical studies is critical in attitude and method and is concerned with power. A third and final characteristic is that it is *interventionist*. That is to say, critical studies is explicitly concerned with *intervening*, or getting involved in problems in order to change the world for the better. A critic wants to step into the lives of his or her readers and give them ways to see and experience the world differently.

The interventionist nature of critical studies is really an outgrowth of its critical attitude and method and its concern for power. We noted earlier that the field of critical studies attempts to show people how to experience life, or how to find life meaningful, in particular ways. That goal implies that people have choices among different ways to live their lives. If people have choices, then they can be influenced or taught to make sense of experience in certain ways as opposed to others. The critic's job is to show how experience might be understood and in doing so to give people options for experiencing their lives. As a critic, you cannot help but be interventionist, because any time you show people different ways of doing things, you have intervened in their lives and changed them in some way.

For example, there are powerful social and political interests in our culture that for decades have encouraged consumption of food, fuel, consumer products, and other goods. From television ads to government and industrial press releases, we are told that it is good for the economy for us to buy as many things as we can. We are constantly urged, for example, to strive to "keep up with the Joneses."

From time to time, however, an ecological movement springs up that urges people to find different meanings in the process of buying and consuming. The current concern over global warming is just such a movement. People are encouraged to see acquisition of one product after another as unnecessary and harmful to the environment. For instance, people are being encouraged to question the wisdom of buying drinking water in disposable bottles. The ecologists who urge people to see consumption in this way are doing exactly what rhetorical critics do; they are saying, "Look at this plastic hamburger carton this new way, rather than that old way," and "Buying a new gas-guzzling SUV every other year means a negative effect on the environment as much as it means a positive effect on the economy."

Good critics do just that sort of thing. They show us how to think about and to find meaning in certain things, how to experience certain texts and artifacts; in so doing, they try to change us. It is almost always liberating to realize that you have more options in deciding how to experience life, to be able to see and understand experience in more than one way, to be able to find many meanings in a situation. For that reason, good rhetorical criticism is liberating. It liberates you, the critic, because it gives you a chance to probe into and develop some of these other potential ways of experiencing and understanding. And good rhetorical criticism liberates your readers and listeners as they share the new insights you have gained. Rhetorical criticism is always judged, therefore, in terms of the insights it provides into how people experience the influences of popular culture, and whether it expands the options people have for ways of experiencing that influence.

We are now ready to consider some of the ways critics go about thinking about the rhetoric of popular culture. This chapter will soon shift into a different mode, so be warned: The following sections do not describe steps to follow in a prescribed order, nor do they give directions for writing or presenting criticism. Rather, the actions described here are ways to think about how people experience life and what their experiences mean.

In thinking about such issues, critics have to make choices or decisions about what to study, what assumptions to make about what they study, and so on. Therefore, the rest of this chapter will lay out choices for you to make, but it will *not* tell you what to do. Critics' choices about what to study, and how to think about those objects of study, will direct their attention in different ways, thus exposing different dimensions of meaning. Thinking carefully about these choices is especially important if the texts under consideration are sites of struggle over many possible meanings; in this case, critics must decide which of those meanings to focus on. In the next part of this chapter, we will examine some of the *continua*, or ranges, of choices that are available to critics.

One important thing rhetorical critics must consider is what the *object of criticism* will be. By object of criticism, we mean the experience that the critic wants to analyze. These objects of criticism are usually, but not always, texts rather than single signs or artifacts. The critic must identify a text and place it in context; we will refer to this identification and placement as *positioning the text*. Obviously, a first step in positioning a text is to find, or identify, a text that you would like to study.

FINDING A TEXT

A fundamental choice in thinking about a rhetorical criticism is that of selecting a text. You will recall from the first two chapters of this book that a text is a set of signs that work together to influence people. Another way to think of a text would be to look for a set of signs that are taken together as creating an interrelated set of meanings. It is important for you to find a text that will be exciting for you to analyze, a text that you will be able to say something about, and a text for which you have some new insights. There are two sources of texts that you should consider.

First, consider your own experience as a source of texts. What have you experienced recently, what has happened to you, what have you seen or heard, that interests you? Have you seen a film or a television show, or read a blog, that "turned on" your critical attitude, for instance—one in which you thought there was something going on beyond the obvious? Can you point to some complex experience, such as going to a wedding or a commencement ceremony, that might usefully be analyzed as a text? Have any of your recent experiences seemed to have something to do with power? Could you point to some magazine article or blog that you recently read that worked to empower or disempower people within its own small space of influence? Finally, have you recently experienced a text that excited your interventionist impulses or your desire to get involved somehow (for example, did you see a movie that you thought was racist in subtle ways, so that you wanted to expose that racism)? These are questions that you might ask in relation to yourself and your own experiences of texts. Remember to look widely for different kinds of texts; we will look more closely at a range of possible choices in a moment.

A second source for finding a text is theory. This term in this context will need some explaining. A *critical theory* is an abstract statement about how people construct meaningful experiences. In contrast, a *criticism* (or *critical study*) is an illustration, or modeling, of that theoretical statement. A theory explains what people do in general, how they make sense of their experiences for the most part. A critical study is an application of a theory—it says, "That generalization can be seen at work here, within this limited frame of space and time."

For example, the critical study that is reprinted in this volume as Chapter 9 began with a theory that said, in a nutshell: Steampunk is a critical and artistic movement that uses images of Victorian England's industrial and imperial past to critique current American and European empire (Brummett, *Clockwork Rhetoric*). This is a theoretical statement designed to explain why steampunk appears the way it does in culture and why so many respond to it. Notice that this theoretical statement is about how people create experience; it makes an assertion about what people do to enjoy and participate in an

©iStockphoto.com/-zakkaesthetic and cultural movement. Notice that the theory is also abstract or general; that is, it talks about how costumes, cosplay, and published images work in general, not about a particular top hat with a stovepipe on it.

The actual critical study that was based on that theory goes to illustrate, or model, that abstract statement with specific examples from steampunk watches and from the movie *Brazil*. The study showed that steampunk manages the power that comes with empire, either by jumping scale up and putting people in a context of overwhelming and stultifying power, or by jumping scale down and creating simulations that seem to put that power within the grasp, literally, of the public. Such strategies include providing a great many highly detailed examples, for instance.

A reader of that study should have been instructed by the study in how to use the theory to understand other experiences, in other contexts. After reading such a study, a reader might forever after be alert to strategies used in other aesthetic and cultural movements, or even in other examples of steampunk more richly, noticing and understanding a little bit more of this aspect of life. A reader might go to a cosplay convention with greater understanding of what goes on when people dress in the trappings of industry or of empire.

Too often, what you learn in one class is never called upon in other classes, especially across disciplines. But in using theory as a source in selecting a text for critical analysis, your own reading and prior education become valuable resources. In psychology, sociology, anthropology, English, and many other kinds of classes, you have doubtless read critical theories (even if the authors you read did not always refer to their works by that name). For example, some theories describe, in general terms, how people behave in businesses or other organizations; such theories might be illustrated with case studies of what happened at IBM corporate headquarters in New York or at a Westinghouse plant in Indiana. Some theories describe how people in general understand poems and will be illustrated by analysis of a particular poem. Some theories describe the steps that people

EXERCISE 3.4

Think about theories you have read in other classes. If you need a reminder, look at the books for those classes and find "theory" in the table of contents or the index. Describe a theory that you have encountered that describes in general what people do, how people behave, how people experience life or find it meaningful. Summarize that theory in a few sentences. When you first read the theory, was it illustrated with a critical study? Did an example come with it? How would knowing that particular theory equip you to understand other experiences

beyond the example provided in that particular critical study?

In other words, suppose you read a theory in a sociology class that made some general statements about the behavior of people in nursing homes. The theory may have come with a critical application, such as studying the behavior of people in a nursing home in a New Jersey town. Does knowing that theory allow you to make interesting connections to the ways people behave in other institutions, such as public schools, summer camps, or the armed forces?

go through in grieving for the dead and will be illustrated by concrete examples of the experiences of particular mourners.

Theories are a useful source for texts because they tell you how to look for a text. For instance, you may never have thought of the stages of a personal relationship as a "text." But after reading Knapp and Vangelisti (*Interpersonal Communication*), you might well be able to see a unifying thread linking several events that have occurred in a relationship that you have had, and that unifying thread might constitute a text. Knapp argues that relationships develop or deteriorate in clear stages; his identification of those stages provides a useful system of categories for analysis. In this way, Knapp's theory of relationship stages calls your attention to a unity of influence among signs, or a text, that you might otherwise not have been fully aware of.

Whether you find a text based on your own experience alone or one that is suggested to you by theory, you will have some important choices to make about how to identify and understand the text. Critical scholars do not always agree about how to make these choices; we will examine some of those differences among scholars in Chapters 4 and 5. Here, however, we will examine some of the ranges of choices that are available to you. We will refer to each range of choices as a *continuum*.

First, you must choose the *type of text* you want to study: discrete or diffuse. As we will see, a given set of signs could be seen as either discrete or diffuse, depending on the critic's intentions. This choice may be represented on a continuum as follows:

The First Continuum: Type of Text

discrete – diffuse

The terms *discrete* and *diffuse* should be familiar to you from Chapters 1 and 2. A discrete text is one with clear boundaries in time and space. A diffuse text is one with a perimeter or boundary that is not so clear, one that is mixed up with other signs. Whether a text is discrete or diffuse depends on how it is experienced, understood, or used. The critic must decide how he or she wants an audience to experience, understand, or use a text. A set of signs that could be seen as making up a discrete text from one perspective might also be seen as only part of a wider, more diffuse text in someone else's experience.

We are used to choosing to see some texts as discrete and some as diffuse just as a matter of habit, but good critics always consider the full range of choices available to them. The texts in Images 3.2 through 3.32 (pages 116–146) are usually taken as discrete texts; it is clear where they begin and end, and it is usually assumed that they will not spill over into the rest of the magazine or website where they began. But a critic could choose to see each image as only one component of a more diffuse text, such as a text comprising a dozen ads of a similar type or a diffuse text consisting of all the issues of a magazine.

The start of school might be understood as a diffuse text, including such signs and artifacts as paying tuition, meeting new friends, finding classrooms, buying books, buying clothes, going to parties and receptions, and so forth. But the critic could choose to take only the first meeting of one class as a more discrete text in its own right. On the other hand, your sister's wedding could be seen as a text with a rather discrete, concentrated core of signs made up of the actual ceremony and the reception afterward. But a critic may choose to include in the text some signs involved with the preparation for, and aftermath of, the wedding, thus making it more diffuse.

It may help you in settling on a text to identify where it falls on this first continuum of discrete to diffuse. What are the consequences of choosing a more discrete or more diffuse type of text? Let's consider discrete texts first. Discrete texts are usually easier to identify because the signs that make up the text are close together in time and space; you do not have to "hunt" for them. The signs that make up the discrete text of the film *Fences*, for example, are all right there on the screen. Because the signs are together in time and space, people are generally accustomed to identifying such a text as a text. Both the sources and the receivers of messages that are discrete texts can count on that agreement; the people who made the large poster advertisement on the side of a city bus, for instance, know that you are likely to perceive and understand it as a text in and of itself. You do not have to work very hard to convince people that the texts in Images 3.2 through 3.32, the television show *Monday Night Football*, and a billboard are texts, each one a discrete thing or event. In dealing with discrete texts, because people are already aware of your text as a text, the insights you have to offer will usually be concentrated on particular details of the text. Your criticism will point to new ways to experience that text and others like it; it will call our attention to meanings that can be found in the text.

©iStockphoto.com/ericsphotography

Diffuse texts are harder to identify. In fact, very diffuse texts may be impossible to identify completely—because they are so diffuse. Your task may be to indicate most of a set of signs that seem to be contributing meanings toward the same influences without being able to identify every sign that could conceivably be part of the set. So, if your diffuse text is the start of school, you may have to give an indication of what the text is by naming several of the signs it comprises rather than every conceivable one. There are many discrete texts within the very wide range of "hip-hop," for instance, but hip-hop itself can be thought of as a diffuse text made up of music, clothing, celebrities, gestures, and so forth—such a huge text that to analyze it one would need to specify limits from the start.

Because you have to work harder to pull together a diffuse text, people generally are less likely to identify as a text whatever you are describing as one. When texts are diffuse, people may not be consciously aware of the unity of influence going on among the signs scattered here and there. Everyone knows that people prepare their income taxes, for instance, but not everyone may be accustomed to seeing that activity as a unity, to seeing all the steps and experiences surrounding that preparation (over weeks or months, at home and in accountants' offices) as a set or a text. Because seeing the preparation of income taxes as a text may be something new for people, the insights offered by your critique are more likely to be both about the text and about the existence of the text itself. You have something interesting to say about the meanings and influences of the signs that make up the experience of preparing income taxes, but you also have something interesting to say in presenting that experience to us as a text.

We have identified a text as a set of signs that work together toward the same influences, which means toward the same meanings. *Identifying meanings* is central to finding a text. What makes a group of signs "hang together" as a text is the fact that you can say that they work together to offer those meanings. But who determines what meanings are? And how do we know what these meanings are? As a critic, you also have choices in determining the sources of meanings that a text might have; these choices are represented on our second continuum, which illustrates the range of possible sources of meanings:

The Second Continuum: Sources of Meanings

broad – narrow

One of the basic principles that we discussed at the beginning of this chapter is that meaning is usually complex and many-layered and may even be self-contradictory. For those reasons, it is rarely the case that a critic can completely explain the meaning of a given text. Instead, critics must narrow their focus to some of the more interesting, influential, or controversial meanings. This second continuum can help to guide a critic in making the choice of which meanings to study. This continuum reminds the critic that some meanings are widely held; we will call these *broad* meanings. Other meanings are held by only a few people, or arise only in particular circumstances; we will call these *narrow* meanings. Of course, it is important to remember that we are dealing with a continuum rather than a sharp distinction here; for most texts, there is a whole range of meanings that are *more* or *less* widely shared in the middle of the continuum.

For instance, what do the book and film trilogy *The Lord of the Rings* mean? A critic who sets out to study that movie must choose which meanings to focus on, because they cannot all be analyzed at once. Widely agreed upon meanings would include simply what the film's basic plot or storyline is. It might be widely agreed upon as a depiction of conflicts among different nations or societies, for instance, and attitudes toward global politics or war in general might shape some of the most widely shared meanings. On the other hand, there are more narrowly held meanings that might be a fruitful object of analysis as well. Since global conflict and war are constantly recurring, people in different eras and locations might attribute narrower meanings to *The Lord of the Rings*. People living during the Cold War of the 1950s–1980s might see the trilogy as meaning the struggle between communism and capitalism. In the early years of the twenty-first century, the trilogy may be read as meaning the global conflict between Western, secular, industrialized societies and fundamentalist, Islamic societies. Affluent people living in suburbs may find meanings in the trilogy that parallel their fears of the movement of drugs, violence, gangs, and poverty out of the city and into their neighborhoods.

What are the consequences of the critic's choice of meanings to analyze? On the one hand, more widely shared meanings are often more important meanings just because they are so common. It may be important to show what most people think a text means, because meaning underlies how texts influence people. More widely shared meanings are also often easier to demonstrate in a critical analysis; they encounter less resistance because they are already understood by many people. However, because such widely shared meanings are already understood by most people,

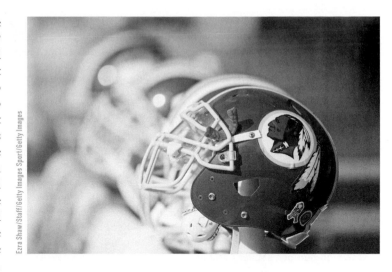

Ezra Shaw/Staff/Getty Images Sport/Getty Images

explaining them further may not go very far toward changing the thinking of those who read or hear the critical analysis. People are less likely to have their eyes and ears opened to a wider range of meaning if they are exposed only to meanings they already know.

Less widely shared meanings at the narrow end of the continuum do have the potential to widen the horizons of people who may never have thought of finding such meanings in a text. For instance, several university and professional sports teams have for years had American Indian mascots: the Cleveland Indians, the Atlanta Braves, the Washington Redskins, the Florida State Seminoles, and so on. The most widely shared meanings for the texts of these mascots were fairly innocuous; they simply "meant" the teams, and occasionally they might have served as reminders of the history of a location and so forth. But critics have begun to point out that a narrower meaning, first held by Indians themselves, is much less innocent. For many Indians, those mascots have "meant" racial insults and a cavalier and patronizing treatment of their cultural traditions. Through choosing to reveal and analyze these narrower meanings, critics have succeeded in persuading some teams (for example, those at Stanford University and Marquette University) to replace their mascots (at Stanford, from the Indians to the Cardinals). That critical effort was not without difficulty; many people claimed to see no derisive meanings in the mascots. In fact, one consequence of choosing to focus on less widely shared meanings is that they are harder to demonstrate to a wide audience of people. But the payoff in terms of changing potentially harmful or insulting meanings that can be attributed to some texts and signs can be greater.

Paying attention to the full range of choices available to the critic, from narrow to broad, is important in revealing texts as sites of struggle. Only by showing what Indian mascots mean (narrowly) to the Menominee or Ojibwa *in contrast* to what they mean (broadly) to many non-Indian sports fans could critics show how those meanings are in conflict, and how Indian mascots are therefore sites of struggle. This continuum reminds the critic of a full range of possible meanings, and thus of the likelihood that those meanings will be in conflict with each other in many texts.

EXERCISE 3.5

One of the clearest examples of signs with both broad and narrower meanings is the cowboy. Look at the advertisement for the "Keep Austin Weird 5k," Image 3.3. Were a broad, national audience to see this ad, they might attribute meanings of fun and excitement to it due to the bright colors. The walking figure seems to be an image of an old country-and-western musician or perhaps a "hippie." The whole thing carries meanings of a laid-back, fun event. Residents of Austin will have narrower and more specific meanings that they read into the text. "Keep Austin Weird" is a slogan widely found around town on bumper stickers and on shirts. Austinites will know that this means south, not north, Austin, which is certainly a narrow rather than broad meaning. Icons specific to Austin in the ad will resonate narrowly with Austinites: beloved stores such as the local Amy's Ice Creams, armadillos, or images of the bats that live under the Ann W. Richards Congress Avenue Bridge. Readers over a certain age will interpret the striding figure as being in the style of R. Crumb's cartoons from the 1960s, which celebrated the hippie culture. In sum, there are several levels of meaning here, from broad and nationally recognizable to meanings specific to narrow segments of the Austin population itself.

DEFINING A CONTEXT

Once a text has been found, the next choice the critic makes in positioning the text is to place it within a *context*. Texts do not occur, and they are not "read," in a vacuum. An important part of being rhetorical is existing in relation to some problem or situation. In other words, signs influence people for a purpose, to some end, in some context. Questions arise, then, of what causes people to construct texts, as well as who is influenced by the texts, why they are influenced, and under what circumstances. Answering these questions entails identifying a context for your text. Here, too, you as a critic have a choice, which is displayed in our third continuum:

The Third Continuum: Choice of Context

original – new

Every text appears or is constructed during some first moment or range of moments in time and space. We may think of that moment (or moments) as the text's *original* context. The people who first gathered to hear Lincoln's Gettysburg Address occupied a moment of time and space that was the original context for that speech; a slightly wider, but still original, context was the nation that would learn of the speech within days by way of newspapers. The "first" use of a text may also, paradoxically, occur across many different moments of time and space. This textbook, for instance, is a text that appears in its original context every time a student picks it up to read it for the first time. The context is made up of the room or library in which it is read, the reading assignment, and so forth. This context will occur (or so the author and publisher hope) thousands of times a year, but it is nevertheless the original context each time. Original contexts are defined by the intentions of those who make or use texts as well as by the "real-life" contingencies of when the texts, in fact, first appeared.

On the other end of the continuum, texts are often moved or appropriated into new contexts, ones that are different from those in which they originally appeared. In the 1980 film *The Gods Must Be Crazy*, an "ordinary" soda bottle falls from its original context, an airplane, into the Kalahari Desert (a new context), where it is taken to be a message from the gods by the Bushmen who find it there. Lincoln's Gettysburg Address is now studied in public schools as an example of beautiful language, succinct and efficient wording, and great ideas; the original context of commemorating a battlefield has been largely lost to the sixth grader who is being tested (that is, encounters the text in a new context) on the address next week. Of course, changing the context of a text also changes many of its meanings, though usually not all of them.

The critic has a *choice* that he or she must make about the context in which to position the text. The text may be considered in its original context, as it was first experienced by people. For instance, a critic might study the meanings that the *Three Stooges* film shorts had for their original audiences in the 1930s and 1940s or their remake as a feature film in 2012. Or, there are two senses in which the text may be considered within a new context.

First, the critic might examine ways in which people, acting on their own initiative or through happenstance, experience texts in a new context. For example, the critic might think about how the meanings of *Three Stooges* shorts change as they appear in the 2000s, as television reruns or on compact discs.

Second, the critic might propose a new context for consideration by the readers of the criticism, even if the text has not actually been experienced by these readers in that context. By suggesting that a text be seen in an entirely new context of the critic's proposing, the critic can often fulfill the important function of showing people more of the ways in which life is made meaningful. For instance, the critic might suggest to her or his audience that they think about the *Three Stooges* reruns as political commentary on the present presidential administration. Clearly, this is nothing like the original context. But if the reader begins to think about how those short features might be understood (or found meaningful) as being about the president, new insights about politics and our present situation might be opened up to that reader. The placement of the Stooges, or any text, in a radically new context like this should not be done capriciously or simply for fun. The new context and text should "fit," and the new placement should teach us more about what both text and context can mean.

This kind of "updating" of context actually happens. In the 1960s, posters of the 1930s and 1940s comedian W. C. Fields were widely popular in college dorm rooms. Fields played characters that were pompous and pretentious but also bumbling and incompetent. In many ways, he seemed to address widely held beliefs that high officials who led the United States into the Vietnam War were just as bumbling as Fields's characters. Of course, that was hardly the original context or interpretation for his films, but they seemed to fit the 1960s in new ways.

In a more serious vein, it would be interesting and insightful for a critic to ask readers to think about Lincoln's Gettysburg Address as being about the ongoing conflicts among nations around the Persian Gulf, especially involving Iran, Israel, Iraq—the desert battlefields of their recurring wars, or those in Afghanistan and Pakistan, and those who fall in those conflicts. The critic can, in a sense, ask Lincoln to speak across the years and miles to a new context. We might learn a great deal about what war means to Americans and how Americans experience war by placing that text in this new context. Correspondingly, we learn more about the text of the speech itself by observing the additional dimensions of meaning that are highlighted in a new context. For many people, the meaning of the speech's original purpose (dedicating a battlefield) has been lost; meaning might be restored to the speech by repositioning it in relation to a new battlefield.

Choosing to place a text at one end or the other of the continuum, or somewhere in between, entails certain consequences. To consider a text within its original context, the critic must do some historical work first to discover what the source of the text (the writer, speaker, film producers, and the like) and the original audiences were thinking about. If we are to think about the film *Gone with the Wind* as a rhetorical text in its original *context*, then we will have to look at the concerns of American moviegoers in 1939 and examine the meanings that the film may have had in that context. It may be illuminating, for instance, to think about the characters and events of the film in light of growing fears over war and destruction in Europe and Japan, and to ask how the film influenced the audience through the meanings it offered given the context of the outbreak of World War II.

A second consequence of placing a text within its original context is that historical accuracy becomes an important criterion for judging a criticism. Whether a criticism faithfully reports the meanings a text had in its original context is an important consideration when that context is where the critic places the text. Today's readers of the criticism will learn about how to experience and to find meanings in life if they can understand the patterns of meaning that were followed at different times in the past.

If the critic chooses to place a text in a new context, especially if it is a context entirely of the critic's choosing, different consequences result. The context will be suggested more by the critic and the critic's insights than by historical research. Historical accuracy becomes much less of an issue, and instead, the quality of the critic's insight becomes a criterion for judging the criticism. What does it teach us, one might ask, to think of the *Three Stooges* films as being about today's political context? Clearly, accuracy is not the issue in that case, as no one is claiming that those films either addressed, or intended to address, today's politics. What matters is whether or not there are insights to be gained; unless placement of a text in a new context is enlightening, it becomes just a game that is best avoided by serious critics.

EXERCISE 3.6

Examine Image 3.4, the advertisement for the Movado watch. In the pages of *GQ Magazine*, its original context, it carries meanings of style. It is surrounded by pages of suggestions on what to wear, how to decorate one's home, how to present an image. But note how simple this image is, how adaptable it would be to many different circumstances. An engineer might study it in appreciation of the machinelike aesthetics. Someone could expand it photographically and make a poster that seems like abstract art for an apartment. You could imagine this image working in a film about mechanization and the power of industry, as a huge and towering icon of machinery. The image is adaptable to many different contexts due to its simplicity.

The last issue that we will consider in thinking about how to position a text is the *relationship between text and context* and how that relationship works. There is no single way to view that relationship; the choices that are available to you are explained in the fourth continuum:

The Fourth Continuum: Text–Context Relationship

reactive – proactive

Sometimes, texts may be analyzed for the ways in which they *react* to a context, which is the left side of the continuum. People have a clear perception that certain challenges, problems, or possibilities exist (creating a context), and that texts are devised so as to react to that context. People may be out of work, racial tensions may be high in a certain locale, perhaps there is a hole in the ozone layer, and so forth. Under such circumstances, texts are designed or are used to react to these perceptions of a preexisting difficulty. For instance, during the 2004 presidential elections, the film *Fahrenheit 9/11* appeared and attempted to influence many people to vote against President Bush, to assign negative meanings to his reactions to terrorism. A presidential election is a clearly perceived existing context for most people, many of whom choose reactive texts in the forms of lapel pins, bumper stickers, and yard signs that react to that context and urge certain meanings upon others. Similarly, at the end of 2012, the film *Zero Dark Thirty* appeared, and it offered what many took to be a generally positive view of the value of torture in fighting terrorism. Both these films may be studied as on the reactive end of this continuum.

At the other end of the continuum is the possibility that texts might be analyzed for the ways in which they are *proactive*—that is, the ways in which they create their own contexts. That is not to say that these texts appear spontaneously or for no reason. Rather, the most important or interesting context within which to consider them is the context that they create themselves. Much advertising works this way. For example, many products, such as the cooking gadgets, mini-choppers, hot plates, wiener steamers, and so forth advertised on late-night television, are simply not needed; they respond to no real-life problems. Instead, they *create* a context of need for themselves, proactively.

Politics often generates texts that are most interesting for the contexts they create. In the 2016 presidential election, candidate Donald J. Trump conducted a campaign that was, by all accounts and as acknowledged on both sides, unconventional. In short order, Mr., soon to be President, Trump himself became the issue. Other candidates and news shows alike began talking about him far more than about his policies and intentions. In most previous campaigns, the nation would have been preoccupied with a candidate's stance on defense, taxes, and so forth. Mr. Trump created a context in which the talk was about him.

Most texts in and of themselves are both reactive and proactive, just as a debater's speech both responds to an earlier statement and in turn becomes the basis for the opponent's reply. A critic must choose which sort of text–context relationship to feature in his or her analysis. But an analysis might address a mixture of both kinds of relationships (a point in the middle of the continuum).

For example, racial conflict is usually a preexisting context of some level of importance in our country, although it varies in terms of immediacy and the amount of attention

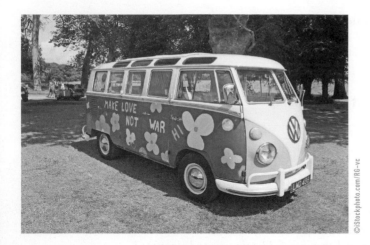

©iStockphoto.com/R6-vc

paid to it. Since the late 1980s, a series of films, such as *Twelve Years a Slave, Hidden Figures, Mississippi Masala, Crash, Remember the Titans, Friday Night Lights, Do the Right Thing, Mississippi Burning, Driving Miss Daisy, Jungle Fever, Malcolm X, Django Unchanged,* and *Falling Down,* have both responded to that perennial context and ignited a new and intensified context of racial concerns. Each newly revived context has generated more widespread public discussion of racial issues. The consequences of choosing whether to identify texts as reactive or proactive to their contexts are important. As a result of that choice, the critic must look either backward or forward—back to a context to which a text or texts react, or forward to determine new contexts that texts create.

Intertextuality: When the Context Is Another Text

One of the most interesting, and commonly occurring, textual strategies that depend on manipulation of context is *intertextuality.* Intertextuality occurs when one text references, makes use of, or actually includes part or all of another text. Any new song

EXERCISE 3.7

One of the clearest ways in which texts are proactive is when they sell the public new technologies. Think of the last time you went to buy a new cellular telephone and discovered that the store was full of appeals to buy the latest and most expensive model, which was full of all kinds of features you never knew existed before entering the store. So it is for most technology. Leisure products often work in the same way. Look at Images 3.5 and 3.6. Both of them are urging the purchase of leisure-time products such as enormous outdoor kitchens, barbecue grills, and patio furniture. If you think about it, few readers are likely to turn to a magazine to find out where to buy such things. The context of desire for these leisure products may not exist prior to seeing the ads. Instead, people are leafing through a magazine and are given a context of desire for these products;

they are invited to imagine what their own scrubby backyards might look like decorated in these ways. A desire for products that did not exist before has now come into being as a result of these texts.

Sometimes texts are proactive in that they introduce an issue to the reader, an issue of which the reader was not previously aware. Image 3.7 is a startling example of this in that many people, especially in the United States, may not know that diamonds are sometimes mined by brutal warlords who control parts of Africa, and that the warlords enforce their authority through shocking means such as cutting off the hands of those who disagree with them. This proactive image may persuade some audiences to look into the connection between diamonds and violence and to change their purchasing behaviors.

that has within it a hook from another, older song is an example of intertextuality. A new T-shirt with an old, recognizable image of a celebrity on it is a kind of intertextuality. Likewise, if someone's outfit seen today includes one element of "hippie" style from the 1960s, such as bell-bottom jeans, the outfit has that amount of intertextuality. The new, container text then becomes the context for the older partial or complete text. In this way, meanings associated with the older text become incorporated into the new text, contributing to its rhetorical impact. Intertextuality can be a powerful and efficient way to create rhetorical impact because it makes use of packages of meaning that already exist in the older text. To some extent, nearly all use of signs is intertextual, since most signs occurred earlier as parts of other texts. Every sentence we speak is intertextual, using as it does words that bring with them layers of meaning from their previous uses. But intertextuality in the sense we are using it appropriates rather specific texts from the past so as to use particular meanings associated with those texts.

Intertextuality can sneak into discourse unannounced. For President Obama's first inauguration, the Reverend Joseph Lowery was asked to give the opening prayer. Perhaps not everyone would recognize the opening of this prayer as some of the lyrics of "Lift Every Voice and Sing," traditionally and historically called the "Negro National Anthem." But for those who did recognize the lyrics, the prayer was a significant gesture placing Obama's presidency in a historical context of struggle and triumph.

One of the clearest examples of intertextuality in popular culture is *sampling*, a musical technique found especially in hip-hop. This has been a strategy used in hip-hop for years. Coolio's "Gangsta's Paradise" samples heavily from, of course, Stevie Wonder's "Pastime Paradise." Wonder's critique of materialism and living only for entertainment provided a stock of meanings ready-made for Coolio's critique of his own urban rapper's culture. Mase's "Welcome Back" begins with a sample of the theme song from the old television series *Welcome Back, Kotter*. That old comedy featured some tough but lovable characters attending an urban high school. Mase's intertextual adoption of the theme song borrowed the lighthearted, comic meanings of the original show, which were rhetorically useful in his attempt to update and repair his earlier "bad boy" image from his *Harlem World* album. Nelly's album *Suit* has a song, "Nobody Knows," that intertextually incorporates an old gospel song, "I Ain't No Ways Tired." Nelly sings of his own history of misbehavior over and around the gospel song so as to make his journey toward stability and prosperity borrow the uplifting moral sentiments of the older song. In that way, he leavens his own "bad boy" image with meanings given by an old religious song, perhaps from the churchgoing days of his youth in Austin, Texas (sorry, St. Loo, he's from the Lone Star State!). Intertextuality occurs in many more texts and on visual and verbal dimensions as well. Critics need to be on the lookout for it, as it imports meaning into a text by making it the new context for an older text.

We have discussed ways to find a text and a context. This has been a process of both discovering a text and positioning it so that we can think about it more usefully—think, that is, about what the text is, what it is trying to do, and the things to which it responds. In every case, the critic must make choices about the most interesting questions to ask about texts in context. Now we are ready to think more carefully about the text itself and about how its component signs work together; for that, we must go further "into" the text.

EXERCISE 3.8

In this exercise, we examine intertextuality. Note how one text has swallowed up part of another text. Some interesting examples of intertextuality may be found in Images 3.2, 3.3, and 3.8. In Image 3.2, note that the part of any text that has the look of a music player—compact disks, portable media players, and so forth—is the image of "play" in the middle with an arrow pointing to the right, and double arrows to the left and right to signal fast reverse or forward. These meanings connected to cool technologies of entertainment are swallowed up into the new text that is the design of the Play fragrance bottle. It is interesting that these controls on a CD, DVD, or portable media player are themselves intertextual echoes of the older technology of magnetic tape players, in which "play" pointed to the right because the tape really did move from left to right, very quickly when in rewind or fast forward. More recent digital technologies are, of course, not moving to the left or to the right (disks are actually read from the inside out, for instance), but the old tape technology was swallowed up intertextually into the new digital technologies to make them more easily understood.

In Image 3.3, the walking figure is intertextual, since images very much like this appeared in old R. Crumb drawings from the 1960s and 1970s. The "hippie" meanings of those old cartoons are transferred to this text through this intertextuality. In Image 3.8, a photo of LeBron James grimacing in athletic exertion has been inserted as an editorial commentary into a photo of a baby. Readers are meant to merge what they know of crying babies with what they know about charges regarding James's behavior when his NBA team does not perform as well as he would like.

"INSIDE" THE TEXT

How can we think about what a text is *doing*? How do texts urge meanings on people, and how do people accept, reject, or struggle over those meanings? We will build our discussion of the dimensions of the "inside" of texts around three categories: (1) direct tactics, (2) implied strategies, and (3) structures. These three categories can be usefully displayed as ranging across our fifth, and last, continuum:

The Fifth Continuum: From Surface to Deep Reading

direct tactics – – – – – – – – – – – implied strategies – – – – – – – – – – – structures

A word of explanation regarding this continuum is in order. This continuum, like the others, represents *choices* that a critic can make in thinking about critiquing a text. This fifth continuum represents whether, or how far, a critic wishes to go beyond studying the explicit and straightforward appeals that a text makes into an analysis of more indirect and less obvious appeals.

Most texts make certain explicit appeals, which we will call *direct tactics*. Texts also have *implied strategies*, which are subtler and not always consciously intended to be perceived; these implied strategies are often the implications of some of the direct tactics that are used.

And finally, any text is put together or organized in certain ways, and its various parts have relationships among themselves. People experiencing the text may not be aware of these deep patterns. These parts and their relationships make up the text's *structure*. Direct tactics, implied strategies, and structures are the sources or storehouses of meaning in a text. Which of these levels of appeals will the critic focus on? That is the choice offered by the continuum. The choice is a continuum because, although we have identified three levels at which texts appeal, the levels are not radically distinct; rather, they merge into each other.

Direct Tactics

Direct tactics reveal the system of meanings, the consciousness, offered by a text most explicitly. A direct tactic is any straightforward request or prompting for you to think or behave in a certain way. It is often accompanied by a reason or rationale for you to think or act as urged. If someone says to you, "Order the steak; the lobster isn't fresh," it is clear that a direct attempt to influence you is being made. The direct tactics used in the rhetoric of popular culture are, in many ways, closest to the reasoned arguments of expositional texts that we studied in Chapter 1. Explicit claims, reasons given in support of the claims, visual images with a clear message in terms of what you are being asked to do or not to do—these are all direct tactics that you might find in popular culture.

Our fifth continuum represents a range of appeals that the critic could choose to analyze. Of all the possible choices on the continuum, direct tactics are probably the easiest appeals to find within a text. Many advertisements are full of direct tactics. In Image 3.9, the list of technological advantages of the BMW diesel may be considered a direct tactic in that it explicitly lays out for a reader why this is the best car to buy. A hip-hop song urging people to fight oppression or a rock-and-roll song telling people to stay off drugs is also using direct tactics.

But not all texts have direct tactics, whereas all texts do at least have implied strategies and structures. In fact, some texts seem almost devoid of direct tactics. We have all seen our share of ads that make no explicit claim upon us, ads that comprise nothing but a brand or company name and an ambiguous visual image. Many soft drink commercials show only the product and images of happy people having fun. Similarly, a street gang's preferred hat style is usually devoid of direct tactics, yet it conveys a powerful message.

Image 3.4, the advertisement for the Movado watch, is nearly devoid of direct tactics. It is heavily visual, creating a feeling of desirability in the reader almost exclusively through the careful choice and arrangement of visual signs. Nowhere in that text is there any direct appeal to go buy the product, nor are there any explicit reasons given to do so.

Because direct tactics are on the surface of the text, the critic who chooses to focus on them should first simply note what the appeals are, make a list of them, and identify what is being urged and why. The critic should think about what support or reasons are given for the direct appeals, remembering that such support might be visual as well as verbal or expositional. Finally, the critic should think about the most likely audience for the appeals and then assess the likelihood of the appeals succeeding with that group.

EXERCISE 3.9

Several of our images illustrate direct tactics to differing degrees. Image 3.10, advertising the Fish City Grill, makes some simple and direct claims about its food and service. It also has a straightforward map to give directions for getting there. These are simple but direct appeals. Image 3.11 is likewise simple and straightforward in declaring its award-winning cuisine and in giving information about its locations. Image 3.12 also shows a more complicated direct tactic of appeal. Information is given about the ecological virtues of Eco countertops. Statistics are used, such as the claim of 75 percent recycled material. Similarly, Image 3.13 touts the high quality of ALNO's products and their construction. And Image 3.14 gives a great deal of information as to what is included in the vacation package it offers. It shows direct tactics in its claims of ease and simplicity of travel, cheapness of fares, and so forth. By comparison, Image 3.15 shows an almost complete absence of direct tactics. It intends to sell its Alyson Jon products visually, through more complex associations that arise from the conjunction of the images shown. It does not explain why an antler-footed footstool goes with the rest of the decor; it simply shows us that conjunction and lets us assemble our own meanings.

Implied Strategies

If critics are not satisfied with examining direct tactics alone (or if few, if any, such direct tactics exist), other choices are available to them. They can examine the implications of the signs, the relationships among them, how they are arranged, and so forth. It may be a little difficult to understand exactly what critics are looking for in examining implied strategies and how such strategies differ from direct tactics. Perhaps a hypothetical example will help. Suppose you had a friend who was working at a bank. Suppose that every time you met that friend, his conversation was punctuated by statements such as, "Embezzling really isn't such a bad thing"; "Gee, I think they probably don't catch embezzlers very often, especially if, you know, they don't really take very much"; and "I've often thought that really smart people could get away with taking their employer's money."

The "direct tactics," so to speak, in the text of your friend's conversation are rather straightforward; these are simple statements about the subject of embezzling. But if you considered only direct tactics, you would probably miss something else that is going on with your friend. Most people would probably realize that the *implications* of your friend's words are far-reaching; they might mean that your friend is swindling the bank where he works (or at least considering doing so), perhaps that he is even in serious trouble. You would arrive at that conclusion because your friend is saying things you would not ordinarily expect and repeating certain things more than is quite normal for conversation. Your friend may not even be aware of his conversational patterns. There are oddities and peculiarities, interesting things that call attention to themselves, in what your friend is saying. So, acting as an everyday rhetorical critic in this situation, most of us would probably do an informal critique of this friend's text and either warn him sternly or turn him in to the police.

Every text has similar interesting quirks and peculiarities—things missing or things too much in evidence—that convey meanings in and of themselves. A critic must choose to focus on these implied strategies. Following the work of rhetorical theorist Kenneth Burke, we will look at three categories of implied strategies, each of which suggests a question that you can ask about texts: (1) *association* (What goes with what?), (2) *implication* (What leads to what?), and (3) *conflict or absence* (What is against what?). These categories overlap somewhat, as we will see. The three questions accompanying them are the basis for how a critic probes a text for implied strategies.

Association: What Goes with What? In answering this question, the critic considers the signs that are linked together in a text. Such linkage may occur when signs are placed in the same place or within the same image so that they seem to go together naturally. The linkage may also occur when signs appear together repeatedly; every time one sign occurs, the other sign occurs as well. For signs that are linked in such ways, the meanings that would usually be assigned to one sign are transferred to the other, and vice versa. Linking signs becomes a strategy of borrowing meaning, of moving signification from one sign to another. Celebrity endorsements are a very common strategy using association. A shoe is shown together with a celebrity in a series of advertisements in hopes that the

©iStockphoto.com/DNY59

EXERCISE 3.10

Which images a text puts together with which other images can tell us a lot about the meanings it is trying to create. In Image 3.16, notice that Stella Artois and related products of Belgian beer are not paired with burgers and fries, as we might see in so many ads for American beer. It is put together with fine cuisine, as pictured in the four images just above the beers. This creates meanings of luxury and classiness for the beer; we are meant to think it is not for chugging with hot dogs at a game. Similarly, "Mexican cuisine" is a complex term and could be read to mean anything from simple street food to a local taco joint to fine cuisine. Image 3.11 shows images of downtown to transfer meanings of urban sophistication to the type of Mexican cuisine offered by the Iron Cactus. Image 3.12 supplements its direct appeal to ecological values by associating its product with images of nature and of recycled glass, such that "green" meanings are transferred

to its product. Image 3.13 pairs an image of a kitchen with that of a fine wine being poured into a tasting glass, borrowing the meanings of fine living and luxury from the wine for its kitchen furnishings. A very common use of association is celebrity endorsement. In Image 3.2, the pairing of celebrity Justin Timberlake with Play cologne transfers positive meanings the reader may have for him to the cologne, which may be new to most readers. Image 3.17 associates the Bentley automobile, long a symbol of luxury, with the Breitling watch, which may be somewhat less familiar as a luxury item. Find other texts that share meanings back and forth between associated signs in this way. Image 3.18 puts the label of a clothing brand into the rubble of a factory building in Bangladesh that collapsed because of unsafe working conditions; clearly the image wants us to associate that brand with its undesirable labor practices.

positive meanings of the celebrity will "rub off" on the shoe. A candidate for public office will want to appear with a popular president in campaign events so that the president's positive meanings will slide over to the candidate.

In another example, the maniacal killer Michael Myers in the *Halloween* movies, particularly the Rob Zombie series, is consistently associated with darkness and with mist or fog. In the brief scenes shot from Myers's perspective, his own vision is foggy and blurred. All the mayhem is done at night; one wonders what he does all day when the sun is out. Think about how meanings of dark and obscured vision are transferred to Myers's character by this repeated association.

Implication: What Leads to What?   Often, several of the elements of a text will suggest, or lead to, some other element. There are two kinds of signs that do this: *keystone* signs and *transformations.* Sometimes one sign or kind of sign, a *keystone* sign, assumes centrality in a text. A keystone is the stone in the middle of an arch over a doorway; it keeps the whole archway up. Without the keystone, the structure would fall. In a text, the keystone sign is key to the overall meaning of the text. That element may not even be the most frequently recurring sign in the text so long as the other signs consistently imply, suggest, or refer to it. Sometimes a keystone sign is the sign that catches the most attention in a text. If a keystone sign were removed from the text, the whole thing would lose its current meaning. The text will not blow a trumpet and announce to you that this or that sign has more importance than others; instead, many of the "roads" in the text lead to or *imply* that sign. If it is visual, the eye will be drawn toward it consistently. If it is verbal, it will be the word carrying the most powerful meanings. We call that a *keystone* sign within a text, and close examination of that sign can tell us a lot about what the text in general means.

EXERCISE 3.11

In this exercise, we look for keystone signs. Image 3.19, the advertisement for D&G, is an arresting image. The conjunction of interesting-looking young men in lipstick, with ripped jeans, old band and military uniforms, and a luxurious old-fashioned library, certainly invites critical analysis. I suggest that one sign in the text is a keystone sign because it pulls everything else into place: beneath the jacket of the man in the middle can be seen, just barely, a shirt with the image of Oscar Wilde on it. Wilde was famous as a late-nineteenth-century aesthete and dandy and is remembered as an early celebrity who openly displayed his homosexuality. That one small part of the whole image pulls everything into place. One can imagine these young men as the very sorts of fellows with whom Wilde hung out. The over-the-top clothing and decorations, the suggestion of "queer" sexual identities, the air of decadent luxury in the room, all come into alignment when we have the image of Wilde as a keystone sign to pull them together. In Image 3.20, we see color by itself as a keystone sign. The distinctive color of the Bombay Sapphire bottle label (although the gin itself is, of course, clear) is infused throughout the image of the ad. It is a cool, quiet, sophisticated yet not boring color and becomes the keystone for the meanings that the ad wants to assign to the product. Image 3.21 is a public service announcement attempting to increase condom usage. The condom in its package is a keystone sign; the eye is drawn to it. The sign is central to the meaning of the text.

For instance, Rick Grimes and Darryl Dixon seem to be keystone signs in the television show *The Walking Dead*. The show's attitude and many of its plot developments lead to one or the other, and the plot keeps returning to them as key figures. The two very different characters provide much of the dramatic tension in the series; between them, they can be taken as an indication of the tone of the show and why it is so popular. In many hip-hop videos, the constant reappearance of guns, cars, attractive women, or ornate male jewelry is a keystone sign; whichever is the key sign for a particular text lends its meanings to the whole of the text.

©iStockphoto.com/Lezh

Another way in which one sign leads to another is by way of *transformation*, or the "standing in" of one sign for another (this transformation can be detected in the iconic, indexical, and symbolic meanings of signs, discussed in Chapter 2). A transformation sign is not what it seems to be; you perceive it and you know that it is standing in for something else. Sometimes the text gives you clear hints as to what you are looking at; sometimes time and care in reading the text are needed so as to figure out what you are looking at.

A widely popular theme in recent movies is the sign of the furiously angry and destructive infected person or "zombie." Someone gets bitten by a zombie and turns into one directly. Films such as *28 Days Later*, *28 Weeks Later*, *I Am Legend*, *Quarantine*, and *Rec* all feature viruses that instantly make the infected rabidly violent. Huge crowds of screaming, furious zombies come pouring over the hill, raging for your blood. The critic might gain some insight by asking, what is this infection, and what are the furiously angry infected, *really*? What are they standing in for? Is it fear of recently emergent communicable diseases such as HIV or varying forms of influenza? Is it fear of strangers? Is it fear of our own unbridled passions overwhelming us? Since the angry zombie is *so* frequently found today, it is likely that this recurring image is a transformation of some concern or fear we have across cultures. On a related note, Michael Myers's character in the long history of *Halloween* movies seems clearly to be standing in for rage itself. He is the embodiment of raging angry, killing for the sake of killing. Another example is Image 3.21, a public service announcement attempting to increase condom sales and usage by transforming the condom into an "accessory," a piece of fashion.

In thinking about the meaning of these transformation signs within the text, the critic should ask why one sign was chosen to stand in for another in the first place, and what meanings are conveyed by such a transformation. For instance, a recurring feature of the *Matrix* trilogy of movies is an enormous Desert Eagle .50AE pistol. It appears to be the standard sidearm for the black-suited bad guys, the "enforcers" of the Matrix. The gun is of a size and clumsiness to make it an unlikely "real-life" carry weapon. It is very difficult to shoot and control. So the question arises, what was such a gun doing in the films—why was that gun used and not a more realistic one? A critic might propose that the massive gun was really standing in for an intense fear of government or police power

Let us look at some transformation signs in our advertising examples. Image 3.22, the advertisement for ASUS computers, shows a string of butterflies being transformed into a computer. A butterfly's light weight, beauty, and portability are turned into the computer, and those meanings are conveyed by the product. Image 3.23 transforms a MasterCard into a toy landscape, the card thereby becoming the underlying basis for an adventure of fun and play. Image 3.9 transforms diesel exhaust emissions into a green, growing plant. This transformation uses meanings of "green" things to make environmental protection claims for the product advertised.

on the audience's part, expressed in a gun that looked awesome and destructive enough to be a transformation of that fear. In the movie *Fences*, most of the film's action leads to the father figure, played by Denzel Washington. It is interesting to ask what the character is standing in for in the film. Various critics have suggested that his character is a sign of the resilience of African-Americans, especially men, in the face of adversity. Others might argue that he is a sign of the tensions involved in patriarchy within any community, but especially that of African-Americans.

Conflict or Absence: What Is against What? The critic who asks this question looks for ways in which the text keeps certain signs apart. Texts do this in three ways. First, texts may *omit* certain signs. When a reader feels this absence, noting that something that should be there is not, a conflict is created between expectations and the actual text. To locate such omitted signs, we ask what the text did not say and compare that with what it did say. We look for what is missing, especially for signs that should be there but are not.

Second, texts may show certain signs in *conflict*. Within such texts, we see explicit pairings of concepts in opposition to each other. Sometimes the text specifically places signs in opposition to each other. Sometimes those oppositions are in the form of contradictions, such as including signs that would not typically go with the other signs that they appear with in the text. Note that in texts of this kind, signs that are usually against or apart from each other have been paired; this unusual combination prompts us to think about the meanings that the odd pairing generates.

Third, texts may put together signs that are *not ordinarily found together*. The match-up of those signs startles or jars us; it is from the potential conflict of signs that the unexpected pairing (and thus, pairing of unexpected meanings) gains rhetorical strength. Complex meanings can be created by these "mismatches." In Image 3.24, both President Trump and Prime Minister Trudeau of Canada are seen looking at Trump's hand, extended in Trudeau's direction. What does the photo say, or more to the point, what can be read into it about this interaction? Is Trudeau snubbing Trump? Is Trump explaining matters to Trudeau?

Almost any night of ordinary television viewing will yield many examples of "what is against what" in the first sense of certain signs that are omitted. For example, women are often omitted as players or commentators from professional sports broadcasts, especially from the more popular broadcasts featuring male-dominated sports such as NFL football. Thus, over time the meaning that "women are not athletic" is built up. Consider also the relative absence of people with physical disabilities on your television screen. Think about the relatively low representation in film or television of people who will be perceived to be gay, lesbian, bisexual, or transgender. When texts rarely link people of varying sexual identities with everyday roles such as store clerks, business office workers, plumbers, and so forth, such texts serve to further a false image of people with those sexual identities as uninvolved in the everyday life of our country.

So, if 90 percent of the successful professionals in the United States (such as doctors and lawyers) are *not* seen to be African-American, Asian, or Hispanic (as television shows would seem to indicate), what does that seem to say about realistic career aspirations for people of color? As the public increasingly depends on television for entertainment—indeed, for a description of reality—what meanings does such an underrepresentation of people of color convey to the public? What effect might those meanings have on the members of those populations themselves?

One major absence on television is a realistic concern about money. On most television programs, you will notice that when people are finished eating in restaurants, they simply get up and leave. In reality, however, people in restaurants divide the bill among themselves, argue over who ate what, ponder the tip, and so forth. When the people on television programs *do* pay for something (such as when they are getting out of a cab), it is done with a hurried grab for whatever is in their purses or pockets. In reality, of course, people count their bills carefully, rub them to make sure two are not stuck together, wait for change, and so forth.

Television's silence about money becomes most obvious in commercials. Commercials are rarely specific about what anything costs; in fact, most of the time the fact that a product costs anything at all is simply not mentioned. There seems to be an assumption that everyone can afford anything; all sorts of products are depicted as being affordable by people from all walks of life.

The second way in which signs are placed against other signs, the depiction of *conflict*, is clear and straightforward. Dramatic television series almost always depict certain groups as in conflict. Terrorists are nearly always presented as Middle Eastern (specifically Arab or Palestinian) and are shown in conflict with Europeans or Americans. The popularity of Saudi or Iraqi "bad guys" on television has grown as the plausibility of Russian enemies (a former TV favorite) slips; spies on television shows now come from the Middle East instead of from the former Soviet Union. Such oppositions, or conflicts, urge upon the television audience a particular view of how the world order is structured.

The unexpected conjunction of signs that would usually be set apart from or against each other is also fairly common. In any election year, for example, we see powerful and wealthy politicians don overalls and flannel shirts to show up at county fairs to eat fried chicken and corn on the cob. Wealthy senators tend not to eat corn dogs on a daily basis. The president rarely goes to 4-H shows in Duluth, Minnesota; thus, when he *does* attend such a show, the intended meaning of that unexpected conjunction becomes interesting and noteworthy. Television commercials often show cheap and ordinary products in contexts of great wealth. That kind of unexpected pairing may create in ordinary people the (false) sense that they can live just as well as the rich folks.

We have been learning about three *implied strategies*: (1) *association* (What goes with what?), (2) *implication* (What leads to what?), and (3) *conflict or absence* (What is against

EXERCISE 3.13

In this exercise, we look for the three kinds of conflict/absence in signs. First, let us look at texts that create explicit conflicts or oppositions. Image 3.14, which we have already examined, draws an explicit contrast (a sort of conflict) between the dense urban environment of New York in the top photo and the elephants of South Africa in the bottom photo. The contrast is meant to highlight the attractiveness of the vacation being offered. This contrast would be appealing to those who want to get away from such an urban environment. Image 3.25 draws a quick and clear contrast between "stinking" and Old Spice products, offering their deodorants as ways to overcome problems of body odor. Does Image 3.25 create other contrasts or conflicts, and if so, why?

Second, let us consider how a text might have something missing, unexpectedly. In Image 3.26, some of the diners in the restaurant are perfectly visible and clear; others are blurs. Why are some of the figures "missing" or absent visually? Although taking photographs in low-light conditions can cause blurring, the magazine could have corrected for that problem with flash, or by taking the photo during the day. Think about what meanings are created by the blurred figures, why some of the diners are only partially there.

The third kind of conflict or absence is when a surprising or unusual conjunction of signs occurs. We do not ordinarily associate young children with jail. In Image 3.27, the stark juxtaposition between the innocence of a young girl and the harsh symbolism of the iron bars produces an especially arresting image. Image 3.28 is an interesting example of a surprising and unexpected mix of signs not usually found together. This is an advertisement for high-end furniture. What meanings are created by putting some of that furniture, with a lavishly set table and two fashionable diners, on a raft in the middle of a river with a bare-chested boatman? Why is this unexpected conjunction created? Image 3.29 offers an image of a beautiful peacock merged with a turtle. Does this unusual mix of signs create the claimed meaning of "stylish and safe"? Sometimes an unusual mix of signs is risky; might this ad also transfer the turtle's meanings of "slow" and "unresponsive" to the Kia (surely not a result intended by the advertiser)? Note that Image 3.30 puts together the unlikely ideas of the moon and growing radishes. This unusual conjunction encourages certain ways of thinking about what American Indian colleges do for their students—think about what those meanings might be.

what?). It may have already become clear to you that these categories sometimes overlap or blend into one another. One thing might "go with" another thing by "leading" to it, for instance, and being "against" one thing will often imply being "with" another thing. As noted at the beginning of this chapter, the categories and questions presented in this chapter are ways to think about the rhetoric of popular culture, and such thinking about real experiences rarely falls into tidy categories. Returning to our fifth continuum, we will now turn to the third choice critics make once "inside" texts: whether to analyze those texts' *structures*.

Structures

When a critic chooses to analyze a text's structure, he or she is dealing with the pattern, the form, the bare bones or organization of that text. Recall that we are considering choices, on the fifth continuum, from surface to deep reading. With structures, we have arrived at the level of form or pattern. Here we do not ask what is said or shown in the rhetoric of popular culture but rather what forms or patterns we can discern beneath the things that are said and shown. At this end of the continuum, signs and texts are examined to discover the most fundamental patterns that organize them and the broad categories to which their elements belong. There are two concepts that a critic might choose to focus on that have to do with structures: *narrative* and *subject positions*.

©iStockphoto.com/AndrewJohnson

Narrative. A number of scholars have suggested that texts can be usefully studied by thinking of them as *narratives*, or stories (see Aden; Fisher, "Narration," "Narrative Paradigm"; Jameson). This is obviously true for texts that do in fact tell a story, as most films do, for instance. But clearly, a number of texts (perhaps most of them) are not narratives or stories on the surface. So what can these scholars mean by suggesting a narrative approach to the criticism of these nonnarrative texts?

They mean that critics can treat these texts *as if* they were narratives. For texts that are not narratives on the surface, this means that the deeper form or structure of the texts should be analyzed, because it is at that deeper, formal level that the characteristics of narrative will be found. What does the critic look for in examining a text for its narrative qualities?

The essence of all narrative is *form*, *pattern*, or *structure*. The phrase "the proud African warrior" is only the germ or nub of a story because it does not flow forward; it suggests but does not follow through on any pattern. But "The proud African warrior looked out across the grasslands as he set out on his quest" is already patterned, in two ways. First, it follows a *syntagmatic* pattern. A *syntagm* is a chain, something that extends itself in a line. We can think of syntagmatic patterns as *horizontal*, as moving in time and space. That kind of movement is what narratives do; a plot is nothing but a pattern chaining out horizontally in time and space, a series of expectations that arise and are either met or frustrated. The appeal of syntagmatic form is the appeal of "what comes next." If you watch a movie in great excitement as to how it will turn out, then the film is appealing to you through its syntagmatic form. Our sentence about "the proud African warrior" asks us to start imagining that warrior as being on a journey, in pursuit of some noble goal, and so we imagine what will come next. We might imagine what that goal is, foresee dangers, and so forth. These expected developments will be revealed to us (or not) as the story moves on.

A second kind of pattern that this sentence follows is called *paradigmatic*. In contrast to syntagmatic structure, paradigmatic structure is *vertical*; it looks at structures or patterns derived by comparing and contrasting a given sign or text with other signs or texts that are like it. We already know that our African warrior is in a quest story; thus, his story can be compared to similar quest stories: medieval knights in search of the Holy Grail, astronauts going to the moon, and so on. Much of what this African warrior means comes from that sort of implied comparison. If you like quest stories, if you like that sort of form, then you will be persuaded by the quest story to pay attention, to follow the text.

In a baseball game, to take another example, what develops when first Smith goes up to bat, then Jones, then Brown, will follow a syntagmatic pattern; events will follow each other in a forward-moving narrative sequence. If it's the bottom of the ninth with the score tied and bases loaded, "what happens next," or the appeal of syntagmatic form, is great. But paradigmatically, when a given batter is up, we might compare that batter's statistics to those of other batters to see how this batter's performance fits into the pattern of other hitters. That second kind of pattern is paradigmatic; we are considering the paradigm, or category, of batters. The relationship between syntagmatic and paradigmatic forms is illustrated in Table 3.1.

There are really two levels of paradigmatic form, and one of them we have already examined in considering direct tactics and implied strategies. When we took a given sign and asked what it went with or went against, we were thinking paradigmatically. A second level of paradigmatic form is the level of structure. We can identify the flow, or pattern, of a given text syntagmatically. But we can also take that pattern as a unified whole and move vertically, to comparing and contrasting it with the patterns underlying other texts so as to construct a paradigm. For instance, one can examine any television newscast syntagmatically to identify the pattern that is followed: headline story, remote broadcast from a reporter, next news story, personal interest story, the weather, and so on. But we can also compare the entire pattern of a particular station's news broadcast paradigmatically with those of other stations in an effort to identify the overall pattern or structure that tends to underlie *all* newscasts. Often, this construction of a paradigm or vertical form is also referred to as the construction of a *genre*.

TABLE 3.1 ■ Syntagmatic and Paradigmatic Forms		
What Smith did in the last game	What Jones did in the last game	What Brown did in the last game
What Smith did last time up in this game	What Jones did last time up in this game	What Brown did last time up in this game
Smith Grounds Out →	**Jones Hits a Double →**	**Brown Singles Jones In →**
What Rivera (of the opposing team) did last time up	What Johnson (of the opposing team) did last time up	What White (of the opposing team) did last time up
What the leadoff batter did in that movie you saw last weekend	What the second batter did in that movie you saw last weekend	What the third batter did in that movie you saw last weekend
The Syntagmatic Flow →		

↑ Paradigmatic Comparisons ↓

Identification of form or structure entails asking the sorts of questions that we might ask of good stories:

1. Is the pattern *cohesive*, and if not, why not? What influence or meaning occurs when the pattern is broken? Humor is often the intended result of deliberate disruptions in narrative patterns that seemed to be following the accustomed groove; examples of such humorous disruptions can be seen in many comedic television shows such as *Saturday Night Live* and *Family Guy*.
2. Is the pattern *recognizable*? What other texts seem to follow the same pattern, and what does their presence in that genre, group, or paradigm tell us about the meanings and influences of particular texts? A number of observers have noted, for instance, that one of the strengths of former president Barack Obama as a communicator is that even when speaking on great state occasions, he seemed to be speaking within the form of a casual conversation; people in the mass audience felt as if he were connecting with them personally.

Subject Positions.   The Marxist scholar Louis Althusser (*Lening and Philosophy*) and others (e.g., Brummett and Bowers; Hall) have argued that texts ask those who read them to be certain kinds of *subjects*. To be a certain kind of subject is to take on a sort of role or character, one that allows you to make sense of the text. But repeatedly assuming certain subject positions may mean that the positions become who you *are*. These theorists argue that rather than having any single, stable, easily located identity, we move from one *subject position* to another throughout our lives. In a sense, then, the power that a text has over you has a lot to do with what kinds of subject positions it encourages (or forces) you to inhabit. Because we develop our ways of thinking by regularly taking up certain subject positions, they imply a *consciousness*, which, as we learned before, is a system of meanings linked to group identification. Thus, there is a patriarchal subject position from which texts of male dominance make sense. Some texts may call for a feminist subject position that entails the adoption of a feminist consciousness, on the other hand.

Whether or not you agree with such a claim, an interesting question that can be asked of texts is, "Who was this text made for—who would fit into the role of audience for this text most easily?" Note that a subject position is not a character in the text itself. Instead, a subject position is who the text encourages you to be as you, the reader or audience, experience that text. Rarely will a text explicitly announce its *preferred* subject position for the members of its audience. Instead, a subject position, like narrative, is part of the *structure* of a text. You can think of a preferred subject position as the missing perspective, the point of view, required for the text to make sense. A preferred subject position is very often a means of control that favors groups already in power in a society. For instance, almost any "real-life crime" television show such as *Cops* will call for a preferred subject position of deference to authority, the assumption that the police are always right, and a sense that justice always prevails. It's simply easier to watch such shows if you can watch them from a preferred position that views them that way. Those ways of thinking also empower current arrangements of power and authority in society.

EXERCISE 3.14

We have already examined the magazine ads at the end of this chapter in terms of direct tactics and implied strategies. Still, or unmoving, visual images such as those found in magazines can also be examined syntagmatically, but such examination can be difficult and usually involves placing oneself in the position of the reader as he or she "moves through" the ad. Yet, very often a "still" image will suggest a story. Image 3.31 says, "It's not what we do or where we go, it's who we are." Does that suggest a story about the church advertised? Is there anything else in this advertisement that suggests a narrative that would be appealing to someone looking for a place of worship? If you look back at Image 3.19, think about stories suggested by the still photo of these men in this context. How did they come to be there? Will they hang around this study posing all day? What will happen next—and how might such a narrative create positive meanings for the product?

Now we will depart from the magazine ad to consider some films, books, and television shows.

This is one form, pattern, or structure that might underlie a text:

a. People occupy a distinct space

b. that they are not free to leave;

c. hostile external forces attempt to attack or infiltrate the space, and

d. they must be repelled or subverted.

Examine, on your own or in class, all of the films, books, and television shows from the following list with which you are familiar. You will find that all share the structure described in items a through d above. For each film, book, or TV show, identify the surface features (actual events, characters, and so on) that match the elements of structure listed in a through d above.

Film, TV Show, or Book	a	b	c	d
Old, classic Western TV shows				
The *Blair Witch* movies				
Movies *Rec* and *Quarantine*				
The Village				
28 Days/Weeks Later				
Any *Star Trek* movie/episode				
I Am Legend				
(your own example)				

What can you learn about the meanings and influences of these texts of popular culture by examining their structures? How does clarifying the "bare bones" of texts, both syntagmatically and paradigmatically, help you to understand the ways that those texts might influence people?

A different structure underlies the following texts. This time *you* supply the description of the structure underlying all of these texts. Then identify the surface features in each that match the elements of the structure you come up with.

a. The Christ story

b. *Dead Man Walking*

c. *Powder*

d. *Phenomenon*

e. *The Brother from Another Planet*

f. *Edward Scissorhands*

g. *E.T. the Extra-Terrestrial*

You can also think of some subject positions as *subversive stances*, positions taken deliberately by the reader in opposition to the "preferred" subject position suggested most strongly by the text. For instance, almost without exception, old "cowboys and Indians" movies strongly encourage a white, law-and-order-based, pro-establishment subject position—in other words, one that will root for the cowboys. It is easier to see such films from this perspective; the films are structured toward that end. But one can also root for the Indians by refusing that subject position and taking an alternative, or subversive, one. In this way, subject positions can often become sites of struggle.

Recently popular television "makeover shows," such as *How Do I Look?*, *Love, Lust or Run*, or *Style by Jury*, clearly encourage a preferred subject position that values style, aesthetics, and a passion for consumption. To make sense of that show, one must think of appearance as vitally important and to think that appearance depends on constant shopping. But one could just as well watch the show by taking a subversive subject position, mocking the smug hosts, sneering at "must-have" styles that will be outdated tomorrow, and sympathizing with the poor guests who are made to throw out their comfortable if frumpy clothing.

Another instance of the possibility of a subversive subject position can be seen in relation to the long-running, now-syndicated television show *Touched by an Angel*. Clearly, the viewer of that show is intended to see the film from a spiritual, even explicitly Christian, perspective, one in sympathy with the "angels" who appear as regular characters. We are encouraged to feel uplifted by the ways in which these angels intervene in the daily lives of the troubled people they encounter; it is easier to take such a sympathetic subject position that delights in miracles and divine revelations. But it is also possible to see the film from the subversive perspective of a nonspiritual or non-Christian person. Such a viewer might "fight back" against the halos and auras of light, the miracles, and the divine interventions portrayed on the show and instead see them as ridiculous, as things to be made fun of. Another subversive subject position at another extreme, which your author has observed in some people, is that of a strongly Christian viewer who takes offense at attempts to portray the divine on television and at ordinary actors claiming (even in a script) that they are angels.

Now, the show itself appears to be trying very hard not to allow you these alternative positions; by the end of each episode, the creators of the series have pulled out all the stops to make you see the angelic characters as good and wonderful and to feel assured that God's in His universe. But because every text has a preferred subject position in which it is trying to place you, it is always possible, at least in principle, to find an alternative, subversive subject position. Doing so may yield some interesting insights into that text.

We have been learning optional ways to think about texts once you, as a rhetorical critic, have positioned them. The kinds of close and careful examinations of texts that we have demonstrated in this chapter have provided choices in considering *direct tactics*, *implied strategies*, and *structures*. Only one more set of choices is necessary to consider before you can begin to produce the actual rhetorical criticism. We will now consider different ways to step back out of the text and to think about how the meanings you have discovered do social and political work.

EXERCISE 3.15

This exercise is in two parts. First, go through the advertisements we have been using to identify preferred and subversive subject positions. We have already considered some of these issues earlier in our examination of the idea of context, or audience, for the images in Images 3.1 through 3.32 (pages 115–146). Recall that we asked who the ads seemed to be speaking to, but we also considered subversive, or oppositional, stances that an audience might take. For instance, it seems clear that the Breitling watch ad in 3.17 calls for a preferred subject position that enjoys luxury, that sees the Bentley and the Breitling as going together, that values high-end consumption. How might a subversive position take a more skeptical, critical view? What role or values might a reader assume that would undermine the premises of this ad? Look at the public service announcement in Image 3.32; notice that it is you and me, the readers of the ad, who are being questioned by the officer. The image insists that we take up a position in relationship to it. On the other hand, we are addressed as "sir." How does this influence the ability of female readers to process and engage with the image?

In part two of this exercise, we turn to your own experience. You have been reading this book for nearly three chapters by now. That much immersion in any text will certainly call forth a subject position. Consider the following questions:

1. What subject position is the preferred one for this book? That is to say, who does this book "call to"? What kind of person, role, or character would find it easiest to read this book? What sorts of characteristics or consciousness are associated with that subject position?

2. Think about yourself as you read this book. You have to adopt a certain subject position in order to read it. How does that subject position differ from the subject positions that other texts—such as the text of a party you attended recently, the text of *Fate of the Furious*, or the text of the *Fist Fight* movie—call you to?

3. Suppose you hated this book, hated the class it had been assigned for, hated the whole subject. Think of an alternative, subversive subject position you could take in reading the book, one its author clearly did not hope for. What difference would that alternative subject position make in terms of the meanings of particular passages, examples, or exercises?

THE TEXT IN CONTEXT: METONYMY, POWER, JUDGMENT

Actually, the ways that we have gone about thinking about texts have always asked you to keep one eye on what is outside the text, on the real world within which texts do their work. What texts do is, as we have discovered, very complex. All the ads that we have examined in this chapter are, for example, trying to influence the meanings that people assign to certain products in order to sell those products. But critics, you will recall, are concerned with power and with how public business is managed in the rhetoric of popular culture. So, in addition to noting how ads sell cigarettes, critics will also ask about the ways in which ads, or any texts, manipulate the distribution of power as they manage public business. (Recall that the management of public business occurs in popular culture as texts influence decisions and sway meanings about important issues.) So this next group of questions will serve largely as a way of reviewing what you have already learned about texts. In considering, generally, what influence texts have in the social and political world, you will need to choose whether to focus on (1) *metonymies*, (2) *empowerment/ disempowerment*, or (3) *judgment*.

Metonymies

You will recall that for reasons of increasing population, technology, pluralism, and, perhaps most of all, knowledge, public issues must be reduced or *metonymized* into the signs, artifacts, and texts of popular culture. Urban problems, for instance, are too complex to consider without reducing them to a series of news stories about particular incidents in neighborhoods and on subways that capture issues of poverty, crime, racial strife, and so forth. Only in that reduced form can people participate in the management of public issues by helping to determine what those issues and their components mean. Therefore, once you have thought about what the texts of popular culture *mean*, it is important to ask how those particular meanings *metonymize* public issues.

An interesting example of the use of metonymies in attempts to manage a public issue occurred during the 2012 presidential campaign and beyond. Mitt Romney, the Republican nominee, was accused by his opponents of being cruel and heartless in his treatment of his employees. Those who made this claim circulated a story, apparently true, that Romney and his family took a trip with the family dog strapped in a crate to the roof of their car. Surely a dog is hardly reason to judge a presidential candidate, but the eagerness with which his opponents circulated the story made it clear that the poor dog was made to stand in for Romney's allegedly mistreated employees and to thus be an indication of Romney's character.

Empowerment/Disempowerment

The category of empowerment/disempowerment is fairly straightforward. It asks us to consider who is empowered and who is disempowered by the meanings that might be assigned to or generated by the text. Remember that empowerment and disempowerment mainly befall large groups of people rather than isolated individuals. Recall also that power is managed in moment-to-moment, everyday experiences (including popular culture) far more often than it is in single, grand events. How does that empowerment or disempowerment result from the way that public issues are metonymized?

In the 2016 campaign of Hillary Rodham Clinton for the Democratic presidential nomination, much public discussion took place over her wardrobe, her demeanor, and her display of emotions. People might have recalled that early in the campaign of 2008, she famously choked up with tears when a supporter asked her "How do you do it?" in reference to her tireless campaigning. Clinton's service as secretary of state from 2009 to 2013 often was discussed in terms of her demeanor and style. In 2016, her followers were described by the metonymy of Pantsuit Nation in an attempt to use one of her favorite styles as a way to characterize them. Throughout her public life, her clothing has been analyzed as being too feminine or not feminine enough. It was clear that the secretary was being used as a metonymy for issues having to do with gender, gender bias, and politics. The secretary and the succession of episodes having to do with her appearance and emotions were used by the public as ways to manage these big issues through her metonymized example. Throughout her career, power and its distribution between men and women had to be addressed rhetorically by Clinton and her aides.

In the 1990s and 2000s, after decades of almost complete absence, gays and lesbians began appearing on television in much greater numbers, often taking center stage in situation comedies such as *Modern Family*, *Will and Grace*, *Ellen*, and *Queer Eye for the Straight Guy*. The cable television channel Logo offers largely gay/lesbian/bisexual/transgender-oriented programming. These television texts have metonymized some life experiences of gays and lesbians into sixty- or thirty-minute episodes. A number of critics have raised the issue of whether the shows are realistic or not. But metonymy, because it is a reduction, is hardly ever completely realistic. Perhaps more important questions would be, who is empowered and who is disempowered by these shows? Are they for the benefit of gays and lesbians or of straights? Do they tend to perpetuate the established system, the way things presently are, or do they encourage alternative distributions of power?

Judgment

The critic is not only concerned about power; he or she is interventionist as well. The critic has some purpose or goal in mind in doing rhetorical criticism—as we noted before, the critic is on a mission. That means that for the critic, judgment of the text is inevitable and unavoidable.

Judgment runs throughout all the insights offered by the critic. In suggesting that a text means this or that, the critic is also judging it. That is because to claim that a text means a certain thing, or calls for a certain subject position, or encourages a certain consciousness, is to take a stand about what the text is doing in the world.

Objectivity is not possible for the rhetorical critic. That is not to say that merely expressing personal opinions is an acceptable alternative for such a critic. All the categories and questions covered in this chapter guard against making criticism merely an expression of personal opinion; instead, they lead the critic into making well-supported *judgments* about the material that is being studied. Such categories and questions direct the critic to give reasons for her or his judgment. Thus, the choices that the critic makes, as illustrated in the five continua presented earlier in this chapter, are not made at random or simply for fun. They are choices that the critic must support with good reasons and evidence in an attempt to persuade the audience who will read or hear the criticism that the meanings the critic asserts are in certain texts are really there.

Summary and Review

The purpose of this chapter has been to help you learn how to think like a critic. In discussing the many things that rhetorical critics think about, we have covered quite a lot of concepts and terms. Does the critic have to use every term and concept included in this chapter in doing criticism? Certainly not. Remember, we have been explaining choices that are available to the critic. What should guide those choices? The critic should ask those questions that help to reveal the meanings that he or she finds most interesting and important. Let's go over some of the more important ideas in this chapter once more in a quick summary.

We began by reviewing two basic principles: that texts wield their rhetorical influence by affecting the meanings that people attribute to the world, and that because meaning is complex, texts are often sites of struggle over what the world means. Therefore, critics are meaning detectives, and their chief task is to show what signs and texts mean and the meanings they urge upon their audiences.

Critics, working within the framework of critical studies, display three characteristics as they go about explaining meaning. We learned that critics are critical in both *attitude* and *method*; that is, they refuse to accept easy answers to the question of what texts mean, and the kinds of questions they ask about texts generally are not best answered through quantifying social scientific methods. We learned that because meaning is complex, difficult to articulate, and often beyond awareness, the specially trained critic is in the best position to say what texts mean. In explaining meaning, the critic shows people new ways to experience life and helps people to expand the ways they have of finding meaning.

Second, we learned that critics have the characteristic of being *concerned with power*. And third, we learned that critics are *interventionist*; they want to change people by changing how they understand the world and the meanings they see in the texts they encounter in everyday life.

Having arrived at an understanding of what critical studies do in general, we explored a number of choices that are available to the critic approaching the study of a text. First, we learned that the critic must position the text. This involves finding a text, for which the critic may consult her or his own experience or theories about texts. One major choice confronting the critic is to settle on a text that is either *discrete* or *diffuse*, or somewhere in the middle of this first continuum. We also learned that the critic cannot study all the meanings of a text and is therefore faced with the choice of focusing on either broad or narrow meanings, or analyzing the text as a site of struggle over meanings. The third choice the critic must make in positioning the text is to focus upon an original or a new context in which to place the text. We learned that the critic may study original or new contexts in which others have placed the text, or may propose a new context of his or her own if doing so will help to illuminate what the text or context means. The critic's final choice in positioning the text involves examining the text–context relationship and deciding whether to feature *reactive* or *proactive* relationships between text and context, or perhaps a mixed relationship between the two ends of that continuum.

We learned that one important consideration for critics is the use of *intertextuality*. Intertextuality

(Continued)

(Continued)

is what happens when one text swallows up, or becomes the context for, another text. We saw that texts might swallow up all or parts of another text so as to borrow meanings that the audience will attribute to the incorporated text.

Once the text was positioned, we followed the critic further "into" the text. Here we saw that the critic's choice is whether to analyze a text's *direct tactics*, *implied strategies*, or *structure*. We saw that direct tactics are straightforward appeals and urgings for an audience to feel or act in a certain way. Implied strategies are subtler and more indirect and are revealed by asking the questions associated with the categories of (1) *association* (What goes with what?), (2) *implication* (What leads to what?), and (3) *conflict or absence* (What

is against what?). Structure is a consideration of the basic form or pattern of a text. Here, the critic examines both *narrative* and *subject positions* so as to reveal the underlying structures of texts.

Has this seemed like an overwhelming number of categories and concepts to consider? It probably has. Yet you should remember that we have been focusing on a critic's choices for just that reason—to illustrate the vast number of choices and options available to the rhetorical critic. No single critical analysis can possibly take into consideration all of the concepts we have reviewed in this chapter. Instead, the critic must make specific choices for how to think about texts and their relationship to the world and then confront the consequences that follow from those choices.

Looking Ahead

This chapter has reflected the strong conviction that critics are deeply involved in helping their audiences to see certain meanings in texts. We began the chapter by arguing that meanings are the basis for rhetorical appeal, and one clear implication of that argument is the idea that critics are also rhetoricians. Rhetoricians argue for particular perspectives and views, often against other perspectives and views.

One might finish this chapter wondering whether critics are in agreement over which meanings to reveal to an audience. This particular chapter has had very little to say about disagreements among critics. And although we have focused on a critic's choices, we have not shown one of the most important choices that critics cannot avoid—the choice of which sorts of "real-life" concerns and commitments to urge upon an audience in revealing the meaning of texts. In Chapters 4 and 5, we will turn to a discussion of the particular schools of thought within which critics work. Consider these questions as you prepare to begin the next chapters:

1. What are the different perspectives or schools of thought that critics work within as they reveal meanings?
2. What specific kinds of changes or new meanings do some critics want to instill in their audiences?
3. How can criticism serve "real-life" politics and social movements so as to help people who are in need of liberation?

IMAGE 3.1 ■ A simple message on a hat becomes a site of struggle

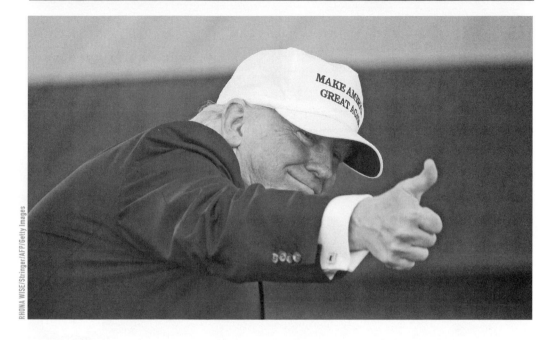

IMAGE 3.2   ■   Givenchy ad for Play fragrance

IMAGE 3.3   ■   We Heart Weird

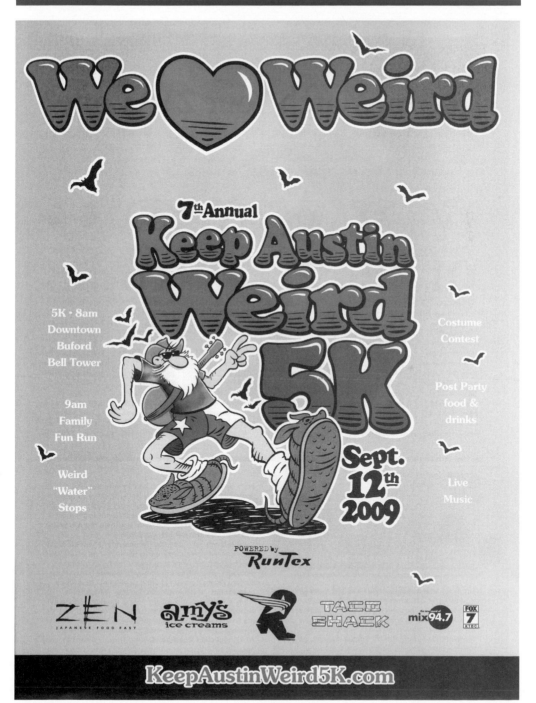

IMAGE 3.4   ■   Movado watch ad

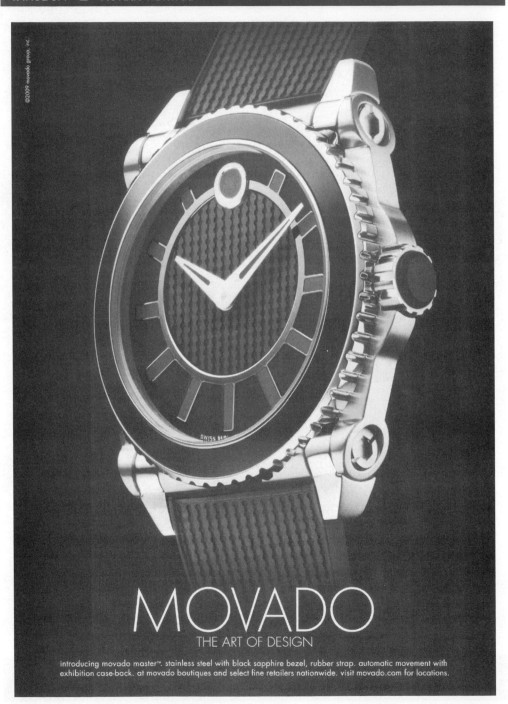

MOVADO
THE ART OF DESIGN

introducing movado master™. stainless steel with black sapphire bezel, rubber strap. automatic movement with exhibition case-back. at movado boutiques and select fine retailers nationwide. visit movado.com for locations.

IMAGE 3.7 ■ A startling juxtaposition of contrary and inconsistent images

For every hand taken in marriage, another hand is taken away.

To ensure that their enslaved workers wouldn't steal them, conflict diamond Guerilla's would often cut off one of their hands. Beauty isn't worth death.

IMAGE 3.8 ■ LeBron James as a baby in a manufactured image accusing him of immaturity

IMAGE 3.9 ■ "Diesel gone good"/BMW ad

Introducing BMW Advanced Diesel with BluePerformance. It's the same technology that helped us win World Green Car of the Year, and it's now available in America in the 335d and the X5 xDrive35d. With up to 36 mpg and an impressive 580 miles per tank, it's as efficient as a four-cylinder with the performance of a V-8. And with 20% less CO_2 emissions, it's also the cleanest, most powerful six-cylinder diesel in America. So you can still enjoy the drive and do it with a clear conscience. Visit bmwusa.com.

BMW 2009
Advanced Diesel

bmwofaustin.com
1-800-334-4BMW

BMW
**The Ultimate
Driving Machine**

Diesel gone good.

BMW EfficientDynamics
Less emissions. More driving pleasure.

BMW of Austin 7011 McNeil Drive Austin 512-343-3500 **BMWofAustin.com**

IMAGE 3.10 ■ Fish City Grill ad

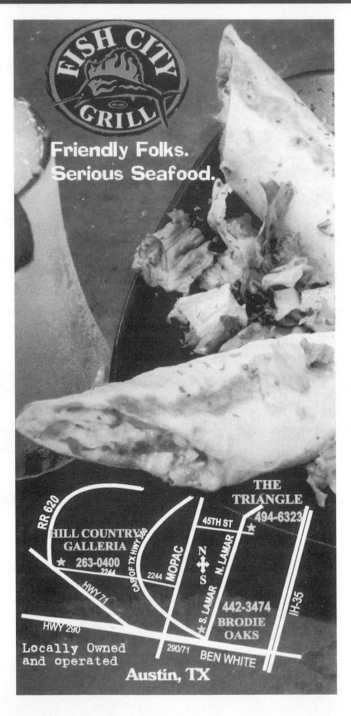

IMAGE 3.11   ■   Iron Cactus ad

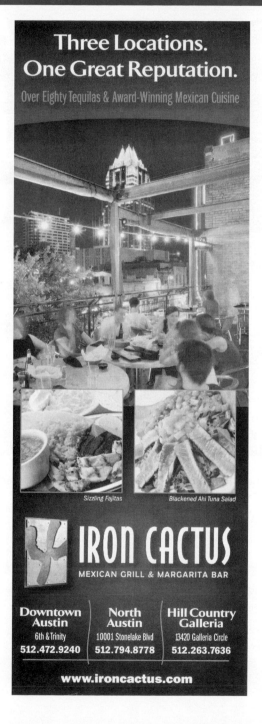

IMAGE 3.12 ■ "The Beautiful . . . Countertops"/ECO

The Beautiful and Eco-Friendly Solution for Countertops

There are eco-friendly surfacing materials in the market today, but no other like ECO™ by Cosentino. New, durable and environmentally friendly, ECO by Cosentino is made of 75% recycled content composed of post-industrial or post-consumer materials and is bound by an environmentally friendly resin which comes in part from corn oil.' ECO performs highly against staining, scratching and scorching and is non-porous; requiring no sealers. Available in 10 beautiful designer colors, ECO by Cosentino will naturally fit into any project or design.

To learn more visit **www.ecobycosentino.com**

Stone Systems of Central Texas
199 Park cover North, Buda, TX 78610
512.295.2950

IMAGE 3.13 ■ The Ultimate Tasting Room/ALNO

The Ultimate Tasting Room

Like a rich, complex, and supple wine an ALNO kitchen also leaves little to be desired. Meet ALNOSTAR HIGHLINE with clean lines and continuous case channels for a seamless effect. This premium collection also features a distinctive high-gloss lacquer finish in four sophisticated color choices. Designed with the epicurean in mind, ALNO kitchens – like fine estate wines – always demand perfection without compromise. Just one of the many collections from Europe's leading kitchen design innovator.

To request a brochure or see more collections please call 512.383.9906 or visit us at www.ALNOAUSTIN.com or call 888.896.ALNO nationwide.

ALNO AUSTIN | In the Design Center of Austin
3601 S. Congress Ave, Bldg. C | Austin, TX 78704
512.383.9906 | www.alnoaustin.com

The Kitchen, Perfected

Savouring Perfection

A CELEBRATION OF BELGIAN FLAVOR

There's a natural affinity between Belgian beers and fine food.
Just as you might pair a dry Chardonnay with raw oysters or a Pinot Noir with
an herb-encrusted beef tenderloin, the exceptional flavors of Stella Artois,
Hoegaarden and Leffe complement a variety of cuisines. So, the next time you're
planning a special meal, elevate it to perfection by choosing one
of our fine Belgian beers to complement the occasion.

Always Enjoy Responsibly.
© 2008 Import Brands Alliance, Importers of Stella Artois® Beer (Malt Liquor in TX),
Hoegaarden® Beer and Leffe® Blonde and Leffe® Brown Ale, St. Louis, MO

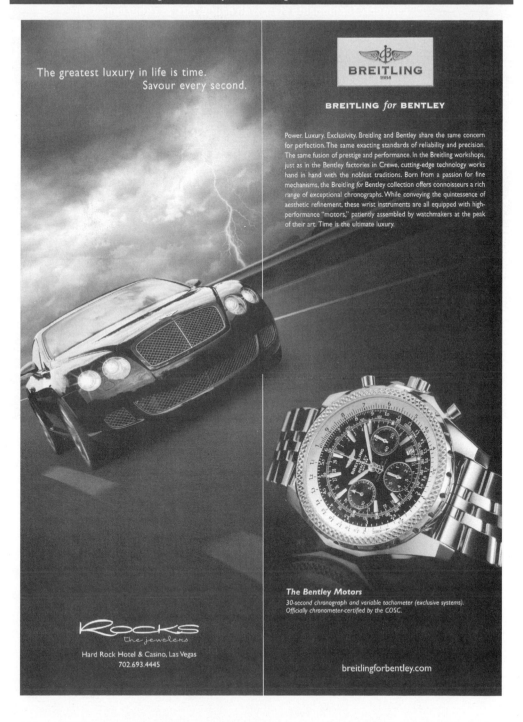

The greatest luxury in life is time.
Savour every second.

BREITLING
1884

BREITLING *for* **BENTLEY**

Power. Luxury. Exclusivity. Breitling and Bentley share the same concern for perfection. The same exacting standards of reliability and precision. The same fusion of prestige and performance. In the Breitling workshops, just as in the Bentley factories in Crewe, cutting-edge technology works hand in hand with the noblest traditions. Born from a passion for fine mechanisms, the Breitling for Bentley collection offers connoisseurs a rich range of exceptional chronographs. While conveying the quintessence of aesthetic refinement, these wrist instruments are all equipped with high-performance "motors," patiently assembled by watchmakers at the peak of their art. Time is the ultimate luxury.

The Bentley Motors
30-second chronograph and variable tachometer (exclusive systems).
Officially chronometer-certified by the COSC.

Rocks
the jewelers
Hard Rock Hotel & Casino, Las Vegas
702.693.4445

breitlingforbentley.com

IMAGE 3.18 ■ A clothing label in the rubble of a Third World factory that exploded connects fashionable style with dangerous working conditions

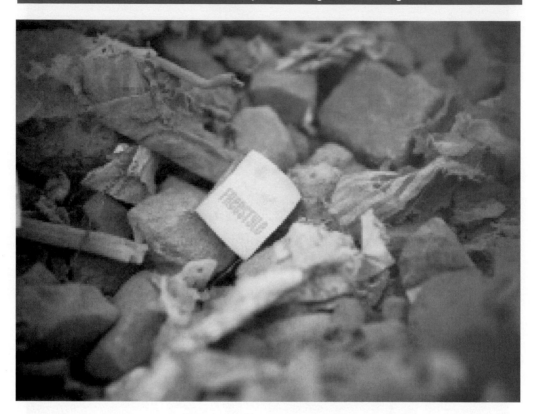

IMAGE 3.19 ■ D&G ad showing pouty young men

IMAGE 3.20 ■ Bombay Sapphire ad

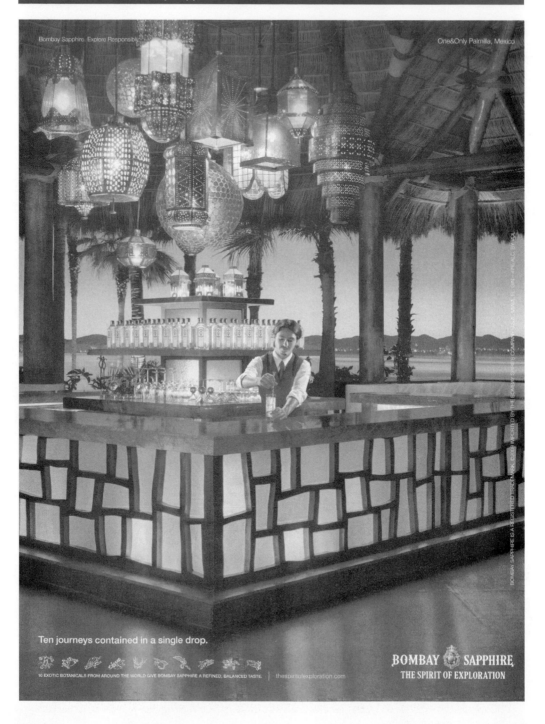

IMAGE 3.21 ■ Condoms and fashion accessories don't usually go together, but this image boosts the allure of the condom

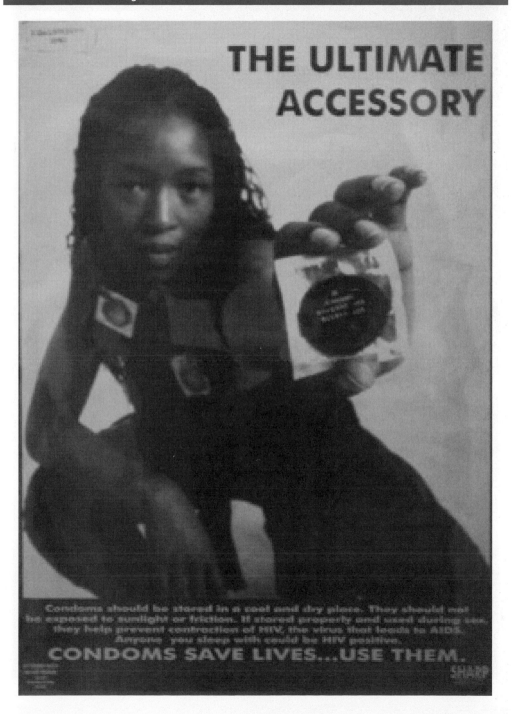

IMAGE 3.22 ■ **ASUS ad**

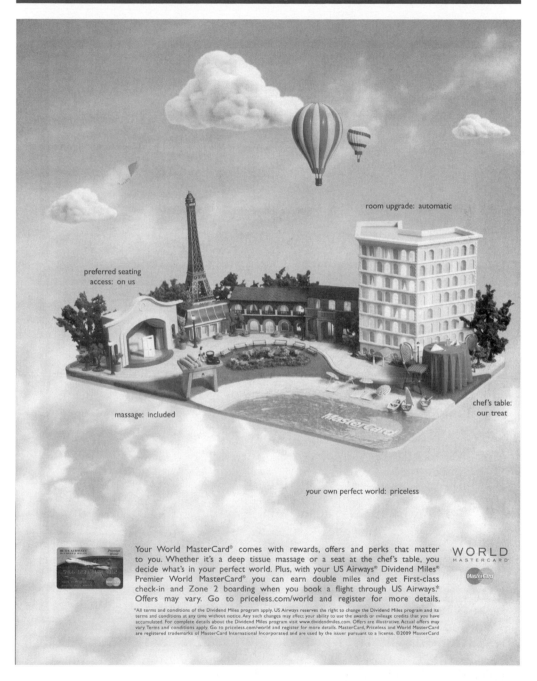

IMAGE 3.24 ■   What are some meanings that can be read into this?

IMAGE 3.25 ■ If You Stink . . .

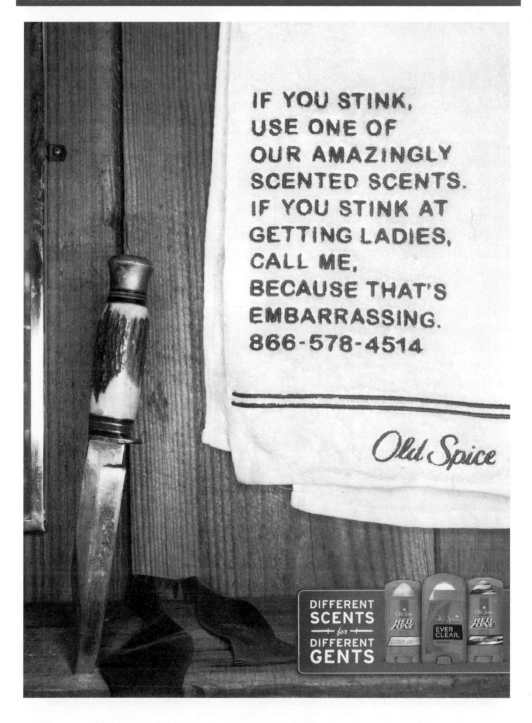

IMAGE 3.26   ■   September dining/Perla's

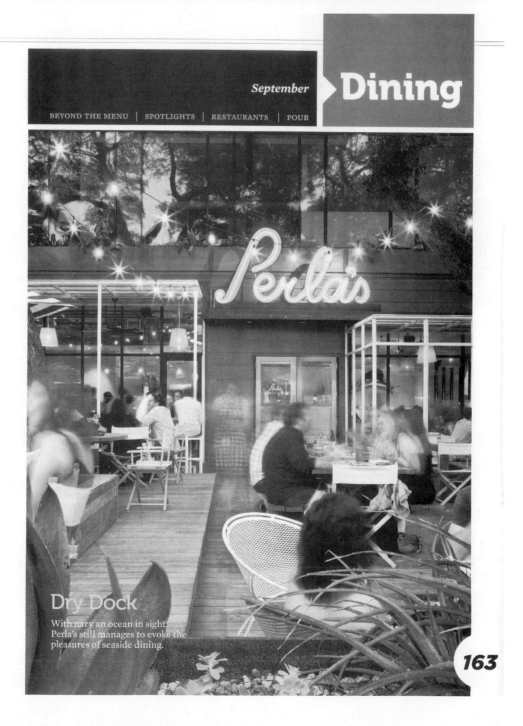

September ▶ **Dining**

BEYOND THE MENU | SPOTLIGHTS | RESTAURANTS | POUR

Perla's

Dry Dock
With nary an ocean in sight,
Perla's still manages to evoke the
pleasures of seaside dining.

163

IMAGE 3.27   ■   What is against what; young children and jail aren't usually associated with each other

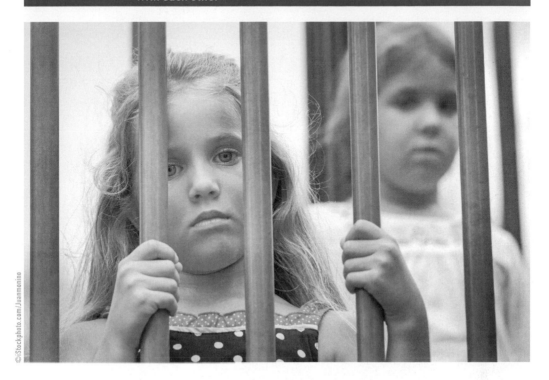

IMAGE 3.28   ■   Bella Dimora ad

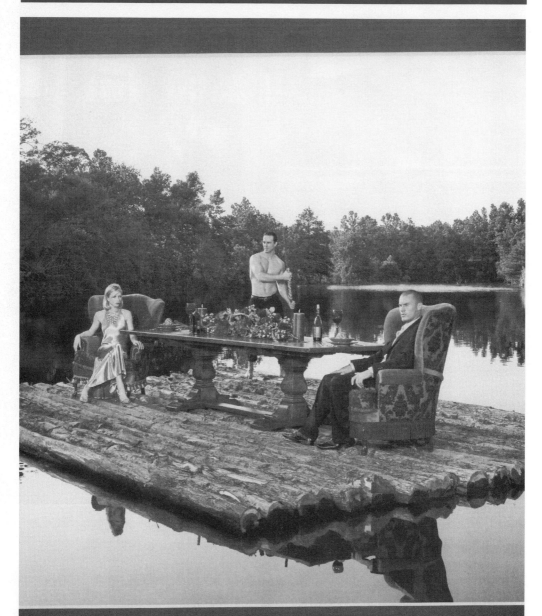

Bella Dimora

Davenport Village   •   3801 N Capital of Texas Highway, Suite D220   •   Austin, Texas 78746   •   (512) 306-8113   •   BellaDimora@austin.rr.com
Fine Furnishings   •   Decorative Accessories   •   Lighting   •   Floral   •   Art   •   Holiday Accents   •   Interior Design Services

IMAGE 3.29   ■   Kia ad with peacock: How is the car transformed in this image?

IMAGE 3.32   ■   You and I are the ones being interrogated

4

VARIETIES OF RHETORICAL CRITICISM

INTERVENTION-Understanding

In Chapter 3, we learned that critics who are trying to understand the rhetoric of popular culture are confronted with choices about the texts they study. These critics are in search of what texts mean and of how those meanings influence people. We have looked at some of the concerns and questions that most rhetorical critics have in common.

Also within the last chapter, the choices that critics make were presented along continua, as evidence that not all critics make the same choices or study texts in the same ways. Texts inevitably have many meanings, and critics may disagree about which meanings and which influences are the most important. Similarly, critics may disagree about which meanings are most influential; in trying to explain why people do what they do and why the world is the way it is, some critics of popular culture will point to some meanings and other critics will point to other meanings. These differences reflect unavoidable differences in taste and philosophy. People simply disagree, and while some think that the world turns because of power, others think that it turns because of biochemistry, sex, God, economics, race, and so forth.

AN INTRODUCTION TO CRITICAL PERSPECTIVES

Another way to express these differences is to say that while we were concerned with *how* texts have meaning in Chapter 3, in this chapter and the next we will consider seven different perspectives on *what* texts mean. There is always more controversy over the latter (*what* texts mean) than the former.

Between this chapter and the next, we will look at seven groups of methods, or seven schools of thought in the rhetorical criticism of popular culture: (1) culture-centered, (2) Marxist, and (3) feminist in this chapter, and in Chapter 5, (4) psychoanalytic, (5) visual, (6) dramatistic/narrative, and (7) media-centered. You might also recall the neo-Aristotelian method that we learned in the first chapter and think of that as an eighth school of thought. You can think of these different approaches to method as different sets of questions for a critic to ask, different categories within which to think, different critical tools, different kinds of meanings to which critics call our attention, and different ideas of what to study in a text.

You will notice a distinction made in the subtitles of this and the next chapter, a distinction between intervention and understanding. Every critical method has at least these two goals: first, to intervene in the world by making it a better place with fairer distributions of power, and second, to increase understanding of how texts work. We have talked about these two impulses in earlier chapters. But some schools of thought will emphasize one of those goals over another. In this chapter, the three methods we study—culture-centered, Marxist, and feminist—emphasize intervention more than understanding (although by no means do they shortchange understanding), and thus this chapter is subtitled INTERVENTION-Understanding. In Chapter 5, the four methods studied—psychoanalytic, visual, dramatistic/narrative, and media-centered—emphasize understanding somewhat more than intervention (while again, not ignoring understanding at all); thus, Chapter 5 is subtitled UNDERSTANDING-Intervention.

We have a second scheme for organizing our methodological schools of thought: methods focused on power, methods focused on self and society, and methods focused on story. All seven of the schools of thought we will take up actually address all three of those subdivisions, but these headings will be helpful in thinking about *emphasis*. The three methods concerned most with intervention, explained in this chapter, are for that reason the most concerned with how power is created and contested: culture-centered, Marxist,

School of Thought, or Method	Major Focus of This Method
TABLE 4.1	
Culture-centered (Chapter 4)	Intervention and power
Marxist (Chapter 4)	Intervention and power
Feminist (Chapter 4)	Intervention and power
Psychoanalytic (Chapter 5)	Understanding and the self in society
Visual (Chapter 5)	Understanding and the self in society
Dramatistic/narrative (Chapter 5)	Understanding and story
Media-centered (Chapter 5)	Understanding and story

and feminist. In Chapter 5, the psychoanalytic and visual schools of thought place a lot of emphasis on the creation of the self in a social context. The dramatistic/narrative and media-centered schools of thought place much emphasis on how stories have rhetorical impact in a society. Table 4.1 may help you understand the logic of organization for this and the next chapter. Let me emphasize again that each school of thought "leaks" into the others, and these distinctions are meant to be helpful but not exclusive in an ironclad way.

Before we start thinking about specific approaches, however, we need to make three observations about them. First, within each school of thought are wide differences of opinion, despite the sharing of a general approach to criticism. Indeed, there is not even universal agreement about the labels that are used to denote the seven groups. (Works included in the reading list at the end of the book will allow you to investigate these differences further.)

Second, there is significant overlap among the seven schools of thought. The fact that one critic might be labeled a Marxist and another a feminist does not mean that they are at odds. Indeed, critical studies often employ more than one approach in combination. So our first two observations could be summed up by noting that any identification of any number of approaches to rhetorical criticism must be somewhat arbitrary and that the boundaries between various approaches are not firm.

Third, not all approaches to the rhetorical criticism of popular culture are discussed in these two chapters. As suggested above, we will deal with only some of the many methods used within each particular school of thought. And some schools of thought, such as deconstruction or fantasy theme analysis, will not be developed here at all. Because our space is limited, we will look only at those approaches that seem most fruitful for revealing rhetorical influences, rather than other dimensions, of popular culture.

You have already noticed how important illustrations and examples are for demonstrating how theoretical and methodological concepts relate to our experiences of popular culture. In these two chapters, we will often use as an example an experience that is surely familiar to anyone who has lived in the United States for more than a few years: watching the 1939 film *The Wizard of Oz*. That movie, broadcast every year on television and widely available on discs and online, comes as close as anything to a universally shared experience of popular culture within the United States. If you have not seen the actual movie from start to finish, then you are likely familiar with bits and pieces of it. You will instantly understand a song or a television commercial that references the yellow brick road. You will be able to hum along with "Somewhere over the Rainbow." In whole or in part, most readers of this book will have been exposed to this film.

METHODS FOCUSED ON POWER

Culture-Centered Criticism

The first approach to the rhetorical criticism of popular culture that we will examine is relatively new and is proceeding on many different fronts. Because attention to a wide range of cultures on their own terms is relatively new in the academy, this method is still in the process of being formulated and clarified by critics and scholars. But, by the same token, it is on the cutting edge of critical approaches and a potentially exciting perspective to work from. It is also highly interventionist, for it calls upon both producers and critics of texts to be sensitive to cultural differences. Whether a culture is ignored or paid attention to is a major factor in whether that culture is empowered.

Cultures and Their Own Critical Methods

A major theme for us in this book has, of course, been the importance of *culture* as a source of perspectives, thoughts, values, feelings, ideas, and ideologies. Culture comprises not only artifacts but also ways of understanding artifacts. Since a way of understanding artifacts is essentially what a method of rhetorical criticism is, it makes sense to say that every culture contains its own methods for understanding artifacts. One rather extreme example illustrates this truth: During World War II, soldiers and sailors from the United States and its allies created temporary, makeshift bases on a number of islands in the Pacific, bringing with them a world of material goods that astonished and impressed the native people who were already living on those islands. With the end of the war, the military personnel abruptly departed, leaving behind odds and ends of military equipment. On some of those islands, there arose "cargo cults," actual religions that centered around the expectation that the GIs would return someday, bringing with them renewed prosperity. The castoff equipment that the military left became infused with religious meanings for the cultists.

Now, for the cultures that developed cargo cults, the helmets, jeep parts, and so forth that were left behind became part of the culture—but so did ways to understand them, ways to interpret them. Those ways of understanding all the castoff items were the religious systems that formed around them. Were a member of a cargo cult to come to the United States, see a helmet in a military relics store, and assume that the store was a religious shrine, we might think that he or she had misunderstood the helmet and what it means. But were one of us to go to a cargo cult island, we would be equally mistaken to identify a helmet placed in a hut as "just a piece of historical junk from World War II." Those of us living in the high-technology world of the United States today have our own "cargo cults" as well. We, too, have not only objects and actions that are peculiar to our culture but particular ways of understanding and interpreting those artifacts, ways that might not be understood by people from another culture. To see the truth of this claim, go to eBay and experience the vast range of oddities and curios offered for sale.

Every culture contains its own methods of critical analysis, its own questions and probes to be brought to bear on the artifact that is being examined. Such methods will be appropriate for understanding artifacts within, or peculiar to, that culture, particularly if we want to know what those artifacts mean for members of that specific culture. If we want to understand what a particular kind of Latvian hat means to Latvians, then we should look at it through Latvian eyes. Of course, this hypothetical Latvian hat will mean *something* to people from Japan, from Great Britain, and from New Jersey. But an awareness of cultures, and of the different methods of critical analysis that cultures give to us, should prevent anyone from assuming that a given artifact has only and always the meaning that one's own culture would give to it.

Ethnocentric criticism is this practice of looking at the artifacts of other cultures and judging them only from the perspective of one's own culture. Ethnocentrism has for centuries been a major tool of racism and imperialism. Soldiers, explorers, and imperialists from European countries would travel to places in Africa, Asia, and South America. Viewing the artifacts of the indigenous cultures of those lands from the perspective of their European cultures only, these European colonialists often labeled the indigenous cultures second-rate, primitive, or savage. Of course, viewing the artifacts of another culture as primitive and underdeveloped becomes a license for oppression. For centuries, people from European cultures used their own ethnocentric attitudes toward the artifacts of other cultures as an excuse to dominate and exploit people of those other cultures "for their own good." A school of thought intended to intervene in ethnocentric criticism is thus very much concerned with power.

Culture-centered criticism is not the same thing as ethnocentrism. Culture-centered criticism grows out of an awareness that cultures are best understood by using the methods of criticism and interpretation that arise from the cultures themselves. Culture-centered criticism understands that looking from one culture to another requires caution about the claims that one makes and an awareness that the culture being observed might well see itself, and its own artifacts, differently.

Culture-centered criticism can, in fact, be an *antidote* to ethnocentrism. This is especially true when the criticism is applied to cultures that have been oppressed socially, politically, economically, or militarily. Such cultures have often been analyzed only through the methods of the very cultures that oppress them. Culture-centered criticism is therefore an important political strategy on the part of cultures that have been oppressed and exploited to recover their own voices and eyes, both for understanding themselves and for understanding other cultures.

Afrocentricity

Culture-centered criticism is being developed on several fronts as Asian, Latino, and other scholars discover and articulate methods of rhetorical criticism that grow out of their own cultures. An approach that is concerned with cultures of African origin is one of the best-developed forms of culture-centered criticism so far. Our focus here on Afrocentric

©iStockphoto.com/fiberville

culture–centered criticism is therefore not meant to imply at all that there are not methods in place suitable for analysis of other cultures.

We noted earlier that culture-centered criticism often serves as a political tool to counter oppression. People of African origin have historically suffered much oppression, culturally and personally, all over the world. An attempt to recapture a particularly African perspective is thus a method of empowerment for people of African heritage. It argues that those artifacts that are clearly part of the culture of African-Americans—such as rap music, the Traditional Black Church, jazz, rhythm and blues, and so on—cannot be adequately understood if analyzed from a European perspective (as they have often been). To understand what the call and response between a black preacher and congregation means, for instance, we must employ methods of critical understanding that arise from within African-American culture.

Here we will focus on efforts in the United States to understand the culture of African-Americans as African-centered. We will turn to three primary sources by scholars who articulate critical principles that are grounded in the culture of African-Americans. In his book *The Afrocentric Idea*, Molefi Kete Asante explains methods of criticism that are fundamentally African in origin. His view is pan-African, looking to that which is common to people of African heritage wherever they may be found around the world. In *The Signifying Monkey: A Theory of African-American Literary Criticism*, Henry Louis Gates, Jr., argues that many methods of criticism and understanding found in the culture of African-Americans developed as defenses against slavery historically and against racism more recently. Gates's concerns are more specifically American, and more directly political, than are Asante's. We will also examine the ideas of Jack L. Daniel and Geneva Smitherman in their article "How I Got Over: Communication Dynamics in the Black Community." Daniel and Smitherman argue that methods of criticism in African-American culture are grounded in the institution of the Traditional Black Church.

All of these scholars argue in favor of understanding the artifacts of African-American culture using methods grounded in that culture. Although these four critics do not all use the term, we will borrow Asante's idea of *Afrocentricity* to refer to a culture-centered method that places "African ideals at the center of any analysis that involves African culture and behavior" (6). Through such a method, Asante hopes that African culture, including its manifestations among African-Americans in the United States, will become "subject and not object" (3), the perspective from which a thing is seen rather than the thing that is seen from some other perspective. Developing that critical perspective is, he argues, a political stance as well, in that it grounds people of African heritage, who have been dispersed all around the world, in an ancient and honorable tradition.

These authors, particularly Asante, are careful to note that they are discussing the ways in which African culture informs African-American culture today. But they do not make the claim that all black people actively participate in that culture. They are making a cultural, not a racial, argument. They point out that there are also African-Americans with a Eurocentric perspective. Furthermore, Afrocentric criticism is potentially something that people of *any* race can engage in by remembering to apply Afrocentric standards when studying an Afrocentric culture. Afrocentricity is not an exclusive club; it is a perspective on how to understand a culture.

©iStockphoto.com/leezsnow

To develop any culture-centered critical method, we must ask what are the values, the ways of understanding and thinking, and the aesthetics that are most characteristic of a given culture. The Afrocentric method identifies a number of ideas, or *tenets*, that are especially important in African cultures and that must therefore be incorporated into the methods used to study cultures grounded in an African heritage. One of the most important of these tenets of Afrocentricity is the value of *unity and harmony*.

Unity and Harmony

Unity and harmony constitute an overarching value that incorporates several component ideas. Daniel and Smitherman identify, among the tenets of what they term the "Traditional African World View," the cosmic values of "unity between spiritual and material" things and "harmony in nature and the universe" (29–30). Daniel and Smitherman also refer to the idea that human society is "patterned after natural rhythms" (31), by which they mean the cycle of social and environmental experiences that are shared by everyone within the culture (rather than individual or private events). The important event of the day, for instance, is not what happens to you personally but what happens to your group as a whole (a town or family celebrating a wedding, bringing in a harvest together, and so forth).

Asante also notes the social value of harmony. Afrocentric rhetoric, he argues, is concerned with creating harmony and balance in the midst of disharmony and indecision (35). According to Asante, the Afrocentric mind is highly communal rather than individualistic and has a distaste for individual achievement that is not related to collective advancement (105). Think of the rhetorical mistakes that a Eurocentric teacher might make, for instance, in encouraging a student from an Afrocentric culture to do well in school so that he or she can get ahead of all the others (rather than, for example,

©iStockphoto.com/JeffBanke

to do well so as to make the whole community proud); that sort of Eurocentric individualism is the wrong rhetoric for the circumstances.

The value of social unity and harmony, of acting together, is an aspect of African culture that can be employed in rhetorical criticism to further understanding of cultures that are grounded in Africa. In the Traditional Black Church, which Daniel and Smitherman take to be "an exemplary form of Black communication" (27), a common pattern of interaction is the "call–response" in which the preacher and congregation will talk back and forth to one another in a way largely unknown among white congregations.

How can we understand this artifact of black culture? Observing it through Eurocentric eyes might lead us to see the congregation as disrespectful of the preacher, as too boisterous or ill-mannered. Such a perspective would misunderstand what call–response means in its original cultural context. Call–response serves to create a unity and harmony between preacher and congregation; instead of a series of interruptions of an individual sermon, it is part of an entire church service that is being created on the spot. Furthermore, Daniel and Smitherman point out that the call–response form can be found in patterns of communication among African-Americans outside the church as well, and in musical forms, such as jazz, created by African-Americans. Participating in these various forms of call–response creates a feeling of satisfaction within the individual as he or she participates with others in creating a unified harmony.

It is possible to overlook what is going on in call–response if we do not think about that cultural artifact with the African value of harmony and unity in mind. But with such a value in mind, we might then look at this and other artifacts of African-American culture to see that value at work. For instance, basketball seems to be much more a part of the experience of African-Americans than does golf (despite the success of Tiger Woods); could that be, in part, because golf is such an individual, isolated game, while basketball requires the close cooperation of team members—harmony and unity—to set up shots, to maintain defense, and to move the ball down the court?

Orality

Another major tenet of Afrocentricity is that it is an oral culture, grounded in Asante's concept of *orature*, or the "total body of oral discourses, styles and traditions." Historically, African cultures have communicated through the spoken word, and knowledge has been encoded in spoken forms of literature. Orature thus depends on *nommo*, defined by Asante as the power of the spoken word, the belief that all power is ultimately that of oral communication (17).

This is an important concept for creating an Afrocentric understanding of popular culture. Eurocentric cultures, argues Asante, see power residing in a given text or artifact that is created by some source. To speak, perform, or present that text is merely to pass along the "substance" of the text that is already there. People of European heritage would, for instance, see a song as essentially and fundamentally the words and notes that are written down on paper; a performer is important, but only for passing the song along to a listening audience. But Afrocentricity regards the song, or any text, as created in its performance or presentation. It must not only be sung by the singer but also heard and reacted to by the audience. Between them, both singer and audience create the text that is the whole experience.

The importance of the spoken word is, of course, quite consistent with the importance, noted above, of unity and harmony. Only the spoken word creates an immediate bond between speaker and listener. The written word, in contrast, can be a communication between even one who is dead and an audience. But when a speaker speaks, a singer sings, or an athlete performs and the audience is there to listen, remark, call encouragement, and make comments—in that moment the text is created, according to the Afrocentric perspective.

The importance of understanding this idea as a principle of criticism is clear. The experience of a text within African-American teen culture, for example, is most fully understood not by the critic simply listening to a Migos or Drake download but by the critic seeing how that song is received and reacted to by a specific audience of listeners. The text of a gospel music service is not fully understood as the words and music on paper, nor even as the singer's voice alone, but rather as the singer's voice *together with* the ways in which the audience joins in verbally and nonverbally. Any text, from an Afrocentric perspective, is "the word revealed in life" (Asante 60). Gates (*Signifying Monkey*) calls this concept the principle of "The Talking Book," describing African-American writing as often highly oral/aural, representing the "black vernacular" or speaking voice in writing and inviting itself to be read aloud.

Signifying

A third important tenet of Afrocentricity—*signifying*—is described at length, and with great complexity, in Gates's book. Gates points to the fact that historically, in much African-American folklore, a figure known as The Signifying Monkey appears. The Signifying Monkey, and the practice of signifying itself, have a great deal of meaning within Afrocentricity and cannot be fully explained here. But one interesting aspect of it is that it is a *strategy of indirection*. It is saying and doing one thing while meaning another, with the full knowledge that one's audience will understand the doubleness or two-facedness of what one says and does.

Gates gives as one example the practice of (in the wording of the time in which he wrote) "toasting" or "the dozens," in which two people will try to outdo one another in heaping insults upon each other's parents and ancestry, economic prospects, physical appearance, and so forth. The words constitute actual insults on the one hand, but on the other hand are really only a game. Gates cites another example of one woman who observes another, obviously pregnant woman and remarks that the latter has been putting on weight. The pregnant woman merely responds that she has, indeed, been getting larger. To which the first woman replies, "Now look here, girl, we both standing here soaking wet and you still trying to tell me it ain't raining" (83). Rain, of course, has nothing to do with it; it is simply a way of taxing the woman with denying her pregnancy but doing it *indirectly*. Indirection—saying one thing and meaning another—is thus an essential component of signifying (Gates 54).

Gates argues that signifying is a practice present in all African cultures and rooted in the mythic figure of "Esu," or the trickster. The trickster figure became especially important among African-Americans, Gates claims, during the time of slavery, when resistance to oppression required an ability to say one thing but mean another. Enslaved Africans had to be able to sing "Steal Away to Jesus," which meant one thing to whites, while understanding among themselves that it meant something quite different, such as a call to a secret meeting. Signifying is thus a strategy for obscuring the apparent meaning, a way to colonize a white sign and make it have a meaning appropriate to one's own culture.

Again, the importance of understanding signifying as a rhetorical critic is clear. An artifact of African-American culture will often be most fully understood by asking whether it has a double meaning, an "in-house" meaning among African-Americans that is specifically and intentionally in contrast to, or in defiance of, the meaning that it might have for white society. Eurocentric criticism tends not to value indirection as highly, and certainly not as a strategy of political survival against oppression. So, for instance, a Eurocentric critic might view the scenes in the *Barbershop* film series, in which highly exaggerated lampoons of inner-city life are presented, as straightforwardly funny. An Afrocentric perspective, on the other hand, might see these scenes as signifying, as having a double and indirect meaning. Perhaps Ice Cube's (and others') portrayals of "ghetto" characters are in fact a burlesque of a "ghetto" dweller *as whites might see such a person* and thus are not only meant to be funny for all audiences of every color but also *oppositional*, set up against whites' oversimplified ideas about people of color.

Other Tenets

Asante, Gates, and Daniel and Smitherman point to many other tenets of Afrocentricity, more than we can consider in detail here. But we will conclude by referring briefly to a few of them.

Oral cultures will trade components of various texts back and forth, because the boundaries between spoken texts are fluid (unlike printed texts, which have firmer physical barriers). Therefore, Afrocentric culture expects that texts will borrow from other texts freely, using a strategy called *intertextuality* (Gates 60). Critics should be on the lookout for that strategy and note that it is culturally appropriate and expected. For example, much of the public speaking of Martin Luther King, Jr., was intertextual. He wove into a speech many brief passages from the Bible, proverbs, maxims, and his other speeches.

Asante points out that *rhythm* and its associated concepts, such as repetition and careful choice of word and gesture, are highly valued in the Afrocentric perspective (38–39). The phrasing of even a single word and the manipulation of pauses for precise effect are aesthetic choices that are not so highly prized in the Eurocentric tradition. In his famous "I Have a Dream" speech, for example, Martin Luther King, Jr., repeatedly used a formal pattern of pausing for effect. Similarly, in one well-known passage of the speech, the phrase "I have a dream" is repeatedly appended to the end of the sentence before it. What is happening here is a manipulation of rhythm, in conjunction with a vivid style, that is very much in tune with the Afrocentric perspective.

Daniel and Smitherman argue that *religion* and its symbols hold a central place in the Afrocentric perspective (30). And Asante notes that *proverbs*, or repetition of the ancient wisdom of a people embodied in sayings, are important in black culture. He also refers to two scholars, Vernon Dixon and Badi Foster, who have suggested seven elements of Afrocentricity. Asante lists them as

> 1) the value of humanism, 2) the value of communalism, 3) the attribute of oppression/paranoia, 4) the value of empathetic understanding, 5) the value of rhythm, and 6) the principle of limited reward. There is, in addition, a seventh element: the principle of styling. (37)

Asante also offers such principles of Afrocentricity as a focus on "1) human relations, 2) humans' relationship to the supernatural, and 3) humans' relationships to their own being" (168).

As we noted above, Afrocentricity is only one example of culture-centered criticism. We have focused on it here because it is one of the more self-aware and best-developed forms of culture-centered criticism. But scholars are also exploring what it means to have a Hispanic, a Chinese, or a Japanese way of understanding culture that is grounded in those cultures themselves. Culture-centered criticism is not negative; it is not a way to negate another's culture. Rather, it is a very positive attempt to show how all cultures contain within themselves the tools for their own analysis.

Whiteness as a Kind of Culture: Analysis and Examples

An important recent trend in critical studies is what has collectively been called "whiteness studies." This approach, exemplified by Nakayama and Martin (*Whiteness*), argues that European cultures are often not understood as having their own special and peculiar ways of understanding the world, just as do Afrocentric cultures. When we forget that "whiteness" is a particular way of thinking about life, culture, and history, we tend to make that way of thinking the default. That means that we regard Afrocentric, Asian-centered, or Latino-centered (and so forth) perspectives as if they were strange and different because they are not Eurocentric. Whiteness studies seeks to bring what it means to be white, and to have a culture informed by Eurocentric values and perspectives, more into conscious awareness. Whiteness studies is an important dimension of culture-centered criticism because it identifies values that may be taken for granted in societies where whites have dominated for a long time. Not everyone in all cultures may share those values or grant as much importance to them. For instance, I once heard an anecdote of a white Peace Corps volunteer from a Eurocentric background who was observing members of an African village carrying water from a lake in a bucket brigade up to the village. The Peace Corps volunteer told the villagers that a mechanical pump and hose would be a much more efficient way to do this. Yes, he was told, but then they could not visit with each other as they did in passing buckets. Here you see a Eurocentric value of efficiency and mechanization come into conflict with an Afrocentric value, already discussed, of unity and harmony. An important concern in this approach is to unmask some of the techniques by which the assumption that whiteness is the "center" of all things has been used as an instrument of oppression in the past. A full exploration of whiteness studies would take many pages, but let us look at one important tenet.

One of the most important themes that whiteness studies has exposed is the assumption of *privilege* that is encoded, usually out of awareness, in Eurocentric perspectives. Texts are examined for ways in which this privilege is asserted and maintained. For instance, in the whole *Indiana Jones* series of films (e.g., *Raiders of the Lost Ark*) and similar texts (e.g., the whole *Anaconda* series of films), there is an assumption that white explorers can go anywhere in the world and find friendly and agreeable "natives" who will be at their beck and call, willing even to lay down their lives for them. Privilege is a state of affairs in which one finds that whatever group or demographic one is in is taken as the "default" or "natural" way to be. Privilege is a condition of not being questioned. In most colleges and universities, for instance, a white instructor will enjoy the "privilege" of there being few if any questions raised about his or her status, qualifications, credentials, and so forth upon walking into class on the first day. A nonwhite instructor does not enjoy that privilege and runs the risk of being questioned about credentials. Similarly, a white person who is appropriately dressed need never fear being questioned or turned away when entering a high-end retail store, while a nonwhite person who is appropriately dressed may well be asked his or her business or at the very least followed. A lifetime of small advantages like this add up to white privilege. Those who study whiteness will be interested in examining texts of popular culture that perpetuate white privilege. How do store employees learn to follow Latino or African-American shoppers around in fear that they may steal something while letting white shoppers wander freely with privilege? What films, videos, and television shows perpetuate that privilege?

Although we may have trouble linking *The Wizard of Oz* to an Afrocentric cultural criticism, surely this one theme of whiteness studies can be shown to expose some of the rhetorical effect of that movie. Is Dorothy not a parallel to the white explorer landing in uncharted territory and instantly winning the assistance of the strange and different beings she finds there? Although the skin colors of the Munchkins are the same as hers, they are obviously physically different, as are most of the other beings she encounters. So many of her enemies are considerably darker in color than she is: the cranky apple trees, the winged monkeys. In the end, it is the whitest (literally) character in the movie, Glinda, who tells her how to get back to white-bread Kansas. A culture-centered critique based on whiteness studies would argue that the film reinforces in a white audience a sense of privilege, of being able to command the allegiance of physically different beings, even in their own homes and spaces, as a matter of right.

MARXIST CRITICISM

At the start of this section, we are in trouble with terms and their connotations, because there is not widespread agreement about what to call the Marxist perspective. On the one hand, some people think of this school of thought solely in terms of ideological or class- and power-based rhetoric. On the other hand, Marxism has far more negative connotations for many people (bringing to mind images of desperate people in North Korea standing in line for hours to receive bread, for example).

We align ourselves with the first group, viewing Marxism as an approach that is concerned with ideology, with class, and with the distribution of power in society. Many of the methods and assumptions with which we think about those issues were first proposed by the German philosopher Karl Marx in the nineteenth century. That is why we label this approach *Marxist*. The term is a handy "umbrella" word, covering all of those concerns and more.

The association of the term *Marxist* with repressive communist governments is understandable but not that relevant to our concerns in this book. The political system in the former Soviet Union and Eastern Bloc nations, North Korea, Vietnam, Cuba, and so forth bears little resemblance to the system of government that Marx actually proposed. Similarly, there is very little connection between those specific governments or economies and Marxist theory as a way to think about the rhetoric of popular culture. Marxism, in the sense in which we will use the term, is a method, or a set of assumptions. So when we refer to Marxist critics, we are referring to people who draw on Marx's theories (regarding class, power, and ideology) in analyzing the rhetoric of popular culture.

Actually, you have already been exposed to many of the methods and principles of Marxist criticism. This approach is one of the most common, and the most mixable, of the seven that we will examine. Therefore, it is the source of many of the ideas and terms to which you have already been introduced. Some of those ideas will be reintroduced here in the context of a discussion of Marxism as a particular approach in rhetorical criticism.

Materialism, Bases, and Superstructure

The philosophy underlying Marxist approaches to criticism is called *materialism*. This philosophy holds that ideas, rules, laws, customs, social arrangements—in short, everything belonging to the world of ideas or concepts—grows from material conditions and practices. That world of ideas is a vitally important one; it includes our ideas of who should govern whom, of who is more or less valuable, of laws and morals, of aesthetics and taste in art and entertainment, and so forth. But materialism holds that those ideas are what they are because of real, concrete, observable actions, practices, and objects. Materialism stands in sharp contrast to *idealism*, a way of thinking that argues that the world is the way it is because of abstract ideas and concepts. Marxist materialism argues just the reverse.

As an example, take the idea of free choice, which many of us value and believe that we exercise. An idealist would argue that free choice is a powerful idea that exerts influence in the real world, and that because it is such a compelling idea, people come to arrange their affairs, their governments, and their everyday practices so as to make the idea of free choice a concrete reality. Marxists, on the other hand, would argue that the present economic and political arrangement of capitalism requires that individuals make purchasing decisions on the basis of their own desires without thinking about the larger good of the community. In other words, our economic system depends on people going out to buy iPods because they want them as individuals, not because they think that doing so is good for others. Because the economic base of our society functions on that model of making "free," individual decisions, Marxists would say that the whole idea of free choice grows out of the economic base derived from those economic conditions. Were we living under a different economic system, so the thinking goes, the idea of free choice might never occur to us, or at least not as such a powerful and central idea in our understanding of our social and economic lives.

Different versions of Marxism have developed different versions of materialism. An early, very basic form of Marxism (now not as commonly held by critics) argued that a *base* of economic conditions (who owns what, working conditions, trading practices, and so forth) simply produced a *superstructure* of everything else: culture (including television, films, and books), ideological institutions (including churches and schools), politics, and so forth. The superstructure of ideas and culture was said to be *determined* by the economic base.

Most Marxists, however, now recognize that churches, rock concerts, and schools (and all that happens there) are just as material as the economic system is. So, for example, the Marxist theorist Louis Althusser has argued that other systems within a society (such as the political and ideological systems), as well as the economic system, operate relatively autonomously; that is, they are all material and they all generate ideas and concepts (*Lenin and Philosophy*). Althusser argued that social relations create ideology as much as economic relations. He argued that a powerful institution, which he called an Ideological State Apparatus (such as family, schools, religion, media, and so forth), can be a source of instilling ideology in the public with a degree of autonomy from economic practices. In trying to explain why people think what they do, why certain ideas become current (including ideas of who should rule, who is valuable, and so forth), Marxists now would more commonly say that those ideas are *overdetermined*, or caused by several material forces acting simultaneously (rather than just the economic forces).

Today, Marxists such as John Fiske expand the idea of what is material to include all the objects, conditions, and practices of day-to-day experience, arguing that ideas, concepts, customs, and the like grow from the material experiences of everyday life (*Reading the Popular*; *Understanding Popular Culture*). More explicitly (and more radically), some Marxists would argue that ideas themselves are embedded in, and take form in, everyday experiences. This view of ideas is essentially the position taken in this book. That is why we have been looking so closely at the "little" experiences of reading magazine advertisements, for instance—because ideas of who has power and who does not have power stem from, take shape in, and are worked out in just such "little," everyday experiences. It is these two concerns—*materialism*, and the way material affects *power*—that together form the core of Marxist analysis.

Our chief example of popular culture in this chapter can help us see the kind of general approach that Marxism takes. The film version of *The Wizard of Oz* with which many people are familiar first appeared on the screen in 1939, toward the end of the Great Depression, when economic conditions (especially in "dust bowl" states such as Kansas) were still grave. The story originally began in a series of books by L. Frank Baum written even earlier, at the start of the twentieth century, and the themes of hardscrabble farm living in Kansas likely resonated with audiences for the first forty years of the books' existence. The year 1939 also saw the beginning of World War II, with Germany's invasion of Poland and France, and the beginning of hostilities between Germany and Great Britain. *The Wizard of Oz* is an extraordinarily rich text, bearing many meanings within the guise of a pleasant children's story. Let's examine just one theme in this movie, considering how critical perspectives that are specifically Marxist might approach that theme: the idea of *home*.

"Home" is the last word uttered in the film ("There's no place like . . ."), and it is the place to which Dorothy is going at the very start of the film (fleeing the evil Miss Gulch). After her one ill-fated attempt to run away from home and her untimely return during the tornado, poor Dorothy spends the entire movie trying to get back home: trying to get into the storm cellar as the tornado approaches, and then trying to get from Oz back to Kansas. Home is a central term, or a central value, in the film.

Marxists might take at least two related approaches to understanding *home* in this movie. First, they would try to understand the idea of home and how it is expressed in *The Wizard of Oz* as a symptom or expression of the economic conditions of 1939. They might note the peculiar intensity with which Dorothy wants to return to her hardscrabble farm; she is not lured for long by the attractions of Professor Marvel's alleged globe-trotting or by the Technicolor beauty of Oz.

Dorothy's desire to return to black-and-white Kansas would be understood by these critics as tied to the economic difficulties of 1939. The economic system needed workers to be happy with home, wherever that was. Home was a metaphor for the established system; it was the job you had, the income you already made. It was important for the public to maintain faith in the economic system and to keep working within it even though it had failed them. The growth of labor unions also threatened to disrupt traditional economic arrangements as working people acquired the means to demand changes in working conditions and distribution of income. Dorothy finds out that a desire for change, even from desperate conditions, results in disaster. The idea of home as the place to be, as the primary object of all desires, is an idea growing out of the established economic system's need in 1939 to keep workers loyal and complacent despite an itch to "roam."

Second, Marxists might see *The Wizard of Oz* as an argument for isolationism or against foreign entanglements (such as a war in Europe); this was the official United States policy and practice in 1939, even as Hitler was gaining power. These critics would note that troubles begin when Dorothy's dog is allowed to run wild in Miss Gulch's yard and grow worse when Dorothy herself goes to foreign parts (Oz). Dorothy learns at the end of the movie to stay "in [her] own backyard." The theme of home as the confines of North America would thus be read by Marxists as emerging from the prevailing isolationist tendencies in the United States at that time.

The idea of home is part of the meaning of *The Wizard of Oz* and part of how its rhetoric works. Marxists point out that any economic or political system not only *produces* goods, products, practices, and ideas but also *reproduces* the conditions under which it produces those things. The tactics by which such an economic or political system induces people to allow it to continue as it is are clearly rhetorical. Thus, part of the rhetoric of *The Wizard of Oz* is the way in which it reproduces its conditions of production—that is, the economic system of capitalism and the political system of isolationism. It encourages workers to stay on the job, dismal though it may be, and it encourages Americans to stay at home and "mind their own business" politically.

The film's meanings are rhetorical because they work to influence the ways that workers regard their jobs and the ways the general public regards overseas conflicts. Marxists today would argue that it is in this movie and in countless other experiences of popular culture (on the job site, in schools) that both economic and political systems are made. In other words, foreign entanglement *is* the trouble that Dorothy gets into, which is accepted as a truth by the audience of this film and added to other, similar meanings encountered in other everyday experiences.

Economic Metaphors, Commodities, and Signs

Today, Marxists look for material causes that go beyond the narrowly economic. But because the history of the Marxist approach began with an attempt to link ideas, culture, power arrangements, and so forth to economic conditions, Marxist critics often retain *economic metaphors* for how culture works. By an economic metaphor, I mean that the way the economy works is taken to be formally similar to how the rest of culture works. Understanding how we buy and sell, for instance, can be used as a metaphor for, or a way to understand, how we relate to each other even in noncommercial circumstances. For instance, Marxists often regard meanings as if they were commodities and discuss the ways in which they are exchanged, traded, bought, or sold. This metaphorical approach can be a fruitful way to think about how artifacts of popular culture are used, since most of those artifacts are in fact bought and sold and possess some dollar value. Marxists supplement the idea of the cash value of artifacts with a notion of their value in terms of *signification*, or meaning.

Take, for instance, simple stud earrings. Suppose you make and sell earrings as a hobby, buying the materials for five dollars and selling the earrings at ten dollars a pair. You are enriched by five dollars per pair. Your customers have ten dollars less, but presumably they feel that the commodity, the earrings, is equal in value to that amount.

But consider the ways in which an earring can also pick up value as a sign, value that can then "enrich" its users socially that can even, in a social sense, be "traded." What does it mean, for instance, for a man to wear such an earring? The meanings are not as charged as they once were (many years ago, for example, the choice of which ear to wear the ring in was supposed to be a sign of whether or not a man was gay—a system that collapsed due to widespread confusion and instability in that particular meaning). But even now, an earring in a man's ear picks up some added symbolic value. It enriches the man who wears it with different meanings: he suddenly has "daring" or "slightly different" or "stylish" added to his other meanings.

Think also about a stud earring worn in the nose. What meanings would that "add" to the "symbolic wealth" of the wearer? We can also think in terms of the exchange value of those signs (just as we might think of the exchange value of money, of labor, or of commodities). To consider exchange value, think about what it would say about you if you were to date, or become friends with, someone wearing a nose ring; what meanings would you have "bought" through such an association? Of course, besides having exchange value, all these meanings should also be thought of as rhetorical; you can clearly influence someone by using a sign in ways that are charged with certain meanings, such as wearing a ring in the nose. We all know that it takes "currency" or money to buy this jewelry. But think of it this way: earrings or nose studs give wearers a kind of "cultural currency," a set of meanings that will "buy" them attributions of coolness, stylishness, danger, and so forth from people in specific social contexts. This is true of most signs. You spend monetary currency to buy a business suit, which then gives you "professionalism" currency to spend by "purchasing" respect in a job interview.

What counts as cultural enrichment, "currency," or exchange value is highly dependent on specific cultural contexts, just as what counts as monetary currency depends on which country you are in. Some prominent hip-hop artists, such as Young Thug, Lil Wayne, and Meek Mill, try very, very hard in their music and accompanying videos to claim the status of criminals just a step ahead of the law, bad gangstas with dark pasts of drug dealing and violence. Of course, if these gentlemen really were *that* bad, they would likely be dead or in jail rather than piling up royalties and enjoying lives of ease. But consider the enrichment that this "gangsta" capital brings these artists; in which "countries" can they "spend" that "currency"? What can these artists "buy" with that image? That image seems to be very popular with young people, especially young males who may try to enrich themselves by purchasing and playing this music. But that currency only works in some contexts, just as specific kinds of money only work in specific countries (e.g., euros work in Holland but not in the United States). Would purchasing a download of the latest Dirty South album get your grandmother very far socially at her bridge club, for instance?

©iStockphoto.com/caracterdesign

And, as a final example, the film *The Wizard of Oz* also contains numerous signs that have picked up meanings that give them a kind of value. Marxists might study the film as a source of such signs, and they might study the ways in which people appropriate those signs so as to spend them and exchange them. The term *Munchkin* has been extracted from the film to serve as a derogatory term, for example. I like to tell people that I can infallibly discover when a certain coworker will come to the office in a bad mood by looking out the window to see if "Surrender Dorothy" is written in the sky. In certain bohemian neighborhoods of cities like New York and San Francisco, you can find T-shirts saying, "Toto, I Don't Think We're in Kansas Anymore." And if you are going to the zoo with a child and the child asks whether you will be seeing lions, you might find yourself adding "and tigers and bears" (to which the child might respond, "Oh my!"). The list goes on and on; *The Wizard of Oz* is a bank of signs to "spend"—to use as wit, as insult, as fun. The ways in which these meanings can be "spent," or used strategically, are an important part of their rhetoric. Such uses are part of the way in which these meanings influence others.

Many Marxist critics look beyond the narrowly economic to identify the ways in which actual artifacts, objects, events, and practices influence power arrangements. Power is, then, perhaps the strongest interest of Marxists. Marxist critics study the ways in which large groups of people are empowered or disempowered. They assume that every society has power structures that privilege some groups while placing others in a relatively disadvantaged position. Such differences in power need not be intentionally planned by any group, nor do they need to be startlingly obvious. But such differences *will* be consistent throughout most of the experiences within a culture. So in the United States today, for instance, second- and third-generation citizens are relatively empowered and recent immigrants are relatively disempowered, men are more empowered than women, and so on. These differences in empowerment are found consistently throughout the culture in everyday, ongoing experiences—because they are created there. In identifying sources of power and its refusal, Marxist critics are highly interventionist. To some extent, by revealing power differences, they give voice to the disempowered and marginalized when such people cannot speak for themselves.

Preferred and Oppositional Readings

More and more Marxist theorists are coming to see the practice of reading texts as a sort of material experience with ideological consequences. One way in which already empowered or established groups and interests maintain their power is through the ways in which the texts within a given culture are read. By "reading," Marxist theorists mean the discovery and attribution of meaning in a text or artifact. Every text, every artifact, according to Marxists, has a *preferred reading*. This is a reading that is the easiest, most obvious one— the one that seems to be *common sense* within a given culture. When the evening news reports that a police officer was wounded in a shootout with an armed robbery suspect, for instance, the public is generally encouraged to assume that the police were in the right and the suspect in the wrong. The robbery suspect is likely to be presented as poor, as a drug addict, as some class of humanity that the public is encouraged to think of as habitually criminal. Notice that this reading perpetuates a system of power in which the already empowered enjoy more police protection than do poor or disreputable people within that system regardless of their level of criminality. Louis Althusser, whose ideas we explored earlier, stressed the power of preferred readings to create ideologies. Ideological State Apparatuses were, he argued, strongly able to impose preferred readings on the public.

In contrast to preferred readings are *oppositional readings*. These are meanings found in a text that are different from, or even opposed to, the easiest preferred meanings. Marxists identify two sorts of oppositional readings: inflections and subversions. An *inflection* is a bending of the preferred meaning to suit one's own needs and situations rather than an outright rejection of those meanings. One possible inflected reading of the preceding example (the officer wounded in a fight with an armed robbery suspect) might come from a National Rifle Association firearms enthusiast who saw the story as evidence of a need for all citizens to be armed. Such a person might "read" this story as showing that armed citizens could have deterred the suspect in the first place or could have aided the officer with additional firepower.

A *subversion* is a reversal, an active undermining or rejection, of the preferred meaning. One clear subversion of the robbery example would be to read the situation as one in which the officer had used too much force, thus obliging the suspect to defend himself. The whole structure of who is right and who is wrong in this story is thus reversed, and the meanings upon which established views of law and order rest are subverted. Note that no given text *must* be read with preferred meanings, nor *must* it be understood oppositionally. Inflections and subversions are simply different ways of attributing meanings to the signs that make up texts.

We have already discussed one of the preferred readings of *The Wizard of Oz* in terms of the concept of home. Let us think about some of the other ways in which the movie is "easiest" to read (we should stress that these are but a few of the possible ways to read the film). There is a tension in the movie between the value of fairness and open dealing on the one hand, and on the other, a respect for law and order. The preferred reading seems to be that law and order should be obeyed, even if such obedience is difficult or repugnant, because fairness and honesty will eventually triumph. The wicked Miss Gulch arrives at the farm with all the force of law behind her ("I've been to the Sheriff. . . . I'll bring a lawsuit that'll take your whole farm!"). She has a legal instrument in hand, allowing her to take the dog, Toto. "We can't go against the law, Dorothy," says Auntie Em in resignation. Dorothy *does* try to do just that by running away with Toto to Professor Marvel's camp, and she pays for it with an injury to the head.

When Dorothy reaches Oz, it becomes clear that a structure of law works there as well. "Rubbish," Glinda the Good Witch tells the Wicked Witch, who threatens Dorothy with mischief; "your magic has no power here." Dorothy's companions follow the Wizard's instructions for obtaining the broomstick, even though they seem hopelessly unfair. But the Wizard, in turn, gets his comeuppance when he is exposed as a fraud. The virtue of each of the four companions who have been following the Wizard's "contract" to obtain the Witch's broomstick triumphs at last. Clearly, even a grudging respect for law and order supports the present system of power and resource distribution. Dorothy and her friends teach the audience to respect that system, even when it puts them at a disadvantage, promising that justice will triumph in the end if we "don't make waves."

One of the movie's easier readings sees it also as a celebration of the value of work. Dorothy is something of a nuisance on the farm at the start of the film because she is the only one with no clear job to do. Everyone else is running around frantically doing chores. "I know three shiftless farm hands that'll be out of a job," warns Auntie Em, to spur the help on to greater efforts. The whole context of the action in Oz is a quest—doing something or working hard so as to earn passage home. At the end, Glinda reveals to Dorothy that she could have gone home at any time, simply by tapping her ruby slippers together, but that she "had to learn it for [her]self." Dorothy and her three companions think nothing of the Wizard's setting them various tasks to do in order to earn "some brains, a heart, the nerve," and a trip back to Kansas. Although it is in his power to grant their wishes (or so they think), they accept the need to *earn* those gifts. For an audience eager to find work in the Great Depression, the preferred reading of the value of work would certainly have been easy to swallow. But the continuation of the established capitalist economy also depended on that desire to put up with a failed economy until its health should be restored; thus, an emphasis on the value of work encouraged people to continue seeking what the system could not, at that time, give them enough of.

The encouragement of preferred readings can be a prop to established power. The Italian Marxist theorist Antonio Gramsci argued that empowered groups and institutions based their power not so much on physical means of rule such as the police, nor on the direct imposition of ideology, but on what he called *cultural hegemony*. Hegemony is a situation in which powerful groups and institutions create in those they dominate the belief that such domination is natural, commonsensical, and the way things ought to be.

We would say that a group exercises hegemony in society when their preferred meanings, the readings of a text that would keep them in power, come to be the meanings that other, even disempowered, groups tend to turn to first. Gramsci argued that ideology therefore recruits the disempowered to participate in their own disempowerment by agreeing to the hegemonic domination of more empowered groups. When people read, or draw meaning out of, texts by drawing on a preferred reading, they participate in one of those everyday, material experiences that perpetuate the existing system of empowerment. The tendency of people to turn first to preferred readings is a product of hegemony. Gramsci's views are usually taken to be in contrast to those of Louis Althusser, whose work we reviewed earlier. Althusser places greater emphasis on the power of the Ideological State Apparatus to impose ideology on people. Gramsci places greater emphasis on the power of discourse to coax cooperation from the public but also the ability of people to resist or inflect cooperation.

Hegemony is a remarkable phenomenon; because of it, oppressed people not only accept but often participate in their own oppression. How is it that some women go about saying that men ought to be "in charge"? How is it that some gays feel contempt for themselves and see their lives as degraded and somehow wrong? Marxists critics are very concerned about examining the ways in which preferred readings induce oppressed people themselves to participate in such oppression.

Marxist theorists note that many of the subtlest means by which power maintains itself are disguised—that is, they do not display themselves as sources or means of power. These theorists would say that the tools of ideology and hegemony tend to be *occluded* (or hidden) as such. In other words, people are not aware of the ways in which they are empowered and disempowered. Clearly, most casual observers of *The Wizard of Oz* would not be aware of the deeper meanings that it is urging upon them or of the ways in which it supports the established system. Marxists therefore tend to be highly interventionist (as we defined that term in Chapter 3), in eager pursuit of the goal of showing people how empowerment works (see Chapter 3, pp. 111–112).

Marxists tend to see many flaws in the established system and to seek changes to it. Therefore, they also try to understand the ways in which texts offer resources for making meaning differently, for being understood in different ways. They do so by encouraging oppositional readings, either inflections or subversions. When texts contain resources for both preferred and oppositional, alternative readings (as nearly all texts do), these texts can be seen as *sites of struggle* (as discussed in Chapter 3). Thus, a Marxist reading of the day's economic news might point out that a preferred reading of stock market news is always encouraged, in which a rise in stock prices is good and a fall is bad. A Marxist reading of that news might encourage audiences to ask how news of a rise or fall in stocks affects unemployment, or worker satisfaction, news that is not reported as frequently. A rise in stock prices might be oppositionally read as empowering only wealthy board members of corporations.

The economic metaphor (discussed on pages 162–164) is often used to clarify the ways in which people construct oppositional readings. Participating within an economic system in legitimate ways (through running a business or buying products, for example) is sometimes likened to choosing the preferred meaning of a text. In that case, oppositional readings become a sort of "black market" of signification, a way of "stealing" signs and using them for one's own purposes.

For instance, there are very clear preferred meanings for a baseball cap; list a few such meanings in your mind. Now, for a gang member to wear a cap in different positions is to "steal" that sign, the cap, metaphorically and make it mean something else—in fact, to make it mean something specifically designed to *offend* the established order and its preferred meanings. The same is true of pop stars' use of signs such as the cross that are, in the preferred reading, religious artifacts; a star wearing the cross as a fashion accessory makes it mean something else entirely. Marxists argue that to turn signs against their preferred usage is a refusal of hegemony, of established power structures.

Let us think of some of the ways in which *The Wizard of Oz* can be read oppositionally. The film has within it the resources to be read in ways that are, in fact, *critical* of the established system. Authority can certainly be read as suspect in the movie. Glinda the Good Witch appears to be the only unambiguously good authority figure in the film, yet even she is fooled by the Wizard, describing him to Dorothy as "very powerful, but very mysterious." Glinda can, however, be read as unfair and even threatening in the way she submits Dorothy and her friends to what might have been a fatal adventure (when she could have told Dorothy from the start how to get back to Kansas). Her power can be read as capricious and arbitrary, apparently exercised for its own sake.

Although there is certainly a preferred reading for male dominance, the movie also has the potential for feminist readings. It centers on a heroine, Dorothy. Two of the most powerful figures, Glinda and the Wicked Witch, are female. Auntie Em is clearly in control on the farm back home in Kansas. All of the adult male figures in Oz are weak, silly, or incompetent. The film is about the quest of a young woman who finds at the end that the resources she was looking for all along were within herself. So, against the dominant male ideology of 1939, it is possible to find resources for female empowerment in *The Wizard of Oz*.

Subject Positions

Another important part of the meanings of texts, also referred to in Chapter 3, is the *subject position*. Subject positions can now be linked with our discussion of preferred or oppositional readings; the two concepts are connected. Just as every text has a *preferred* reader that it implies or "calls to" (or, in Althusser's terms, interpellates), so there can often be *subversive, negotiated*, or *oppositional* subject positions. Marxist critics try to discover the kinds of roles or characters, or subject positions, that are most strongly suggested by texts, but they also try to identify the resources within texts and within people's experiences that would enable the construction of inflected or oppositional subject positions.

For example, there is clearly a preferred way to read NFL football games: you think they are important, you follow all the statistics, you understand when drama and conflict arise. But there is also a preferred subject position for NFL football games. We may call this position "the fan." To make NFL football work for you, you have to take on that role. Think about the different patterns of talking, moving, and dressing that you enter into when you become a fan. But not everyone can be a fan. Some people hate NFL football, and so if they were forced to watch a game, they would take a subversive subject position, one of skepticism and grumpiness. Their reading of the text would likewise be oppositional, seeing the game not as a heroic contest but as a lot of huffing and puffing and running around to no great purpose. Subject positions and readings go hand in hand.

From our discussion of subject positions and readings, it should already be clear to whom *The Wizard of Oz* "calls." It is easiest to watch the movie as an honest, hard worker, as one who admires fair dealing and openness, as one who values doggedness and determination, and as a good citizen who obeys even unjust authority. From that subject position, one does not find it strange that Dorothy risks her life to earn passage back to the dreary workaday world of Kansas. That subject position makes it easy to despise the false Wizard at the end. The "good citizen" subject called to by this film will go along reluctantly with the decision to hand Toto over to Miss Gulch, while hating Miss Gulch for throwing her weight around. The "good citizen" will not be surprised when Dorothy and her companions sorrowfully turn to leave the Wizard's palace after first being rudely turned away. Much of the rhetoric of the film lies in these subject positions; they were recognizable to much of the film's original audience and easy for these people to step into. The preferred readings of the text felt comfortable for many people, and the meanings found in those readings were easily accepted by them.

There is much more to Marxist rhetorical criticism than we have space to explore here. The Marxist critic is concerned with the ways in which popular culture influences people to accept established arrangements of power and economics, and it tries to discover ways in which people find resources for influencing themselves and others to change undesirable power and economic arrangements. Some of the methods that study ways in which power and goods are distributed are visual, psychoanalytic, and feminist criticism, all close cousins of Marxist analysis.

Standpoint Theory

Standpoint theory is a perspective widely shared across many feminist and Marxist perspectives (e.g., Collins; Hartsock; Kenney and Kinsella). To sum up a very complex and diverse school of thought, standpoint theory argues that the world may be known only in partial perspectives given to us by where we are situated in the world in terms of class, race, gender, geography, sexual identity, and so forth. All of these perspectives are partial, but some are more partial than others. The perspectives of the empowered are more limited, this theory argues, because *not seeing* inequality and injustice is an important way to perpetuate inequality and injustice. The perspectives of the disempowered are usually more inclusive, not only because being able to see the world from a broader perspective is a survival skill for those at risk but also because seeing that which power wants to hide from general view is useful for those who seek to share that power. In other words, the wealthy and empowered need not be able to consider the standpoints of others if they have enough resources, high enough walls, and responsive enough guards or police to afford to ignore other standpoints. The poor and the dispossessed need to know how the world looks to others just to be able to negotiate that world better.

Standpoint theory in general works to show how different texts are produced from different standpoints grounded in class, gender, and so forth, and it works to expose those different points of view to each other. Standpoint theory exposes the partisan sources of much everyday ideology by asking whose standpoint is privileged in a particular text or image. Standpoint theory inquires as to the point of view assumed in a text or image, and how the object would be different were it made from a point of view that was connected to a different ideology or way of life.

Standpoint theory could help inform the debate over the confirmation of Supreme Court justice Sonya Sotomayor in 2009. During the process of debating Justice Sotomayor's background, qualifications, and previous judicial opinions, one comment in particular that she had made was widely discussed. She had once said that a "wise Latina woman" would have more insights into injustices caused by racism, sexism, and class oppression than would someone from a different background. Many accused the justice of racism in that statement. But standpoint theory would confirm what she said, arguing that membership in any group that has been marginalized—whether that means being female, Latina, African-American, gay, lesbian, transgender, or the like—gives one a special understanding of how power and social processes work. Rhetorical critics can be enriched by standpoint theory to examine texts from the perspective of the margin and to find the insights given in texts produced by those who are marginalized.

FEMINIST CRITICISM

Varieties of Feminist Criticism

Feminist criticism is a wide-ranging group of approaches to rhetorical criticism. All feminist critical thinking begins from the assumption that there is gender inequality between men and women, particularly in today's industrialized economies, and thus power differentials. Feminism tries to explain how such inequality is created and perpetuated through popular texts. But it also examines texts to discover sources of female empowerment, to explore ways in which inequalities may be refused and overthrown. We discovered that Marxist critics believe there is an established system of power already in place in any society and that the system tries to perpetuate itself even as some people try to oppose it. Feminist critics make a similar assumption; they argue that there is a male-dominated system of power in place, and they call that system *patriarchy*. They want to intervene in patriarchy to level out the playing field.

Of course, many observations about the inequities between men and women can be made on the basis of fairly obvious evidence. In general, men are paid more, they hold more positions of governmental or corporate power, and so on. The critical approach that draws attention to these kinds of inequities between men and women is often called *liberal feminism*. *Liberal*, in this sense, means attempting to increase participation within a democratic system. Thus, the liberals of nineteenth-century politics tried to change the laws so that more people could vote within the established political system. And liberal feminists today are concerned with involving more women in the already empowered echelons of business and government. Some rhetorical critics do adopt a liberal feminist perspective in order to study the ways in which inequities are created and maintained in a patriarchal system.

©iStockphoto.com/ecliff6

But as we have discovered, critics do their most uniquely valuable work in revealing what is not obvious. And that which is "not obvious" is very often that which props up power differences, especially those founded on class differences. *Marxist feminism* critiques the ways in which the intersection of class and gender creates structures of empowerment and disempowerment. One of the major tools of patriarchy is economic disempowerment, which is studied by this branch of criticism. The scholar bell hooks has explored these issues in many of her works (e.g., *Where We Stand*).

One branch of feminism, *radical feminism*, is often allied with the kind of psychoanalytic critique we were discussing earlier. Radical feminist critics point out that it matters little whether a female executive gets the same salary as a male executive if deeper inequities are built into the very social being of men and women. These critics assume that the most important, and most fundamental, bases of inequities are to be found in the creation of the psyche, in the unconscious and its repression. Radical feminists thus use psychoanalytic theory (discussed in the next chapter) to point out how the present system itself *creates* men and women inequitably. But this inequitable "creation" occurs through the repression of desire in the unconscious; in other words, it happens in ways that are "beneath the surface" and thus require the efforts of critics to reveal them.

Radical feminists may also take a biological perspective and argue that inherent biological differences between males and females create unbridgeable differences that underlie social arrangements and ways of thinking. These differences may be found encoded in texts and in ways of communicating as well. This may be exemplified by a branch of feminist criticism that is not directly linked to psychoanalytic theory, a branch that might be called *foundationalist* or *essentialist*. Liberal feminism sometimes takes this form. This school of thought argues that there are a number of desirable characteristics that are essentially female, regardless of the culture in which one lives. Essentialist feminists maintain that these characteristics need to be reclaimed in a world dominated by those male characteristics that are undesirable. They argue that it is fundamentally female to be communal (rather than individual), noncompetitive, and nonviolent; these desirable characteristics are perceived as inborn, part of the nature of being female.

Of course, those arguments raise the issue of whether gender identity, or sex itself, is natural or socially constructed. Many feminists have found the work of French psychoanalyst Jacques Lacan helpful in approaching the question of which characteristics of the psyche are "natural" and which can be attributed to patriarchal culture. Although his work is far too complicated to explain fully here, we will note the distinction Lacan makes between the *Imaginary* and the *Symbolic*. The *Imaginary* is the pattern through which the psyche is organized for everyone, regardless of culture. It includes very basic structures of perception and experience, the "mirror stage" (referred to on page 200), in which children learn how images and representations work, is one component of the Imaginary.

Lacan refers to the ways in which particular repressions are carried out, or the particular issues that one culture worries about, as the *Symbolic*. The Symbolic varies from one culture to another. It is the set of parameters available within a given culture for making individual psyches. This concept is important, because feminists identify all of patriarchy as being within the realm of the Symbolic. By doing so, these theorists are saying that an ability to recognize images, for instance, is something that people in all times and places must acquire (and therefore part of the Imaginary). But the repression of desire does not *have* to occur in such a way as to privilege patriarchal signs; that particular form of repression, a patriarchal problematic, occurs in some but not all societies (through the Symbolic of the particular culture in which it occurs).

Another theorist who addresses the question of whether gender is biologically natural or constructed is Judith Butler (*Bodies That Matter*). Her view of gender as *performative* provides the basis for some interesting feminist critiques. Her work traces the ways in which all of us perform our gender roles. That perspective emphasizes a discursive or textual basis for gender. If gender is textual and discursive, then it is changeable and manipulable. Texts can be analyzed for the ways in which they show or support performances of gender, advising audiences on how to "do" different kinds of male or female roles. And performative roles may also blur, blend, and transgress traditional boundaries in ways that can bring about social change.

How Do Patriarchal Language and Images Perpetuate Inequality?

Feminist critics identify specific textual strategies that contribute to patriarchy. Vigilance to the presence of these components of texts is an important task for the feminist critique of popular culture. Through identifying these strategies, critics can explain how popular culture may perpetuate patriarchy and also ways to intervene against it.

Language and Images That Denigrate

Often, language and images will be used in texts within a patriarchy in ways that *denigrate* females, often without the creator of those texts intending that result. Feminist critics argue that patriarchy may be so deeply ingrained in a society that one need not consciously set out to disparage women for a text to be created that does so. Such denigration needs exposure. One very fertile ground for such analysis is today's hip-hop music and videos. Constant use of denigrating terms such as "bitches" and "hos" and depiction in music videos of women as only sexual objects, as existing only to serve the desires of men, can certainly be analyzed as tools of patriarchy. But less obvious and extreme uses of languages and images may be identified as well. Consider how the identification of films with romantic or relationship themes as "chick flicks" subtly restricts female interests to the sappy and sentimental. Consider how the ongoing use of the masculine pronoun *he* in application to people of both genders subtly argues that males are the "default" gender. Feminist critics are on the lookout for such denigrating use of language and images across texts of popular culture.

Silencing

Texts also *silence* women by denying them a voice, by creating no space for the expression of the female experience. Feminist critics might examine the ways in which some religious texts speak of God as only biologically male, excluding and silencing the female spirit. Feminist critics might note the heavy imbalance of leading characters and heroes in film and television, in which most of the strong characters are male. That which is heroic and female, or those female traits that may be considered strong and heroic, are thus effectively silenced through lack of expression in texts.

Lack

We will spend a little longer examining the ways in which feminist critics explore the patriarchal use of *lack* in texts of popular culture. This observation is connected to psychoanalytic criticism, which is discussed in the next chapter, in that it is grounded in experiences of early childhood. If one observes little boys and girls, it appears as if the boys, possessing external genitalia, have something that the little girls *lack*. Of course, females lack nothing in terms of reproductive organs, but this too-easy external physical difference *can be exploited by patriarchy*, feminist critics argue. The more internal and less easily observed female sexual organs do not count, so to speak, when it comes to serving as signs, simply because they are not immediately visible. Our culture, which privileges sight as a route to knowledge, tends not to value what it cannot see, hence this symbolic strike against women. Texts that prop up patriarchy, building on this false observation, perpetuate the myth that females lack something men have. The idea of a lack is then translated into other traits stereotypically attributed to women, traits that parallel a lack. Passivity is a lack of activity, docility is a lack of initiative and command, and so on. Of course, these critics are not arguing that women universally or naturally have such traits. Rather, they are pointing out that such traits are attributed to women, or more precisely to the female role, under a system of patriarchy.

One important way in which the myth of a lack is perpetuated is in how texts are constructed from a male perspective. We noted above, in discussing point of view, that films suture the audience into their storyline by putting the camera, and thus the viewer, into the space occupied by Jack and by Jane, the characters in a film. However, the audience is more often encouraged to occupy Jack's space. This is because, as feminist critics would note, popular culture much more often makes women into *objects* rather than *subjects*—and this too is the assertion of a kind of lack, for objects lack the power of action and initiation. That is to say, women become something to be looked at, talked about, worried over, desired, and so on. Men, on the other hand, are more typically made into the lookers, the talkers, the worriers, the ones who desire—in short, into subjects. (As another way of thinking about this distinction, consider the grammatical roles of the *subject* and the *object* in a sentence.)

In terms of the position of the camera, the storyline, and the audience's sympathies, movies more often present a situation that assumes, or suggests to the audience, that men are subjects and women are objects—that men act, desire, and decide, while women are acted upon, desired, and decided about. This is true not only of film, feminists argue;

feminist critics point to many different texts of popular culture to illustrate this subject–object distinction. Of course, women *are* occasionally portrayed as subjects in some texts, but in these cases they are often punished for occupying such a position.

The real rhetorical effect of this ingrained subject–object distinction, argue feminist theorists, is to encourage men to act mainly as subjects and women to act mainly as objects. The rhetoric of popular culture occurs daily, from moment to moment, as first children and then adults are taught how to be men (subjects) and women (objects). The work of feminist critics involves locating that subject–object distinction (and many others as well) in the experiences of the texts of popular culture.

Feminist critics trace the presence–lack structure of textual arguments even into visual images in popular culture. They might argue that under patriarchal systems, culture will be organized around signs of empowerment that are phallic: signs that represent the penis and the male sexual function. You may have heard the term *phallus*, or *phallic symbol*, before. We refer to the phallus as a symbol or sign, rather than to the actual penis itself, as a way of referring to a wide group of signs that *represent* the penis and the male sexual function (including, for example, rockets, skyscrapers, guns, oil wells, the Eiffel Tower, and so forth).

Signs that are phallic will be more favored or valued; signs that are linked to female sexuality will be less valued. Relationships between signs that express male or female sexuality will mirror the relationships that the culture favors between men and women. That is because those real, cultural relationships are already in place when the infant is born, so the repression of aspects of male and female sexuality follows those cultural patterns. The system of patriarchy (like the economic and political system as understood by Marxists) reproduces itself by creating in the individual unconscious the patterns of empowerment between the sexes that are found in actual practice.

How Can Texts Empower Women?

Feminist critics are not entirely gloomy. Their vigilance for texts that disempower is balanced by their attention to resources for female empowerment and equality that may also lie in texts of popular culture. In pursuit of textual strategies of empowerment, feminist critics look for *alternative rhetorical forms* and for *alternative ways of seeing* the world expressed in texts. Standpoint theory energizes this goal as well, for it argues that the worldviews of the relatively disempowered are not only different but also often more inclusive than the worldviews of the empowered. Feminist critics look for the ways in which broader and more inclusive points of view grounded in female experiences and bodies provide resources for empowerment.

Alternative Rhetorical Forms

Feminists observe that patriarchy is propped up not only by what is said or shown within texts but by the nature of texts themselves. In Chapter 1, we learned that the history of rhetorical theory has often ignored texts that occurred in forms not used by empowered elites. This continues to be true. Feminist rhetorical critics identify those texts that by their nature seem to be instruments of patriarchy, and they identify alternative forms of texts that have the promise for restoring more gender equality.

For example, so many texts of popular culture such as films and television shows are produced by enormous corporations that are owned and controlled by men, and we would thus not be surprised to find that these texts often denigrate or silence women or portray them as lacking something. Hierarchical power is central to patriarchy, and these corporations are extremely hierarchical, with a few powerful individuals (usually men) controlling the production and distribution of texts from the top down. Feminist critics might point out that women's experience throughout history has typically been more democratic, more local, less hierarchical, and so they may look for textual forms that are more congenial for those forms of experience. Feminist critics might argue that women's rhetoric is most powerfully found in, and expressed in, local and democratic forms of communication, such as small social clubs, reading or writing groups, performance in local and community theatre venues, the sharing of journals and poems, and so forth. Texts of popular culture are found not only at the theater or on television, these feminists might assert, but in other forms more consistent with the life patterns of many women. An excellent example of this approach is in Foss and Foss (*Women Speak*), who argue that a wide range of local, democratic textual forms, such as mother–child interactions, holiday greetings, dress, gardening, baking, and children's theatre, are important rhetorical forms for female empowerment.

Feminist critics identify empowering texts also by identifying texts that embody different ways of seeing. The French feminist Hélène Cixous, for instance, argues that the most essentially and typically female perspective, or standpoint, is one grounded in the experience of the body (Sellers). It is a patriarchal strategy, she argues, to foster a heightened sense of the abstract, of that which is utterly removed from the here and now. Women's thinking must return to being grounded in the body, she argues. A feminist critic using this particular perspective and searching for empowering texts might therefore identify texts that appeal to the physical experiences of women as texts that can articulate a woman's point of view.

Queer Theory

Queer theory is an interesting and relatively recent critical approach that was developed by critics and activists in a number of disciplines, including feminism and gay, lesbian, bisexual, and transgender studies. Seminal scholars include Eve Kosofsky Sedgwick (*Epistemology*), Judith Butler (*Bodies That Matter*; *Gender Trouble*), Sara Ahmed (*Queer Phenomenology*), and Judith Halberstam (*In a Queer Time*). Queer theory has both political and theoretical underpinnings. What is key to queer theory is exploration of the violation of tidy, established categories of social thinking.

The word *queer* has in the past been used as a derogatory term for those who were not heterosexual (and it continues to be used that way in some quarters). A time-tested strategy for groups that are oppressed and marginalized is to "turn" a sign of their oppression, often a derogatory term, to their own purposes. In this way, over the last few decades, African-Americans, for instance, have turned the derogatory term *nigger* into the more empowering and inclusive term *nigga*. The same has happened with *queer*. Within the last couple of decades, what used to be a derogatory and negative term has become embraced by people of gay, lesbian, bisexual, and transgender identity and used as a term of empowerment. One could even argue that it has gone mainstream, as one can attend academic conferences or publish in scholarly journals with *queer* in the titles, and queer theory has become a respected way to think about some important issues. In this way, queer theory has had political underpinnings of liberation and refusal of marginalization.

The term also has scholarly underpinnings. Feminism was an important source of these foundations. The work of feminists such as Judith Butler began to question what seemed like tidy, natural, and necessary categories of gender: male and female. Gender, Butler and others argued, is something that is performed rather than a given. For that reason, a wider range of gender identities may be socially and rhetorically created, going beyond simply male and female. What is key to this theoretical stance is a *questioning of categories*. If one can disturb the tidy division of male and female, one can then interrogate all sorts of other categories, asking how alternative systems of categorization are constructed socially and rhetorically.

Sexualities that are nonheteronormative (that is, that do not assume that heterosexuality is normal, natural, and the way things ought to be) are by their very nature breakers of categories. In a heteronormative world, men and women are supposed to be sexually interested in each other, men pursuing women and vice versa. Men pursuing men, women pursuing women, men and women crossing over into the other gender category as well as into other categories of sexual desire—that is a "queer" world because it destroys tidy categories that have been made to seem natural. Of course, any rhetoric of what is natural and normal is hegemonic and an instrument of power, as we have discussed before; to assume that the world has in it unambiguous men who sexually desire women and unambiguous women who sexually desire men empowers some groups but not others. If most people can be persuaded to accept this situation, then you have heteronormative hegemony.

Gay, lesbian, bisexual, and transgender sexualities not only disturb heteronormative categories of who "should" desire whom sexually. These sexualities also disrupt gender categories. In Western cultures, at any rate, these nonheteronormative sexualities are often publicly presented through manipulating categories of gender. Gay males may present a public style that may be hypermasculinized or another style that is feminized. There are "lipstick" lesbians who mine signs of femininity and "butch" lesbians who appropriate signs of masculinity. Gender identity and sexual identity are closely connected, and queerness in one set of categories is likely to entail queerness in another.

Queer theory has evolved to a point where it is interested not just in sexual or gender queerness, but in the queerness that comes from any disturbance of normative, accepted categories. In this sense, whatever calls into question our hegemonic categories of race, class, age, and so forth can fruitfully be understood as queer. One might think about beauty pageants for little girls as queer in this sense, since the behaviors one finds in beauty pageants are often more "normal" for much older women. The film *Little Miss Sunshine* and the television show *Here Comes Honey Boo Boo* both question child beauty pageants and point out their strangeness, which could then be understood as queer. To be clear, queer theory no longer concerns itself exclusively with gender or sexuality, although those continue to be important concerns.

A critic would use this expanded sense of queer theory to study the ways in which texts of popular culture either affirm widely accepted views of what normal categories are or challenge these categories. In this sense, Tiger Woods and President Obama may be studied as queer, although both are likely unambiguously male and heterosexual. But their ethnic and racial identity is queer—it defies easy categorization. Texts in popular culture about both men are therefore going to do the work of challenging tidy categories of race. Woods has called himself "Cablinasian" in reference to his category-busting identity of Caucasian, African-American, American Indian, and Thai heritage. President Obama jokingly referred to himself as a "mutt" (while his family was searching for a new dog to occupy the White House). His background is Caucasian-American and African, but not African-American. He was born in the exotic and distant state of Hawaii and spent much of his youth in Indonesia after his mother married an Indonesian man. Obama defies easy categorization. Rhetorical critics might track struggles over defending or breaking racial categories by studying texts about Woods or Obama.

Dr. Ben Carson, 2016 presidential candidate and President Trump's first secretary of housing and urban development, is a bit "queer" in this sense in that he defies expectations (those expectations being racist). He is a highly regarded physician and occupies a powerful seat in government; both of those break categorical expectations that people may have for African-Americans. A rhetorical criticism grounded in queer theory, then, is interested in the ways that texts question and disturb "normal" social categories.

Analysis and Examples

What would feminist criticism show us in *The Wizard of Oz*? A number of feminist readings could be made of the film; let's examine just a few examples of insights that this approach might bring us. Some interesting observations can be made about the movie by thinking about shapes: elongated or pointed phallic signs and rounded signs that remind us more of the relatively rounded contours of the female body (of the ova, the breasts, and so forth). Glinda the Good Witch, the ruling female of the film, comes and goes inside a giant round bubble, for instance. One instrument of the Wicked Witch's power is the crystal ball, in which we see mainly women (Auntie Em, the Witch herself). The false Wizard, exposed largely by the female Dorothy, is whisked away at the end of the movie in a round, hot air balloon that he cannot control ("I don't know how it works!").

In contrast to these and other female shapes are the film's phallic signs. A sign of great power is, of course, the tornado that takes Dorothy to Oz, a possible phallic sign. The city of Oz rises up in elongated form on the horizon as the travelers draw near to it; in it they will find the supposedly powerful male Wizard. The Wicked Witch, of course, is a somewhat problematic female. She has stepped outside the bounds of acceptable power for women; she is bony and angular and entirely outside conventional standards of female beauty. Her castle is also phallic, and Dorothy and her friends are finally trapped by the Witch's soldiers in a guard tower, rising erect above a wall of the castle. The ruby slippers themselves, although a blood red (menses?), are both elongated and the source of the power that Dorothy was seeking all along. They are hollow, and containers, as the female body may be interpreted in patriarchy. Think for a moment about the effects or influences created in the audience by the interplay of these male and female symbols. What do they say about differences between men and women, and about the status of women?

Let us consider another set of signs in the film. As noted above, the tornado is rather clearly a phallic sign: long and sinuous, snaking its way across the plains of Kansas, doing violence. Dorothy is taken up into the tornado and is eventually expelled from it. She lands in a place populated by child-sized Munchkins. Is it possible to find a link between Dorothy's dramatic expulsion (ejaculation?) from a phallic sign and the sudden presence of children? Dorothy is the focal point of a struggle between a good woman (Glinda) and a bad woman (the Wicked Witch) for the rest of the film; but in her experiences, she meets men almost exclusively. Those experiences constitute a quest, a yearning, to arrive at the place that she has deemed to be right for her. What can you make of this structure of the film as a quest story, given the signs of sexuality and procreation that began Dorothy's journey in Oz? What meanings do these signs offer within the context of a quest? Does it mean anything that Dorothy ends the film lying in a sickbed? For instance, one might read that final scene, in the context of other sexual imagery in the film, as a suggestion that Dorothy is not really sick but has experienced childbirth and is in bed for that reason—that the acquisition of sexual knowledge and maturity is the real payoff of her journey.

The Wizard of Oz is certainly a queer text. Oz is a queer place. The Munchkins are not the expected size for adults. The Lion, who ought to be valiant, is cowardly. The Tin Man is a queer conglomeration of parts. The winged monkeys change back into people once their enchantment is ended by the death of the Wicked Witch. The Wizard is not what he seems to be. This is a text that would benefit from a detailed study of the ways it violates expected categories. How might all these disruptions of established categories affect an audience's social and political views? I think a good case can be made that the film gently undermines an audience's faith in categorical divisions and in the surface appearances on which they are based. The Lion is not after all cowardly, nor the Tin Man without a heart, nor the Scarecrow without brains—quite the contrary. The Wizard is not a real wizard, and Dorothy was not helpless all along; she need only have tapped her heels three times. If the audience may be led to question appearances, they may be led to question established categories generally.

Summary and Review

In Chapter 4, we have learned about three schools of thought in the rhetorical criticism of popular culture: (1) culture-centered, (2) Marxist, and (3) feminist. Chapter 4 was about methods that emphasized INTERVENTION somewhat more than Understanding, while not at all shortchanging the latter. In the next chapter, we explore four more methods: (4) psychoanalytic, (5) visual, (6) dramatistic/narrative, and (7) media-centered. We should expect to continue to see both differences and overlap in the way these schools approach their subject.

5

VARIETIES OF RHETORICAL CRITICISM

UNDERSTANDING-Intervention

I n Chapter 4, we learned about three schools of thought in the rhetorical criticism of popular culture: (1) culture-centered, (2) Marxist, and (3) feminist. In this chapter, we explore four more: (4) psychoanalytic, (5) visual, (6) dramatistic/narrative, and (7) media-centered. We should expect to continue to see both differences and overlap in the way these schools approach their subject.

Let's return to the organizational plan for covering our seven schools of thought or families of methods. Chapter 4 was about three methods that emphasized INTERVENTION somewhat more than Understanding while not at all shortchanging the latter. In this chapter, we look at four methods that feature UNDERSTANDING more, although all of them also provide a basis for Intervention. In this chapter, the four schools of thought are further divided into two groupings. Psychoanalytic and visual criticism are two schools of thought that contain methods focused on self and society. These try to understand how individual selves are rhetorically, socially created, and then how those selves function in society. Psychoanalytic criticism focuses a little more on the creation of selves that then function in society, whereas visual criticism examines one major dimension of our shared social life together, and that is shared ways of *seeing*. Dramatistic/narrative and media-centered schools of thought contain methods focused on story. Not only are stories widely found in popular culture, but thinking about many texts *as if* they were stories or plays is often a useful critical method. How stories are conveyed to people as well as consumed by people is of interest to media-centered criticism, which considers the dimension of the *medium* in texts of popular culture. As noted in Chapter 4, all of these methods "leak" into one another; our divisions and categories are meant to help you understand the rhetoric of popular culture but are not completely exclusive.

Bettmann/Contributor/Bettman/Getty Images

METHODS FOCUSED ON SELF AND SOCIETY

Psychoanalytic Criticism

Psychoanalysis began as a method for analyzing and treating mental illness. It was founded by the Viennese psychiatrist Sigmund Freud in the late nineteenth and early twentieth centuries. Today, few psychiatrists use Freud's methods as their main approach to treating mental illness, but rhetorical and cultural critics have found Freud's approach very useful in explaining certain things about culture in general. Today, the term *psychoanalysis* is used more broadly, in reference to a theory about how the individual mind, personality, or psyche is constructed and then enters social contexts.

Of all the methods of critical studies, the psychoanalytic may be the most "suspicious," for it takes nothing at face value. Psychoanalytic criticism assumes that all the artifacts of popular culture—in fact, all signification—has something "behind" it, some other reality or significance beyond just itself. Those deeper meanings, the ones that psychoanalytic critics are especially interested in, have to do with the ways in which the mind is constructed. Let's examine a few of the basic principles of psychoanalytic theory.

Making Minds and Selves

A central question for psychoanalytic criticism is, how are the human mind and personality formed? The answers that practitioners of this method give define its distinctive characteristics. A theory of how the mind is formed can be adapted to a theory of how to appeal to those minds rhetorically. People who study film especially have found psychoanalytic criticism useful. As we will see later, much of what we study in psychoanalytic criticism can also be applied to the criticism of visual rhetoric. So, as noted, all of our schools of thought connect to other approaches. You will recall that the organizational structure for these seven schools of thought looked like this:

School of Thought, or Method	Major Focus of This Method
Culture-centered (Chapter 4)	Intervention and power
Marxist (Chapter 4)	Intervention and power
Feminist (Chapter 4)	Intervention and power
Psychoanalytic (Chapter 5)	Understanding and the self in society
Visual (Chapter 5)	Understanding and the self in society
Dramatistic/narrative (Chapter 5)	Understanding and story
Media-centered (Chapter 5)	Understanding and story

Psychoanalytic critics assume that the mind is never formed in isolation. We become human personalities in relationship to other people. The newborn infant is not yet aware of itself as a separate person. We become fully formed personalities, we form minds, as we come to realize that we are distinct individuals. The child must come to understand that she is not her parent; she must place herself in relationship to her parent to become a person. This process continues throughout life as we continue to construct and maintain our sense of self by situating ourselves in relationship to others.

Another way to put this is to say that who we are is always defined in relationship to something external to us, specifically something that is social or that has social implications. We become people in relation to another. This self-creation process is carried out using verbal and nonverbal *signs* or *representations*.

A number of psychoanalytic critics, following the work of the French analyst Jacques Lacan, argue for the importance of *visual images* or nonverbal signs. Let's remember this link to the visual in our discussion a little later of visual rhetoric. Lacanian theory argues that an important stage in child development is the child's learning about images or representations, and that one way in which this happens is by the child's discovering its own reflection in a mirror. The child is delighted to find that when it moves, the image or representation of itself moves. In other words, the child learns about connections between images and reality. Images become something the child can count on as tools of knowledge and discovery. At the same time, the child learns about himself, about his separate existence as a distinct human, from these external visual images. A crucial link is formed: for the rest of her life, the child will turn to those external signs to derive an understanding of self.

The process of self-creation is also carried out through the process of learning *language*. Here, too, the child is taught that she and the things that are important to her can be represented through external signs. When she learns the words that represent herself and her parents, her pets, her favorite toys, and so forth, she also learns what those things are, and she learns who she is. In the world of language, which is external to the child, the child comes to know herself and the things of her world.

To arrive at a sense of the self and of other things through language and images creates frustration, for signs and images also separate us from the world—and from ourselves. The child learns that he and "mother" are separate, indeed that they exist at all, by mastering words and images for self and mother—but mastering words and images for mother will never match the original closeness of the child's first, physical connection with mother. Forever after, the child will live in a world in which signs—words—seem much more accessible, much closer, than the things to which the words refer.

Some signs and contexts seem to promise a closer reconnection with that original state of unity than do other signs. The experience of watching a film, some critics argue, comes close to duplicating that early mirror or language-learning stage. The film viewer is "cradled" in a soft and comfortable chair, much like a parent's arms. The darkness of the theater is also comforting and soothing. And finally, most films that we see today are examples of what has been called *realist cinema*; that is, they are designed to put the viewer into the actual action of the movie. You may or may not know that a movie is filmed in small pieces at a time. For instance, if Jack and Jane are talking to each other, all the shots of Jane's speaking might be filmed at once, with the camera standing where Jack would have been standing, and then all the shots of Jack's speaking might be filmed with the camera in Jane's position; the film is then edited to give the illusion of Jack and Jane speaking back and forth. That technique has the effect, psychoanalytic theorists argue, of *suturing*, or binding, the audience into the actual film itself; Jack and Jane appear to be talking to you, the viewer, as well. Furthermore, psychoanalytic theorists argue, that experience of finding yourself "sewn up" within these images on the screen parallels the child's delightful discovery of appearing in the mirror's image; this, they argue, is why film is so rhetorically appealing and influential. We will easily see the connection between psychoanalytic criticism and the focus on point of view when we get to it in visual rhetoric studies.

Just as a side note, one area of interest within the study of popular culture is the ways in which the *apparatus*, or specific physical means of production, of a particular medium works to create influences and effects, and psychoanalytic theory is often called upon to explain those influences (see, e.g., Cha). For example, television shows must be taped in a hurry to meet the industry's voracious need for programs, and so in the cheapest productions its cameras are often (not always) placed out front, where a stage audience would be, so that the actors can simply play their parts once through (a lot of daytime television or "soap operas" are shot that way; think *Days of Our Lives* or *General Hospital*). Psychoanalytic theorists argue that this kind of television is therefore less influential and less appealing than are movies or TV shows recorded from an audience's point of view, because the audience is merely a spectator rather than sutured into the image itself. Note that a focus on apparatus connects to media-centered criticism, which we will study later in this chapter.

In sum, the sense of self that most of us have was originally created through the painful process of learning that we are separate from other things and people in the world, a process carried out by learning the meanings of signs. As we continue throughout our lives, our sense of self is constantly being formed and maintained in external signs and representations. Those signs are powerfully motivating, and to understand why is to get at the heart of psychoanalytic rhetorical theory. The power of signs comes from the motivation of *desire* in at least two ways.

Desire

Signs appeal to us, first, because they appeal to a *desire for wholeness*. Remember, language and nonverbal signs create awareness of ourselves and of the world, but they also separate us from the baby's original sense of happy unity with the world. *The most powerful signs are those that offer people a chance to return to that original state of being a whole, complete person*, a state before we knew ourselves to be separate beings. This principle can be applied very successfully to the advertising of many products. How is it that, upon seeing an ad for two-toned saddle oxford shoes, you suddenly conceive an intense desire to buy those shoes (when two minutes earlier you had no such motivation)? Psychoanalytic critics would urge us to examine the text of the advertisement for ways in which it offers the customer identity, a way to be a whole person. "You can complete yourself as [pick an identity] if only you will buy [name a product]" is how this appeal works. Think of how that works in your own mind: "I can be more (cool/professional/attractive/macho/feminine) if I buy that. I can complete the person I want to become."

One can also see this kind of appeal in *The Wizard of Oz*. The audience is, of course, invited to identify with Dorothy, and Dorothy's entire experience in the film can be seen as a process of separation and yearning after wholeness. Early in the film, Miss Gulch threatens to separate Dorothy from her dog, Toto. Dorothy must separate herself from her family so as to keep her bond with the dog intact. At Professor Marvel's camp, she grows sorrowful over that separation and is determined to return to her family. But the tornado creates the grand separation of throwing her into Oz, and the rest of the film will see her struggles to return to the wholeness she experienced back in Kansas. Each member of the film's audience is, according to psychoanalytic theory, likewise yearning for some kind of wholeness, each in his or her own way. Dorothy's experience is so appealing to so many people because it seems, at a fundamental level, to parallel the experience we all have of separation and yearning to become whole again.

A second way in which signs appeal to us through desire is through the fact that *desires must be repressed*. Newborn babies experience only pure and uncontrolled *desire*. When they want something, they cry for it, reach for it, or crawl for it. They have no self-control, nor do they know about social inhibitions. When they are hungry, they want to eat then and there; when they wish to urinate or defecate, they do so at once, no matter where they are. If they are angry, they express that anger at once. Infants live for gratification of desire; Freud called this characteristic of infancy the *pleasure principle*.

Yet from the moment of birth, social inhibitions and controls also begin to curb the infant's actions and expressions. The child learns that there are times and places to be fed, that not everything may be grasped, that the elimination of waste must be strictly controlled, and so forth. In contrast to the pleasure principle, the child comes to learn the *reality principle*: that the world will disapprove of and even punish certain actions. And so the child comes to *repress* more and more of its desire for gratification so that its behavior is acceptable and it can live with others in a society. Such repression is widely regarded as a necessary step in human development. People, being social creatures, cannot go about seeking gratification in totally uncontrolled ways and still live with others in civilized groups. It is "common sense" that adults cannot go about eating, defecating, and urinating whenever and wherever they please.

The *psyche*—the mental equipment that everyone has, the mind in all its complexity—is a product of both desires and the ways in which desires are repressed. Who we are, how we think, what we come to value, and so forth are all created by what our parents and society at large tell us that we can and cannot do, think, or feel—but also by our powerful desires to do, think, and feel those things nevertheless.

The desire for gratification, although repressed in favor of reality, never goes away. Instead, in its repressed state it takes on a different form, the structure within the psyche that Freud called the *unconscious*. The unconscious is formed by the process of repression. The unconscious keeps trying to make its desire for gratifications felt; it keeps trying to break through to conscious awareness and action, all the while remaining continually repressed. Despite this repression, the unconscious exercises enormous influence on how we think and feel, how we act, and how we relate to other people.

Let us consider one example of psychoanalytic explanations for behavior. Infants, of course, want to defecate—and to be honest, the experience of defecation remains mildly pleasurable for adults as well. But that desire must also be repressed at certain times. The question is, how is it to be repressed? Some psychologists argue that young children should be praised for the production of feces in appropriate times and places (and anyone who has raised a child knows how proud they are to be able to learn how to use the toilet). But more important, some psychoanalytic theorists argue that this particular method of repressing desire—the use of high praise—results in adults who are highly productive in many ways, people who freely and confidently produce whatever counts as production in their respective fields (sales records, art works, engine blocks, and so forth). In other words, the key to happiness and productivity lies in the way in which the desire to defecate was repressed; productivity at work is in part the result, within the psyche, of proper toilet training.

One major theme of psychoanalytic criticism is the ways in which particular, whole cultures repress desire. Desire repressed makes up the unconscious, and much can be learned about why people do what they do by studying the patterns of repression that are peculiar to their particular cultures. Some cultures may disapprove more of some desires than of others, and the ways in which infants are taught to repress certain desires will also affect the development of the unconscious.

Psychoanalytic theory strives to explain certain characteristics that seem to be common to most members of a culture. Taking the idea of American culture very broadly, for example, it has often been observed that ours is a highly pragmatic and highly competitive culture. Getting ahead and doing whatever it takes to maximize the bottom line is a theme that has always been strong among most Americans. Practical results often count more than do self-improvement, ethics, or other principles. Psychoanalytic theory would try to locate the sources of this distinctively American trait in the ways in which the unconscious is built out of repressed desires.

Such an explanation is also a rhetorical theory, however, for it explains what is desirable, or what is sought after, within a particular culture. And of course, what is desirable and sought after is what will be influential, or rhetorical. A psychoanalytic theory of American competitiveness, for instance, could explain why video games that feature aggressive, assertive behavior are so popular, games such as the *Grand Theft Auto* series.

If you are wondering what toilet training has to do with the rhetoric of popular culture, the point is this: texts of popular culture satisfy our desires if they are successful. They take us through the routines and processes that we have found pleasurable before. A psychoanalytic critic will want to know what a culture, what an individual, desires and why—and will then identify promises to express that repressed desire in texts.

Let's suppose you are viewing one of the films in the long series that began with *Fast and Furious*. The theme is, of course, racing fast cars, usually on city streets, usually in defiance of authority both domestic and legal—what are some other consistent themes in that series of films (*Fate of the Furious*, etc.)? A psychoanalytic critic would study the ways in which the films appeal to the repressed desires of the audience: to rebel against authority, to extend the self into a mechanism of great power, to conquer foes, and so forth. A psychoanalytic critic might also be interested in looking at the expression of repressed desires from the other direction, so to speak. Begin with the repressed desire of violence: people generally cannot have tantrums and throw things and lash out whenever they like. All right, but then what are some texts in popular culture that give expression to that repressed desire? The expression of those desires is a major part of the rhetorical appeal of such texts.

One possible explanation for *The Wizard of Oz* is the fine balance it strikes between the expression of desires the audience is likely to have and the repressions they are likely to have experienced. The dog Toto wants to run free, even if it's through the Gulch garden, and Dorothy wants to let him do that. Repression of those desires in the form of Miss Gulch, Auntie Em, and Uncle Henry brings the hard facts of life and the law down upon Dorothy. Desire reasserts itself as she flees, but repression in the form of the authority figure of Professor Marvel sends her back home. In Oz, an ongoing drumbeat of desire to return home is constantly frustrated by the repressions offered by adversaries and the hazards of the road. The film can thus be read as presenting in archetypal form the balancing of desire and repression. The audience can read their own repressed desires into the film.

Psychoanalytic criticism is such a large school of thought that here we have merely scratched the surface. If the general approach intrigues you, I encourage you to read further and learn other facets of this method. We now turn to the second, and related, method having to do with the self and society: visual rhetorical criticism.

VISUAL RHETORICAL CRITICISM

Of course, we are living in an increasingly visual culture and, as we learned in Chapter 2, more and more of the management of important public decisions is carried out using images. The study of visual rhetoric has therefore become increasingly popular recently, and critical methods for the study of images and primarily visual texts have been devised (Barnhurst et al.; Finnegan; Hariman and Lucaites). The visual is a major way in which people develop a sense of self, of who they are. But it is also a major point of connection to society, as visual rhetoric appeals to shared visual experiences.

Images as Focal Points of Meaning Attribution

Let's suppose I say to you, "I have a poodle dog at home." Certainly, even such a simple statement may be interpreted in several ways by different listeners based on their own experiences and cultural backgrounds. But language, especially declarative, argumentative, or expositional language, has a tendency to impose restrictions or parameters on how it is interpreted. Hearing my statement, you are unlikely to think I am using a metaphor, for instance, although I might be—the language simply doesn't appear to be asking you to think of it metaphorically. Other interpretations—that I might be referring to my lunch, for instance—are certainly possible, but the way the language is presented makes that interpretation less likely also. Although linguistic statements and arguments always leave room for interpretation and multiple meanings, they have means to guide those readings. Now the question is, do visual images similarly guide how people find meaning in them?

Compare what happens when you hear someone say, "I have a poodle dog at home" with what happens when you see a picture of a poodle. Some (e.g., Postman) argue that an image makes no assertion in the way that language does, that the picture simply "is" and for that reason cannot be part of the give-and-take of rhetoric. I believe that point of view is mistaken. *Images, like language, have a structure—they appear in context—and they must be interpreted so as to extract meaning from them.* Images, like verbal utterances, are focal points for the attribution of meaning. That is to say, people will rarely just leave an image alone, especially one found in popular culture. We read those images and attribute meanings to them.

Images can also be constructed, as is the case with any text, so as to encourage certain attributions of meaning and to discourage others. A picture of a starving baby in Africa is likely constructed and presented rhetorically (perhaps by a relief agency asking for contributions) in ways that strongly encourage some attributions of meaning and not others. Yet how images are structured may be different from the ways in which linguistic texts try to impose certain meanings on audiences. Images may be constructed and presented in the full knowledge that control over attribution of meaning may be less than is the case for the spoken or written word. And clearly, many images are accompanied by language that affects the attribution of meaning. In sum, images can certainly be part of the give-and-take of rhetoric, and they can be structured in ways that encourage some meanings but not others. But overall, *images are relatively more ambiguous than is language.* This ambiguity can be a resource for rhetoric in the hands of a skillful persuader.

One cause for the relative ambiguity of images lies in their circulation. Especially in an era of YouTube and other digital media, we know that once an image is "released" into the world of popular culture, it can be reproduced in a dizzying variety of texts and contexts, and often not in ways consistent with the meanings attributed to the image when it first appeared. You may be familiar with the idea of a *meme*. A meme is very often visual, whether a still image or perhaps a short video clip, that is circulated, reproduced over and over. In 2011, students "occupied" the campus of the University of California, Davis, in protest of its economic policies. A photo of a police officer in full riot gear sauntering by and pepper-spraying helpless students sitting on a curb during this occupation was widely circulated. The image of the officer appeared over and over, sometimes in humorous contexts, sometimes to criticize the unjust use of police force in other contexts. The image was a meme. Soon, the mere fact of its circulation gave it power: people recognized it, recognized its connection to police power, and so forth. But, on the other hand, many people in the country were opposed to that occupation and to similar protests. To them, the meme may not have had such sinister connotations. When images are torn from their original texts and contexts and circulated widely, their very ambiguity can give rise to differing attributions of meaning. Think for a moment about currently popular memes and how their circulation may depend on ambiguity.

Images are structured, especially those that are carefully crafted for rhetorical purposes. By structure, here you might understand everything that was said in Chapter 3 about *implied strategies*. The image of the poodle is or is not paired with other images, is or is not put into conflict with other images, is or is not a keystone sign or transformation of another sign. When the critic applies those three complex categories of implied strategies to images, she is examining the ways that the images are organized. That organization is rhetorical in that it helps to guide the attribution of meanings to the image. Is the picture of the poodle paired with a dog show setting or is the poodle out in a hunting field? "What goes with what" in the picture helps you to attribute meanings to it. If you have previously thought of poodles as having big, poofy haircuts and you see a poodle with a close trim all over, the absence of such a showy hairdo will shape your attribution of meaning. If the poodle is a keystone sign in a photograph of a luxurious apartment, then that way of organizing the image will shape your attribution of meaning to the image. Persuaders who use visual images in texts know all this, and they take great care to present the images in ways that facilitate preferred readings. What is key in visual images, if they are found alone in texts, is that they must be structured so as to influence viewers' attributions of meaning without the help of language that says, "This is a pampered, spoiled poodle." Because images alone don't have that linguistic help, they are relatively more ambiguous.

Context may be relatively more important for how we reduce ambiguity and interpret images, even as it is also important for how we interpret language. Images occur in contexts that affect the attribution of meaning to them and reduce their ambiguity. In 2017 and for a few years before, a terrible war in Syria caused a tidal wave of immigrants to flee north into Europe. Much of this news was conveyed by way of images of desperate, Third World people grieving their terrible losses, pleading for food and water, carrying dead children. Americans, and people from all over the world, responded differently, some with donations of aid, some in fear that the refugees would swamp host countries. But strikingly similar photos of desperate Third World people have circulated for decades in Western media; for example, victims of war in the Sudan. There is never any shortage of war and natural disaster around the world, and we see such things daily on the evening news. So Americans were seeing images of great need that were visually identical to what they had seen before. Yet viewers reacted with more interest and involvement, on one side or another, to the Syrian refugees. Clearly, the different context of a sudden, dramatic tsunami with intense media coverage versus the more usual context of ongoing poverty, war, and economic exploitation made a difference in how meanings were attributed to these photographs. In 2016, news media were preoccupied briefly with horrific images of a deadly fire in a warehouse housing an artists' community in Oakland, California. Although these images were widely circulated, they were almost always accompanied by media newspeople suggesting what the images meant and how to interpret them. Those media commentators provided a context for the public's viewing of the images, especially for those not from Oakland.

Consider the visual images we are shown of natural disasters. Hurricanes Katrina and Rita in 2005 and Hurricane Ike in 2008 caused great devastation to the Gulf Coast. Katrina especially is infamous for the destruction it brought upon New Orleans after the levees broke. In that context, charges of government inaction at all levels were rampant. National suspicion grew that relief agencies were not doing enough. In that context, thousands of images flooded the media, especially after Katrina, and they were manipulated to serve different purposes. Photos of evacuees in the New Orleans football dome were sometimes put into a context of sympathy, sometimes into a context attributing criminal behavior to those people. Filmmaker Spike Lee's HBO documentary *When the Levees Broke* makes powerful use of images in the aftermath of Katrina to indict political leaders whose actions and responses were allegedly inadequate in the crisis.

Photographs, like language, must thus be interpreted so as to extract meaning from them. Rhetorical critics should not assume that an image just "is," or that it conveys clear and obvious meanings to an audience. Images may be thought of as placeholders for a meaning that the audience must assemble. Critics should explore the ways that images are organized, and the contexts within which they are viewed, so as to understand the interpretations that may be made of them. And, in doing so, critics should always be aware of the potential of images to be sites of struggle among competing interpretations.

Critics of visual rhetoric should identify the *kind* of logic or rationale behind the structure that orders images or classes of images, for this can tell us a lot about how the images are rhetorical. The critic needs to ask what sort of visual world is being created, and how the "rules" of that world affect the audience. A logic of glorifying materialism seems to underlie a lot of hip-hop music videos, for instance. A logic of beautiful violence seems to inform

©iStockphoto.com/Pgiam

many video games. How images are consistently organized in these ways across texts tells us a lot about the rhetoric of the texts. The critic might observe that in *The Wizard of Oz*, the images are organized so as to create rather stark contrasts between Kansas and Oz. But the images are also organized around a contrast between simplicity and grandeur. The witch and the wizard both have grand castles; Dorothy has only a simple farmhouse back in Kansas. Yet simplicity of image aligns here with goodness, while grandeur is either suspect or downright evil. How does that contribute to the rhetoric of the film?

Images as Focal Points of Collective Memory and Community

Images are in need of interpretation, and they draw attributions of motives just as does language. An important difference between the rhetoric of the image and the rhetoric of the word, though, is that images are *relatively* more flexible at allowing differing, even conflicting, attributions of meaning to the same text. For example, nearly anything that someone might *say* about the Vietnam War is likely to be controversial even decades after it was fought; any utterance is likely to draw sharp agreement or disagreement. But the Vietnam War Memorial in Washington, DC, is primarily a visual text, a long, black, stark shape engraved simply with the names of those who died; no argument, no claims, no expositional text. Unlike a statement such as, "We could have won in Vietnam" or "We had no business being there," the monument gives the public nothing to counter, nothing to object to; it simply exists as a visual, material statement. Visitors to the memorial may come together and find common ground regardless of their feelings about the war; it is a focal point for collective remembering, and thus it can be a way to further community by overlooking differences of opinion.

In Johannesburg, South Africa, there is a museum in commemoration of District 6. District 6 was a thriving black community that was destroyed during the apartheid era of the 1970s to make way for white-owned businesses. The destruction was so heinous that there was very little actual development, and so it sat empty for decades, bare ground razed of all buildings (the rubble from the buildings was dumped into the sea to create the foundation for a high end, white-owned shopping mall). But the museum contains many images of the old neighborhood, and the floor is actually a map of the district. Images that once might have meant "economic progress" are now a focal point for commemoration of a terrible period in history. Former residents of the district come to the museum, often in tears, to find where their houses were on the floor map and to grieve over the old photographs. Clearly, the meaning of the images has been turned to something other than a celebration of progress by the context of the museum.

Have you ever wondered why so many old American cartoons from the early days of animation were of animals and not people (Bugs Bunny, Porky Pig, and so forth)? It was because portraying animals instead of people let Warner Brothers, Walt Disney, and other studios avoid the issue of race. Audiences of every color could go see cartoons as a shared experience because the image glossed over differences. Animal images were chosen because their ambiguity could be exploited in regard to race; they allowed people to avoid difference and controversy. The ambiguity of images thus served a strategic purpose even as it provided a way for people of all races to attend the cartoons and identify with them.

This is not to say that people always agree on how to interpret images; it simply means that the images themselves can become the basis for community precisely because they allow a feeling of shared, collective memory and common ground even when real agreement may be illusory. Images are relatively more ambiguous than is language, and thus images can more easily resolve conflict and contradictions within the public. It is true to say that "the United States is a diverse nation with racial tensions," yet such a statement expresses a contradiction: celebration of diversity and tension over diversity are at odds. There is no shortage of images in advertisements, for instance, of a racially diverse group of people happily hanging around wearing the same clothes, consuming the same products. In that way, images of, say, Old Navy clothing being worn by a diverse group of young people become significant points of social connection insofar as they present a picture of people coming together who might not do so with such enthusiasm in real life.

The rhetorical critic of visual images therefore looks for ways in which the ambiguity of images allows appeals to social solidarity, seems to create collective memories, and resolves social conflicts with rhetorical effects. On the other hand, rhetorical critics can look for ways in which images are structured so as to encourage more specific meanings, even meanings that may lead to social divisions. You may recall that Image 3.19 from Chapter 3 was organized in such a way as to convey meanings of gay sexual identity, and that the inclusion of the keystone sign or image of the famous (and decadent) gay author Oscar Wilde helped to structure the image in that way.

Perhaps one reason for the ongoing appeal of *The Wizard of Oz* has been that, although it appears as if all the actors are white, the creatures they become while in the land of Oz are largely deracialized. One white actor becomes a man whose skin is made of tin; another white actor becomes a nonracial lion. Many of the bad guys are monkeys; others are cranky apple trees (although we will think of the colors of these "villains" later on in this chapter). Compare the ongoing popularity of *Wizard* to that of another film that came out the same year, *Gone with the Wind*, in which racial differences are clearly portrayed and in stereotypical ways that may be uncomfortable for today's audiences.

Point of View

One last rhetorical strategy employed by images is the point of view they create. Just as texts call forth a subject position, so images position the viewer in specific ways. In the movie *Sixth Sense*, the camera always has the psychiatrist, Dr. Crowe, in view. It is as if the whole story is told by putting the audience in Dr. Crowe's shoes. We take his point of view for rhetorically charged reasons: it increases the shock of the surprise at the end when Dr. Crowe (and we) discover that he has been dead, and a ghost, for most of the movie. In movies about zombie attacks, such as *World War Z*, *28 Days Later*, and *28 Weeks Later*, the point of view is always that of the people who are fleeing or hiding from zombies, never from the point of view of the zombies themselves. In contrast, Rob Zombie's *Halloween* films shifts point of view, sometimes showing us what the world looks like through Michael Myers's fogged night vision. Consider television coverage of a presidential speech. If the president is speaking from his desk in the Oval Office, the camera gives the audience the point of view of a visitor to the president, perhaps sitting across the desk in a chair.

That point of view makes the communication seem more intimate and informal. When the president addresses Congress, the camera nearly always gives the audience a point of view below the president, looking up at the chief executive, even though many in-person viewers such as those in the gallery might actually be looking down. This point of view is rhetorical because it honors the office and its incumbent, putting the viewer in a subordinate stance.

Another dimension of point of view can be the difference between intimacy and distance. One effect is created if we see something as if from afar, another if we are up close and personal. In a film featuring lots of destruction, such as those in the *Chronicles of Riddick* or *Resident Evil* series, including movies like *Pitch Black*, some terrific explosions are seen from afar. They are beautiful and artistic, and the audience can rejoice in the image of glorious, spectacular violence. Other explosions happen in the near vicinity of the camera, often as it puts the audience into the point of view of the hero, and then the explosion is terrible, something to be feared and fled from. Point of view can thus encourage the audience to react in one way or another to the same kinds of events.

In *The Wizard of Oz*, the camera nearly always follows Dorothy. The viewer is given her point of view. The audience is placed on her level, never very much above or below. In this way, we are put into the movie from her perspective and are meant to experience the wonders and dangers of the film as she does. In understanding any text, the critic should consider the point of view created by the image to be occupied by the viewer.

METHODS FOCUSED ON STORY

Dramatistic/Narrative Criticism

This perspective on the rhetorical criticism of popular culture is a broad, loosely connected school of thought. Many different critics and theorists have worked within the field of dramatistic/narrative criticism. What unifies this approach is a shared understanding of basic human reality and motivation.

The first several perspectives that we have studied, as well as most others, carry an understanding of what "makes the world go around" in terms of human reality, perception, and motivation. Culture-centered critics understand people to be motivated by their cultural contexts. Marxists see material, economic conditions as fundamental, as the reason for why we see the world as we see it and why we are motivated as we are. Visual critics focus on our increasingly visually oriented world and how visual texts work. Psychoanalytic theorists would argue that early childhood experiences, especially those based on sexual difference, make people do what they do in later life. For feminists, many texts can be explained in terms of their representations of gender. So, what is key for dramatistic/narrative critics? *Language* is the answer.

Language as a Grounds for Motives

Dramatistic/narrative critics believe that *language and other sign systems* are the grounding for human reality and motivation. We have seen earlier in this book how signs, especially as they function symbolically, take on a life of their own. They can impart meanings that are not connected in a necessary, one-to-one relationship to any material objects or actions. Critics using a dramatistic/narrative approach (which we will abbreviate as D/N throughout this discussion) argue that we see the world in certain ways and react to it with certain motivations because of and through the symbols that we use. In other words, the most fundamental reality is the symbols we use, especially the larger structures, such as *drama* or *narrative*, into which these symbols are arranged.

Pursuing that idea further, these critics go on to examine the ways that signs (especially symbols) change, interrelate with one another, lead from one to another, and suggest or discourage linkages to other signs. They study those symbolic operations because they assume that they are the sources of perception and motivation. They argue that the "dances" that signs go through because of their intrinsic characteristics are the same moves that perception and motivation go through. For instance, the intrinsic similarity of the English words *God*, *guide*, and *guard* cause us to see them as linked in terms of their meaning or motivation. The words look and sound alike in English, and hence our motivations concerning what the words mean might be linked as well: we see God as a guide, as a guard (as a goad, as good, and so forth).

Because language and other symbol systems are so complicated, D/N critics use many critical tools that call attention to the many meaning- and motive-generating functions that language performs. Here we can review only a few of the major categories of analysis. We will turn chiefly to the great dramatistic theorist Kenneth Burke for the ideas that we will study here.

D/N critics assume that people create and use texts so as to help them understand and formulate responses to problems they encounter in life. An author, poet, or political speaker puts symbols together in an essay, poem, movie, oration, or other text as a way of trying to understand and respond to certain problems in life. Once a way of understanding and reacting to a problem is encoded in a text, that text becomes a place to which others may also turn for motivation and perceptions. Readers, film and television viewers, and others who share similar problems may use the same texts for help in confronting those problems. In Kenneth Burke's words, D/N critics assume that "literature is equipment for living" (*Philosophy of Literacy Form* 293–304).

Because the source of perceptions and motivations is the symbols themselves, it is assumed that anyone who understands the symbols and how they work within a given system will have access to the perceptions and motivations they generate. If one is unhappy with one's present life, dramatists would argue, it is because one is using a dysfunctional set of symbols; the key is to find different motivations by using a different set of symbols. To quote Burke again, "motives are shorthand terms for situations"—if you want a different situation, use different "shorthand terms" (*Permanence and Change* 29). The label "evil empire" for the former Soviet Union once summed up widespread American sentiment toward that country. Descriptions of Russia or the Ukraine as "impoverished," "struggling," or having a "crumbling economy" are shorthand terms that describe our new motives and new perceptions of lands that were once part of the USSR. Now, those who violently oppose their national governments, especially if those governments are allied to United States interests, are often termed "insurgents" in the media; think about the effects of using that term instead of such alternatives as "revolutionaries," "criminals," or "political activists."

Sometimes the focus of D/N analysis is at the level of the individual symbol, sentence, or other small unit. You have already studied some of the critical methods used by D/N analysis in Chapter 3, especially in the section on "implied strategies," in which you were urged to consider "what leads to what," "what goes with what," and so on. As we discussed in that section, the fact that a given word leads to another word indicates that the motivations suggested by that word lead to the motivations suggested by the next word. This kind of critical strategy is very much in keeping with the principles of D/N criticism.

Key to the dramatistic/narrative perspective is the idea that human thought and action can be understood as if it were a drama, a narrative, or a story. Drama is a good metaphor for understanding human experience, these critics argue, because what is a play but a bunch of words? Scenes, movements, and actions are all structured around language. Language is the skeleton, the framework, of stories, and thus all language, from this perspective, can be understood as if it were a play or a story.

Terministic Screens

In studying individual symbols, or sets of them, a central concept for D/N criticism is that of *terministic screens*. The idea here is that the vocabularies that people typically use allow them to think and to do certain things but prevent them from thinking and doing certain other things. Therefore, a terministic screen is, in Burke's words, a "trained incapacity" as much as it is an enabler to see the world in certain ways (*Permanence and Change* 7). You can get a glimpse of the terministic screen that most Americans use to perceive other people if you look at the categories named in the personals ads of newspapers or websites. Terms for race, gender, and professional status loom large as the "boxes" within which we categorize people.

To see this point in another example, consider how, in the United States today, our ways of talking about the success of people or groups tend always to be embodied in terms having to do with money. The success of movies, for instance, is measured in box office sales as expressed in the total dollar amount. This practice leads us to see contemporary films such as *Batman v Superman* or the *Finding Nemo* animated film series (with a ticket price of nine dollars or so) as doing very well when compared to movies (such as *Gone with the Wind*) that first came out when admission to theaters cost far less. When it comes to films, we are simply not attuned to talking in terms of numbers of viewers; instead, we talk in terms of total dollars. In a related example, we are quite accustomed to measuring a person's career success in terms of salary dollars, but we simply have no convenient way to talk about success in terms of personal satisfaction, low levels of stress, and so forth. We must talk around those points, or talk about them at great length, while it is much quicker and easier for us to talk about salary figures.

Teleology

When D/N critics examine individual symbols, another important concept that they use is *teleology*, or the idea of the development of a symbol (Burke, "Language as Symbolic Action" 16–20). Teleology refers to the perfection of a thing—the idea that within every concept or representation of a dog, for instance, is the concept of a perfect dog, which is the *telos* of that dog. One important thing that any narrative or drama does is to develop symbols, often in the direction of its telos. The great Russian playwright Anton Chekhov, for instance, once said that if a gun appears in the first scenes of a play, it must be used by the end of the play. That is because a gun is not perfected until it is fired; the shooting gun is the telos of the gun lying on the table. That idea or symbol of a gun yearns to be fired. This idea of development, or teleology, comes from the characteristics of the symbol, not from any material reality itself. The gun lying on a table, as far as it is concerned, can stay there until it rusts. It is the human idea that guns tend toward a perfection in being fired that calls for its firing.

D/N critics would therefore look for key individual symbols in a text to track their development throughout a narrative or drama and to show how that development happened as it did because of teleology. Because such texts are "equipment for living," D/N critics would explain ways in which the teleology of symbols intersects with real-life problems and solutions. For instance, nuclear weapons are the perfection of harm. They are the worst thing that can be done to a person or people or place. It is interesting to note the times when the texts of popular culture call for the use of nuclear weapons against enemies and when they do not. Saudi Arabia, for instance, has often been viewed with distaste by people in the United States because of its system of control over women, but no one has called for its nuclear destruction. Yet conflicts with Iran and North Korea have repeatedly been dealt with in popular culture by invoking this perfect symbol of harm, the nuclear weapon.

Because we have already discussed some of the other principles of D/N criticism in relation to individual symbols, vocabularies, and other small units of discourse in Chapter 3, here we will focus on understanding larger units of texts within D/N criticism. Sometimes D/N critics focus on the whole structure of a text, on the forms and patterns within it, the type of text that it is, and the ways in which the structures within the text relate to one another. We will turn now to just a few of the major categories of analysis that D/N critics follow in looking at how larger structures of texts work.

Narrative Genres

D/N critics view texts as *stories* or *dramas*, even if a given text is not explicitly such, because they argue that the characteristics of stories and dramas underlie all symbolic behavior. Stories and dramas usually occur as examples of types, or *genres*. A story might be a mystery, a romance, or a spy thriller, for instance. The text will include indications of which sort of genre or type it belongs to, leading the reader to have certain *generic expectations*. For instance, if a detective and a murder appear within the first twenty pages of a book, the book is in a way "asking" to be considered a mystery. Sometimes some parts of the context of the text will alert us as to its genre or type. If you are attending a college graduation, you know that the genre of "commencement address" is likely to be the type of speech that you will hear from the featured speaker, and you will expect the speech to include some sort of uplifting advice for people about to enter the world outside academia. Another part of a text's context might be the person or people who had a hand in producing it. If you hear that Stephen King has a new book out, you can make a pretty good guess as to the genre that book will fit into.

All texts of popular culture can be viewed in this way, by placing them within a genre. It is important to understand that a genre describes a set of expectations that an audience might have about how a text will interface with the audience in a certain situation. A genre does *not* describe a set of hard-and-fast rules that texts must follow. For instance, if you are at a dance and are told that the deejay will next play the latest song from Kings of Leon or Them Crooked Vultures, you will certainly expect a hard-driving, loud, heavy beat and assertive lyrics. That is not to say that you will, without any exception, get such a thing. Suppose the song is a soft ballad done to singing violins. Go on, try to imagine it. In this case, the idea of genre would still be useful, because it would describe the expectations that such a song would *violate*. The people at the dance may find the song a wonderful and interesting change, or they may shout it down. But their reasons for doing one or the other are likely to be influenced strongly by their generic expectations.

Comedy and Tragedy

In several of his books, Kenneth Burke takes the idea of genre a step further to argue that the standard, classical genres of literature underlie all texts that one might encounter (even those of popular culture) and that those standard genres provide important but unsuspected "equipment for living" to their audiences (*Attitudes toward History*, part I). Burke reviews many genres such as the epic, the satire, the burlesque, the ode, and other classical categories of literature. Two categories particularly well developed in Burke's analysis are the two broad categories of *comedy* and *tragedy*.

To understand what Burke means by comedy and tragedy, we must understand some of his views about the real-life problems that people face (*A Grammar of Motives*; *A Rhetoric of Motives*). Burke argues that people are threatened by differences. We do not like to think that others are strange and alien, and when we perceive differences between ourselves and others, we work to overcome them. The condition of being different and estranged from others is referred to as *mystery*, and Burke argues that we try to overcome mystery.

Differences are overcome by entering relationships that are organized around certain rules and principles; these relationships are called *hierarchies*. By "playing by the rules" of the hierarchy, we find common ground between ourselves and others and are able to keep mystery at bay. The common ground that is established in hierarchies is a way to achieve *identification* with others, which is something that people generally want. For instance, the rule-bound and highly structured organizations within the business world provide a way for people from different racial, religious, ethnic, and age groups to relate to one another. Similarly, people may be from very different backgrounds, but if they are attending the same football game together, the structure of watching the game from the stands is a source of identification for them. And a man and woman may be different from each other, but through the structure of a marriage they can achieve identification.

The problem is, nobody can follow the rules of any hierarchy all the time. We are always violating the rules or at least thinking of violating them. Such violations create feelings of guilt, and the violations must somehow be dealt with so that the hierarchy may be restored. Sometimes we observe others violating the rules, and those violations must also be dealt with so that others do not destroy the hierarchies that ground identification and keep mystery at bay.

So the question becomes how to handle the inevitably recurring guilt that comes with living in hierarchies. This guilt is an inevitable, real-life problem. For example, we may think racist thoughts and feel guilty because we know that those thoughts violate the principles of equality that many of our hierarchies insist upon. We realize that we are not working as hard as we have agreed to at our jobs and feel guilty because we know that we are violating the rules of that particular business hierarchy. What can we do?

Burke says that discourses (by which he means the texts of popular culture, among other things) are available for people to turn to in devising means of dealing with guilt. Guilt may be handled in three ways. The first way is through *transcendence*: to see our guilt-inducing action as not truly a source of guilt because it is required by a different, higher, or nobler hierarchy. If you need to work late every night of the week, for instance, your family may complain and you may realize that you are guilty of violating expectations that you will come home at a reasonable hour. But one way of dealing with that guilt is to say, to yourself and to your family, that by working late you are earning more money for *their* benefit, for the greater ultimate good of all. In another example, a president may deal with the guilt of having lied to Congress by saying that he did so because the higher considerations of national security compelled him to do so.

A second way of dealing with guilt is to punish it in oneself. This simple and straightforward method Burke calls *mortification*. Sometimes, the guilty party finds a way to punish his or her own guilt through some related, atoning action. This way of dealing with guilt, through punishment, is, of course, common in religious faiths; a particular sexual sin, for instance, might be punished by some form of penance such as fasting, prayer vigils, or giving money to the poor.

The third way of managing guilt is described as *victimage* by Burke; it involves finding some other party that can represent one's guilt, and then attacking the guilt in that other form. (You may be more familiar with this general phenomenon under the name of "scapegoating.") Of course, if one is concerned about the guilt of others in the first place, then victimage is a convenient way to handle their guilt as well. And now we come back to *comedy* and *tragedy,* two kinds of texts that illustrate the two forms victimage may take.

Comedy is a kind of text that pictures the guilty act in question (either one's own or another's) as being committed by a *comic fool.* The text treats this misbehaving individual as mistaken and embarrasses him or her by revealing the error of the action to all. Comedy also typically shows its audience that the guilty act was inevitable insofar as it was a common human failing. In this way, the comic fool is reintegrated into the social hierarchy. But more important, if the fool's guilt mirrors a person's own guilt, then by experiencing the comic text, that person has vicariously reintegrated himself or herself back into the community, and the hierarchy, as well.

Tragedy is a kind of text that pictures the guilty act in question as being done by a *tragic hero* (*hero* is simply a technical term here and need not mean a "good guy"; in fact, some tragic heroes are rather objectionable). According to a tragic text, the guilty action is something that needs to be punished, as, by extension, does the tragic hero. The hero is depicted as engaging in actions that are inevitable insofar as they arise out of situations or character flaws that members of the audience might have as well. But instead of treating the guilty hero as simply mistaken and in need of correction, tragedy treats the hero as in need of punishment or even destruction. When audience members experience a tragic text, then, they see their own guilt purged by seeing it punished and destroyed.

This theory of comedy and tragedy, as well as Burke's theories of other categories of literature (the epic, the ode, and so on), may sound rather esoteric but is meant to explain how people experience all kinds of discourses and texts, including those of popular culture. To see the relevance of this theory, consider two ways in which the problem of racism in the United States is handled in popular culture. Racism is, of course, a violation of hierarchy by any measure; it threatens to destroy the fabric of civility and tolerance upon which life in a diverse society depends. One way to treat racist acts symbolically is to laugh at them, to treat them as absurd and ridiculous. We see this comic treatment of racism in the comedy monologues of Chris Rock, George Lopez, and Cedric the Entertainer. Another way to treat racist acts symbolically is to punish them, having their perpetrators killed, locked up, or defeated in significant ways. This happens to the racist characters in *District 9*, *Monster's Ball*, and *The Green Mile*, for example.

A similar choice between tragedy and comedy confronts viewers of the long-term comedy series *The Big Bang Theory*. The peace of the group of friends in an apartment building is constantly threatened by the social awkwardness, control mania, or eccentricity of the main character, Sheldon Cooper, yet the "family" order is generally restored at the end of each episode. But some viewers may occasionally watch the program in an altogether different mood, hoping for the more "tragic" solution of simply whacking Sheldon a good one. Someone who yells, "Just smack him!" at the screen is not only in a grumpy mood; she is taking a tragic perspective.

In the summer of 2013, George Zimmerman was acquitted in his trial for the alleged murder of Trayvon Martin in Florida. Most of the reactions to the trial were tragic on one side or the other, either calling for Zimmerman's quick conviction or saying that Martin deserved death for having provoked Zimmerman. Some reactions are comic, attempting to treat Zimmerman as a ridiculous fool. In either case, one does not have to look far to read into these reactions some expression of the public's own guilt at residual racism, violence, and fear of others in urban environments. The incorrigible Zimmerman returns to the news on a regular basis for some violation of the law, and similar reactions may be voiced about him each time.

The Pentad

Another major tenet of D/N criticism, particularly in Kenneth Burke's work, is called *pentadic analysis* (*A Grammar of Motives*). We noted previously that D/N criticism argues that people formulate their perceptions of the world through symbolic systems, especially through language. One important way in which the world is understood through language is through the explanations we make to ourselves for what caused a particular situation or experience to occur. This is an important aspect of how we understand the world, because through these explanations we formulate our own motivations. If, for example, someone thinks the world is the way it is because of money or economic circumstances, he or she will be motivated in a very different way than will a person who thinks the world is the way it is because of God's will.

Burke argues that when people explain the world to themselves, and thus formulate motives for acting in the world, they do so by anchoring their explanation in one or a combination (a *ratio*) of five basic terms, called *the pentad*. The five terms of the pentad are

1. *act* (actions, things that are done, willed or intended undertakings)
2. *agent* (people, groups, beings with the power to choose and to act)
3. *agency* (the means, tools, or techniques with which something is done)
4. *scene* (the physical or social environment, or context, for action)
5. *purpose* (the guiding ideas, goals, or motives for choice and action)

Pentadic criticism operates on the assumption that texts, and authors of texts, will tend toward explaining the world consistently by using one or a simple combination, or *ratio*, of these five terms. Texts as a whole are studied for the ways in which they tend to suggest that the world is the way it is because of a term or ratio between terms. The overall vocabulary of a text, the development of ideas or plot, the kinds of events that occur, key signs—all are studied to discover an underlying, and often not obvious, tendency to key an explanation of the world to a term or ratio.

For example, a concern for many people these days is that some children do not acquire skills in reading by the time they graduate from high school. The oft-repeated question "Why can't Johnny read?" is a question of why this aspect of the world (reading skills) is the way it is. But in answering that question, people will also formulate motives for responding to the problem. One answer that people might give is that Johnny can't read because he is in a poor or underprivileged environment, surrounded by noise and squalor, exposed to few positive role models; this is a *scene* explanation. Another answer is that Johnny can't read because his kind of people just can't, that there is some sort of inbred genetic or dispositional deficit preventing his reading; this is an *agent* explanation. One might give an *agency* explanation, answering that Johnny can't read because he has not been given books that would interest him, or that he is being exposed to the wrong agencies (e.g., video games), which do not encourage reading. One could give a *purpose* explanation, arguing that Johnny can't read because he is simply not motivated and has no inner drive or desire to read. Finally, perhaps Johnny can't read because he has never been taught, because nobody has ever done anything to instill in him an ability or desire to read; this would be an *act* explanation.

Burke argues that the great philosophies of the world are complex ways to explain experience and to formulate motivations by using the terms of the pentad. Charles Darwin's concept of survival of the fittest (which argues that adaptation over the long run to the environment determines which creatures are fittest and therefore more likely to survive) is *scenic*, for instance. Mystic explanations of the world, including those of many religions, are *purpose*-centered, argues Burke. Because people construct such explanations of how the world operates for themselves, they respond favorably or unfavorably to similar explanations that are offered in discourse, including the texts of popular culture. A pentadic analysis can therefore be a useful explanation of the rhetoric of popular culture; the public may or may not respond to a text of popular culture because of their acceptance or rejection of its key pentadic term or terms.

Analysis and Examples

The Wizard of Oz is a text that can be analyzed through the methods of D/N criticism as well. Here, we will try out two of the methods suggested above. First, the movie offers a good illustration of how guilt is dealt with in both comic and tragic terms. Note that both the Wicked Witch and the Wizard are hierarchy breakers. The Witch is guilty in all particulars, acting against all the rules of the societies of Munchkin land and Oz. The Wizard is guilty in terms of the society of Oz and the pact that he makes with Dorothy and her companions. The Wizard is treated as a comic fool, however. His guilt is unmasked, literally unveiled, as Toto draws the curtain away from him while he works the controls of the machines of deception in his palace. It becomes clear that he is not who he claims to be and cannot do what he claims to do. Once the error of his ways is revealed, however, he is restored to the community. In fact, he and Dorothy together plan to journey back to Kansas, but his incompetence gets the better of him in the end as the balloon takes off with him helplessly inside.

The Wicked Witch, on the other hand, is treated tragically and is destroyed in the end. It is inevitable that she does what she does, being a wicked kind of witch. But it is precisely her guilty acts that are her undoing; if she had never trapped the four companions in her castle, Dorothy would not have been there to throw water upon her, thus melting her.

Remember that in handling guilt comically or tragically, *The Wizard of Oz* was vicariously handling guilt for the audience through victimage. Consider the sorts of guilt that the Wicked Witch and the Wizard could represent for the audience. Perhaps one reason for this film's enduring popularity is that the guilts that are handled comically and tragically are really very ordinary and very common guilts. Many of us claim to be what we are not and would like to hold power over others despite our failings. The temptation to strut and posture, and to impress others with empty phrases and bluster, is strong in many of us. These are the Wizard's failings, and we see our everyday selves in him. Similarly, few guilts are more common than a lust for power, for control over others, for getting our way, for having a castle full of possessions and an army to defend them. These are the crimes of the Wicked Witch, and these darker guilts are shared by many in the audience. In understanding how guilt is handled through the texts of popular culture, D/N critics must always ask how the audience for the text is being given equipment for living through their own particular guilts.

The Wizard of Oz can also be examined using pentadic analysis. One possible argument, for instance, is that the film is *agent*-centered. Let us examine several components of the movie to see why that may be so. Notice that between Kansas and Oz, each of several characters reappears in different disguises but as essentially the same person (and portrayed in the film by the same actor). It is as if the underlying person, the characteristics of the agent as agent, are strong enough to survive the transition from reality to fairyland and back: Professor Marvel and the Wizard are both genial humbugs; each of the farmhands seems to lack what the corresponding Scarecrow, Tin Man, and Lion lack; and Miss Gulch is as evil and grasping as is the Wicked Witch.

Another aspect of the agent-centered quality of the movie is the centering of the plot around ways in which the four companions are deceived about who they are and what powers they have and how they overcome those deceptions. Dorothy has the power to go back to Kansas immediately by tapping the heels of her ruby slippers three times, but she must discover that about herself. It is clear that each of her three companions already has the personal characteristic that he thinks he lacks. The Scarecrow thinks he needs brains, but it is he who invents a plan to get into the Witch's fortress. The Lion thinks he lacks courage, but he leads the charge in the ensuing battle. The Tin Man thinks he lacks a heart, but he has to be admonished not to cry for Dorothy, "or you'll rust yourself again, and we haven't got an oil can."

When they finally return to the Wizard, the Scarecrow, Tin Man, and Lion are each given what the audience knows to be a meaningless trinket; yet through that trinket, each suddenly "discovers" the thing he or she was "missing." It was there all along, as Dorothy discovers of her own heart's desire; what they have found is not brains, heart, courage, or home, but *themselves*. So the movie seems to advise the audience to look within themselves, to the kind of people (or agents) that they are, to discover the truth about the world.

D/N criticism, then, looks to the ways in which symbolic systems, and especially language, work. It assumes that motivations work the same way, insofar as they are derived from those symbol systems. The texts of popular culture are studied in order to determine how the signs they are made of "work," interact with one another, and create motivations within themselves that are then available for audiences to use in confronting real-life problems. In focusing on language, D/N criticism takes the stance that language use is inherently dramatic or storylike and can best be analyzed from that perspective.

MEDIA-CENTERED CRITICISM

You will have noticed that, as predicted in Chapter 4 and also earlier in this chapter, strict lines of separation among the schools of thought studied here have not been possible. We discussed some feminist ideas when considering Marxism, for example. The next perspective we will discuss, that of *media-centered criticism*, has also been alluded to earlier in this chapter within the discussion of psychoanalytic criticism. You may recall

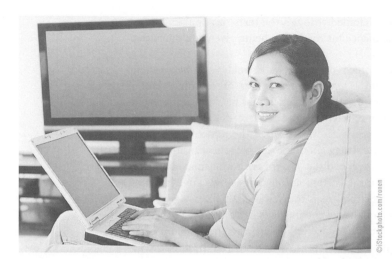

©iStockphoto.com/ronen

that we considered the ways in which experiencing a film duplicates the mirror stage of childhood and the argument that this duplication of a pleasurable experience in childhood is one reason for the rhetorical effectiveness of film, for why it is so popular. That argument is a good illustration of media-centered criticism. Just as culture-centered criticism (which we discussed in Chapter 4) argues that texts of popular culture should be analyzed using concepts taken from the culture in which they occur, media-centered criticism argues that texts of popular culture should be analyzed using concepts that take into consideration the *medium* in which the component signs of the text appear. Because mediated communication in popular culture so often takes the form of stories, the question of how media interact with stories rhetorically is central to this school of thought.

Here we will focus on three media. We will look at the medium of the computer for obvious reasons: it is the medium of the century, a technology of communication with which everyone is familiar. We will study the interconnected medium of handheld devices such as smartphones. We will also examine the medium of television, because television is clearly a popular and important medium in the United States, Europe, and even most of the Third World today. Much of popular culture comes to us through the "tube," and that which does not is often obviously influenced by television. For instance, the newspaper *USA Today* (founded in 1982—well into the television age) is designed to be highly visual, with bright colors and many graphics, and it is sold on street corners in a box that looks like a television set. Media-centered criticism would therefore caution critics to consider the characteristics of television as a medium and to show how those characteristics affect many other dimensions of how texts are created and received.

What Is a Medium?

We must first understand what is meant by *media*. A *medium* is sometimes defined as a channel of communication, a way to move signs from one person to another, or as the material in which the signs of communication are manifested. The book you are holding is a medium through which some signs that your author has made have come to you. Sometimes medium is defined more narrowly as a *technology of communication*, such as television, radio, or film. A more inclusive definition, one that underlies media-centered criticism, sees a medium as a *technology* of communication in combination with its typical *social uses*. According to this definition, a medium is both (1) a means of producing and reproducing signs and (2) the ways in which a given society or culture typically makes use of that means of production.

For instance, television in the United States is a medium that comprises not only a certain technology (the screen, cable hookups, stereo sound, sometimes a Blu-ray or video game player, Netflix, and so forth) but also a certain pattern of usage: televisions are usually found in the home, and if not in the home, then in enclosed places of informal social gatherings (such as a bar). We are so familiar with that way of using television that we may lose sight of the fact that the same technology could have been paired with very different social uses. In the very early days of television, for instance, Adolf Hitler planned to place large sets on street corners and in other public places in Germany as a means of official propaganda; in this case, there was no intention to have people keep televisions in the home. You can see how different television as a medium would be today were the technology with which we are familiar put to that different social use. To see a medium as both technology and social usage requires the critic to examine the ways in which technologies are used in culture and in the everyday lived experiences of people.

The computer is a medium that is used in particular ways. In the early days of the *personal* computer, many machines were plugged in and never used because people could not imagine significant uses for them. All that changed, and largely through the Internet, which now anchors computer applications of all sorts. The Internet is a particular way of using this machine, but it would not have to be that way; computers could be used only for word processing, only for calculating numbers, and so forth. But since people all over the world use the computer to access the Internet, then the social connections inherent in the Internet become integral to the computer as a medium.

Media Logic

Media-centered criticism can take any medium as its focus, showing how the medium influences the texts it carries and the audiences it addresses. Since many if not most of those texts in popular culture are stories, the questions we are asking are how media logic shapes stories and which stories do better in certain media because of their logics. Many scholars are working on developing media-centered criticism, but two of the most interesting critics in this area are David Altheide and Robert Snow (Altheide; Altheide and Snow; Snow). Altheide and Snow use the concept of *media logic* to explain what media-centered criticism is attempting to do. Underlying the idea of media logic is the assumption that as people become accustomed to a technology and to the social uses to which it is put, they internalize certain ways of thinking and perceiving.

For instance, suppose you spend most of a day downloading music onto a device such as an iPod. Suppose that at the end of the day, you turn on your radio and hear a song you particularly like. You start to reach for the right button so you can hear it again and are caught up short, because of course radio does not have an ability to repeat or rewind as part of its "logic," as the iPod does. What has happened, say Altheide and Snow, is that you have internalized the iPod logic, so much so that you come to expect to find replays everywhere. If you really have internalized that logic completely, you may even start looking for "skip track" or "delete" buttons as you read boring textbooks!

Media logics can become deeply sedimented in our consciousness. There are several software programs that allow you to download audio or video files onto your computer and play them back. The screen that comes up on your monitor for most if not all of these programs is designed to look exactly like an old-fashioned audiotape or videotape player, with the controls one might have found on such a machine. The "play" button, for instance, is usually an arrow pointing to the right, as it was for these older tape machines in which the tape went from left to right to play. Take a look again at Image 3.2 from Chapter 3 to see an example of how this logic is perpetuated even in products having nothing to do with music. Fewer and fewer people have anything to do with audiotape or videotape machines, but the logic of their controls is being continued beyond the actual existence of the machines.

Think for a moment about how consumption of stories might be affected by different media logics. The arrows on old tape machines give a linear sense to consuming stories. The arrow points us through the story to the end. And, sure enough, years ago people used to attend to stories straight through from beginning to end with *relatively* less variance or interruption. Today, with technologies like the computer or the television remote that do not have the "arrow" logic, people are much more likely to jump around, to consume bits and pieces of the stories they encounter in the media, to assemble their own kinds of stories. These differences are relative and not absolute, but they are surely influenced by the different media logics many of us use to access stories now.

Of course, we do not always "transfer" the logic of one medium to another. But one medium does tend to become dominant in any given society. In the nineteenth century and into the twentieth century in this country, the dominant medium was print (books, newspapers, letters, magazines, and so on). In the latter half of the twentieth century and to some extent today, television has been the dominant medium, affecting the ways that people habitually think about their everyday problems and experiences. Today, however, the computer is becoming a dominant medium, especially insofar as it is connected to the Internet. Notice how media-centered criticism describes media as the fundamental factor in culturewide perceptions and motivations, just as Marxism identified the material and economic as fundamental and feminist criticism identified sexual difference as fundamental.

Characteristics of Television as a Medium

Media-centered criticism is not restricted to television or the computer, but we will focus on those two because of their importance to our culture. Media-centered television criticism tries to explain some central characteristics of each as a medium (in terms of both technology and social use together). Let us briefly consider some of the characteristics of television that this approach has identified.

Commodification

One characteristic is *commodification*. A commodity is a good, something that is bought and sold, something with intrinsic value that can be traded economically. There are several reasons why television in the United States today has a logic that includes commodification. The first and most obvious reason is that television broadcasting is a commercial enterprise and is constantly selling commodities to the public. Television programming is saturated with advertisements. Often, advertisements blend into the regular programming because (1) ads have production values that are as high as or higher than the shows themselves, so that the ads are interesting and eye-catching and therefore resemble the program; (2) the same actors will appear on both programs and advertisements, thus linking the two (actor Dennis Haysbert appears as a strong and authoritative salesman for insurance services in television commercials and also portrays strong and authoritative characters in many of his film and television roles); (3) ads and programs often employ the same formats, such as that of a music video, thus blurring any clear distinctions between the two; and (4) ads and shows are interspersed with each other with increasing frequency. The end result is that the selling of commodities becomes increasingly inseparable from what one sees in general in watching television.

Another reason why television is heavily involved in commodification is that the audience itself is a commodity. We do not often think of ourselves as commodities, but in a sense we are. Television as organized in our country depends on advertiser support, and advertisers are more interested in buying time during programs that have large audiences. For that reason, programmers are able to "sell" an audience to a commercial sponsor. We as that audience are, in a sense, sold to an advertiser for fifteen seconds at a time on the expectation that we will be there in front of our television sets to watch a commercial at that time.

Television also commodifies because, increasingly, the content of the shows themselves displays the "good life" as one that is rich in material goods (or commodities). Murder mystery shows will almost invariably involve the death of a rich and famous person. A story about the murder of an ordinary librarian living in an upstairs duplex in Cleveland is unlikely to become a TV episode because it does not give programmers a chance to show fine furniture, Waterford crystal, oil paintings on the walls, and a Rolls Royce in the garage. We have shows about the lifestyles of the rich and famous, not the middle class and obscure.

Finally, television commodifies because the set itself is an owned commodity. It is something that the viewer holds as personal property and is thus a sign of one's economic status. It is interesting to note how all these forms of commodification interrelate. For instance, television sets were initially sold so as to provide an audience for commercials. In other words, ads came first, and people were encouraged to buy sets so as to become audiences (commodities) and be sold themselves to advertisers.

The impact of commodification is that it creates an intense concern for commodities in the minds of those who use television a great deal. Material goods come to be considered one of the most important things in life. People may come to think that having a lot of material goods (like the people they see on TV) is the natural way to live and may therefore think that poverty is somehow unnatural or a moral defect. Media-centered critics would examine texts of popular culture, especially those on television, to trace the effects of commodification in the perceptions and motives those texts offer.

Realism

Another important characteristic of television is its *realism*. This characteristic has been well explained through George Gerbner and his colleagues' work with the concept of *cultivation* (Gerbner et al.). Cultivation refers, in this sense, to the ways in which television cultivates perspectives on what the world is like.

Television cultivates a sense of its own reality in viewers. It seems to be a window on reality for at least two reasons. First, it is a *visual* technology, and in our culture, seeing is believing. Television shows us pictures of things, and many Americans think that pictures cannot lie. Thus, what we see on television, we assume to be real. We may know that a drama is staged and being presented by actors, but the distinction between drama and real life is increasingly blurred on television. News broadcasts, for instance, may present pictures of a prison hostage crisis that look exactly like the fictional drama on the same topic that you saw the night before.

A second reason why television seems to be so realistic is that it is so much a part of our lives. We generally take it for granted, regarding it as a part of our homes, located in our everyday surroundings. We would never question the reality of what we see out our living room windows; in the same way, we take television to be a realistic window on the outside world. In fact, television has become a guarantee of reality. "How do you know?" we might ask of a friend who has told us an unbelievable story. "I saw it last night on TV," she responds, thus clinching her argument. Much television *is* in fact about real life; we are used to live broadcasts and video journalism bringing actual happenings into our home, making these events much more present and alive than any newspaper article could.

Television is becoming increasingly intertwined with reality (or at least the claim and appearance of reality) through shows like *Pawn Stars, Survivor, Top Chef, Cops, Naked and Afraid, Chopped*, and *Cold Case Files*. These are programs that merge dramatic reenactments or staged talking head shots with candid videos of live action. Because television seems so realistic, the perceptions and motivations portrayed in its programming cultivate a similar sense of reality in viewers. Gerbner and his colleagues have found, for instance, that people who are heavy viewers of police shows on television come to grossly overestimate the amount of violence that actually occurs in their communities (Gerbner et al.). The world looks more violent than it actually is to them because they think that they are seeing that real world on television. Media-centered critics would look at these and other perceptions and motives offered by television and identify ways in which they cultivate unrealistic or distorted views of reality. These critics would study the "world" that television creates and then judge the effects of that world on the larger society.

Intimacy

We will examine one more of television's central characteristics: *intimacy*. Television is highly concerned with that which is small, personal, and person-oriented. Furthermore, media-centered critics would argue that television serves to make these small, intimate concerns paramount in many aspects of our lives.

As we have noted, television is a technology that is interwoven with our personal lives because of its place in the home. Many people have more than one set so that they can watch TV wherever they are in their homes, even in their bedrooms. The home setting of most television viewing would naturally make it an intimate medium. But of course we often read books and newspapers at home, also. To understand television as an intimate medium more fully, we need to think about what kind of programming tends to succeed on television.

Most television screens are rather small compared to film. Big HDTV sets are becoming more available and cheaper, but even the largest screens are small compared to film. For that reason, large and complex images do not work as well on television as they do on film. What television does best is to show relatively simple scenes with only one or a few objects on which to focus. Thus, television does very well in showing people. The human face is a relatively uncomplicated thing to watch, and it does not require a large screen to be seen. In fact, some of the extreme close-ups that we see on television would not work well on film; nobody wants to see a face that is thirty feet across, pores and warts and all. But the human face and form do well on television because the small screen keeps them human sized.

This suitability for portraying individual people helps to explain the specific ways in which television portrays events. Notice that some scenes that you would not ordinarily think of as involving shots of individual people often do just that. If a car chase scene is depicted, for example, television will keep returning to show the faces and bodies of people in the car as much as or more than it will show the cars themselves. Sports provide another example. Television actually does not do very well in showing two opposing strategies in football as they unfold across a one-hundred-yard field. That is why the camera will focus on individuals as much as possible, following receivers as they run downfield or backs as they run with the ball. In between plays, the camera will zoom in for extreme close-ups of players as they walk back to huddle or writhe in pain on the field. So when television is portraying panoramic action, it keeps pulling back from the broad view to show what it shows best: the people within the action.

Because of its location in the home, and because of what its size and technology can do best, television calls our attention to people. Furthermore, it focuses on people's concerns, experience, and problems. In this way, it is an extremely intimate medium. Joshua Meyrowitz has shown persuasively how television has robbed public figures of truly private lives (*No Sense of Place*). Because TV demands a focus on the person and the personal, it is good at showing—or at pretending to show—the intimate facts of the lives of those whom it portrays. In an age of television, we know all about the president's colon and kidneys; such a state of affairs was unknown in the less intimate age of print.

Furthermore, television's intimacy tends to turn public attention toward the personal dimensions of any event of great public importance. Hostage crises do very well on television because they are about people; the larger political and social issues behind the hostage taking, however, are likely to go unexplored on television. The reasons why various factions in the Middle East are constantly at war with one another is difficult to explain on television, but if a U.S. citizen is taken hostage in the Middle East, the person's grieving family can be interviewed intimately, even in their homes. Thus, television will opt for the latter far more often than the former. To cite another example, conflicts in countries of the Middle East such as Israel, Syria, Iran, and Iraq are very complex and may be hard to portray or to understand on television. Therefore, a news special on those changes will likely focus on one or a few individuals, showing what their everyday lives are like and the problems they face.

Media-centered critics argue that the American public increasingly tries to understand public problems by examining the experiences of individuals, and that this shift to the personal is a direct result of the dominance of television in our culture. Critics would examine texts of popular culture to show the ways in which complex political and social issues, especially when portrayed on television, are transformed into personal images. The problem of Mexican nationals crossing into the United States for work becomes the story of Raoul and his family; the problem of toxic wastes becomes the experience of Betty, who lives within a mile of a dumping site; and the problem of the homeless becomes the plight of Amos, a man who sleeps on hot air grates in the sidewalk. (Recall that in Chapter 3 we described this as a process of understanding complex problems through *metonymy*.)

Analysis and Examples

The Wizard of Oz, though originally a film, is actually a fruitful example for thinking about media-centered criticism, particularly criticism that addresses the effects of television. Interestingly, the movie did not do as well as a film as it has on television. It did not win any major Academy Awards, for instance, and was widely discounted as merely a children's movie by the critics of the late 1930s. Twenty-five years later, however, it was firmly established as a television institution, being broadcast once a year to enormous family audiences clustered around the set. Now it is broadcast even more often on a variety of cable channels, and it is widely available on DVD and videotape. Although this is certainly not the only question that a media-centered critic would ask, it would be interesting to consider why *The Wizard of Oz* has done so much better on television that it did as a film.

We might consider the characteristics of television in answering our question. First, the movie is visually lush and splashy, especially when the Oz scenes are contrasted with the dull black and white of Kansas. Of course, many movies that do well as movies are colorful and gaudy, but it could be that a television audience, attuned to commodities, will better understand how commodity-rich Oz might be a place of wonder to Dorothy Gale from Kansas ("Can I even dye my eyes to match my gown?" "Yes." "Jolly old town!"). Good and bad in the movie seem to be aligned, respectively, with commodification and a lack thereof; the Wicked Witch's palace, although huge, is a bare and spartan place, while the "best place," the city of Oz, is encrusted with precious metals and jewels. In fact, the companions' first experience in Oz appears to be an enrichment with commodities, as the Scarecrow is restuffed with the finest straw, the Tin Man is waxed and polished, and the Lion and Dorothy have their hair and nails made beautiful.

Power is also signaled by commodities. The audience does not see where Glinda the Good Witch lives, but the other two most powerful figures—the Wicked Witch and the Wizard—have enormous palaces. The Witch's commodities are ugly and not anything we would want, but it is clear from the sheer bulk of her castle that she is rich in commodities. And the (seemingly) powerful Wizard's palace has enormously high ceilings and halls that stretch for miles.

Can we say that *The Wizard of Oz* did better on television because of television's realism? Notice that "real life" in the movie—the scenes in Kansas—are in unrealistic black and white. The realism of living color does not appear until Dorothy gets to Oz.

Your author is of an age to recall when color television sets began to replace black-and-white sets as standards in American homes. Like a slow tide, the acquisition of color sets spread across a neighborhood. And I can also recall from my youth the anticipation with which the first color viewing of *The Wizard of Oz* was awaited, because now the audience could participate in the Kansas-to-Oz transition (the move from black and white to color) with Dorothy. The family with the new color set had in fact gone from Kansas to Oz (no matter which programs they were watching) when they bought their new set.

But even for viewers who did not experience that transition from black and white to color, television's realism may in fact provide a more satisfactory answer for what is, after all, a central question in *The Wizard of Oz*: was it real? Did Dorothy really go there or was it all a dream? It is easy to imagine that Oz is a fictitious place as you leave the movie theater, because after all, you leave the movie behind. But the television stays right there in your home. It has been showing you realities all along and thus makes it easier for the young at heart to imagine that Oz was, in its turn, real.

Finally, consider the heavy emphasis in *The Wizard of Oz* on *characters*, on people and pseudopeople. Practically all the action is portrayed through close-up shots of people and creatures. Furthermore, these characters are all extremely telegenic and interesting in close-ups. The mythical creatures, such as the Scarecrow, the Tin Man, and the Wicked Witch, need to be seen up close and personal so that the realism of the makeup jobs can be appreciated. On the other hand, especially for children, a Wicked Witch the size of a movie screen might well be overwhelming. In sum, *The Wizard of Oz* found its right "size" on the television screen.

Media-centered critics study the texts of popular culture with an eye toward the media that present those texts to the public. In many cases, these critics would argue, the characteristics of a particular medium itself may be more important than are the texts displayed through that medium. Media-centered critics trace the effects of the medium that may be found in an audience's ways of thinking about and processing stories.

Characteristics of Handheld Devices as a Medium

It sometimes seems as if our everyday lives are completely dominated by handheld devices. Increasingly, that means smartphones. Observe any large group of people walking around, say downtown or at a college or high school campus, and the odds are good that most of them will have their eyes glued to the phone in their hands. The phenomenon is even coming to be seen as a social danger, and many cities and states are passing laws against using such devices while driving a car.

The uses for these devices are many: checking email, sending texts, Twitter, Instagram, using GPS to navigate, and so forth. Smartphones perform many of the functions of computers, and yet they are small and powerful enough that we can carry them around with us. Together with their content, or the kinds of things you can do with them, handheld devices constitute a kind of medium. Their characteristics blend with some of those of the computer and Internet, as discussed in the next section, but let us consider some key characteristics found most clearly in handheld devices. We will focus on connective power and context mobility.

Connective Power

A smartphone connects you to global information resources. No longer do you need to wonder who won the 2011 World Series; you simply look it up. Navigating streets and cities with which you are unfamiliar need hold no terrors; you simply call up the GPS application on your device. You can talk to anyone in the world, and if they don't answer you can leave them text messages. Your author visits the People's Republic of China regularly to teach and lecture, and his smartphone has the WeChat app that lets him send texts to friends all over China. If I need to speak to someone in my office while I am away, I can reach the person in seconds. Sadly, my dean can reach me in the same amount of time!

This kind of connective power creates a new sociality, or a new way of being social with others. Many people would rather send texts than telephone someone, because it is time consuming and uncertain to call; perhaps nobody will pick up. We have instead become accustomed to asynchronous interactions in our social world with others, whether friends, acquaintances, or online sources of information. The days of having to go see someone to make a connection or ask a question are long over. You make connections in a virtual world that is now disconnected from time. Power no longer comes from who you know but from what you know about making connections. Since the connections are asynchronous, you make the connection or seek information or leave a message on your time. You rarely need to find a time to talk that is mutually agreeable. So the kind of connections given by handheld devices at least create a feeling of personal empowerment. Whether the empowerment is real may still be a matter for debate.

Context Mobility

It seems obvious to say it, but handheld devices give the user total mobility. With the exception of airplanes or tunnels in which signals are lost, there are few places where one cannot connect, seek information, and communicate. What this means is that context is less important as part of the process of communication. People are freed from their contexts in ways they were not even just a few years ago.

Suppose you are having dinner with friends. Are there some topics that are considered inappropriate for that context? Of course there are. But if you get a call in such a context, the phone allows you to excuse yourself and step away from the table to take the call. The device allows you to create your own context. Of course, we all know people who will not leave the table or a meeting but will continue to talk about their latest medical results as if other people were not there. This practice, while offensive to many, is another kind of context creation. The handheld device allows the user to imagine that a new context has been carved out around her, specific to usage of the device. The context dissolves when the call is ended. To take another example, people can seek refuge from boring meetings by surreptitiously turning to their smartphones so as to check email, send and receive texts, even do some online shopping while the speaker up there finishes the quarterly report. These are contexts easily dissolvable by turning from the device to the physical context at hand.

Power lies in the ability to control context. Those who want to control others will control context, as prison wardens have understood for years. On a less drastic terrain, teachers, lecturers, and business executives conducting meetings will often demand that handheld devices be put away or turned off because they want to shape the context for themselves and their audiences. With handheld devices, the ability to create context is movable. It goes way beyond the control found in, say, the ability to decorate your own apartment. You can create your own context anywhere.

We may be hard-pressed to link *The Wizard of Oz* to a medium like handheld devices that was scarcely yet imagined when it was filmed. But we see evidence in the movie of a yearning for

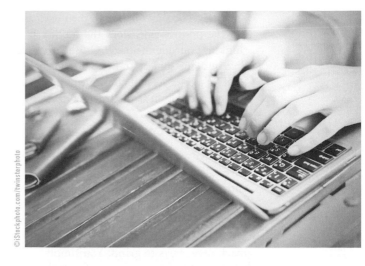

that kind of connectivity. Professor Marvel pretends to be able to access information from a distance with his crystal ball. The witches, good and bad, likewise use crystal balls or devices like them to see events from afar. In handheld devices we see an early culmination of a human yearning that has been around for a long time.

Characteristics of the Computer and Internet as a Medium

As noted earlier, to think of any technology as a medium, one must think of it as it is used socially. Computers, of course, are a cluster of technologies with wide-ranging applications. But here let us consider the medium the computer has become insofar as it gives access to the Internet. People access the Net constantly from home and work, for business and personal pleasure. What are some (we cannot explore them all) characteristics of that experience's media logic? Bear in mind that we will see some overlap here with other media, especially handheld devices.

Fluidity

One of the most striking characteristics of the Internet is its fluidity. Regardless of which URL (or webpage) you are currently using, you are usually at most but a couple of clicks away from another webpage, and another beyond that, and then another. Most pages have several links that will take you to different sites, where of course there are links to take you to other sites, and so on.

Think about how the fluidity of the Internet compares with reading a book. When you read a book, you are in a sense immersed in the "space" of that text. Of course, you can put the book down and do something else, but the idea of instantly going from a novel to a mathematics textbook to a book of poems is completely foreign to the book as a medium. The Internet offers a completely different feel of fluidity, of ease of movement across texts. That means, of course, also a fluidity across subject matters. You can read about the history of the West and go instantly to a site selling boots and then immediately to a history of shoemaking and then to a site on exotic leathers. If this way of moving across texts becomes habitual, then so does the way of thinking that comes in its wake. On the positive side, does the fluidity of the Internet contribute to creative ways of thinking "outside the box"? On the negative side, does it create an inability to focus, to dive into one subject and one text for hours (as one does while reading a book)? What kinds of stories are best consumed through such a fluid medium? These are questions that will need attention as the Internet develops as a medium.

Speed and Control

Earlier we referred to the work of Altheide and Snow. An interesting concept they have called our attention to is the centrality of the *keyboard* as a kind of super-medium, cutting across many different technologies. Telephones, blenders, food processors, remote controls, and computer keyboards—these are members of that family of technologies. What they have in common is that they allow instant command over processes that are sometimes quite powerful. The fingers push a few buttons and great machinery starts to grind. You simply press your thumb on the remote control and a whole world of entertainment flashes by you. Keyboards give us very quick control over experience.

Surely the computer is among the most common keyboards in use today; only the telephone/smartphone/PDA may surpass it. The ease of access granted by manipulation of the fingers makes speed and control a central characteristic of the computer. The processes controlled by these manipulations are the fluid movements across sites and texts. This is also speed of shifting from one interest to another; it is speed of access to information. In the days before computers, if you wanted to know who the sheriffs were in the state of Idaho, you would have to take a trip to the library and spend some time hunting down that information. Any reasonably competent user of a computer today could get that information within five minutes maximum, even if his or her server was having a slow day. This creates expectations for speed and control that may apply beyond the world of the Internet. As more and more functions of everyday life fall under the control of the Internet, we may become less and less patient with what seems like endless waiting in lines or with being placed on hold while phoning.

Dispersal

With so much power at the fingertips of computer users on the Internet, it is not surprising that another central characteristic of this medium (the last one we will review here) is that it disperses people away from physical, social contact into another kind of social contact facilitated online. It is not the case, as some might allege, that computers on the Internet isolate people at home in front of their own tiny screens. Those people may well be making contact with others across the globe. Virtual communities spring up in bulletin boards, instant messaging connections, and Usenet groups. Bloggers become the core of communities that may be truly global as they report on political crises or natural disasters in their own parts of the world. Virtual communities centered in games such as *World of Warcraft* sprout up across the Internet.

But note that these communities are dispersed communities. They situate the individual in connection to others through technology. Whereas people used to gather in physical spaces to meet and talk, now people are dispersed into physical isolation at the same time they experience social connection. We are only now beginning to understand the new, wider ways of thinking that the dispersal of the computer and Internet create, ways of acting that continue as a media logic once we turn the computer off. But is it any wonder that increasingly people wander around among strangers talking to people they know on cell phones? That phenomenon looks strange to people whose patterns of thought equate physical proximity with social connection, for here is a person next to me talking into empty space and not talking to me!

Analysis and Examples

It would be difficult to apply the Internet-connected computer's media logic to *The Wizard of Oz*, since the film has been so little viewed as an entire text online; we watch it at home on TV. Instead, we might think about ways in which this medium contributes substantially to the nature of another kind of text. Consider, then, what becomes of the experience of going shopping (which can be thought of and analyzed as a text) when it goes online.

Shopping malls and stores contain a kind of fluidity already, but it is a fluidity across categories of merchandise rather than within a category. If you are physically in J. C. Penney looking for shoes, you have the fluidity of going to the undergarment section a few steps away and the overcoat section a few steps from that. But there is likely to be only one shoe department per store and certainly only one price per type of product. You can go to a different store, but now it gets to be more difficult, for you must walk or drive to the nearest competitor.

But online shopping adds a much greater amount of fluidity to that experience. You can click links that will take you from one shoe site to another. If you use some online services such as NexTag or Bizrate, you can move quickly from one merchant to another who is selling the very same shoe. One effect of this fluidity is to concentrate on the task at hand at the expense of inattention to the context or surroundings of the task. Fluidity creates, as Meyrowitz noted early in the days of the Internet, "no sense of place." In person, shopping or any other task must usually be considered in connection to its context, but online the task stands nearly alone. Consider how useful an effect this is for marketers as the consumer becomes a floating consciousness, freed of the constraints of context and free to focus only on the task of buying a product.

The speed of online shopping should also serve the interests of business. Speed and ease are combined in the ability to purchase items after entering only a few numbers from a credit card or, if one is using PayPal or other payment services, just clicking a few links on the screen. Notice that the speed of online shopping is all at the point of purchase. Once the product is purchased, it may take a week or more for it to actually arrive at your doorstep. Consumers become trained to wait patiently for those products. Thus, online shopping flips the usual expectations in which it takes time to shop but you have the product instantly. Again, this new structure of expectations benefits business entirely, as they have your money immediately, and as long as you do not complain, and you rarely do, business does not mind if you wait for the goods.

Finally, notice that the experience of shopping in person is often social. Hanging out with friends often involves hanging out at the mall. Online shopping disperses people into solitary consumers. Such dispersal may well also benefit business, as we have no friends around to curb our impulse buying or to keep us from becoming fashion victims. Lost alone in the hyperstore of the Internet, the consumer consults only his or her desires in making purchases.

Summary and Review

We have studied seven schools of thought, or approaches to criticism, in this chapter and in Chapter 4. It is important to realize, however, that in many ways the things you have learned in this chapter are less crucial than the things you learned in Chapter 3. By that we mean simply that the particulars of any given approach are not as important as the act of criticism itself—the act of revealing, through any approach, that which is not obvious about texts.

In these two chapters, we have learned about different perspectives on what texts mean. In a sense, we have reviewed differing views on which meanings critics should look for as they study texts. We began with three "warnings" about the critical perspectives we would discuss: (1) there are differences of opinion within perspectives, (2) there is agreement among perspectives, and (3) not all perspectives are covered here.

With those warnings in mind, we began by organizing our seven schools of thought into those that emphasize INTERVENTION over Understanding, and those that emphasize UNDERSTANDING over Intervention, although all our perspectives are concerned with both. Chapter 4 focused on three schools of thought or methods concerned with power: culture-centered, Marxist, and psychoanalytic. Those three methodological approaches heavily emphasize intervention. Chapter 5 looked at four schools of thought that heavily emphasize understanding. It began with two schools of thought that attempt to understand the self in society: psychoanalytic and visual

criticism. This chapter ended with two schools of thought that attempt to understand story in popular culture: dramatistic/narrative and media-centered.

In studying the critical perspective of *culture-centered* criticism, we learned that this perspective is opposed to ethnocentrism because it argues that the texts of a given culture should be studied using the critical methods and assumptions appropriate to that culture. We focused on the specific perspective known as *Afrocentric* criticism, which studies the texts generated by African-centered cultures. When critics study texts of African cultures, they look for expression of certain themes or values, including *unity and harmony, orality, signifying, intertextuality, rhythm and style,* and others. We also noted that *whiteness studies* can usefully ground a critical analysis when it exposes the assumptions that are embedded in Eurocentric cultural perspectives, assumptions that often go unnoticed yet may ground forces of oppression and domination.

Next we turned to *Marxism*. We learned that Marxism is based in the idea of *materialism*, that perceptions and motives are grounded in material experience. Marxist critics look for ways in which texts reflect, or are symptoms of, those material conditions. Because of this concern with the material, a Marxist perspective often draws on *economic metaphors*, treating signs and texts as if they were commodities that could be traded. Marxism is also very much concerned with power. It shows how texts encourage *preferred readings* that support the *hegemony*, or dominance, of groups of people who are already empowered. But Marxism also reveals resources for *oppositional* readings, either *inflections* or outright *subversions* of preferred readings. We also learned that Marxists identify the *subject position* encouraged by texts, an idea we encountered earlier, and we connected subject position to preferred or oppositional readings. Standpoint theory provided a useful, general way to think about what Marxist and also feminist critics look for in texts, as it argues that marginalized perspectives are often the richest in understanding culture.

The third perspective was the *feminist* method. We explored a number of different kinds of very basic feminist points of view: liberal, Marxist, and radical. We saw that feminist critics explore ways in which texts perpetuate patriarchy through denigrating women, silencing them, and exploiting the idea of a lack.

We also saw that feminist critics identify sources of female empowerment and equality in texts of popular culture. Based on the assumption that many texts of popular culture embody a way of thinking and communicating that inherently favors patriarchy, feminists look for alternative forms of texts that are more grounded in feminine patterns of local, democratic experience. And we saw that some feminists look for texts that present a view of the world from the female experience of the body in a grounded way as opposed to patriarchal texts that encourage abstractions. One offshoot of feminism and of political activism that we studied was queer theory.

The fourth perspective we examined was the *psychoanalytic*. This perspective is grounded in the psychoanalytic idea that a person's *desires* are always being *repressed* in socially acceptable ways and that repressed desire accounts for much of our motivations at an unconscious level. Fundamental

desires that are repressed in childhood account for especially strong motivations, and among these, the repression of sexuality has a particularly powerful impact. Feminist criticism takes up at this point, focusing on the ways in which fundamental differences between males and females are defined and ordered by different cultures, especially a *patriarchal* culture that oppresses women. Gender differences, we discovered, are encoded in signs, with *phallic* signs both expressing and perpetuating male dominance. We discussed some controversies over the extent to which those differences are natural and unavoidable or created by cultures and thus manipulable.

The fifth perspective was concerned with *visual rhetoric*. We learned that visual images are focal points of meaning attribution; that is to say, they never generate meanings or references automatically or necessarily. Instead, images work much like language. They have a structure that affects the ways in which people read meanings into them. And, as with language, images may then become sites of struggle over meaning.

However, because the meanings of visual images are *relatively* less constrained than are the meanings of words, visual images can become the focal points of community and collective memory. A picture of a widely known leader may be acknowledged as a leader by people who do not agree on the meanings of leadership they attribute to the person. People may hold the sight of a great house of worship as the center of a community even if the specific beliefs held by people, beliefs grounding meanings, vary widely. Images and monuments may become the center of loosely connected collective memories because the visual does not require the specificity of linguistic signs and can thus accommodate a much wider range of meanings. We learned the importance of point of view, as texts position readers to see the world in

(*Continued*)

(Continued)

ways that empower some groups and disempower others.

The sixth perspective reviewed was the *dramatistic/ narrative* method. This wide-ranging school of thought is grounded in the idea that for humans, the use of signs is our fundamental reality and source of motives. Thus, the vocabularies, or *terministic screens*, by which we order our world are an especially important object of study for critics. The tendency of signs toward their perfection, or teleology, is one characteristic of signs that generates motives. We noted the importance of studying the type, or *genre*, that texts belong to. In particular, we learned about Kenneth Burke's theory of how hierarchy is maintained and guilt kept at bay through the related narrative structures of *comedy* and *tragedy*. We also reviewed Burke's *pentad* and saw how texts may be studied as if they were keyed to act, agent, agency, scene, purpose, or some ratio among those terms.

We turned finally to *media-centered* criticism. We noted that a *medium* must be understood as both a technology and the social uses to which that technology is put. The idea of a *media logic* calls the critic's attention to the inherent characteristics of a medium and how habitual use of a given medium creates distinctive ways of thinking in an audience. We identified three media to study for their logic: *television, handheld devices*, and *computers and the Internet*. Focusing particularly on the medium of *television*, we identified three characteristics of its media logic as *commodification, realism*, and *intimacy*. We saw that texts on television can be studied for the ways in which they reflect, or embody, those characteristics of the medium itself. We thought about the logic of handheld devices that allows for *connective power* and *context mobility*. We identified three characteristics of the computer and Internet's media logic as *fluidity, speed and control*, and *dispersal*. The effect of those characteristics upon the textual experience of shopping was studied as a way to understand how media-centered criticism pays attention to the effects of the medium itself.

Looking Ahead

In the Looking Ahead sections of the first three chapters, we formulated specific questions. Here, only one question really remains: How does the critic use these perspectives in actual critical practice? In Part II of this book, you will read some critical studies that apply the methods and techniques you have been learning to actual texts of popular culture. Thus, you will find several examples of how to "do" criticism. One thing you should note as you read these studies is how they make use of the ideas held by the different approaches to criticism described in this chapter.

Remember that no one study is limited or restricted exclusively to one approach. Your goal should be to explain the texts of popular culture, not to establish some sort of orthodox plan for following a prepackaged form of criticism. An approach to criticism that rigidly applies the terms of a single method or perspective to a text is sometimes referred to as a "cookie-cutter" approach. Always try to avoid an inflexible, cookie-cutter approach to rhetorical criticism. Instead, let the methods and techniques you have learned guide you in generating your own insights about a text. And as you read the following studies, note that while they are linked to the perspectives you have studied, they avoid a rigid application of the methods of any one perspective.

Chapter 6 applies techniques of the dramatistic/narrative perspective to a study of media coverage of two disastrous house fires in Milwaukee. We will see how some unavoidable characteristics of rhetorical texts themselves create paradoxes for how we talk about social relations. Chapter 7 uses psychoanalytic and visual rhetoric perspectives to study the rhetoric in the experience of attending gun shows. Chapter 8 uses culture-centered and feminist critical techniques in an analysis of the film *Groundhog Day*. Arguing that a major characteristic of American culture is a preoccupation with simulational experiences, the chapter studies the movie as a commentary on simulation. It also shows how attitudes toward women are struggled over in that text. Chapter 9 is a media-centered and visual-centered critique of the popular aesthetic and cultural phenomenon of steampunk. The chapter shows how some texts of steampunk manage power by subjugating individuals to state and corporate power, or on the other hand put that power within the imagined grasp of the individual. Chapter 10 combines dramatistic/narrative criticism and media-centered criticism with a bit of culture-centered critique to study the phenomenon of the "bad resurrection" in American life and culture, in which evil beings, objects, and events that we thought we had defeated and banished nevertheless return, more powerful than before.

APPLICATION

In this section of the book, we will apply some of the critical methods we learned in Part I. As you will see, sometimes a rhetorical critic focuses on one of those methods, and sometimes the critic will use a few in combination. Generally, the idea is to understand how the text influences people and to suggest an intervention if that is your goal. If methods are used in combination, they should fit together, and there should be a good reason for the combination. You will also note that we do not use every part of any given method. To do so would be to use a "cookie-cutter" approach, the lockstep application of a method without using good judgment as to what works. Let these serve as examples of how you might do your own rhetorical criticisms, for class and in life.

6

PARADOXES OF PERSONALIZATION

Race Relations in Milwaukee*

One idea that you should have gained from reading Chapters 4 and 5 is that criticism is *not* meant to be a cut-and-dried, lockstep procedure. You do not conduct, say, Marxist criticism by slavishly following the "five easy steps to a Marxist analysis." In fact, the best critical studies will be those in which the critical machinery is not too obvious. You should use the concepts and

*SOURCE: Adapted from Brummett, B., *Rhetorical Dimensions of Popular Culture*, copyright © University of Alabama Press. Reprinted with permission.

categories that a theory or method offers, but you should not feel that you cannot bend those rules. You want your reader to learn about your subject matter and the insights that you bring to that subject. When criticism too obviously announces, "Now I am doing the first thing you do for feminist criticism; now I am doing the second thing," and so on, its power to change people's perceptions is diminished. The real payoff of criticism is insight into what texts mean. Critical methods should serve that end.

Also, as we noted in Part I, schools of thought in criticism cross over into each other, borrow from each other, and often work well together. It can be unnecessarily limiting, therefore, to determine in advance that a criticism must be only dramatistic or only media-centered. On the other hand, some focus of attention is needed in criticism, too, so that the critic can help the reader to focus on certain issues.

In this chapter, the focus of the critical methodology will be largely *dramatistic/ narrative*. We will be concerned with some of the motivations that arise out of some of the operations that public discourse performs. We will begin by thinking about what happens when we personalize any important, wide-ranging social issue; in this case, the issue has to do with race and race relations. Since we cannot engage big social issues in their entirety, we must use textual, discursive means to approach the subject. Personalizing a current social issue is one way to do that: we turn an abstract issue into one we can personally relate to, and we do that through texts, through talking about it. However, when we personalize, that kind of discourse inevitably involves paradoxes that can derail our efforts to understand. This chapter illustrates dramatistic/narrative principles in that it looks at the textual, linguistic, and discursive mechanisms of personalization and the paradoxes that arise from that use of language.

Let me also note that the events occurring in this chapter took place some time ago. Sadly, the problems of race relations and the personalizations we use to approach that issue are ongoing. This study therefore illustrates how timeless rhetorical criticism can be, how relevant it is to long-term problems. I am certain you can hear today's news stories in much of the story that follows.

THE PROBLEM OF PERSONALIZATION

One of the most serious problems that democracies face today is a gap between the locations of democratic decision-making and the problems about which such decisions are made. Increasingly, events that powerfully affect individuals are occurring at an international level. For example, today, decisions about world trade tariffs made in the U.S. Congress may very well have profound effects on shoe factory workers in both Italy and Massachusetts. And the good people of Anytown, USA, may be asked to vote on the performance of their senator regarding arms treaties with Russia and human rights in China.

The average citizen is required to make decisions about a wide range of issues today. Those decisions are either made directly, as in voting on referenda, or indirectly, as in voting on the performance of elected leaders. In either case, the citizen must find ways to understand problems that may be distant (possibly even international in scope) and are likely to be extremely complex for that reason. Perhaps two hundred years ago, the citizens of Bent Whistle could concern themselves only with local politics and affairs. But those days are gone. A French conglomerate is thinking of building a factory in Bent Whistle, and if the citizens are to be certain about whether or not they want that factory, they must acquire an understanding of business and international commerce, environmental impact, and many other issues.

The challenge for the average citizen today, then, is to *personalize large and complex issues* in ways that make them understandable without distorting those issues so much that good decisions cannot be made. We personalize issues when we translate vast and impersonal problems into smaller, more manageable images, stories, and texts. Personalization, in other words, is a *strategy of textualization or narrative.* We understand the problems of the Middle East by seeing them compressed into stories about specific hostages who have been kidnapped, or by making certain leaders the embodiment of good or evil (depending on our politics). The kind of textual strategy that is used in personalization is called *metonymy*, or *metonymization*. Metonymy occurs when something complex is reduced to a more manageable sign of that complex thing, as when the complexities of British government are reduced to the public figure of the prime minister or the reigning monarch.

Any public issue is in principle personalizable (or not); whether or not an issue becomes personalized is an entirely subjective, perceptual matter. I may know that environmental problems are important but be unable to personalize that issue for myself; that is, I may be unable to imagine what ecological disaster would mean for me, what choices I might make now to undertake direct action (by stocking food or boycotting certain products, for example) or indirect action (by voting for senators on the basis of their ecological records, for instance). So I may avoid personalizing that issue and instead remain at the fringes of the issue, as a spectator.

On other issues, I may be motivated to personalize a public problem to a much higher degree. It would be possible to feel closer identification with war victims in El Salvador, for instance, if we shared the same religion. I might try to understand a conflict in Central America by personalizing it into images of its victims—by reading all I could about them and by forming my attitudes and opinions from stories about them. If we are able to personalize a distant and confusing issue, we are then in a better position to participate in decision-making about that issue.

In the United States, people have often personalized race relations. Race relations is both a vast and complex issue *and* one on which every person is required to participate in decision-making. Even whites who actually encounter African-Americans in the flesh no more than once a week may still entertain the most passionate and vocal opinions about them, while African-Americans and other nonwhites are understandably sensitive to the ways in which public issues near and far might affect their personal abilities to get and keep jobs, live comfortably and with dignity, and so on. And all of us "encounter" different others in media—film, television, Internet—on a regular basis. Ours is a very race-conscious society. The issue of race relations therefore provides particularly good examples of the ways in which large public issues are personalized or brought to more manageable size.

The personalization of race relations must be done textually, through discourse or narrative, by way of metonymy. Someone who wants to understand his or her place in any large public problem cannot have immediate access to the whole of that problem. Instead, that person looks for ways in which the problem is expressed in texts and narratives. Someone who wants to understand the problem of pollution cannot examine all pollution; that person must turn to texts that personalize pollution and express it in a manageable way. In this chapter, we will see that the strategy of personalization generates two troubling paradoxes. These paradoxes arise from the very act of personalizing vast, abstract problems; they arise as those problems are textualized and dramatized in metonymy.

The vehicle for our exploration of race relations in this chapter will itself be personalization, based on the author's experience. We will focus on race relations during the 1980s in the greater Milwaukee area and on the relative economic, social, and political status of African-Americans and whites living there. I am white and used to be a resident of the Milwaukee area. I lived in a western, largely white, suburb close to the center of the city, and I drove to work at a university on the other (eastern) side of town, situated next to another suburb. My route to and from work took me through the part of town in which most African-American residents of Milwaukee live (some 97.5 percent of African-Americans in the greater metropolitan area lived in the inner city at that time). Many of my personal friends were white (although many were not), so I could observe the general tenor of discussion in the community. My situation therefore paralleled that of many white Milwaukeeans; I was placed in a good position for understanding how many people in that city (or in other similar cities) might use texts to understand the large, confusing issue of race relations. Therefore, I will self-consciously assume the position of a white exposed to an average mix of texts in the city of Milwaukee, and I will attempt to show how whites might personalize race relations there. Although the incidents reported here happened some decades ago and in one particular city, many of the racial dynamics studied here are still with us, and not only in Milwaukee. You may think as we go about more recent parallels that you have experienced. I keep up with news from Milwaukee, and I fear that the news stories and the talk about them that we are about to study recur on a regular basis, even now.

In considering both the theory and the ethics of personalization, I will explore some paradoxes of personalization that arise specifically in the area of race relations (though I think these paradoxes may be generalizable to other public issues that entail personal involvements). I will focus specifically on the ways in which the complexities of race relations in Milwaukee were metonymized in the public discourse revolving around two disastrous, fatal house fires within the African-American community. One of these fires killed twelve people on the night of September 30–October 1, 1987; the second killed six people on the night of October 14–15, 1987.

I began gathering public discourse from the press concerning these two events and for a period of about two months kept track of stories with any mention of the fires, African-Americans, or race relations in general in Milwaukee. My research led me to take note of a great many texts, not all of them explicitly about racial issues, but all of them "fuel" for metonymizing complex racial issues. Most of my material is taken from the print media, especially newspapers. Although some television broadcasts are included in the texts I examined, logistical problems involved in obtaining ephemeral news broadcasts kept those texts to a minimum. I believe, however, that the printed material I gathered is representative of material found in other media as well.

Finally, I want to be very clear that the personalization—the metonymies—that I construct are from my assumed position as being representative of other whites; I do not attempt to say how October and November of 1987 looked to African-Americans in Milwaukee. Therefore, what follows is a reconstruction of how race relations probably look to most whites in Milwaukee; you may take nearly every sentence as preceded by, "In one likely white perception of events . . ." The conclusions I reach will be directed at how whites might reevaluate some of the ways in which we understand personal roles in race relations through metonymy and personalization. Let me now don the persona of the Average White Observer and begin.

THE SCENE AND FOCAL EVENTS

The context of race relations in Milwaukee is a particularly rich one, drawn from vivid memories and much public discussion of problems between African-Americans and whites. One does not have to live in Milwaukee very long to get a sense that African-Americans here face economic and political trouble, largely perpetuated by a white power structure, and that racial strife is a decades-old context for present woes. Longtime residents remembered the racial discord of the 1960s, in which actual armed tanks rumbled through the suburban streets and Father James Groppi led African-Americans on protest marches into predominantly white (and violently outraged) residential areas. Within the recent memory of residents was the controversial tenure of a "law-and-order" police chief who was notorious for organizing squads to investigate political activists and dissidents, especially civil rights activists. Within the two years prior to these incidents came indictments of numerous real estate agents for practicing racial discrimination by attempting to protect traditional racial boundaries between neighborhoods.

Problems in the African-American Community

Milwaukee's sizable African-American community was lured to this town of Germans and Eastern Europeans by the growth in industry in the 1940s and 1950s. Unlike African-Americans in other Northern industrial cities like Chicago, African-Americans in Milwaukee have no long-standing political base. Furthermore, the construction of Interstate 94 in the early 1950s destroyed the core of what had been a vital African-American business and residential area. Consequently, the failure of Rust Belt industry in the 1970s and 1980s has had exceptionally severe consequences for the African-American community. A Milwaukee Urban League study released during the period under study here details the resulting unhappy statistics: 77.6 percent of African-Americans born in Milwaukee in 1986 were born to single mothers, and 29.9 percent of the African-American population lived below the poverty line, with an unemployment rate of 25.9 percent (Cole; McCallister).[1] Furthermore, these figures do not reflect the widespread *underemployment* and inadequate compensation of those African-Americans who *were* employed.

---

[1] I have observed a special convention for references in this chapter. All of the articles here are so short as to be no more than one or two pages; therefore, I have not included page numbers in the citations within the text. (Page citations for all print references do appear in the bibliographic listings at the end of the book.)

In addition, residents of Milwaukee have available to them countless press reports of crime from the African-American community that seem to outweigh stories of disturbances anywhere else in the city. It is the policy of the major newspapers, the *Journal* and the *Sentinel*, not to specify race in any news stories unless it is relevant to the issue. But race is often implicated by other information provided in stories. Milwaukee is a "city of neighborhoods," a euphemistic way of saying that it is highly segregated. Therefore, any address from or reference to the north, near north, or northwest side of the city may be read as likely to involve African-Americans, while references to the south side (except for the near south, which is heavily Hispanic) and suburbs will suggest conservative, blue-collar whites and references to the east side will hint at more liberal, white-collar whites.

Also, Milwaukee's ethnic makeup is such that some names are highly identifiable as white names; Hyrniewicki, Czysz, Kuemmerlein, and Anagnastopoulos, for example, are names that prompt readers to view their owners as Central, Eastern, or Southeastern European in origin. In general, of course, no such marker exists for African-Americans, except for those few names that seem to have been associated somewhat more frequently with African-Americans than with whites in recent years (Jefferson and Washington, for instance, were two family names of persons killed in the fires) or names that seem to be chosen strategically as alternatives to traditional European names (Shanika, Shavonda, and Sharinda were names of children killed in the fires). Therefore, the seemingly neutral texts provided in crime stories are often racially marked or at least racially suspect and thus guide the ways in which people personalize the environment of race relations. If Anton Drabowicz runs amok with a meat ax on the south side, one is likely to read that as a story about a white. James Jones murdering his mother downtown is hard to peg, but Chavarte Jefferson assaulting his wife on the near north side will quite probably be read (correctly or not) as an African-American crime.

In sum, then, the media feature many crime stories that point—by way of location or, less often, by way of name—to the African-American community, thus facilitating the perception of African-Americans as living in a violent context. So it was around the time of the two fires in the fall of 1987. For instance, one story depicts a struggling family on the near north side in which the mother was found by the father shot to death; according to the father, "it was like walking into a nightmare, only worse" (Sykes). A picture some weeks later confirmed the race of the family as African-American. The continuation of this story on an inside page accompanies another story, with a picture, of an African-American woman who was slain at home ("Funeral Set").

News reports on the day of the second fire include a story about African-American suspects arrested for killing a white ice cream delivery man (Gribble) and another about Milwaukee Brewers' player Gary Sheffield, an African-American, who was arrested for drunkenness and violence in New York (Faust). Other prominent news reports around this time included renewed interest in a recent killing of an African-American child by African-American children in nearby Beloit (Ward), another story of a stabbing in the African-American community (Cuprisin and Lisheron), and the tale of a mother in the same neighborhood who was so incapable of caring for her children that she did not understand how to flush a toilet (Knoche). In short, the picture painted by the press about life among African-Americans is grim and unflattering. Thus, the social context for the period under analysis here is likely to be perceived as one of poverty, violence, and failure for African-Americans.

Violence against African-Americans

African-American crime and hopelessness did not make up the only ongoing story at this time. Violence and discrimination against African-Americans and other minorities by whites was also a prominent story. On the Madison campus of the University of Wisconsin, recent racial incidents had prompted a march by three hundred protestors (Esposito, "300 Protest Racism"). The issue was not resolved, and doubts persisted about the ability of the university administration to control racist fraternities and curb individual acts of racial violence (Jones, "UW Dean"). Other press reports (Jones, "Dean Defends," "Racial Incident") cited long lists of insults and attacks—both verbal and physical—on African-Americans and Jews in Madison, a town and campus that had always prided itself on its liberal atmosphere. One African-American parent was prompted to wonder in print, "Is my child even safe at that place?" and called the incidents in Madison an "unconscionable blight" on the state (Short). Also prominent in the news at this time was an ongoing attempt in the United States Congress to allocate reparations to Japanese-Americans who had been stripped of property while in internment camps during World War II (Cunibert), which added to the context of racial tension and white guilt.

The School System

Another important part of the racial context was concern over the quality of the Milwaukee public school system, which was widely perceived to be failing, especially in its work with minority students (Bednarek, "Education of Minorities"). A long-standing and costly lawsuit among several parties had raged for months over the issue of how to arrange court-ordered busing for integration. The suit was settled amid mistrust and suspicion on all sides during the two-month period studied, further intensifying the focus on racial issues (Bednarek, "Integration Lawsuit Settled").

Stockbyte/Getty Images

White Political Attitudes

A final factor in constructing the context for the fires is the taxation and social service mix in the city and state. Milwaukee and Wisconsin have traditionally been high-tax, high-service, liberal Northern polities. But an election the year before the fires had replaced a liberal Democratic administration at the state level with a moderate Republican one. This change was based largely on the mood reflected in a letter to the editor of *The Milwaukee Journal* complaining that middle-class people "haven't received raises in years and some of us have taken huge cuts in pay. . . . Without our hard work there would not be money for welfare, food stamps, or heat assistance" (Dlugi). Another disheartened taxpayer complained that "it just is very disturbing to me and my husband, as taxpayers who have worked continually for 32 years, to read in the newspaper about a 38-year-old woman who has 13 children and five grandchildren. . . . I am really getting fed up with going to work every day, paying my federal and state income taxes, and for what?" (Conrad).

This resentment of welfare recipients and the poor—specifically, resentment at having to support them in the midst of a faltering Rust Belt economy—led to such measures as Republican governor Tommy Thompson's "learnfare" proposal, which would have tied welfare payments to regular attendance by schoolchildren (Schultze). Although the plan was defeated by the legislature during this time (Gill and Romell), it highlighted the issue of public support for social services and an attitude toward the poor that was frequently expressed at the time. (A revised version of the plan was later passed.)

TRAGEDY AND METONYMY

Into this scene of texts featuring images of African-American oppression, failure, violence, disadvantage, and plain hard luck came two events that could serve as centers around which a text of race relations in Milwaukee could be written. The first was the worst house fire in Milwaukee's recorded history: Twelve people, ten of them children, died during the night of September 30–October 1 (Romell). Most of the victims were members of an extended family living in the house, though some were merely guests for the night. A little more than two weeks later, six children in a family were killed in another house fire less than a mile from the first ("Six Children"). In this fire, the oldest victim was a teenage sitter who was caring for five children while their mother was in the hospital giving birth to another child. The fact that all victims were *identified* as African-American (actually, five of the second set of victims were biracial; more on this in a moment), the close proximity of the houses, and the long-term economic problems of both sets of victims allowed the two fires to become a metonymy for the problems of African-American Milwaukeeans in general.

Metonymizing the Tragedies

It was clear from the start, even before the second fire, that the potential for metonymizing complex social problems through the image of this disaster was great. A newspaper report of the first fire clearly linked the general state of African-Americans in Milwaukee with these particular victims: "The pre-dawn fire Wednesday that killed 12 people, 10 of them children, is tragic evidence of Milwaukee's need to do something about decaying Inner-City housing and hard-core unemployment, officials said Wednesday" (Romell). A newspaper headline following the second fire further signaled a clear pattern of metonymy: "Diverse Social Ills Had Role in Tragedy" (Gill and Romell).

Soon articles discussing the trend among poor people of doubling up on housing, with resultant dangerous overcrowding, began to appear (Hajewski). Noting that "the similarities are chilling" between the fires—among them that "the families in both fires were on welfare"—another article referred to the deteriorated condition of inner-city housing (Kissinger). Some letters to the editor used the two sets of victims as symbols for the effects of Governor Thompson's cuts in welfare (Deshotels). Although it was apparently not the case that playing with fire caused either blaze, an article discussing pyromania in children also appeared, explicitly linking the two fires with a larger social issue in its statement that "many of these [pyromaniac] children come from chaotic families or single-parent homes" (Wilkerson).

Even articles not directly linked to the fires could nonetheless be incorporated into a metonymy insofar as they bolstered the distorted image of African-Americans as poor, wretched, violent, or victimized. One article reviewed the centrality of "suffering" in the lives of Malcolm X and Martin Luther King, Jr. (Kren). Another article described a group home for delinquent teenage boys, and the accompanying pictures showed only African-Americans (Norris). According to this article, these unfortunate youngsters seemed not to have much going for them: "Bill . . . is struggling with deep psychological hurt. Jerome uses joking to cover immaturity and insecurity. Robert angers quickly and is given to lying."

Telecasts concerning the second fire followed that story with one segment after another depicting failures and heartbreaks that could be read as hardships specific to the African-American community. Channel 12's story (*Ten o'Clock*) was on a "scared straight" program at a local jail, featuring footage of (predominantly) African-American inmates bemoaning their wasted lives. Channel 4 emphasized that the fires were within the same neighborhood, thus implicating the African-American community directly as a site of tragedy (*News 4*). Channel 6 (*News at 6*) covered the failure of the National Football League strike, including footage of its unsuccessful (and African-American) leader, Gene Upshaw. In short, it was apparent that the fatherless family configuration and economic suffering of the victims of these two fires were being used to symbolize widespread concern over illegitimate births, high crime, and welfare dependency within the African-American community.

Metonymy and Paradox

Let us consider metonymy itself a little more closely. Metonymy can be either positive or negative. For instance, a single person can be made to stand for whatever is good or bad about an entire group of people. Thus, metonymy is clearly a rhetorical strategy; indeed, it is one of the "four master tropes" explained in Kenneth Burke's *A Grammar of Motives*. When metonymy moves broad public issues into images of and about people, the metonymy has the effect of personalizing. When metonymy motivates individual actions and attitudes, it also serves to personalize. And when metonymy turns people into icons toward whom one may act, that is personalizing as well.

In short, the issue of race relations in Milwaukee became symbolized in the image of these particular fire victims, who became a set of signs around which all the other discursive texts of violence, economics, and so on revolved. Milwaukeeans participated in that metonymy by reading press reports or viewing telecasts and then formulating actions and attitudes for their own lives in response to what they saw and read; in this way, race relations became personalized for many white Milwaukeeans in the fall of 1987.

What happens when personalization occurs through narratives of metonymy? Some paradoxes are inevitably entailed when such metonymy takes place—paradoxes with ethical implications.

THE PARADOX OF IDENTIFICATION

Public problems often involve large groups of people, and to the individual person those groups can easily remain faceless. A nuclear accident in the Ukraine or a chemical accident in India is a terrible thing, but the individual American can easily remain aloof from such a problem that confronts people who are foreign and anonymous. The same is true of problems that the ordinary white person will perceive as afflicting African-Americans in Milwaukee. In the absence of close personal contact with an entire demographic group, the response to stories of hardship and crime is likely to be along the lines of either (1) "What's the matter with those people?" or (2) "These people are in serious trouble." Neither response, however, is likely to call up much personal involvement or action or any real understanding of the complex issues involved (though it may motivate calls for collective action; more on this in a moment). For the average white person, formulating some sort of response to the perceived problems of African-Americans is much like formulating a response to the problems of nuclear power, the destruction of the rain forest, or acid rain. Many such problems remain beyond the ken of individuals; that is, they seem too bewildering or complex for us to understand.

The complexities of drought and political oppression in Ethiopia remain beyond the understanding of most people, too. But television footage of starving Ethiopian children in the 1980s galvanized public response, motivating personal and individual action in response to a public issue. One of the most important ways in which contemporary public discourse metonymizes complex issues is by presenting them in images with which the public can *identify*. In *A Rhetoric of Motives*, Burke argues that identification fuels all motivation; showing the public the ways that they as individuals can connect to broad social issues is, therefore, a primary way of mobilizing motivation for individual action. When people identify, they make a link between the self and the other. That link also calls forward a political stance toward such larger issues as nuclear power, discriminatory practices in South Africa, and environmental destruction.

Identification and Race

So it is with the issue of race relations. To the extent that whites can identify with the travails of African-Americans, whites will be motivated to overcome their own racism. Clearly, then, identification is also a strategy with ethical implications insofar as it enables or discourages moral choices. As Burke reminds us, identification will occur if people see that they are like other people, that their interests are joined.

Resources for identification were present within the wider context surrounding the Milwaukee house fires in 1987. For example, much of the discussion over the racial incidents on the Madison campus of the University of Wisconsin at the same time offered the possibility of motivation through identification; a number of images of African-Americans and of their motives that enabled white identification emerged from that discussion. An African-American writer of a letter to the editor noted that the heartache of racism

> comes from your child's description of the knife held to his throat by a white bully in grade school. It comes from watching your baby struggle proudly to pronounce the "big words" someone painted on the front of your house during the night: filthy epithets! It comes from watching that person you love dearer than life get passed over and put down and treated as if her skin were the only part of her that matters. And even with these realities, your child still earns a 3.0 and he still makes the football team and he still beats out the others to play first chair in the high school orchestra. (Short)

It would take an alienated heart indeed not to identify with the universally relevant anguish and pride in that letter writer's powerful sentences. The racial problems in Madison were similarly metonymized in the plaint of Geneva Brown, a first-year student at the university: "To have someone physically threaten me just because I'm African American is something I've never [before] encountered" (Jones, "2 Stories"); most whites have also probably never before been threatened on the basis of their race. Racial problems are represented in Charles Holley's statement that racism "hurts down deep, because I'm a human being" (Esposito, "2 Stories"); it would, presumably, hurt whites as well. Similarly, the pain of racism is evident in this excerpt from an interview with California congressman Norman Mineta, a Japanese-American who recalls being separated from his family during the time of the World War II internment camps:

> "I didn't want to be separated from my parents," Mineta said, faltering. He had been recounting the story over lunch in the House members' dining room, but stopped altogether as he started to cry. Listening in, one of his young congressional aides also started to cry. The congressman composed himself. "We should have done this in the office," he said. (Cunibert)

These examples from the period under study illustrate the ways in which complex issues, such as racism on college campuses and reactions against Japanese-Americans in World War II, are metonymized into issues—the anguished parent, the frightened child, the shock of unexpected indignities—with which whites can identify.

But the particular issues that the victims of the two house fires stood for highlighted certain problems for identification through metonymy, which become clear as we move from context to more focused texts relating to the two disasters. Metonymizing a complex problem into a concrete symbol can give the public something with which to identify, but if the metonymy involves the strange, foreign, or frightening, it may also give the public concrete images that threaten identification. The first fire victims were presented in terms that placed them on the knife's edge of this paradox of identification. Enough facts about the victims were provided to allow a middle-class white audience to identify with them to an extent, yet enough difference (especially difference based in race) was still evident to forestall a complete identification.

Enabling Identification

Let us consider the texts that served as resources that *enabled* identification first. The victims of the first fire were portrayed positively and along many dimensions with which whites could identify. Morvay writes of one victim, "'Thomas was a church-going man,' his niece said." We are told that Thomas worked for the city, and a picture of a loving extended family is painted. We learn that the family spoke by telephone every evening with a grandmother in Miami. This same grandmother is quoted as piously avowing, "'I know God took my grandchildren and my daughter right on back to heaven. The Lord is too wise to make a mistake.'" And the distraught mother of two other young victims is quoted as saying what any parent would say under such circumstances: "'Let me go see my babies . . . just let me go. I've got to see them.'" Christopulos quotes another grandmother in mourning: "'Why couldn't it have been me instead of my poor little baby? . . . When I got there, I kept praying Anthony would be all right.'" A white audience can sympathize with such grief, and with the rudeness of a funeral home representative who interrupted the interview to force a card on the bereaved woman. We can also sympathize with the heroic efforts of neighbors to rescue the children, which were foiled by the intense flames (Romell).

Reports of the second fire also contained material encouraging identification by way of the children who died in the fire. All three evening news telecasts interviewed teachers and principals of the children, who gave sincere and positive praise for them, and printed news reports typically gave brief, upbeat biographies of each child (Ahlgren). Channel 12 focused mainly on the impact of the children's deaths on their neighbors (*Ten o'Clock*). One neighbor was quoted as saying, "'They need to do something for these kids, these people, or there're gonna be a whole lot more bodies to come get.'" This was the only station to report that neighbors could hear cries for help coming from the house, a horrible fact that must surely have drawn universal sympathy. Channel 4 (*News 4*) described the human face of "people who are stunned, who want to do something"—as the white audience surely would.

The metonymizing of human misfortune into heartbreaking images of children was the best chance for identification offered by coverage of the second fire. An older brother of the victims is quoted as saying at the funeral, "Each of them was going to be somebody. They were just beginning. Not a one of them had a chance for nothing" (Mitchard, "Rise Up"), displaying a kind of pride and sense of loss that people of all races could understand. Mitchard ("Grief Will Come") quotes a Sunday school teacher of the children who had seen them only that evening: "'The big kids were on the porch last night with the babies at 9 p.m.,' she said reasonably, 'and so they can't take them . . . you can't spare . . . you just can't. . . .'" The collapse of this woman's narrative into anguish speaks eloquently of the pain of losing children. Mitchard quotes another neighbor who showed the kind of shock with which many could identify when she said, "'It's a strange thing when children perish and you cannot cry. I would dearly love to cry, but I can't.'"

Other stories focused on the predominantly white firefighters who had dealt with both blazes, and the effects the fires had on them were forcibly presented to a white audience as the reactions they themselves might have had (Kissinger and Rummler). They quoted one firefighter: "All I could think of was 'not again.' It's harder this time, when it happens so close together." Gleisner, who had a nine-month-old son at home, said, "The first thing I did was that I went out and bought four more smoke alarms." Finally, a photo essay ("A Time") showed pictures of the funeral, of the lost children, and of weeping family members.

Forestalling Identification

But consider how fine is the knife's edge of identification, for texts that allow identification may quickly turn into texts that discourage it. Gilbert's story ("Fire Victims") of the funeral for ten of the victims, held in Miami, begins on a theme inviting universal identification: "A mother and nine young cousins killed last month in Milwaukee's worst house fire were laid to rest. . . ." But the story then moves on to a description of the funeral service that marks it as appropriate for a traditional African-American church service—and therefore unlike anything that most staid whites (and Milwaukee *is* heavily staid Lutheran and Catholic) observe on Sunday morning. Gilbert describes the funeral as "a searing service marked by raw grief and uncontrolled outburst" and "a roller-coaster, gospel gathering, elevated by passionate displays of faith and family togetherness." Whites are further reminded of the difference, or otherness, of these metonymized people by their nontraditional, non-Anglo names, such as Shanika, Shavonda, and Sharinda (Romell).

Many reports of the second fire also provided ample symbolic resources for tilting the paradox of identification in the direction of difference. Although there was much to spark white identification with the victims of the second fire through a metonymy of tragedy and loss, such positive texts were countered and overwhelmed by the spectacle of the victims' unfortunate mother, who was giving birth to her thirteenth child at the time of the fire. This poor woman and the family's general circumstances became a metonymy for white resentment of what is perceived as African-American welfare dependency, high illegitimacy rates, and other problems noted earlier. The family is depicted by Romell and Gill as "plagued by poverty"; their article chronicles a dreary history of the father of most of the children as an unemployed alcoholic and child abuser. The mother, Diane Washington, was a thirteen-year-old runaway when she first came to live with this man, and since divorcing him she had become attached to the father of the rest of the children, a man from Chicago who had been arrested on felony firearms charges. One child described the quality of life in the Washington family as "baloney and crackers . . . It wasn't all the time, but sometimes we ran short of food, you know." The family is described as moving at least once every year because of their inability to meet the rent. The mother is said to have no intention of marrying again. Her desperate circumstances lead her to describe her life in ways with which no middle-class white person could identify. "'I live the life I want to live,'" she is quoted as saying, "'and go and come like I want to.'"

This mother in particular became a symbolic lightning rod for white frustration stemming from the context of the fires, a metonymy for allegedly self-inflicted problems that befall many poor African-Americans. Ahlgren depicts Mrs. Washington as producing one child after another with reckless abandon and declaring at one point, "'Now I guess I'll quit. I have my football team and my basketball team.'" News reports noted that the family was eligible for government aid that could have paid their gas bill, but that for some reason this help had not been requested. Payment would have allowed the gas company to resume service, thus doing away with the need for the space heater that had caused the fire. Clearly, the implication was that the mother was not even capable of obtaining the welfare to which she was entitled (Kissinger; *Ten o'Clock News*).

Press reports concerning Mrs. Washington were riddled with seemingly unintended irony. The child born just before the fire was named Passion'ate Love (Mitchard, "Rise Up"), and Gill and Romell quote her as saying, in all innocence, "Like my mother told me one time, I made my bed; I have to lie in it." The temptation in both cases, for any reader not inclined toward identification with her, is to say in exasperation, "Yes, that's just the trouble."

As a metonymy for poor and helpless people, Mrs. Washington clearly encouraged reactions that were the opposite of identification. As one letter complained, "she loved children and wanted her own football team. I find my senses reeling! . . . The problems of poverty that embrace so many of our neighbors are certainly not helped by increasing the numbers of a family" (Richfield).

Another letter similarly noted,

> Diane Washington "loves" children and so do I. But how, in all justice to the children, can she keep producing while her children are at the public's mercy? Her 16-year-old pregnant daughter, with a 9-month-old baby, is following her mother's example. When will this end? (Tessler)

Resentment was also expressed in this landlord's complaint:

> There is absolutely no justification for 13 or 14 people living in a two-or-three bedroom home, using a penny for a fuse. You can rest assured that the landlord did not know they all lived there. (Thomas)

Mr. Thomas's letter is clearly metonymizing general problems into the images of the fire victims, for the actions he describes match neither set of fire victims; yet he is explicitly writing about the fires.

The Persistence of Race

An important dimension of the texts of race relations is the role of race itself as a fundamental category for classifying humankind. It must be said that in most of the United States, and perhaps in Milwaukee particularly, race is a factor that will always interfere with identification on the part of some people, no matter how much material there is to foster identification. Race is a marker of a difference that will make *all* the difference, and for these people, the racial category into which a person falls will color, so to speak, any and all of their judgments about that person.

At precisely the time of the second fire, unrestrained identification occurred with another child in dire straits, young Jessica McClure of Texas, who was being rescued from a well over the course of two or three days (*News at 6*). Although she was farther away, concern for this white child among white Milwaukeeans was undiluted. But as noted above, sympathy was not so unreserved for those involved in the two fatal fires. Thus, racial prejudice led to a judgment structured by the rhetoric of racial categories, illustrating the fact that in the United States today, *any* discourse with racial components is a discourse that will divide people.

Another interesting dimension of the texts of racial categories is that for many whites, and perhaps for African-Americans as well, an individual falls into the category of *African-American* for possessing any detectable amount of African-American racial makeup at all, sometimes for merely associating with African-Americans. In this case, the work of the texts of racial division is also extended to those who are white but who have very close connections with African-Americans.

In the case of the Milwaukee fires, there were two instances in which the public was allowed, perhaps even encouraged, to think of individuals as African-American because of their involvement with people of that racial category rather than on the basis of their own physical appearance or heritage. It turns out that Diane Washington, mother of the second victims, is identified (in only two instances) as actually being white (Romell and Gill; *A Time*). And Jill Schreck, mother of some of the first fire victims, bears a name that sounds German (in this town of German heritage); she also looks Caucasian in a picture published in the newspaper ("Survivor"). Yet the overwhelming sense created by press reports about the fires was that everyone involved was African-American—despite the presence of whites, and despite the fact that the children in the second fire were as white as they were African-American. Diane Washington's own identification with African-Americans puts her on that "side of the fence"; she is able to stand in for irresponsible African-Americans even though she is white. African-Americanness seems to be a difference that cannot be overcome by similarities.

The peculiar rhetorical insistence in the available texts upon the importance of the category of African-Americanness is also echoed in other news stories that were linked to the fires. On the very day of the second fire, a white Milwaukee alderman was convicted of accepting a bribe from an African-American attorney, a story carried immediately after coverage of the fire on all three television stations. And a newspaper article about the alderman's downfall at the hands of the African-American attorney (Bargren) appeared on the same page as (1) an article about African-Americans who had slain an ice cream delivery man and (2) a story about the firefighters involved in both disastrous fires. All three stories were continued together on the same inner page. In short, the introduction of African-Americanness into a mix of texts such as this turns it into a category which, for many whites, will be an insurmountable barrier to identification.

In sum, the identification engendered by images of dying children might easily have been outweighed by the persistent accumulation of press reports depicting Mrs. Washington as an irresponsible bearer of children at the taxpayers' expense—as the very epitome of the hopeless and incorrigible welfare mother. In the case of the second fire, metonymy may have countered, rather than furthered, identification. Metonymy is thus a risky strategy for motivating personal involvement in public issues. If you make what is abstract, or far away, more concrete through images of a child, a fire, or a welfare mother, you either court identification with the image or you risk the confirmation of your audience's worst fears about "those *other* people."

The person attempting to metonymize complex issues into an understandable text is therefore faced with a choice about how to see "those people" and how to place ourselves in relation to them. This is an ethical choice insofar as it concerns how we treat and define others. When we metonymize, we are responsible for the outcome. Identification is therefore not a passive occurrence but a chosen action, and management of the paradox of identification is an ethical choice.

THE PARADOX OF ACTION: THE PUBLIC AND THE PERSONAL

We have been considering connections between broad public problems and personal implication in those problems. To move from the public to the personal requires a risky metonymization that may, in the end, scare the personalizing individual back to considering problems impersonally; the person might then see problems as interesting but not personally relevant, just as we might know, for example, that election results in France will affect us in *some* way but not in a way that will motivate us to see any kind of personal involvement in the matter. Another route of movement from the public to the personal can be seen in the distinction between public initiatives or legislation and individual perceptions or action. It is one thing to think to oneself that "there ought to be a law," another thing to go out and actually do what one thinks needs to be done, or to alter one's deep-seated opinions and prejudices. You might think that the state should finance soup kitchens, for example, but simply *thinking* that is different from volunteering to work in a soup kitchen. The latter is a form of personalization.

The two fires in Milwaukee often called forth the first, nonpersonalizing kind of response in the form of demands for legislative action to address a particular problem. The city council quickly passed a law requiring landlords to maintain smoke detectors in rental property, and U.S. senator Robert Kasten fired off a letter to the newspaper announcing legislation to help the poor heat their homes in winter (Kasten). And around the same time, in response to the racial incidents on the Madison campus, a plan to grant free or reduced tuition to minorities was introduced (Deger).

But the disasters also called forth texts that enabled personalization, urging specific personal action and a change in attitudes. One writer of a letter to the editor, who was from an almost entirely white suburb and bore an Eastern European name (Jankowski), described her own experience as a volunteer at the second funeral; she also called for individual involvement in the long term, writing, "We as a community should experience the grief and work toward improving Inner City life so this need not happen again."

Personal Action and Loss of Vision

The paradox of action lies in the fact that the shift from public policy to individual action can sometimes be accompanied by a loss of the political vision, available at a broad and public level, that should guide individual action. To think in terms of broad sweeps of history, of the relations of large groups of people, and of economic and political trends, is to think in terms of underlying *causes* for misfortune and oppression. Institutionalized racism, for instance, is not something that can be grasped by looking just at this or that specific example, isolated instances that can almost always be rationalized on a case-by-case basis. Institutional racism is grasped by thinking at precisely the level of broad, public issues, to see how thousands of acts of oppression (by the police, by the class system, by the schools, by other institutions) cumulatively take their toll in shaping broad patterns of social relations. That is a kind of understanding that simply cannot be grasped if I restrict my vision to a particular African-American woman, no matter how many insults and slurs she may suffer; one cannot understand her experiences as embedded in broad patterns of oppression unless one backs off to connect her experience with that of millions of others.

The paradox at the broad, public level is that political action and involvement can then take the form of simply "letting Congress do it," thus refusing individual responsibility and involvement. The paradox at the level of personal decision and action is that such involvement may proceed in ignorance of the broader forces that have caused problems to occur in the first place. And the risk of that kind of ignorance is that it can turn political action and involvement into patronization. Action directed toward those less fortunate than ourselves, if uninformed by the *causes* of those misfortunes, can turn into a kind of "alms-giving" that soothes our consciences but blinds us to our implication in those causes for misfortune. The paradox of action, then, can threaten to paralyze us, preventing the ethical choices involved in metonymizing complex issues into the personal.

The Paradox in Milwaukee

One can see this paradox occurring at the level of individual action and attitudes in Milwaukee. A representative anecdote of such a paradox is the story of a white woman who was going to buy some cigarettes with two dollars and heard of the second fire (Gill and Romell). This woman went directly to the neighborhood of both fires, knocked on the door of a complete stranger, and gave the two dollars to the African-American woman who answered the door as a token of her concern. One can sympathize with the motive for personal, individual action in response to this tragedy, not as an isolated instance (in which case the donation would be irrelevant) but as a metonymy of long-term racial problems. Evidently it was the metonymization of social problems into particular people living in a specific neighborhood that gave the cigarette smoker a place in which to act. But one can also read in this story (though I found no direct acknowledgment of it in the newspaper article) how patronizing the woman's action was—how little it cost her, how proud she may have felt about her "gift," and how that gift may have served to blind her to her own involvement in the broader forces that led to the fire in the first place.

Of more concern, however, is the implication of African-Americans themselves in such patronization. For it turns out that the African-American woman favored with the two dollars was touched by the gesture: "That $2 meant more than the smoke alarm legislation," she said (Gill and Romell). The paradox is that on the one hand, the public policy action of the smoke alarm legislation stands a good chance of saving lives, yet it invites no personal action to overcome problems; on the other hand, the personal action of giving two dollars may seem more involved, but it is also too easy and leads to an avoidance of uncomfortable questions.

A similar example reported at about the same time described a white man who sought to do something to help untrained and jobless African-American teenagers. He hired a skilled African-American carpenter to remodel inner-city houses while simultaneously teaching his skills to those teenagers. On the surface, it seems like a worthwhile, concrete action on the part of the white man. Yet it was reported that "Wigdale [the white man] believes that young African American men don't have enough role models and recognized one in Coleman [the African-American carpenter]" (Lynch). Disturbing questions arise in response to such a statement: How can Wigdale know what it's like to be a "young African American man"? Who is he to judge that Coleman would make a good role model for the young men? Will Wigdale then hire those young men once they are trained? What responsibilities for African-American joblessness must be borne by the construction industry in general, and how might Wigdale's actions allow him, and others, to overlook those responsibilities?

African-Americans "In Need of Help"

The paradox of action at the personal level is intensified by news reports of African-Americans "in need of help," particularly reports that portray such help as coming *not* from African-Americans themselves or from within African-American culture, but from the white community. One telecast concerning the second fire (*News 4*) featured an older brother of the victims who turned directly to the camera and instructed the viewing audience to avoid space heaters at any cost. He claimed personal responsibility for having turned off one of the smoke alarms and absolved the white landlord from any blame in the fire. Such claims, even if true, hide the broader forces, such as unemployment and substandard housing, that led to this family's problems in the first place.

Even more pointed was an interview during this time period with a group of African-American students who were attending a predominantly white school on the south side of the city, far from their homes. One student described her previous, neighborhood school as "too roguish. It's bad." Another said that teachers in predominantly white schools "are more educated," while another claimed that predominantly African-American schools are "a lot of trouble" (Gilbert, "Blacks Count"). The message of this interview was that African-Americans are *in need* of whites, an attitude that intensifies the patronizing stance of some who would become personally involved in racial issues. Within such a context, even those arguments for self-help made by African-Americans themselves become fodder for those who would focus more on the idea that help is needed. As one African-American leader is quoted as saying about his own culture's statistically lower performance on tests of academic achievement, "it has nothing to do with ability. It has to do with work. We watch more television than anyone else in America" (Mulvey).

The specter of African-Americans "in need of help" extended beyond Milwaukee in the discourse available at the time of the fires. During this same time period, Michael Jackson's album *Bad* was released, as were numerous publicity photos depicting the startling changes that had been wrought in him by cosmetic surgery. In short, Jackson's appearance had taken, since his early days with the Jackson Five, a marked turn for the Caucasian. Guensburg reported the shocked reaction of African-American teenagers in Milwaukee: "He looks like a ghost. He looks like the bogeyman" and "He's lost some of his soul." Famous African-Americans such as baseball player Ozzie Smith were quoted as saying, "I don't mind a guy trying to look different, but Lord, there's got to be a limit." African-American psychologist Diane Pollard noted, "I find it psychologically interesting. It's really eccentric behavior. It does send a negative message about being African American" (Guensburg). An accompanying article described Mr. Jackson's eccentricities, including sleeping in a hyperbaric oxygen chamber and attempting to buy the bones of the "Elephant Man" (De Atley).

Stories about Michael Jackson, like the story about the African-American teenagers attending a white school, portray African-Americans "in need of help"; such stories also suggest that African-Americans get that help not from themselves or their culture but from whites and white culture. Such an undercurrent supports a stance of condescension and patronization by whites who might become personally involved in racial issues; in turn, any action taken by these whites becomes a missionary involvement—a stooping to conquer, a "giving of alms" to those who have no other resources. Such is the stance created for those who would metonymize racial problems into images of desperate, incompetent, or eccentric African-Americans who seem incapable of succeeding without white help.

SOME SOLUTIONS

The problems of identification and action, and the paradoxes one encounters when attempting to personalize broad public issues, are complex. Such problems are closely connected to the ways in which people order the world for themselves. Certainly, other people may be constructed as "like me" or "unlike me," thus aiding or hindering my identification with them. But because people are complex sources of texts, the ways we construct others as like or unlike ourselves include how we construct stances, or roles, for others and for ourselves.

Let us now consider how the paradoxes of identification and action may be minimized through a conscious awareness of how people, whites in particular, understand the general public problem of racial issues and construct a personal role for themselves within those issues. I believe that with this set of problems, as with any others, an awareness of how we use the texts of popular culture—and of *other* ways in which we might order our experience—is liberating and subversive. And as argued in Chapter 3, that is the highest calling for the critic and teacher of rhetoric: to make people aware of both how we now, and how we might in the future, understand complex problems (in this case, those revolving around race relations).

Reciprocal Personalization

Racial issues tend to be reciprocal. That is to say, what one says about African-Americans can and should imply actions or attitudes appropriate for whites. But that reciprocity does not always occur *explicitly, consciously, strategically*. What happens in the readings of the fires offered above is that the *fire victims* are metonymized as certain images, but those doing the metonymizing are not. Whites construct explicit positions for African-Americans as victims—as helpless, violent, and irresponsible—yet they construct no explicit positions for themselves. Whites are implicitly constructed, then, as patrons or superiors, as those who can give alms or advice, like benevolent aunts and uncles. Whites constructed Michael Jackson as a dancing bear, but they did not consciously see that they must reciprocally define themselves as bear baiters.

It is this willingness to metonymize others, combined with a failure to see oneself as a metonymy (a symbol of larger forces and issues), that contributes to the paradoxes of identification and action. In regard to the paradox of identification, for example, when others become metonymized images that are strange and different, the strangeness is always in relation to an idealized vision of the self that is very likely an unexamined one. To look to my own side of the equation or inequality requires me to "unpack" that vision of myself—to confront it and make decisions about whether I wish to retain it or not. The ethics of creating one stance or subject position or another are in that way brought to my attention, and I am able, then, to make a conscious ethical choice.

Metonymizing Yourself

In regard to the paradox of action, individual action is divorced from larger social issues if I refuse to see myself as acting as a metonymy, a metonymy in relation to the metonymy that I construct for African-Americans. For to see myself as a metonymy would require me to ask, "A metonymy of what?" With the particular issue of race relations, constructing a position for myself within a metonymy might lead me to see that I too am implicated in the social conditions that I metonymize into concrete images of African-Americans. Since those are the images that will guide and motivate my action, an awareness of my implication in them could preserve a useful tension between my own individual action and my social awareness.

Such an awareness, and such a tension, might lead me to realize that I benefit from reduced competition for adequate housing, for example. I also benefit from inadequate wages paid to produce the products I buy and the stores that I shop in. I benefit from the excess profits made at the expense of workers and the poor by companies, the stocks of which support my universities and retirement funds. I benefit from a pool of cheap, even desperate labor willing to do jobs that I would not do under any circumstances. Among some of the people I identify as family and friends are people whose racism contributes directly to the oppression of people of color. I have received the benefits of a disproportionate allocation of public school resources to the schools I attended and to the almost exclusively white college preparatory courses in which I was enrolled within those schools.

None of these reflections need lead to guilt on my part, since I did not cause or initiate the system that brought them about. These reflections should, however, spark a crisis of ethical decision about the extent to which I participate in reproducing such a system. I did not invent racist oppression, but I can become aware that I lie safely cradled in its benefits to whites. To see myself as having something to do with the death of more than a dozen people crowded into a house that burned in the inner city, and to see myself as implicated in some of the reasons why Diane Washington could not pay her gas bill and had to rely on a faulty space heater, can lead to a change in my ability to identify with the people involved in the fire. And it can also change the role of my personal political action from something designed solely to help *them* into something designed to help *me* as well.

Metonymizing Others

A second strategy for minimizing the paradoxes of identification and action is to metonymize more strategically, more carefully, and with more awareness. One of the prime ways to do so is to find images that correspond to smaller and more carefully differentiated groups. Very few of the press reports I studied during the period under analysis attempted to differentiate among African-Americans either explicitly or implicitly. Heightened public awareness of the problems befalling African-Americans in the inner city focused on poor, inner-city African Americans as stand-ins for a whole race, an entire demographic category. The overcrowded household in the first fire and the large and seemingly irresponsible Washington family in the second fire came to represent not just the limited category of impoverished African-Americans but African-Americans in general.

When one over-metonymizes in response to the two fires, such over-metonymizing exacerbates the paradoxes of identification and action. It is difficult to identify with entire social groups. If an entire group is metonymized with a negative image, the public is left with few symbolic resources for localizing the damage—that is, for understanding that the group is actually complex and that only one aspect of it is represented by the present image. Recognizing that such an image is limited can mean that failure to identify with the image will then not be read as failure to identify with an entire group; in this case, hope for future identification with other parts of the group may be kept alive. Action directed toward specific images or situations may be less likely to be turned into patronization if people remain aware that the action is directed toward a limited goal and that other people who are like the target of this action in some ways may *not* be in need of help, may indeed be in a position to give help as well. If my actions are no longer perceived as "helping African-Americans" but instead are understood as helping a specific group of people, then I am less likely to see my actions in a grandiose light. But I am also aware, then, that there remains a large group of other African-Americans, and the resources of African-American culture itself, that my actions do *not* affect. And those other resources may then be seen as vaster and more meaningful than my own efforts in this one isolated case.

Resources for Careful Metonymy

Some articles available to the public at the time of the fires did provide the potential for reminding readers of such differentiation among African-Americans and, consequently, of the potential for self-help and resourcefulness within the African-American community. A historical article by Donald Jackson describes an African-American dean at Boston University, representing a more restricted group of well-educated urban African-Americans, moving into an area of Beacon Hill (a neighborhood in Boston) that was populated by African-Americans in the eighteenth century. The move is a reclamation of African-American history, by African-Americans. Closer to home, St. Mark's African Methodist Episcopal Church in Milwaukee is portrayed as a strong, financially secure institution that serves the community and is a bastion of self-help and self-reliance within the inner city (Breyfogle).

As construction of images moves toward smaller and more differentiated categories, metonymy moves toward synecdoche—that is to say, from reduction toward representation. Synecdoche is a trope of representation rather than reduction. The Washington family as a metonymy of all African-Americans must always remain just that, a metonymy. But it may very well work as a synecdoche for poor, divorced, biracial families in the inner city, if that kind of representation is the only symbolic task to which it is put. Synecdoche gives way to metonymy when our images stand for issues or problems that, in their entirety, are too large to comprehend from any perspective. Breaking up those issues into manageable categories that can then be represented through synecdoche may be the best symbolic strategy to pursue.

STEPPING BACK FROM THE CRITIQUE

Let me now step back and become critically self-conscious for a moment: What good has this criticism done? If these reflections on the paradoxes of identification and action seem sensible to you, then your ability to see how some texts work in popular culture has been expanded.

Students want relevance in their education, though they may not often have an explicit desire to be *changed* by relevant education. From the perspective of rhetorical criticism, relevance in education has to do with showing students how they are constrained culturally in the ways they experience the texts that surround them. Relevance means showing students alternative ways to remake the world into something fairer, more just, and more equitable. Ancient rhetoricians trained their students to manipulate meaning in the forums of the day. Today, meaning is managed on many fronts besides that of the public speaking platform.

Meaning is managed by the people of Milwaukee as they read their newspapers and watch their televisions. How that meaning is managed will affect, I think, whether we sit passively and allow our experience to be shaped for us, whether we rouse ourselves to give two dollars to African-American strangers in the inner city, or whether we see the real possibilities for change in ourselves, in how we experience our lives, and in the worlds we make together. The equipment for living that you as students have is not neutral machinery. It is morally and ethically loaded, and critics who study how the rhetorical dimensions of popular culture work as that equipment serve as symbolic engineers.

We might also think of how the criticism in this chapter has used the dramatistic/narrative critical perspective. You will recall that the key idea to that approach is that discourse itself will generate certain motives as a result of how language or other signs work within the discourse. In other words, the dances and moves that words go through are actually what motivates the users and receivers of the words. In this chapter, we have noted that to personalize public issues requires turning those issues into discourse, or "textualizing" the issues. We have to talk or write about complex issues such as race relations in order to get a handle on them. But what happens in the talking or writing? When we squeeze real life into metonymies, what do the metonymies do to how we think about and react to the real-life situation? This chapter has shown how paradoxes arise, not just from "real-life" experience but from the textual, discursive act of metonymizing itself.

NOTES FROM A TEXAS GUN SHOW

This chapter makes use of two kinds of methods. The first might be obvious: culture-centered criticism. The chapter does that in complex ways. You may sometimes hear the expression "gun culture" applied to those who own, collect, appreciate, and use firearms in the United States. A central aspect of gun culture is the gun show. The chapter is also culture-centered in that it examines the specific culture of Texas and its relationship to guns, as experienced through gun shows. A second kind of method is visual. Note the use of images, the reporting and critique of what it looks like to attend a gun show, and the meanings facilitated by those images. With these two methods in mind, let's begin.

©iStockphoto.com/YuriyS

TEXAS AND GUN CULTURE

Gravel, concrete, and discouraged patches of grass turning to mud . . . an armada of pickup trucks and SUVs . . . men in denim and camo jackets. This is what you see as you drive up to Texas gun shows. You may find such shows offered on a monthly or bimonthly basis in cities and burgs all over the Republic. From Odessa to Houston, no matter the size and wealth of the city, the gun shows are pretty much the same. They will be in old, converted warehouses, failed K-Marts, third-tier local arenas. Faded paint announcing businesses of yesterday are covered over by big temporary banners declaring "Gun Show today!" The shows are remarkably the same. The look and feel of a Texas gun show reflects a consistency of the culture that supports them. What is that culture?

That culture, which just for convenience we might call gun culture, is as strong in Texas as anywhere else in America, maybe stronger. The popular image of the pickup truck with the shotgun rack over the rear window, of the shirt bulging with the concealed weapon underneath, of rifles standing inside closets and revolvers on the nightstand, may be more widely true in the Lone Star State than in any other. Never mind that some of that lore happened in Arizona or Minnesota; get on a horse with a gun, you are in Texas. This is the state where country singer Billy Joe Shaver could shoot a man in the face in a bar and get acquitted on what is popularly known as the "some ol' boys need shootin'" defense. How guns work in American culture may be well and fairly assessed by coming to ground zero of firearms and their culture, Texas.

Gun culture nationally, in an important sense, *is* Texan. When cowboys ride into the sunset on their horses, six-gun securely holstered on a hip and a lever-action Winchester housed in the saddle scabbard, when the wind whistles down the sendero and coyotes howl, when this vision plays out in movies, television, country-and-western songs, or daydreams, the location is Texas, never mind what the official plot says. Cowboys roamed the Badlands of the Dakotas and the prairies of Kansas, the OK Corral was in Arizona, but in a sense they were all Texans. The armed cowboy, the tall, lean sheriff, the desperado, the small rancher defending his land (it's always a "he"), these images all merge into Texas identities.

There are very few real cowpokes still around, and some of those may be found in Texas, but they are as rare as a live armadillo by a highway. Most people don't run into them much anyway. Oh, you can see the guy in the Levi's and Western-style shirt with the big belt buckle and the cowboy hat in stores and such, especially in the South and Southwest, but real cowboys doing cowpokish things . . . not so much. One can see movies—mainly old movies—of the cowboy life, and country-and-western songs still echo with the scream of the wild cougar, but to really be immersed in the fantasy that is the armed cowboy, one has few places to go. But you can go to the gun show to get as close as never mind.

Clearly, the gun is key to the cowboy image. The gun may morph into the black rifle of today's military conflicts, into the snub-nosed revolver of film noir or the various weapons of first-person shooter video games, but their common ancestor is the cowboy gun, whether six-shooter pistol, double-barrel coach shotgun, or lever-action rifle. Every modern gangsta film like *Scarface* is the shootout at the OK Corral in drag. Some people who collect (or accumulate) guns specialize in one genre or another, but I think most gun enthusiasts will have a variety of types. As dogs are all basically wolf, from Shih Tzu to Great Dane, so guns are all essentially where they began in modern form, and that is, especially in America, with the post–Civil War cowboy and buffalo hunter guns. What that means is that there is a unity of feeling and affect in guns, and resonance with one is at some level resonance with them all, of all eras and circumstances.

Probably the central gun culture consistency I want to stress is that the cowboy myth and its variations are all working class. Likewise, gun culture in the United States is working class. Certainly, people of means have firearms, but the popular imagination puts them in the hands of poor and middle-class working people. This is consistent right across the range of gun-representing popular culture. The cowboy in fact and on screen is not wealthy, in fact is little more than an itinerant seasonal worker. The marshall or sheriff is not wealthy and is likely to sleep in the back room of the jail. Rarely one will see a person from a wealthy or privileged background (e.g., in the film *The Ghost and the Darkness* [Hopkins]) connected to guns, but it is usually in a context of work and poverty (e.g., building a railroad in Africa). The title character in *Scarface* (De Palma) lives by the gun and become wealthy, but he begins life in poverty and his riches buy him only wretchedness. Guns in the American imagination—and I think likely in fact—are connected to the working class.

There are two paradoxes in gun culture today that I want to mention. The gun is deadly for real and in earnest; these things are meant to kill something, and they do. However: Hunting, yes, often. But people, bad guys, them varmints, not so much. When it comes to the killing associated with the cowboy (or gangsta, etc.) myth, the gun is a contradictory bundle of restrained potential. It fairly hums with the power for dealing death and the realization that you'd better not do that. For all the violence in the media, and in particular for people linked to the gun culture at gun shows, these instruments of death that are found everywhere hardly ever deal death although that's their main purpose.

A second, related paradox is that gun culture, in particular as found at gun shows, is both performative and simulational. By performative, I mean people are projecting an image. It may be a true image, but it's a carefully crafted image, just as the manager of an office may perform a managerial role. If you get up and put on certain kinds of clothing to project an image, if you walk and talk in a certain way, if you groom yourself in predictable ways, then you are performing an identity, even if that identity really is "you." And by simulational, I mean that much of the performance of gun culture is sort of like a video game in that it isn't "real." It's a simulation. You may be performing a cowboy, but odds are that you are not really a cowboy. This loops back to the idea that guns are deadly serious instruments of death but hardly ever used for that purpose on other people. The gun enthusiast who collects six-shooters and cowboy coach shotguns will never face down Wild Bill in the street, but be assured that a fantasy of doing so plays through that person's head regularly. The doomsday prepper who arms for the zombie apocalypse will likely never experience that catastrophe but nevertheless invests a lot of thought and emotion in planning and mentally rehearsing for it. These fantasies make gun ownership highly simulational.

Put these observations together with my claim that gun culture is working class and we see strong parallels between that class position and gun culture. Working-class people are likely to experience life in terms of frustrated potential, the first gun paradox I discussed above. Many of the working class think with good reason that they coulda been contenders, but circumstance and class restrictions prevented them from doing that. And when these working-class people go to gun shows, where they may display their tail feathers for their kind to see, it is the working class that they perform. This is true no matter how much they may have in the bank, and so often the performance of the working-class status is simulational. To participate in American gun culture, you need to be willing to project some kind of working-class image and perhaps even identity.

Everybody has opportunities to perform the dimensions of their identities that are most important to them, that seem central to who they are or want to be. Think of the gun show, in Texas or elsewhere, as a mini convention for performance and simulation of the cowboy, working-class identity. The old boys who go there perform their knowledge of guns. If they are veterans, they wear insignia to let you know that. Jeans, cowboy hats, gimme caps, belts with big buckles, Western shirts, the whole nine yards, you find it here. It would take special circumstances and a hard skin to show up at a gun show in a suit and tie; probably nobody would say anything to you, but you would know you were performing the "wrong" identity for this occasion. As people perform these cowboy identities, they do so in a simulated environment that is sealed off from the twenty-first century outside. Nowhere else will you find so many guns, knives, holsters, and scabbards or so much camouflage gear and clothing, military surplus, tooled leather, and the like. To enter the gun show is to enter into a simulation that, while you are there, is encompassing. By way of illustration, let me walk you through what you might experience at the gun show in Texas.

But first, who am I to be walking you through a gun show? I don't have the knowledge or discipline to say that I collect guns, but I accumulate them. I have more of them than I have years. I hunt. I was a Life Member of the NRA until I resigned over what I took to be its racist actions. I have a concealed carry permit in the state of Texas, and I carry whenever and wherever I legally can. As a youngster I dreamed of being a cowboy, a fantasy fueled by my father's origins in the panhandle, and was never without a cap pistol. I am a gun nut. You are in good hands.

AT THE GUN SHOW

I have never been to a gun show in a new, tidy, well-kept facility. Without fail, these shows are in minor, failing local arenas, or in defunct big-box stores and warehouses opened just for the event. Parking lots are fields of broken concrete. In a real sense, this is the lone prairie transferred to the context of cities and middle-sized towns (it seems not to be worth the while of gun show operators to hold events in small rural areas, despite the rural resonances of the cowboy image). It is a low-overhead environment entirely in keeping with a working-class sensibility.

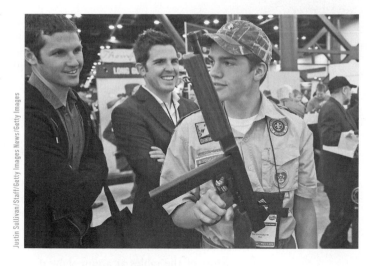

Justin Sullivan/Staff/Getty Images News/Getty Images

You park your car and walk through the rank-and-file of pickup trucks and utility vehicles. If gun show patrons own sports cars or hybrids, they don't drive them to the shows. Many of these trucks sport stickers and decals expressing memberships in sports or firearms clubs, conservative political opinions, or military experience. You will find a few men—and it's almost entirely men who come to the shows—in the parking lot coming to and from the venue, sometimes with sons in tow. Some of them carry guns they want to sell into the building; some are coming out with the day's haul.

People at the gun shows dress in working men's garb: denim, overhauls, cowboy hats or gimme caps advertising agricultural or firearms products, belts with enormous detachable buckles, and so forth. On the way in, a few take some last pulls from their cigarettes and leave them in the sand buckets by the entrance. Signs generally forbid even legal concealed carry, likely for insurance reasons since the clientele are surely offended by such notices. If there is an election pending, there will be campaign signs here and there as you enter.

You walk in and pay your fee, usually around five dollars or a little higher, and get your hand stamped as proof that you have paid so you can get back in if you leave the building temporarily. A table nearby is manned by police officers who are inspecting guns that people bring in, usually for sale or trade, to make sure they are not loaded. Here and there other police officers stand by, friendly and watchful—they seem not to be expecting any trouble.

And so you are in, and the world of the gun show lies before you like the pleasant land of Counterpane. Tables displaying goods for sale are laid out in long blocks stretching nearly the length of the hall. To work a gun show systematically, you start on one side and walk up and down between the blocks. Vendors sit in folding chairs within these blocks. They are there for the long haul and have brought coolers, boxes, and cases for selling their wares. Many have dogs. These vendors form a community within the community of the gun show. Most are friendly with one another; most will watch another's table if someone needs to go to the bathroom. They have paid a modest fee for the right to rent tables, usually for two days. Many of these men have wives or daughters with them, but it is predominantly a male group of vendors. If you ask a question of a woman, she may call to the man in charge. She is there mainly to take money and make sure nothing gets stolen.

Many of these vendors are federally licensed dealers. Some are ordinary citizens who may sell their guns legally so long as they are not making a living at it. Thus, you will find the fellow who is retiring, or downsizing a collection, or moving house, and wants to shed some guns, knives, gunleather, oddly assorted ammunition, knives, and such. The licensed dealers must follow all the rules any other dealer does, including requiring firearms buyers to fill out federal forms and wait while the information is phoned in to Washington. A private individual is not bound by these rules and may sell to anyone he thinks could otherwise legally buy a gun—but this assumption is never really checked on. This is the so-called gun show loophole, which is a misnomer. You may go next door in most states and buy a gun from your neighbor without having to pass a background check so long as your neighbor is not a licensed dealer. All a gun show does is bring together such private individuals for greater convenience of sale. It is in that sense a market but not a black market. The gun show is thus a mishmash of authority and legal constraint and individual citizen action on the edge of the law. In that sense, it somewhat resembles the Wild West.

Most of the tables at a gun show display—who knew?—guns. But many of them display knives, some mixed in with guns. There are some larger knife dealers with extensive displays of only knives, machetes, and so forth. There will be several tables displaying military surplus clothing and equipment: boots, jackets, vests. Some tables will have trays of surgical equipment, no doubt for sale to doomsday preppers equipping themselves for amateur bullet extractions. Some tables will sell holsters of leather or synthetic fabric for pistols or long guns. Some of these will sell bandoliers for carrying lots of readily available ammunition across the chest or in belts. A few vendors will sell books of militaria, cowboy history, gun lore, and so forth. Perhaps the most marginal of the vendors still linked to gun culture per se are those who sell bumper stickers and posters, all of them of a conservative bent—castigating President Obama, declaring an intention to shoot trespassers, and so forth.

A feature of every gun show I've ever seen, which I can't claim to comprehend fully, is the presence of distinctly non-gun vendors. Someone is usually selling roasted nuts or candy, jams, meat jerky, homemade honey, and such. Reliably you can find at least one vendor offering porcelain figures or women's jewelry, and a more out-of-place commodity for a gun show can scarcely be imagined. Are these gifts to take home to placate a spouse for yet another gun purchase? Are they an echo of the civilizing touch the schoolmarm brought to the frontier town? Your guess is as good as mine, but the consistency with which you find these unicorn vendors is remarkable.

The aisles between the blocks of tables are packed tight with gun enthusiasts threading their way slowly past the displays. This is no stroll through luxurious surroundings; it is more like the crowded saloons of the Westerns to which the dusty cowboy goes after a season in the wide-open spaces. Gun people are fond of repeating the old chestnut that an armed society is a polite society. We hope it is true, at any rate, but some attention to manners is required as one winds through these tight spaces. Every now and then passage must be created for a man in a wheelchair, maybe a veteran facing long recovery from wounds. One constantly begs pardon for the inevitable jostling needed to progress through the crowd. This physical proximity to others reinforces a sense that there is nothing fancy about those in attendance. You will never smell cologne. You will from time to time get a whiff of body odor or clothing that has been worn to work in. You will physically encounter people up close and personally.

If manners are expected to be performed while squeezing through the aisles, a more rigid code of conduct is in force for interaction with the vendors selling merchandise, specifically those selling guns. Sometimes these rules are expressed in signs that are posted; more often they are just commonly understood. Chief among them is that one should ask permission of the vendor to pick up a gun on display. Vendors selling guns, especially the licensed dealers, will have scores of pistols, rifles, and shotguns on display, sitting in boxes if new, sitting out on the table if used. It is considered bad form to simply pick up a gun and examine it. Sometimes it's not physically possible to do so because a security cable will be running through many of the guns and must be disconnected before an examination is even possible. One may be reprimanded if one forgets to follow this rule.

If the dominant performance of gun culture is working class, then it is white working class. That is by far the overwhelming demographic of the shows. Occasionally one will see an African-American or Asian. In Texas, one will see Latinos not infrequently, but still not in proportion to their share of the state's population. This demographic fact is consistent with the cowboy myth if not the cowboy reality. In fact, many historical cowboys were African-American or of Mexican heritage, but try to find those groups represented in classic Western movies. It's all white cowboys and their deadly enemies, the Indians, with the occasional tragic half-breed to spice up the plot line. I have never seen outright racism or microaggressions at a gun show, but the performative message is strong that this is a white-dominated culture.

The buzz of conversation at the shows is in earnest. Accents are Southern or Southwestern in Texas. Even in the North, accents will never be perceived to be upper class. Vocabulary choice also is working class, simple and straightforward. I don't at all mean to imply that people at the shows are unlearned; I am friends with a Mensa member and organization officer who frequents the shows and points out to me vendors from that group. It's that people express themselves plainly and simply. You will hear snippets of hunting stories as you walk along. Some buyers or vendors may be discussing hunting dogs they are training, selling, or buying. A few are growling out conservative political views, which is consistent with the bumper stickers and posters available at some tables, which dish up a fair bit of vitriol toward President Obama, the United Nations, Michael Bloomberg, and the like. These are good ol' boys, and they talk like that.

When you do hear a specialized talk with technical vocabulary, it will be in discussions of the guns themselves. Most of the men here, whether show patrons or vendors, have some kind of specialized knowledge of history, firearms, or ammunition. It is genuine knowledge, carefully assembled from a lifetime of experience and learning about the subject. You will hear historical stories of particular guns, of notable feats of marksmanship, of the use of certain guns in war or law enforcement or on the frontier, and so forth. You will hear the technical merits of different guns and cartridges discussed in exquisite detail. Some of this talk is the performance of expertise and knowledge, a display of mastery within a very specific field of knowledge. Here, the old and middle-aged are generally in their glory, drawing on lifetimes of experience and learning to create performances of expertise.

The gun show is an escape from restrictions and conformities of big business, in many ways. If one goes to a brick-and-mortar store for firearms, the selection is inherently limited. Most such stores will be stocking dealers for the big names in firearms manufacturing: Ruger, Browning, Glock, and the like. There may be many varieties of guns offered, but they will all be what is current and newly available on the market. Gun shows, on the other hand, draw private individuals who have combed through their closets to find old, strange, discontinued guns, obsolete cartridges, and so forth. The "kitchen table" licensed dealers who show up are always doing business on a much smaller scale than are their brethren in the big-box stores, and so they must supplement their stock in trade with a wide range of used guns taken in trade or purchased used from customers. In fact, you can always find customers walking the floor who are selling their own guns, and they wear signs advertising the fact. What this means is that the odd, strange, wonderful, and even legendary in guns, cartridges, and gear may be found at a gun show much more commonly than at a regular store. You will simply not predictably find an old Colt Peacemaker revolver in a regular store, but you can at a gun show. You will find obscure guns brought back from the European or Pacific theaters of World War II, or the Korean or Vietnamese wars, and you will be able to talk to the veteran who brought them back—but you can't do that at a regular store. The gun show is therefore a site of the unique, the individual, the storied. To reference a distinction made by Walter Benjamin, you will find guns that began as mechanical reproductions but have through age and history and association become nearly unique works of art (*Illuminations*). The gun show is a kind of museum, an archive, of individuality and uniqueness that I think can speak very strongly to the working-class individual who dreams of riding free through the Western wilds. It is a kind of escape from the regulation and repetitive drudgery of most workplaces today.

CONCLUSION

If I attend a gun show with someone I know personally from other contexts, I am always impressed with how that person and I manage to conform ourselves so as to belong to the crowd. Whether one is "fronting," though, I claim that the gun show is perhaps the most simulational and performative focused site in the country. A parallel example might be the annual motorcycle rally in Sturgis, South Dakota, in which all manner of upper-middle-class professionals perform outlaw motorcycleness alone with the "real" outlaw motorcycles. That is performative and simulational. But, for the most part, the gun culture crowd is always performative and simulational because those firearms are so rarely pulled out and used.

We may then think of the gun show as a great site of yearning: yearning to be a cowboy, a Texan, a rude mechanic, a member of the working class. People yearn to master the power and violence of the gun. They yearn to fling defiance in the face of authority. Yet none of this really happens at the gun show. It is highly performative and bound within the parameters of a simulation, much like Helmglot's apocryphal porpoise (Brummett et al.). It is a place where grownups can go to exercise their imaginations, but imaginations only.

Perhaps in some way this truth informs us of other dimensions of Texan culture. Much of what we do when we barbecue, ride pickups, wear the cowboy gear, pile our hair up like beehives, is a yearning for an identity that is hard if not impossible to actually achieve. The fatuous threats and hints that Texas may secede and become its own republic again are understood even in Texas to be so much hot air. This is Texas: We have our dreams, and they are strong ones, but the dreams do not always survive the morning light.

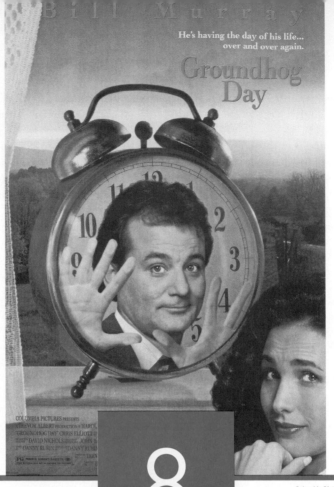

He's having the day of his life...
over and over again.

Groundhog
Day

8

SIMULATIONAL SELVES, SIMULATIONAL CULTURE IN *GROUNDHOG DAY**

W hen we discussed techniques of culture-centered criticism, we learned that any particular scheme of analysis uses only a partial list of the characteristics of a culture. Earlier in this book we also learned that cultures are complex and overlapping and may be defined in

*Source: *The World and How We Describe It*, Barry Brummett. Copyright © 2003. Reproduced with permission of Greenwood Publishing Group, Inc., Westport, CT.

different ways. In this chapter, we consider culture in a very broad sense that is nevertheless historically specific. Industrialized cultures with capitalist economies that have a heavy dependence on electronic media for entertainment—cultures such as those in the United States, Western Europe, Japan—share a significant characteristic, and that is that they are increasingly *simulational*. The simulational nature of such cultures, including the broad, national culture in the United States, affects how texts are understood and the impact they have. In fact, it is as a component of capitalist cultures today that simulation has become so powerful. Simulations are integral to these cultures.

SIMULATION

What do we mean by the simulational (Brummett, *The World*)? A simulation is an experience that is self-contained, referring mainly to itself. The classic case of a simulation would be a video game. To play a video game, you must enter the world of the game. There you will see many signs that have some sort of reference to objects, ideas, stories, and so forth outside the simulation, but the main purpose of these signs is not to tell you something about what is happening in that "real world." You may see a sword in a simulation, for example, and know that the image of the sword represents that cutting instrument in the real world. But the sight of a sword in a simulation is meant to be taken only on its own terms within the context of the game. Nobody assumes that it has reference to some real sword someplace and that you are receiving information about that sword.

A video game is a world unto itself into which we enter when we play it. When we are done, we turn the game off and it goes away. Anything that happens in the game stays within that little world. That sealed, self-referential nature of an experience is key to simulations. Because a self-contained world may be repeated over and over, the ability to make copies of an experience is also key to simulations. Hitting the reset button on a video game gives you a copy, if not of the same events, then of the same little world. You may have that same world over and over again as often as you wish.

A number of observers (Brummett, *The World*) have argued that a key characteristic of industrialized cultures, including that of the United States, is that they are becoming increasingly simulational. For instance, the enormous preoccupation with sports that one finds in so many countries today reminds us that a given game has to do with very little outside the game itself. Sports itself is highly political, but the games themselves are relatively simulational. What happens on the field or in the arena stays there and "goes away" once the game is over. Clearly, spectator sports are highly simulational today. People who live their lives for sports may thus be said to spend a lot of time in a simulational world. And to the extent that a whole culture is preoccupied with sports (Super Bowl, anyone?), we may say that simulation is becoming a cultural characteristic. Let us recall that although our fourth chapter focused on culture-centered criticism in terms of racial categories (e.g., Vietnamese culture), culture need not be seen as defined exclusively by color.

Similarly, a lot of leisure environments are created these days that are little worlds unto themselves. Theme parks, water parks, amusement parks, even shopping malls are environments we enter and enjoy while we are there, but they have little connection elsewhere and outside. Inside the simulational environment, little else matters. When we are done, we leave the world with few consequences. The ability to have roughly the same experience reliably, as copies, is a big part of the appeal of these simulational environments.

A society that is engrossed in entertainment generally may be said to be simulational. Think of the encompassing nature of movies, for instance, with lavish special effects and surround-sound systems. A little world is created into which we enter, and whatever happens in the theater has very little effect once the film is done. And if you go see the movie again, you will see an exact copy of the experience, which is simulational. In short, we live increasingly in simulational environments. Film in general gets more simulational as its technological excellence increases. We are only a few years away from the *Star Trek* holodeck.

This chapter studies a film that rhetorically critiques the simulational nature of culture today, and thus we need to look at it with an understanding of that cultural characteristic. As it makes that critique, it also has some things to say about how women are regarded, and especially how women might be regarded within a simulational culture. The movie studied, *Groundhog Day* (Ramis), is not a new one, but it is evergreen and well worth watching if one has not seen it. This chapter thus combines *culture-centered* and *feminist* techniques of rhetorical analysis to study the message this film brings us about our simulational world. From a feminist point of view, the film offers female empowerment as an antidote to an obsession with simulation.

SIMULATION AND *GROUNDHOG DAY*

Clouds roll across the sky, taking shapes in which one can see dogs, elephants, or what you will. Clouds are among the earliest venues of simulation for us, pictures that are not pictures, shapes that morph into other shapes. These instruments of fantasy stream by in fast motion, animated by cinematic technology.

What better way to begin *Groundhog Day*, a film that depicts and critiques the never-ending loop of a life into which a self-centered denizen of postmodern culture has magically fallen. This film suggests that many of us are Narcissus and in danger of falling into that pool. Using the rhetoric of simulation (although never using that term), the film is a metaphor for a life of social disconnection and self-absorption. A simulational culture is built upon, and builds, the simulational self, the film tells us, and until we can break out of that self-referential loop, we are doomed to the same old, same old every day.

Pittsburgh television weatherman Phil Connors makes clouds his business. We find him doing a weathercast with animated gestures in front of a totally blank blue screen. His demeanor suggests a fascination with high-pressure systems and a comradely bonhomie that seasoned television audiences have been taught to wink at. He stands in profile and talks about things that the audience, in reality, cannot see. It is not until the film screen fills with another smaller screen, that of a television, that we see the technologically created fantasy in which he works. A map of Pennsylvania appears where once we saw only blue, and it is busy with moving weather symbols. Connors mimes blowing, and clouds move in response across a map of the Northeastern region, an approaching storm in microcosm. An icon for a cold front appears, which he refers to as "one of those big blue things." Phil knows he is in a fantasy world. It doesn't matter to him, nor to us, for we are used to this simulation, we understand this world and its larger context: "Coming up next: sex and violence in the movies," says the news anchor. The media report on the media. This "news" will be no more real than the clouds.

The anchor reveals that Phil and a technical crew will travel to Punxsutawney, Pennsylvania, the next day, Groundhog Day, to report on the annual emergence of Punxsutawney Phil, *the* groundhog of Groundhog Day. Phil has done this several times, he tells the producer, Rita, and a hint of leaden desperation is clear in his voice. He has a running start on the repeating loop that the next day will become— and we may recall that endless, closed repetition is a characteristic of simulation. Phil will wake up the day after Groundhog Day and discover that it is still Groundhog Day—and similarly the day after and the day after. That is the whole premise of the movie: how do we live a day—a life—that is a never-ending copy? It is a question that a culture might face that is becoming deeply entrenched in simulations.

Off camera, Phil's good humor dissipates like a cloud, showing him to be bad-tempered, ironic, and cruel. He is especially and pointedly cruel toward women in this film. An important part of the rhetoric of this film is to link denigration of women with a simulational environment. As long as Phil lives a simulational life, taking nothing seriously, a major symptom of his malaise is that he does not take women seriously either.

Examples of Phil's bad humor, especially toward females, abound. He insults the anchorwoman. Phil's assistant weatherman promises him "excitement" in his trip to Punxsutawney, especially since he will be going with Rita, a new producer at the station: "You guys are gonna have fun," the assistant says, to which Phil sarcastically replies, "She's fun, but not my kind of fun. I won't be there for fun." Whether he has fun or not, the valorization of entertainment as the main issue in anticipating their trip is characteristic of a world of simulation, and it is linked to the insulting of women.

Phil and his crew pile into a high-tech van loaded with the latest equipment. Simulation often depends on today's advanced technology, and they have plenty of it— they are an ark of simulation. On the way, Phil complains bitterly about their assignment and says, "Someday somebody will see me interviewing the groundhog and think I don't have a future." That, of course, is precisely what will happen; Phil's confrontation with the groundhog will bend time from a straight march into the future to a circle turning back upon itself. Besides being a closed loop, a simulation is endless repetition, and so are both the annual emergence of the groundhog and Phil's pilgrimage to cover the event. The technician in the van fondly recalls earlier assignments in which he covered the yearly return of the swallows to Capistrano, which he compares to the groundhog's yearly emergence. A template of endless return has been established, and Phil is going to join it.

Who is this Phil Connors, weatherman, who is heading toward a day that will cycle and recycle for what may well be decades, even centuries? He is the groundhog, Punxsutawney Phil, who comes back year after year. Punxsutawney Phil is, of course, a fantasy, a simulation. He is the "same" groundhog, and has been the same groundhog, for decades as well. The occasional deaths of the real, material groundhogs involved are irrelevant. There is no Phil IV, Phil V, or Phil XXIII. Every year, the reset button is hit on this particular video game, and the simulational rodent emerges from his den. This fate is awaiting Phil Connors. In case the film's audience doesn't get this equation, on the first day of repetition Rita will call a bewildered Phil by name, which prompts the response by two local men nearby, "Phil?! Like the groundhog Phil?" Another sign that Phil is the groundhog is that on the first, "real" Groundhog Day, as the officials prepare to open Phil's den, the film audience can barely hear the crowd chant "Phil! Phil! Phil!" But the next day, the first day of the repetition, the film audience hears that chant much louder— for now the crowd in the movie is calling to Phil doubled, man and rodent merged.

The Phil Connors who is about to enter the loop is a thoroughly unpleasant person. He is completely self-absorbed. All his conversation is about himself, his career, his prospects in life. He cares little for others and insults people habitually, carelessly. If he approaches women, it is for his personal gratification. His exploitive stance toward women is clearly linked to his heedlessness of consequences generally. The dominant trope in his life is irony, which detaches and distances him from others. This is the kind of life the film comments upon. Showing the dangers of such a life is the point toward which this critique of simulation is directed. *Groundhog Day* will depict self-absorption as simulation, and simulation as bad. It will connect both self-absorption and simulation with the mistreatment of women. It is only as Phil learns to turn out of himself that he escapes the cycle at the end.

Comes the dawn of Groundhog Day, and the camera shows the digital clock at Phil's bedside click over to 6:00 A.M. "I've Got You Babe" swells up from the radio, and two jolly, chatty radio deejays banter about the day and the weather. We are seeing the props for the temporary eternity that Phil will spend here, and intimations of an endless cycle emerge early: "It's cold out there," says one announcer, to which his partner replies, "It's cold *every* day; what is this, Miami Beach?"

Phil, lodged in a large bed-and-breakfast, goes downstairs to eat. Mrs. Lancaster, the kindly old landlady, says, "There's talk of a blizzard." Phil goes right into his television act, standing at right angles to an imaginary screen and gesturing, running through his spiel, the gist of which is to deny that there will be a blizzard. It is a telling act, for it highlights both the technological, simulational nature of Phil's professional life and the disconnection that his constantly ironic demeanor brings to his life. He is mocking the bewildered Mrs. Lancaster's well-meant social comment on the weather, but her polite comment will turn out to be more true than his mockery. Refusing that social connection, he then asks her if she *really* wanted to talk about the weather. She asks if he is departing that day, and he replies within the frame of his television discourse to tell her the changes are one hundred percent, as if giving a prediction of rain. We see the link between an age of simulation and an age of irony in the distance both create from real connection with others.

As Phil begins to move through the day, we encounter more of the pieces of the scene in which he will be trapped. Insurance salesman Ned Ryerson, who knew Phil in high school, accosts him on the street. Phil's first and instinctual response is to assume that people relate to him not at a personal level but in terms of his fame within the simulational world of television: "Thanks for watching," he tosses out, and keeps on walking. Ned will not be put off and begins ticking off reasons why Phil should remember him, punctuating each reason with "Bing!" Ned, like many members of the television public, like the film's audience, is so accustomed to living within a simulational world of special effects and video that he must provide sound effects for his discourse.

Arriving at the scene of the groundhog's emergence, Rita greets Phil with, "This is fun!" expressing a dominant value of simulation. Phil is rude to all and sundry. He behaves himself on camera: "Once a year, the eyes of the nation turn to this tiny hamlet in western Pennsylvania to watch a master at work"—as if it were the same groundhog, over and over, year after year. And off camera Phil the weatherman grumpily expresses that very sentiment: "Then it's the same old shtick every year." Back on camera, he lapses into his habitual, detached, ironic mode: "This is one time when television fails to capture the true excitement of a large squirrel predicting the weather."

The high-technology van heads back to Pittsburgh, but the scene quickly grows colder and snowier as they proceed. Eventually they are stopped just outside of town by state troopers who tell them that the road is closed and they must return to Punxsutawney. "Haven't you listened to the weather?" asks the officer. An outraged Phil replies, "I make the weather!" and once again goes into his on-camera act, gesturing at a nonexistent weather map and predicting that the storm will blow over, despite the fact that he is shaking with cold and dusted with the falling snow. He simply cannot escape what is clearly professional engrossment in a simulation, disconnected from the real blizzard that rages around them. Back in town at a gas station telephone, Phil gradually gets closed off from any outside reality: "Come on—all the long-distance lines are down? What about the satellite? Is it snowing in space?" Technology cannot free him from the closed world he is entering, nor can his manufactured celebrity. Pleading that the phone company must keep *some* lines open for celebrities and emergencies, he declares, "I'm a celebrity in an emergency."

At this point, a passerby with a snow shovel whacks Phil on the head; is this his entry into simulation? Is this the window blowing in on him that will send him to Oz? The film never says, and there is never a point of awakening from a coma late in the film that would bracket the endless cycle of Groundhog Days as a hallucination. The film gives a nod to this standard cinematic/televisual convention of putting a character into a simulation but refuses to separate that entrance into fantasy from everyday experience. In this way the experiences of Phil Connors that are about to unfold become a commentary on all our everyday experiences and a warning to be alert for their simulational dangers. Back at his bed-and-breakfast, a grumpy and ironic Phil is last seen heading for his room after a cold shower—which should have awakened him from unconsciousness if anything could.

Comes the dawn and the bedside clock is seen ticking over to 6:00 A.M. "I've Got You Babe" awakens Phil. Is the song speaking to his childish ego now? "They say we're young and we don't know, won't find out until we grow." He notices the similarity in this morning's radio patter to yesterday's and expresses it in technological terms: "Hey, storm boys, you're playing yesterday's tape." He clearly doesn't think much of their dramatic inventiveness. Phil anticipates their lines already and calls them out: "chapped lips!" But he soon starts to recognize the scenes he sees as yesterday's experience: "What the hell?" he cries upon seeing a snowless street from his window. "Didn't we do this yesterday . . . what day is this?" he asks a man on the stairs whom he encountered the day before. Mrs. Lancaster asks him the same questions and makes the same comment on the weather. In reply he asks, "Do you ever have déjà vu, Mrs. Lancaster?" On the first, real Groundhog Day he had told her that his "chances for departure" were one hundred percent. Today he is not so sure and responds to her query about his plans by downgrading it to eighty percent.

As he moves toward the broadcast site of the groundhog's home, he meets the same people—a bum, Ned Ryerson—and he steps in the same puddle of water. He tells Rita, "Something's going on; I don't know what to do." Rita asks, "Are you drunk or something?" Phil replies, invoking The Main Value of simulation, "Drunk's more fun. . . . I'm having a problem—I *may* be having a problem." His on-camera monologue begins more tentatively, with dawning awareness of his fate: "Well, it's Groundhog Day . . . *again*." The film quickly cuts to Phil back in his room that evening, still trying to phone out and being told that service will be restored tomorrow. "Well, what if there's no tomorrow?" he replies. "There wasn't one today." Any character in a video game might say the same.

The bitter truth is made clear to Phil as he awakes the next morning to the same day. Arriving at the groundhog site, Rita tells him, "You've got work to do." "No, I don't," he replies, "I've done it twice already." He tries to explain the situation to Rita later in a restaurant: "Rita, I'm reliving the same day over and over. Groundhog Day. Today." Nobody understands him. He goes to a psychologist who says, "I think we should meet again. How's tomorrow for you?"

This day will be pivotal in Phil's understanding of his simulational circumstances. Later, drinking in a bowling alley with Gus and Ralph, two down-and-out locals, Phil recalls an idyllic day he once spent in the Virgin Islands with a beautiful woman. "That was a pretty good day. Why couldn't I get that day over and over?" His stance toward his recurring day, just like his stance toward life, is entirely selfish and hedonistic. Fun is the only value by which he judges life. Phil poses a question to his drinking buddies: "What would you do if you were stuck in one place and every day was exactly the same and nothing that you did mattered?" Ralph burps, stares into the middle distance, and says, "That sums it up for me." It sums it up for many in the film's audience as well, who may be as detached, self-absorbed, and caught in a pointless loop as is Phil.

The conversation leads Phil to pose what may be the key question for the whole movie to these friendly philosophers: "What if there were no tomorrow?" One of his new friends gives the key answer: "No tomorrow . . . that would mean there would be no consequences, there would be no hangovers, we could do whatever we wanted." And one truth about what simulation really means dawns on Phil: "That's true, we could do whatever we wanted." Before long, he takes a first step in exploring this hypothesis by leading the local police on a merry, drunken chase in Ralph's car.

Why should a simulation appeal to people? Why would it be "fun" to live in a world without consequences, in which pushing the reset button or waiting for 6:00 A.M. makes all things new? What prompts the film's *audience* to escape real life and sit for two hours in a simulation? Careening around town in Ralph's car, Phil articulates a vision of control and order from which one might well flee into simulation's total freedom: "It's the same thing your whole life: clean up your room, stand up straight, pick up your feet, take it like a man, be nice to your sister." He runs the car onto the railroad tracks, police in hot pursuit. "I'm not gonna live by their rules anymore! You make choices and you live with them"—and in this last assertion he must be referring to real life because, as he will discover, you make choices in simulation and you need not live with them at all. Swerving off the tracks in front of an oncoming train, Phil knocks over a giant plywood groundhog on his way to crashing into some parked cars. If he is the groundhog, he has knocked any firm foundation out from under himself in his decision to live life without rules and consequences. He enters simulation in spirit as well as in fact. The police descend upon Phil and his friends, and his stance is still ironic: he orders hamburgers as if the officer were a waiter. Predictably, control and order reassert themselves. The final scene of this day is of a forlorn, doubting Phil behind iron bars.

But he awakens the next day to an awareness that his recklessness of the night before indeed has no consequences. "Yes!" he cries, pumping his arms as he springs out of bed and launches into a day of pure piggish indulgence, which at a spiritual level is exactly what he has been doing all his "real" life. The obnoxious insurance salesman Ned Ryerson gets punched out cold. We see no evidence at all that Phil showed up to give his on-camera monologue. He sits in a café behind a table groaning with piles of fattening, greasy food and tells an astonished Rita, "I don't worry about anything anymore." He begins a recurring pattern of asking women for information about themselves that he can use the "next day" to make it seem as if they have some connection from the past—all this in aid of seducing them. His only approach to relationships with others, given his new freedom, is selfish and manipulative.

A pattern begins in which Rita, the female lead in the film, becomes his sounding board for his troubles. Several times he will try to persuade her of the impossible situation in which he finds himself. Later in the film he will devote all his days to seducing her. The film positions the female in the empowered position of being able to validate his experience. It is only toward the end of the movie as Phil moves from attempts to control women to a more equal and loving relationship that Rita comes to believe him. It is that equality that will save him. The film thus positions authentic relationships with women as an antidote to a simulational obsession. In this way the film not only questions the culture's simulational obsession but offers a reexamination of attitudes toward women as a way to overcome that obsession.

©iStockphoto.com/ZargonDesign

The next day Phil puts his plans for seduction and exploitation of women to work, approaching a woman (Nancy) as if he knows her. He uses the information he got the day before to act as if they were in high school together. His strategies work. But we see his real desire; as they tumble about on the sofa, he calls her Rita both before and after he offers up this lie: "Nancy, I love you. I've always loved you." When he *does* make human connection, it is with the "wrong" person.

So for a while we pursue this rake's progress, beginning with the alarm at 6:00 every morning. The film never indicates that Phil dreams. Instead, he seems called from a sound sleep into wakefulness. But perhaps by beginning each new/old day by pulling Phil from sleep, the film presents its action precisely as if it were a dream; it is only on the last day that 6:00 brings a true awakening.

The film ceases to document each specific day's pattern of recurrence (for he will be here for years and years) and instead points to the fruits of his piggish labors: he robs an armored car because he has had days to study its patterns and pick the right moment of lapse in security. With the proceeds from this theft, he plunges even deeper into simulational fantasies: he buys a Rolls Royce and emerges from it dressed as, and imitating, a Clint Eastwood cowboy character, with an attractive woman in tow. Phil is playing out other simulational fantasies within his simulation, and perhaps the audience envies him. He is in a cycle of complete self-absorption and indulgence, which is the fate of those in simulations, the film would seem to say.

Turning his attentions to the real object of his desire, he asks Rita, "Rita, if you only had one day to live, what would you do?" She doesn't know how to respond, so he asks her an important question: "So what do you want out of life, anyway?" It is a question he needs to ask himself, since never-ending life is all he has, but he is squandering this opportunity and pursuing personal gratification and sexual seduction instead. He is seeking information about her personal preferences and longings as he did with Nancy and will use them in an attempt to get Rita into bed. The film continues to show Phil's dependence on women for wisdom and understanding, yet his inevitable failure to attain wisdom and understanding as long as he exploits women.

We begin to see one iteration after another of Phil's ever more manipulative strategies with Rita. He takes her to a bar and discovers her favorite drink, and so we see the same scene the next day in which he surprises her with ordering her favorite drink, but then he must discover her favorite toast, which he offers up the next day—and on and on. The audience, as is Phil, is treated to one copy after another of the same scene, each one altered only slightly as he attempts to get it right. We see calculating looks in Phil's eye as he salts away one new revelation after another about what will please and seduce Rita, to be used the "next day." At one point, ironically, Rita asks Phil, "There is something so familiar about all this. Do you ever have déjà vu?" Is the power of his simulation leaking over into her real life? Ever distanced by irony, Phil replies, "Didn't you just ask me that?" When, back in his room, she says that she should go, he applies to her the standards of his own life: "Where would you go? Why?" But sooner or later she detects his strategy every day and in each repetition: "Is this what love is for you?" Phil relies on a false rhetoric of reality: "No, this is real, this is love." Rita replies with the main truth: "Stop saying that! You must be crazy. I could never love anyone like you, Phil, because you'll never love anyone but yourself." We are shown a long, long series of failures for Phil to achieve his goal of seduction, metonymized by a quick series of slaps she gives him at the end of each day. Rita has named the very problem that keeps Phil in a simulational loop, and that may well trap a narcissistic audience as well: he loves only himself. An important way in which that is manifested is in his exploitation of women. The simulational closed loop of self-centeredness is clear to Rita, but it may be something experienced by many in the audience as well, and the film warns us of its consequences.

What would count as success for Phil in his pursuit of Rita? Even sexual triumph would not be the love, the personal connection, that would spring him from his prison. The burden of endless repetition with no real consequences weighs heavily on Phil. A close-up of the digital clock's clicking over to 6:00 makes the stroke of that hour seem like a massive wall falling, with appropriate sound effects. Phil looks haggard and desperate. Unable to orient his life to any meaningful purpose and unable to seduce the woman he really wants, he spends his days watching endless television, participating in the pointless, simulational cycle of recurring shows to which so many in the audience subject themselves. Sitting in a forlorn living room with a group of aged pensioners, he appears to know every answer to the quiz show *Jeopardy*—which earns him polite applause.

Anger at his simulational prison begins to take over. He tries smashing the bedside clock, to no avail. He gives his on-camera monologue in rage and bitterness, speaking of his own eternal repetition: "There's no way that this winter is ever going to end. As long as this groundhog keeps seeing his shadow, I don't see any other way out." What is it, to see one's shadow? In the context of this simulation, it is a preoccupation with the self and the self's dark representation. Note that the legend holds that if the groundhog sees its shadow, bleak winter will continue for six more weeks. Only if the groundhog does not see its shadow, is not given a token of itself and can thus look to other matters in the world around it, will there be an early spring.

But both Phils are still locked into the eternal contemplation of their shadows, so Phil Connors decides to take matters into his own hands. "He's gotta be stopped," Phil says of Phil, "and I've gotta stop him." Phil kidnaps the groundhog, steals a pickup truck, and leads the police on a chase to a quarry outside town. Phil Connors is still in the simulational world of fantasy, television, and entertainment, for he tells his victim, "Well, we mustn't keep our public waiting, huh? It's show time, Phil"—and drives into the quarry's abyss, plunging to the bottom in a fiery explosion. The rest is silence. But Phil has only ended until the tape can be played again. Phil despairs when he awakes, alive and well and back from the dead, the next morning at 6:00. There follow several ingenious attempts at killing himself, by electrocution, stepping in front of a truck, and leaping from an upper story. These suicides have no more consequences than do anything else he has ever done in this simulation.

So Phil tells Rita, "I'm a god . . . not *the* God, a god . . . I'm immortal." He shows her that he knows each detail of what will happen in the café they sit in, who people are, their sexual orientations and life histories, who will say what, when a dish will fall, and so forth. He knows *her* in detail and tells her all about her own life and hopes. But it all seems like yet another show, an artifice, to Rita: "How are you doing this?" she asks in wonder, as if viewing a magic trick. Phil replies, "I told you, I wake up every day right here, right in Punxsutawney, and there's nothing I can do about it." They spend the day together discussing his plight. Rita has a naïve view of how to see simulation: "Maybe it really is happiness," she says tellingly, for who in the film's simulation-sodden audience would not grasp for the same irresponsible existence? Who in the film's audience did not delight at Phil's ability to stuff himself without shame or to pursue seduction like a single-minded goat? It seems as if it ought to be happiness, but the film is showing us it is not; it is pointlessness because it is simulational.

Phil begins to feel some genuine closeness to Rita. As they sit companionably on his bed, Phil tries to teach Rita how to toss cards into a hat, and lets it be known that he has spent six months, four or five hours per day, doing nothing but perfecting this dubious virtue. "Is this what you do with eternity?" she asks. What else would he do, having tried self-indulgence and death? His greatest sadness, Phil tells Rita, is that she will not remember this day tomorrow, but "it doesn't make any difference. I've killed myself so many times, I don't exist anymore." Rita replies, "Maybe it's not a curse; just depends on how you look at it." It's an offhand comment, but key. She is inviting him to live his recurring life in a way that will break the simulational loop. She prepares to leave, saying it was a nice day. "Maybe if it's not too boring, we could do it again sometime," she says, not quite having understood Phil's situation. But tiredness overtakes her. She falls asleep next to him in bed, but for once he does not try to seduce her. It is an important first step in his recovery. He tells her sleeping form that she is the "kindest, sweetest" person he knows, and he expresses love to her, but she is asleep and does not hear. Awaking suddenly, she asks, "Did you say something?" But he only replies, "Good night." Phil has come close to breaking away from his self-preoccupation. But the words he has spoken that can take him out of simulation and into real relationship were spoken to a sleeper, perhaps one in a dream; he could not say them to a real person, fully awake.

The next morning he awakes again in the same day, but he has turned a corner. He walks through life with a new purpose, keyed to helping others, to reaching out of his loop into the lives of those around him. He gives money to a beggar he has passed thousands of times. He buys his crew coffee and pastries, is helpful and kind to them. He reads literature and takes piano lessons, learns Italian, masters ice sculpture, and is generally pleasant to everyone. We see the new Phil getting better and better at his piano lessons and sharing that skill with others.

The hard realities of the actual world begin to draw Phil out. He discovers that the beggar he has helped is doomed to die in the evening of that day from old age and long dissipation. He pursues many strategies to help the man, feeding him and even giving him mouth-to-mouth resuscitation when he finds the man dead in a trash heap. He takes the beggar to a hospital, but nothing helps; the Great Reality is too strong. "Sometimes people just die," says a nurse, consoling him. "Not today," Phil replies bitterly, although his resolve is still not enough to save the man. This confrontation with a reality beyond himself changes Phil even more. He delivers a stirring, eloquent on-camera monologue on life and winter that draws the entire assembly at the groundhog's den to gather around him in profound respect and admiration.

Phil now spends his days helping people, being on the spot to change tires for elderly women in cars, catching children falling from trees, giving the Heimlich maneuver to a man who chokes on steak every night, and playing the piano for parties. We know he has studied the pattern of the city and its residents for a long time so as to know when to be on the spot with a helping hand. Phil's new way of living is entirely selfless, for he cannot benefit from any of his actions. To some extent he is still stuck in a simulational loop, though, for his actions cannot ultimately benefit those he helps, either. The boy will fall from the tree again tomorrow, the tire will go flat, the diner will choke. Phil has not taken that last step out of himself to establish true connection with others. His simulational self helps but then moves on. He is a hit-and-run philanthropist. He has emerged from his own preoccupations but has not yet crossed over deeply into others' lives. It is clear that he has lived in this limbo for a long time, as he shows mastery of medicine, foreign languages, and arts to a degree that bespeaks decades or more of study.

Then comes yet another iteration of the dance held on the evening of Groundhog Day, and this time he dances with Rita as many people come up to thank him and praise him for the help he has rendered them that day; two of them call him "Dr. Connors." An astonished Rita asks, "What did you do today?" To which he replies, "Oh, same old, same old." A bachelor's "auction" ensues, and Rita bids all the money she has in her wallet to "buy" Phil. As they leave the hall, Ned Ryerson runs up to gush about all the insurance Phil has bought from him. "This is the best day of my life," he says, and both Phil and Rita respond, "Me, too." This particular Groundhog Day *has* been the best of Phil's life, for he is finally learning to reach out in real love to others. Phil tells Rita, "No matter what happens tomorrow, or for the rest of my life, I'm happy now, because I love you." This time he means his expression of love, and she responds, "I'm happy, too."

The next morning the clock ticks over to 6:00 and "I've Got You Babe" comes on as usual. The deejays inside the radio are stuck inside that musical loop. But Rita is lying in the bed with Phil! He's *got* her, his Babe. "Something is different," he says slowly. "Anything different is good. This could be real [pause] good." He is right, it is *real* good, and good because real. He turns to Rita: "You know what today is? Today is tomorrow. It happened. You're here." Her being there, the human connection he made and maintained, has pulled him over into February 3. Rita says that last night he just fell asleep; even his old plans for seduction were set aside. He asks her, "Is there anything I can do for you— *today*?" He is oriented toward another person and her needs now. And what he does for her today will be real, it will make a difference. They go out and he says, "It's so beautiful. Let's live here." And then, thinking again: "We'll rent for starters."

CONCLUSION

Groundhog Day enacts a rhetoric of simulation, showing the audience Phil Connors and his life as a mirror for so many of us. People today are preoccupied with self and selfish interests, obsessed with entertainment and its technological underpinnings, unable to make real human connection. That problem is particularly highlighted in terms of dysfunctional relationships between men and women. *Groundhog Day* is this predicament carried to its logical conclusion, a simulational paradise with no consequences in which total selfish piggishness is *possible*. But the film uses the most negative meanings of simulation to advise its audience that such a life, if possible, is not desirable. Nor is selfish exploitation of women by men desirable. The real harm of patriarchy and simulation, it argues, is loss of real human connection through inauthenticity of being, refusal of love, ironic detachment. And for a culture lost in simulation, the film advises a recovery of that connection and authentic being.

Although produced some years ago, the film continues to be popular and is widely available on disc and online. Just as its popularity has continued, so have issues of simulation and relationships between men and women continued to be important in American culture. The continuing popularity of the film may have to do with its relevance to these issues of enduring importance.

©iStockphoto.com/Ellerslie77

9

JUMPING SCALE IN STEAMPUNK

One Gear Makes You Larger,
One Duct Makes You Small*

Steampunk is an aesthetic style grounded in the Victorian era, or the age of steam. It borrows the clothing of that era, but what is most reliably distinctive is its use of a machine aesthetic based on steam engines, locomotives, and early electrical machinery: gears, pistons, shafts, wheels, induction motors, and so forth. The aesthetic was first articulated in literature during that

* SOURCE: "Jumping Scale in Steampunk: One Gear Makes You Larger, One Duct Makes You Small," by Barry Brummett; originally appeared in *Clockwork Rhetoric: The Language and Style of Steampunk*, edited by Barry Brummett, published by University Press of Mississippi, 2014.

period in the works of Jules Verne and H. G. Wells. The American West has contributed images to the aesthetic, many of them grounded in the revolvers, locomotives, and rifles of the second half of the nineteenth century. It has found common aesthetic cause with Goth style among young people. Steampunk images are found widely in the films of Tim Burton, such as *Edward Scissorhands* and *Coraline*, in the film and television series *The Wild, Wild West*, and in many iterations of the television series *Doctor Who*. In many ways, it imagines what our world might look like if the internal combustion machine had never been invented and instead steam power had been refined over two centuries. Steampunk thus makes use of public memory through its appropriation of images of the past, but it changes those memories in its rhetorical applications.

Steampunk has wide popular appeal, even among people who may not have heard that term. A Google search for "Steampunk" generates on average over twenty million entries each time. There is also a budding scholarship on Steampunk, some examples of which may be found in the online journal *Neo-Victorian Studies* (http://www .neovictorianstudies.com/). There are several studies on the subject, including Etienne Barillier's *Steampunk!*, Art Donovan's *The Art of Steampunk*, Jay Strongman's *Steampunk: The Art of Victorian Futurism*, and Jeff VanderMeer and S. J. Chambers's *The Steampunk Bible: An Illustrated Guide to the World of Imaginary Airships, Corsets and Goggles, Mad Scientists, and Strange Literature*. Here, I invite you to think about the rhetorical appeal of Steampunk. Steampunk is a unique popular culture phenomenon; it is also a unique opportunity for rhetorical criticism. The overall question arises, what rhetorical effects do Steampunk texts have for different contexts and audiences?

STEAMPUNK AND JUMPING SCALE

In this chapter, we will combine elements of the *visual rhetoric* and *media-centered* critical approaches with a nod to some *dramatistic/narrative* considerations. A recurring characteristic of Steampunk artifacts is that they often "jump scale" from the original grounding and size of steam engines and related machinery, and the process of jumping scale in this particular aesthetic form is usually visual. Often, scale jumping is accomplished either through manipulation of images or through the production of actual objects whose visual appearance, whether outsized or tiny, is key to the rhetorical effect.

Steampunk is conveyed through images in a highly visual medium. It is meant to be seen. Its practitioners are very much into cosplay conventions in which they dress up in Victorian trappings of factory or empire with the express purpose of being on display in public. Artists produced highly colorful, elaborate images of futuristic airships powered by steam, and so forth. Steampunk depends on the creation of visual simulations, that is to say, imaginary worlds in which the viewer can "get lost" in the image, becoming engrossed in the terms of the spectacle that is presented. For that reason, in this chapter we focus on the media characteristic of the visual that is the creation of simulations. A highly visual medium is designed to pull the viewer in as if she were actually there.

Steampunk imagines the steam engine grown tiny or huge. Michael Nevin Willard has developed the idea of jumping scale as a useful analytical instrument. "Whenever a place is constructed—both architecturally and socially—" he explains, "scale is also produced" (466). We see this on many levels: "Scale is open-ended and extends in an indefinite series of nested levels from the smallest scale of the body to the largest scale of the global" (466). Scale has rhetorical power, as those in positions of power, in designing public and private spaces, "produce scale that limits the extent of [the disempowered's] social activity and everyday life" (466). Therefore, to jump scale can be a way to challenge the social, physical, geographic arrangements made by people and institutions in power. Jumping scale is a way to claim a different identity and a different social organization from that which hegemonic power has assigned:

> Jumping scale is a process of circulating images of self and community that can be cast broadly to the rest of the social hierarchy. This is the basis for the production of larger scales that insure continued inclusion in, and ability to shape, urban spaces. (Willard 467)

Willard's specific concern is with urban skateboarders, who refuse the scale that urban planners have assigned to their activities and may be found skating in a wider, expanded space, in places forbidden to them.

Beyond the example of skateboarders, one can see jumping scale as a way to claim an identity and social construction, sometimes by the empowered and sometimes by the disempowered. The huge writing of graffiti in public spaces, beyond the scale of the human body writing on paper or a computer, jumps scale. The political leader who constructs enormous statues of himself, who speaks in halls and on podiums far larger than needed for the human frame, has jumped scale. The typical consumer delights in the arc of electronics development that produces telephones and computers and so forth that are by now so much smaller than their originals that they have practically jumped scale.

We see many examples of jumping scale in Steampunk. An eBay search for "Steampunk wristwatch," for instance, generates quite a few collections of tiny, used watch mechanisms and parts, evidently for use in making jewelry such as cufflinks (also for sale on eBay, or on Etsy). The watches themselves are made with tiny (often fake or nonfunctional) tubes, hinges, cogs, and other apparatuses copied from the era of enormous steam machinery. Such a search also reveals "skeleton" watches in which gears, levers, and springs that one may find on a much larger scale in steam engines are visible as the clockworks of these watches. On the other side of jumping scale, the aesthetic of a geared engine blown to enormous proportions may be found in the eponymous film *Howl's Moving Castle*. The film features a steam-powered machine that is as large as a castle. The Corliss Engine for the Centennial Exhibition in Philadelphia of 1876 was based on an ordinary-sized steam industrial engine (large enough on its own terms) that was blown up to tremendous, monumental size. This working engine could be walked through by those attending the Exhibition, and reportedly caused the faint of heart to swoon. Such an effect could not be achieved except through the power of visual images that facilitated a simulational experience in the viewer. The aesthetic for both the enormous and small images noted above is clearly Steampunk.

What is the rhetorical significance of jumping scale? How does it work rhetorically to influence audiences specifically in Steampunk? These are the questions I will address in this essay. To do so, I will engage in a close reading of several elements of the film *Brazil* that are clearly Steampunk and have jumped scale "up" to a size beyond the human, beyond the activities contained within them (Gillam). And I will examine some products offered on eBay that are explicitly identified as Steampunk but have jumped scale "down," shrinking the world of massive steam machinery to the human scale and below. Let me begin with a brief consideration of the aesthetic dimensions of Steampunk so we can know how to understand what happens when scale is jumped.

The Aesthetic of Steampunk

I have previously published a book studying the rhetoric of machine aesthetics (Brummett, *Rhetoric of Machine Aesthetics*). Unaware of Steampunk as a distinct aesthetic at the time, I described the aesthetics of what I call *mechtech*. Clearly, this aesthetic, although it goes beyond Steampunk, subsumes it:

> . . . a machine aesthetic keyed to gears, clockwork, lawn mowers, revolvers, pistons, hard shiny metal, oiled hot steel, thrumming rhythms, the intricately choreographed blur of a spinning camshaft, and the utilitarian shafts and pipes running through the steel box of a factory. (29)

Several dimensions of mechtech aesthetic are found in Steampunk (Brummett, *Rhetoric of Machine Aesthetics* 33–48). The first is a "dimensionality" of *depth and surface together*. One can see into a mechtech machine, can see its inner workings. I argued, "Mechtech dimensionality is the machine in context, gears and pistons within the frame of their housing, the dialectic between them being a part of the aesthetic" (34). Key to this aesthetic is *knowledge of how something works*, for "seeing past the skin and into its depth is a revelation, an epiphany, an avenue to knowledge" (34). Therefore, "as a path to knowledge, the dimensionality of mechtech is also a means to order. . . . Knowing what is inside something is an act of ordering what is inside" (34). One may not actually understand the engine, but the ability to see into it with depth gives the illusion of knowledge, and at an *aesthetic* level gives an illusion of understanding the machine. This illusion of knowledge may be understood as a kind of simulation dependent on manipulation of images.

Another dimension of the mechtech aesthetic is the sense of *personal empowerment* one gets from operation of a machine. Given the great potential for power in most mechtech—and Age of Steam—machines, the operator of the machine must perforce exercise a great deal of kinetic and psychological identification with the machine. Anyone who has operated heavy machinery knows the feeling of power that comes from merging with the machine, being as one with it, in a kinetic way that is rarely found when operating, say, a computer. Another aesthetic dimension has to do with the mechtech machine as object. It is an object of *precision*, its beauty is *geometric*; there is nothing ambiguous or biological about an Age of Steam machine. A steam engine, unless it malfunctions, does thus and so in precisely the same way each time. This is the ethos of the *factory*, which is the imaginary context for the mechtech machine, where efficiency and precise procedures rule.

The ideal of production in mechtech aesthetics is that of *fragmentation and precision*: the machine is designed to perform one part of a larger overall process of production, but to do that one function with great precision and power. Uniformity and reproduceability of product are important components of this dimension. Finally, in explaining the mechtech machine, I pointed out that machines are gendered with typical gender roles under patriarchy, and that the engenderment of the mechtech machine is *male*, with the persona of the operator being that of a *warrior*. Think of John Henry wielding a hammer. Think of the male driver of a battle tank. Having noted these aesthetic dimensions of mechtech, let me also point out that another kind of machine aesthetic I described as *chaotech*, or the appeal of the decayed machine, overlays much of Steampunk. There is a light wash of decay over the Steampunk machine as object. Many of them show or simulate signs of long use. They are just a bit rusted, just a little brown from age and pollution. Often, this chaotech dimension serves as the bona fides of actual use or its simulation; the machine looks as if it has been in hard use for a long time. The Steampunk machine is thus an aesthetic object of great power with a hint of corruption about it that may reinforce an aesthetic sense that it is a real machine that actually works. The corruption reinforces the sense of reality that is key to creating a simulational experience.

In sum, insofar as Steampunk machines are what I described as mechtech, they are sources of knowledge and personal empowerment, especially on a male dimension, and of the persona of the warrior. A Steampunk aesthetic is one of precision and great power at doing very specific tasks. Add to that a hint of decay, a whisper of rust and age as the bona fides of actual use, and you have the aesthetic potential of the steam engines, locomotives, old revolvers, and so forth that Steampunk borrows from the Age of Steam. I now want to take up the question, what happens to these aesthetic dimensions when scale is jumped? What are the rhetorical effects of a text that shrinks the Steampunk machine and its parts down to a human scale or below, to a scale of easy personal appropriation and use? What are the rhetorical effects of a text that blows up the Steampunk machine to gargantuan proportions, raising these aesthetic dimensions to monstrous size? I take those questions up first in an analysis of two Steampunk wristwatches and a set of cufflinks, and then in an analysis of scenes from the film *Brazil*.

One more observation before I begin, keyed to the dramatistic/narrative approach. In *A Grammar of Motives*, Kenneth Burke observes that the scene of an interaction, of a drama, is powerfully definitive of what happens and what may be found within it:

> Using "scene" in the sense of setting, or background, and "act" in the sense of action, one could say that "the scene contains the act." And using "agents" in the sense of actors, or acters, one could say that "the scene contains the agents." (3)

When we jump scale, we shift scene. In what follows, I want to keep in mind the idea that jumping scale down makes the human and human uses of objects the scene for "tiny" Steampunk. And jumping scale up makes the Steampunk machine or object itself the scene for the human and human actions. This distinction will prove to be useful in understanding the different rhetorical effects of jumping scale.

Jumping Scale Down

If you go to eBay and do a search on "steampunk wristwatches," "steampunk clocks," "steampunk cufflinks," "steampunk jewelry," and the like, you will find hundreds if not

Barry Brummett

Barry Brummett

Barry Brummett

thousands of items on offer identical or similar to those that form the texts I am examining here for jumping scale down. On this page, the top photo is of a pair of cufflinks I purchased from eBay; as you can see, they are old watch movements, case, face, and hands removed, otherwise very little altered other than to be glued or soldered onto a cufflink base. The middle and bottom photos are two wristwatches I purchased from eBay. These are works of art that are somewhat more manipulated than the cufflinks. They are actually working watches in a manufactured setting cleverly designed to look like Age of Steam engines and mechanical parts. The middle photo in particular shows tiny, entirely fake, hoses, gears, dials, metal tubes and the like as if the watch were powered by, or were part of, a tiny steam engine. Both watches are truly tiny, the watch face in the middle photo being smaller across than a dime, the watch face in the bottom photo being about the area of a nickel.

An aesthetic experience is more than merely representational; it is simulational. To hear the thunderstorm passage in the *William Tell Overture* is not simply to be told of a passing storm; it is to create a simulational experience for the audience. Nonprogrammatic music perforce creates a simulational experience, evoking emotions apart from direct connection to an external context. Aesthetic experiences are powerfully moving, and thus powerfully rhetorical, and this is in large part because of the highly simulational nature of the aesthetic experience. We take moving passages in literature not as factual references to war, love, loss, and so forth; we enter into the experiences aesthetically.

In this way, the aesthetic dimensions of mechtech machines, Age of Steam powerful engines, locomotives, and so forth are re-created simulationally through the visual power of Steampunk artifacts. When the Steampunk object jumps scale downward, through images it puts the power of those aesthetics within a frame of the human scale. Clearly, an engine the size of a watch face would in actual experience, were such a thing possible, make very little clatter, roar, and commotion. But the aesthetics of Steampunk jumped scale down to the tiny puts the power, energy, precision, and other dimensions of the large mechtech engine simulationally within the human scale and under the control, in the possession of, the human agent.

The aesthetic of precision in a mechtech/Steampunk engine is paradoxically amplified by jumping scale down. The dead clockworks in the top photo in particular show tiny little gears and cogs, all fitting tightly, all the works tightly packed into a small space. Even this dense array of mechanicals gives some depth of perception, as we can see into the machine somewhat even if we cannot understand how it works. A dense thicket of otherwise incomprehensible parts is made more comprehensible precisely by the shift of scale that puts the complexity of machinery into a tiny package that can fit on the human wrist. It is ours and we subsume it, which gives a kind of mastery over it even in the absence of actually understanding how a clock mechanism works. In our possession and shrunk to a scale where *people* are the context for the machine, the clock mechanism of the cufflinks gives a simulation of actual use. One is using it, even if only to close a shirt sleeve, and this aesthetic use is then a simulation of the sense of power that would come from an operator becoming one with a powerful, throbbing machine. Notice too that in the cufflink on the left in the top photo, a faint hint of decay seems brushed over the mechanism. This clockwork is just a bit rusted, not burnished as brightly as the one on the right in a place or two. A hint of use amplifies the simulation of a machine that is powerful and actually harnessing vast energy. A touch of decay tells us the machine has been used, and is thus usable, and that bolsters a simulation of power. The effect is then one of the power of the Age of Steam machine jumped down below the human scale and put at the simulated disposal of the human. The rhetorical effect is a feeling of micro-empowerment.

If the cufflinks in the top photo show a dusting of age and wear, the two watches in the middle and bottom photos have been on the railroad to Birmingham and back for decades. The bona fides of rust and use, telling of a "real" machine in real use, lie heavy on the scuzzy surfaces of these watches. Unlike the cufflinks, however, both are actually working watches. Battery run, they tell time perfectly. Thus, every time the wearer checks the time, the wearer is performing a tiny simulation of the merger with the machine that is key to the mechtech aesthetic. The aged appearance of each watch is, of course, entirely simulated. Although each is made by hand in limited lots, each is completely new. But the simulation created by the appearance of age is of a machine in long use, generating great power at the hands of the user for decades.

The aesthetic of surface and depth, of an ability to peer into the machine and achieve some understanding of its parts, is greater in the middle and bottom photos because they are more sculptural than are the cufflinks of the top photo. The actual watch part of the bottom photo is cantilevered at an angle up off the plane of the watch band. One wears it so that it sits at about a forty-five-degree angle facing one. One can see beneath and around the actual watch. The plane of the base for the watch, beneath it, is a simulation of hoses, tubes, pipes, steam pressure dials, and the like. None of these actually work, of course, but they contribute to a simulation that one can see into a machine and know how it operates. The watch in the bottom photo has hands that actually tell time, but the cogged, barred plate over the face makes telling the time quite a feat. One must peer from more than one angle, and discount the movement of the second hand, to make out that it might be 2:15. It's not an easy machine to use, and in that way simulates the difficult mechtech engine barely brought under the control of the operator. An effort must be expended, and the effort is then rewarded by knowledge. If the knowledge is of the time rather than of the engine that gives the time, close enough; a simulation of the mechtech engine is maintained. The watch of the bottom photo, in contrast to the complicated simulated machine of the middle photo, is fairly simple. An impression is created that the whole thing is one gear, a part of a larger machine pulled out and functioning on its own.

In sum, the sense of controlling and understanding powerful machines that one may obtain by mastering a mechtech engine is made easy, and brought within the scene of human operation, by jumping scale downward in the top through bottom photos. Simulations of tiny, workable parts—the fact that some parts *do* work, productively—and the appearance of age and use are simulated guarantees of an actual, productive, mechtech machine. Yet this machine, by jumping down in scale, is brought entirely within the scene of the human agent. In simulational rather than real terms, the effect is an impression that one has the power of the locomotive, of the steam engine, literally on one's wrist or in one's hand. The rhetoric of Steampunk aesthetics in jumping scale down is therefore bound up in simulations of empowerment.

Jumping Scale Up

Terry Gilliam's 1985 film *Brazil* is surely one of the most prescient movies ever made. Sixteen years before 9/11 and its aftermath, it depicts a society obsessed with terrorism, dominated by tyrants, where the greatest threat to life and happiness is an overreaching, inefficient, and highly bureaucratized government. Low-level technocrat Sam Lowry realizes that one Harry Buttle has been wrongly arrested, tortured, and killed on suspicion of terrorism—all caused by an insect crawling into the creaky works of a government machine, thus creating an error. As Lowry works to right this wrong, he himself, and the woman of his dreams (literally), themselves fall under suspicion of terrorism. Lowry is arrested and taken to the torture chamber, where the stress is too much and he loses his mind. Images of this society wracked by pollution, never-ending war, willing to settle for cheesy simulations and corrupt politicians, might be taken from today's headlines.

Steampunk images, grounded in a mechtech aesthetic, are plentiful in *Brazil*. The film is constantly threatening to jump scale up. Excess and hyperbole lie around every corner. Everything is bigger than it needs to be. Everything is clunky and mechanical, a society developed in a mechtech rather than electrical direction. It is eerily reminiscent of our world, deviated in the direction of Steampunk a few decades ago. First, I will review the ubiquity of Steampunk images in the film. Second, I will point to many cases of excess in the film, which are consistent with a theme of jumping scale upward, even if they are not technically such a move. Finally, I will point to the clear cases of jumping scale upward, and the meanings created by such a move.

Steampunk images permeate the film. If there is one image that dominates, it is that of the duct. Old-fashioned, clunky television sets in a shop window all show advertisements for ducts in the opening scene. Ductwork snakes through every room, every building. Ducts are all over the key Ministry of Works and the Department of Information

Retrieval. Otherwise elegant salons have ducts running through them. When walls and ceilings are cut into, coiled ductwork bursts out of them like the intestines of a beast. When Lowry goes back to his apartment after work one day, an apartment that has been sabotaged by a vengeful Central Works team, he finds it unlivable, festooned with ducts of every size and condition so that one can hardly move through it. The cleaning machines in the Ministry of Information are trailed by enormous long ducts.

Computers are mechanical-electrical devices; the screens are distorted magnifying lenses over small, old-fashioned television picture tubes. The keyboards of these computers are from old-fashioned typewriters, and one can clearly see into the works of the computers. But these works are unambiguously in a Steampunk register: pipes, hoses, tubes, dials, pressure chambers, and the like protrude from behind the keyboard and beneath the monitors. Often the monitors are held up by clunky iron brackets. Nothing looks quite new, quite shiny; these "electrical" machines seem at least as much mechanical, and they have seen hard use.

Clothing and decoration is from the late Age of Steam, reminiscent of a range from Edwardian times through the 1930s. The bureaucrats wear suits that could be found any time during that range. The clerk who manages the abduction of Buttle early in the film has an Edwardian bowler hat and a suit from that era. But the police all wear goggles, a key Steampunk accessory, and their uniforms are covered on the outside by pipes and tubes. The heating and cooling anarchist engineer, Harry Tuttle, is likewise dressed in clothing laced with pipes, tubes, and small ducts. When Sam dreams of himself as an avenging angel, his costume and wings are actually supported by a scaffolding of brackets and steel girders. Similarly, the secretary in the outer office of the torture chamber, typing the screams and cries of the victims as fast as she can, has her hands encased in a scaffolding of steel to enable faster typing. Clothing and the coverings of bodies are often clearly Steampunk. Living quarters often reference Victorian through prewar times as well. Old Mrs. Lowry's apartment is floridly Edwardian. Even the humble Buttle flat looks turn-of-the-twentieth-century. Central to the aesthetic of mechtech, shared by Steampunk, is the image of the male warrior, and the film is simply full of such beings, in gaudy and exaggerated military uniforms. The Ministry of Information's basement floor is populated by men in exaggerated Nazi uniforms. Women seem largely to have the task of shopping and getting elective plastic surgery. This is a male, and thus a mechtech/Steampunk, world.

The film is a riot of excess and exaggeration, which is akin to the spirit of jumping scale upward, even when scale is not actually jumped. Images of Steampunk of *ordinary* scale, or of other mechanicals, abound, and always just on the edge of bursting out of scale into enormity. The terrorist bombing campaign that is the context for the society of the film is in its *thirteenth* year, but they are still experiencing, as a deputy minister says, "beginner's luck." Breaking into living quarters to abduct residents, as with Buttle at the start of the film and Sam Lowry himself near the end, is way overdone: not only are doors rammed in but holes are cut through ceilings and police slide down firemen's poles as well as bursting through doors and swinging in through windows. Harry Tuttle, the guerrilla heating expert, comes and goes by sliding down buildings on a zip line instead of simply knocking on doors. Going to the Information Retrieval office for the first time,

Lowry observes a surreal stampede of bureaucrats following their leader at a run up and down the corridors of the building while he barks out orders at a staccato pitch. Horrific explosions from terrorist bombs are taken by the characters in their stride; the wounded and bleeding writhe on the floor while the Lowrys and their guests continue to dine in the restaurant that just blew up. In short, everything is just about to burst from absurdity, from excess. Even when the film is not jumping scale physically, it is doing so discursively with exaggerated and ridiculous scenes.

When the Steampunk images truly jump scale upward, the rhetorical effect is clear. The human characters are swallowed up in the belly of the beast, and it is a mechanical beast. Steampunk pushes your face in its mechanicals; when the mechanicals are gigantic, then Steampunk inserts the human into the aesthetics of Steampunk. The control, the power, the precision of Steampunk is thus ascribed to the state, and the person is consumed by it.

The Ministry of Information, which seems to be the very seat of government, is in a building that is enormous, monumental beyond all telling. In the basement of the Ministry are the biggest ducts of the entire film, watched over by the men in Gestapo uniforms. Twice Sam must creep along through this wonderland of fantastically large ductwork. Upstairs, walls of television monitors are found within the lobby, and it also crawls with machines of surveillance. These machines are clearly Steampunk, exposing their inner workings as much as any Tim Burton film does.

Sam Lowry rides in a ridiculous little car that is hardly larger than he is on an errand to the Buttles' apartment complex, and it is nearly run off the road by enormous, grungy vehicles fitted out with ducts, hoses, and pipes. It is in one of these vehicles that he attempts a getaway with Jill Layton, the woman of his dreams, and they are swallowed up by the obvious, visible mechanics of the gargantuan vehicle. Driving into the countryside, we see that the human scale is dwarfed by acres of enormous pipes, tall industrial towers, and huge storage containers, all of them as rusty and used-looking as the vehicles.

At the end of the film, Sam Lowry is captured and winds up in the mechanical belly of the beast. He is locked in a padded cell that is so huge we cannot see the ceiling. Then he is taken to the torture chamber, a wonder of Steampunk jumping scale up. The distant walls of this chamber look like the inside of a machine, and they show signs of industrial use and wear. Here also, the ceiling is so high we cannot see it. A single catwalk crosses acres of scaffolding out to the platform on which the victim sits strapped into a chair, machines and instruments of torture with their workings, hoses, pipes, and gears clearly visible. The victim is inside a machine, and the machine is the state. Such is the aesthetic power of this image that many of the victims die or, like Sam Lowry, lose their minds in fear and desperation.

CONCLUSION

Steampunk shares the aesthetics of what I have described as mechtech, an aesthetic of power, of knowledge of the means of power, of control and precise production, of male and military domination. Steampunk uses that aesthetic in two ways: it gives a simulated, entirely aesthetic feeling of dominance and mastery over that power when it jumps scale down and puts simulations of Age of Steam mechanics literally into or on the hands of people. And it cows, warns, and frightens the viewer when it puts the ordinary human into the jumped-up scale of truly monumental, enormous aesthetic simulations of that power, knowledge, mastery, and domination. The aesthetics remain fairly constant; the differing results come from the direction in which scale is jumped. Therefore, part of the news of this essay is to stress the importance of jumping scale, and the direction of the shift, in creating rhetorical effects.

This essay may have served to clarify some of the rhetorical effects of the aesthetics of Steampunk. I hope I have also illustrated the utility of thinking about shifts in scale, and the varying meanings that all sorts of aesthetics and simulations might have as they jump scale up or down. Further research might consider the effect of jumping scale on other aesthetics: Christian, Art Nouveau, and so forth. And further research might consider other examples of jumping scale in Steampunk, and the different rhetorical effects created by shifting scale in other contexts.

10

THE BAD RESURRECTION IN AMERICAN LIFE AND CULTURE

Our lives are patterned. Were that not so, we would be constantly exhausted by the pressures of adapting to constantly new situations and challenges. We could not rely on any habits, any previously successful ways of negotiating life. Life itself would be chaos.

We see the truth of that claim in small ways. If you move to a new city and find yourself driving on unfamiliar streets, you know how stressful that can be, until you fall into a "rut" of going to work or school, coming back home, and so forth. When you travel to a foreign country, especially if it is your first visit, you know how hard you have to work to manage the language, the money system, local customs in shops and on the street. Stay there a while and you find you are settling into some patterns that make life easier.

We might call these patterns forms. Forms in life help us get through the day. There are forms in texts also, as we discovered in the third chapter. We know how to communicate, enjoy music, watch movies, and so forth because very few such experiences are totally new each time. They follow patterns. Sometimes we know to avoid certain texts if we know we are not fond of the pattern running through it. These patterns may lie beneath the surface of a text—a surface we can call content or information—and cut across a wide range of texts even outside our awareness. Sometimes patterns are of types of texts like fairy tales, sometimes of certain patterns within stories, such as the recurrent pattern of Helmglott's apocryphal porpoise, which rises only to rise and rise again (Brummett et al., "NSFW"). There is a pattern in texts we might call the "Romeo and Juliet" pattern in which two lovers from very different backgrounds come together, often with disastrous consequences. Movies from *West Side Story* to *Avatar* and beyond embody that pattern. Yet how many people watching 2005's *Guess Who* (Sullivan) were consciously aware that they were watching the pattern of Romeo and Juliet?

The same patterns running across different texts may also run across real-life experiences. Perhaps some of you have experienced the Romeo and Juliet pattern in your own lives. Shared patterns are a major way to link texts with experiences. In fact, patterns in such cases may be a major rhetorical resource, because a text (say, a movie) that follows the same pattern that someone encounters in everyday life can rhetorically *advise* that person as to what to do. One movie following the Romeo and Juliet pattern may finish it out as in the original Shakespeare with death and destruction, thus warning you against such an entanglement in your personal life. Another might vary at the end into a happy ending, encouraging you to go out and find your Romeo or Juliet. A pattern that cuts across texts and experiences is called a homology. Some critics have made successful use of the idea of homology (Brummett, *Rhetorical Homologies*). Homologies are especially useful in helping a reader to think about hidden patterns, perhaps hidden just because they underlie so many different texts and experiences (Brummett, *Rhetorical Homologies*).

A homology is a formal parallel across different objects, actions, modes of experience, and so forth—depending on the sort of homology one is explaining. Mathematicians (Atiyah), literary scholars (Goldmann), anthropologists (Leach; Lévi-Strauss), and scientists (Lorenz) all use the idea of homology as a speculative instrument. Lévi-Strauss, for example, identified formal parallels among myths across cultures around the world. In my own book on the subject, one homology I identified was a shared formal pattern of *ritual injury* across professional wrestling, Laurel and Hardy films, tales of saints' martyrdoms, and so forth (Brummett, *Rhetorical Homologies*).

People identify homologies, although likely not by that name, in their everyday lives. It may seem to you as if your supervisor at work acts like a queen. That suggests a formal parallel between what your supervisor does and what a queen does. Many of us may identify family patterns recurring across generations and locations. Perhaps some of your relatives seem to act like queens as well. Note that these homologies are formal; they are patterns rather than assertions of literal equivalencies. You are not suggesting, probably, that your supervisor or grandmother goes around in an ermine robe and a crown as queens literally do (I suppose), but rather that a pattern of behavior connects how he or she acts at work to what we think of as patterns undergirding queenly behavior. In the same way, Robert Hariman's excellent study of political style suggests that recurring, formal patterns of behavior in leadership may be found across government, business, and beyond.

What is key in using a homology is identification of the mechanism creating the formal parallel. So widely different cultures share similar patterns to their myths: Why? What creates that homology? Different scientists and scholars will give different answers to the question about the homologies they study, depending on their disciplines and the conceptual tools they are using. Maybe myths share similar patterns because human brains are hardwired similarly; maybe because human experiences (life, death, the seasons, etc.) are fundamentally similar; maybe because linguistic structures recur in different languages. Different scholars of homology identify different engines of similarity creating those forms.

When one is studying a *rhetorical* homology (Brummett, *Rhetorical Homologies*), the mechanism creating the formal parallels is the nature of discourse. This idea is grounded in much of the work of Kenneth Burke. In rhetorical homologies, experiences and texts follow formal patterns inherent in language and its systematic use. Characteristics of discourse itself create a form that generates similarity across the variable content of different experiences and texts. Enough formal similarities among members of a homologous set must be established to persuade an audience of reasonable readers that a form rather than mere chance underlies the similarities. Once a homology is established, the critic can then dig down into some members of the homologous set to see whether new characteristics that are discovered may also be found in other members. In this way, homological criticism may be a way of understanding wide ranges of texts and experiences. For instance, if you find your supervisor's and a queen's behavior to be formally similar, then unpacking more dimensions of queens may suggest that you look for the same dimensions in your supervisor—and you may learn more about queens by digging down into your boss's patterns of behavior.

To pay attention to the form of a discourse is very much within the dramatistic/narrative school of thought in rhetorical criticism. It argues for the rhetorical power of the text itself, and of the forms within texts. Especially when the critic reveals a homology underlying texts and experiences in unsuspecting ways, dramatistic/narrative thinking can be powerful in helping audiences come to an understanding of how they might be influenced in ways beyond their conscious awareness.

Media, especially entertainment media, can play a major role in linking texts to experiences homologically, and that is because the media of film and television especially do not call their own operations to the audience's attention. Audiences are supposed to lose themselves in film and television, in the high-quality simulations they present, and so movies and television shows try to be engrossing to audiences without revealing their own constructed, artificial nature.

The main method used in this chapter is therefore dramatistic/narrative, and when we turn our attention to film, as we will a fair bit, we are also attending to that medium's ability to create engrossing simulations for people to enter uncritically. Thus, we use some media-centered method here also. The homology we will track down here I will call "the Bad Resurrection." I want to show in the pages that follow that quite a few texts and experiences in American life and culture follow a particular recurring form. The experience is common, but the form is likely out of the conscious awareness of most people experiencing it, whether in texts or in life. When studying a homology, it can be useful to pare the form down to its bare bones, its most abstract description. Then, armed with that description, the critic can show her or his audience how the form underlies the texts and experiences in which it emerges, and which it ties together.

So, what is the Bad Resurrection? To put it as formally as I can, there is some evil entity (a person, a spirit or demon, a monster, a group, an affliction) that threatens vast harm. Conventional authorities seem powerless against the threat. The threat must be opposed unconventionally. A small but powerful agent takes on the threat and appears to defeat it. But no matter how thoroughly vanquished the threat may be, there is a Bad Resurrection: it comes back, sometimes more powerful than before, and so the cycle must be repeated. I will show how, in American culture, this pattern underlies texts and experiences of cancer, terrorism, certain movie series such as *Halloween* and *Friday the Thirteenth*, and the *Fast and the Furious* series. In this list, if I mention an experience (cancer), there will be texts about that subject that follow the pattern. If I mention texts (*The Fast and the Furious*), it can be shown that those texts follow some common, shared experiences in American life. The one homology of the Bad Resurrection cuts across them and advises audiences on how to respond to the unpleasantnesses we encounter.

CANCER

Of all the diseases that people can get, cancer is one of the—if not the—most dreaded, and it is perhaps the disease most likely to recur. It is universally demonized and moralized. Susan Sontag argues that it is the foremost moralized disease of the twentieth century (*Illness as Metaphor*). If you hear that someone has lung cancer, or esophageal cancer, one is likely to ask what the person did to bring the disease on. In this sense, cancer matches other instances of the Bad Resurrection in that it is supremely evil, regarded as almost an autonomous threat, and is very much connected to moral issues. Sontag notes the persistent moralization of cancer at least throughout the twentieth century, and one could argue that this remains true today. Having cancer was in many ways thought to be shameful, a sign of some character flaw or moral failing. Your author's maternal grandmother died of ovarian cancer in the 1960s, and the family was strictly forbidden to tell her what was ailing her for fear that the shame would be too great a burden. We have

©iStockphoto.com/TommL

not far to look for other attributions of evil to cancer, such as, "But have you ever thought that there are cancer diseases caused by evil spirits? You may not believe it but there really is!" (Takano). Agency or planning, a prerequisite of moral accountability, is ascribed to cancer by calling it an "evil genius" (Walsh).

One may think of other diseases as cured or as chronic, but nothing tops cancer for being a disease that often might seem to have disappeared but in fact can recur, and when it does, with devastating consequences. As one website reports, "there's no way for doctors to know that all of the cancer cells in your body are gone, which is why many doctors don't use the word 'cured'" (WebMD).

A sense of recurrence in a cycle, of the reappearance of evil to blight hope, is expressed exquisitely in this passage from an article by Sean P. Smith:

> Half of all men in the developed world are destined to end up with some kind of cancer. A coin toss. Most cancers are treatable; others, you're doomed from the start. My father's four-year "battle" was a familiar story: An operation. Convalescence. A fishing trip where we have to turn around before we get to the river. Metastasization. Impossible hope in some celebrated new technology. A flight and a hotel and a hospital. A thank-God-we-have-insurance treatment. Home. Recovery. Remission? A fishing trip. Shit, he threw up on the fly rods. Another doctor, this one with pill—lots of them; better get one of those weekly organizers with the little boxes labeled M, T, W, ... Wait. Metastasization. Let's try radiation. Don't worry about his hair; it didn't grow back after the operation. Fishing? We wish we could do lunch. If he's awake by then. Bedtime is 6pm. Let's just try walking by a river. OK, the park. The goddamn backyard. Metastasization. (29)

Cancer is also a threat that, while advances have been made in conventional modes of treatment, is often addressed in nonconventional ways. Despairing of the ability of medical authorities to prevent its recurrence, patients often turn to treatment modes found in other parts of the world, or modes grounded in unconventional spiritual systems. One patient reports:

> I live in Southern California and I'm very blessed to be alive today. I certainly wouldn't be here today if I took the medical advice of my conventional oncologist. He simply said oncology couldn't do anything else for me because of my near death reaction to their poisonous chemotherapy. (Cancer Research Awareness)

A Swiss center for alternative cancer treatments says:

> Conventional medicine concentrates mainly on the removal of the tumor and on so-called pre-screening methods while largely forgetting the primary causes of cancer. But it is known to us that the development of cancer is associated with chronic infection and inflammation. (Paracelsus)

Cancer is a paradigmatic example of the Bad Resurrection. It is highly moralized, and often regarded as an enemy with active agency. People despair of the ability of conventional authority, in the form of the medical establishment, to counter the threat. And so people turn to alternative sources of medical care for help. And it returns, implacably. "Remission" is often the best hope that is offered to cancer patients, and the word "cure" is rarely used.

TERRORISM

It should come as no surprise that American culture often speaks and thinks of terrorism as a kind of cancer.

Surely terrorism is, metaphorically and so far, the cancer of the twenty-first century. Like cancer, it may well be caused by an external agent but is in many cases an experience of the body—the body politic—gone badly wrong. One medical doctor declared, "Invading, spreading and destroying: Terrorism is cancer. A malignant growth, it corrupts healthy cells, yielding fear, pain and death. It lays waste to resources and lives. Every place, every organ of every society, is threatened" (Salwitz). One need not look far to find discussions in popular culture equating terrorism to cancer (Sharira; Westphal). One source compared campaigns against cancer with campaigns against terror:

> For example, some of the current approaches to terrorism, such as large-scale military action, stigmatize large populations of innocent civilians in order to target terrorists harbored in their midst. This kind of broad-based attack often harms both the terrorists and the innocent civilians who surround them. So it was with the first effective chemotherapeutics used to attack cancer: The toxic drugs did not discriminate, but killed both normal and cancerous cells alike. In essence, these drugs targeted rapidly proliferating cells, and that meant they also killed normal, fast-dividing cells throughout the body. The result was modestly improved patient survival, at the cost of terrible side effects. Even worse, original chemotherapeutic drugs often induced secondary cancers because of the very nature of their toxic effects on normal cells. Similar broad-based responses to terrorism have in some cases led to radicalization of small subsets of local populations exposed to systemic retribution. (Westphal)

And it is a given that terrorism, like cancer, is uniformly and without exception bad and often moralized. There will be no usage whatsoever claiming that terrorism is anything but evil. If one thinks a given act is not evil, one will not call it terrorism.

It is significant that the "doctors" treating terrorism are no more successful, perhaps even less so, than those treating cancer. Officialdom pours billions if not trillions of dollars and thousands of lives into the fight, and still the bombs go off in the great cities of the West. In 2003, President George Bush stood on the deck of an aircraft carrier to declare, infamously, "mission accomplished" in the war against terror in Afghanistan and Iraq. The president was so disastrously wrong that the expression has entered culture as a kind of joke, a way to declare an utterly forlorn confidence in success against a hard adversary. In 2016, for instance, a web article argued that a high percentage of prisoners released from the Guantanamo Bay prison for terrorists return to their assaults (Hoft).

J. SCOTT APPLEWHITE/AP/Associated Press

Today, we have no confidence that terrorism is in any place defeated or even defeatable. Again, parallels to cancer abound. A loose but invisible cluster of cancer cells is the Bad Resurrection waiting to happen, and is it merely coincidence that popular usage describes small and hidden groups of terrorists as "cells"? Note the emphasis on invisibility in that wording, which is key to the Bad Resurrection, for the evil is as potent and present as it is hidden in every example of that form.

The public hears from time to time of mercenary forces involved in the fight against terror, but of course we don't hear much. After almost two decades of trying, conventional authority in the form of national governments and armies seems to be making little headway. Terrorists wage war in southwest Asia and launch attacks in major cities, and there seems to be little visible progress. This is consistent with the Bad Resurrection's despair in the effectiveness of conventional authority.

The best we can hope for is local remissions. Note our recurring experience of being exhorted to practice a kind of alternative medicine, the medicine of citizen vigilance. One cannot sit in an airport today for five minutes without being urged to report suspicious occurrences, abandoned items, and so forth. We may have little faith in the reporting of abandoned briefcases as effective in the fight against terror, but this kind of alternative medicine seems at least no more ineffectual than the efforts of the authorities, who appear to be helpless to stop recurring terrorist attacks all around the world. Meanwhile, doomsday preppers and local militia stockpile guns and durable foodstuffs in preparation for when evil will come to their cities. Terrorism is a prime example of the Bad Resurrection playing out on our screens every day.

We have studied the Bad Resurrection in two "real-life" kinds of recurrences, cancer and terrorism. But we find the form across many kinds of discourse as well. In the next two sections, we look at examples of the Bad Resurrection in movies. Its popularity in popular culture, not only in experiences, tells us something about how widely recurrent the form is in American life and culture. And we may begin to consider how films that follow the pattern may speak rhetorically to our real-life experiences.

The *Fast and the Furious* Movies

The *Fast and the Furious* films are a series that chain out a long and loosely connected story. At this writing, *Furious 7* (Wan) has been out for two or three years, with an eighth installment, *Fate of the Furious*, due to be released soon. We will focus on *Furious 7*, then. As in discussing terrorism we pulled forward some parallels with cancer, so it is that terror is central to the developments in *Furious 7*. *The Bad Resurrection* crosses over from experience to texts and back again. Part of the importance of identifying homologies is to note that rhetorical texts such as film can "speak to" real-life situations that are formally similar and can advise audiences as to how to confront real-life situations.

©Universal Pictures/Photofest

The themes of terror and resurrection intertwine throughout the movie. And the themes stretch back into previous installments of the franchise. In the previous film, *Fast & Furious 6*, for instance, the girlfriend of Dom Toretto, Letty, presumed to have died in an even earlier installment, was resurrected in a sense. It was revealed that she actually escaped death, despite the apparent evidence to the contrary of a grave and headstone. She continues in *7*. In *7*, she and Dom go to visit her supposed grave, and Dom wants to destroy her headstone, but she prevents him from doing so. She is more poignantly a resurrection as she stands there looking at an indication, however false, of her death.

In the sixth film, Dom and his crew of hired mercenaries had foiled the efforts of what is described as an "international terrorist" in the form of Owen Shaw, who was not killed despite appearances to the contrary but is found at the start of *7* in a hospital bed, watched over by his equally evil brother Deckard. His improbable if tenuous survival is a kind of Bad Resurrection. Deckard vows revenge on Dom and his crew and stalks out of the hospital, threatening the doctors and nurses with violence if Owen should die.

In one scene after another, Dom and his crew attempt to secure a vastly powerful piece of software while Deckard and his explicitly terrorist allies try to reach the software first. It is worth noting that one of Dom's crew is portrayed by the actor Paul Walker, who died in an automobile accident just as filming was ending (a kind of real-life parallel to the ubiquitous fast and dangerous driving throughout the entire series). A few of Walker's scenes had to be finished through digital graphics, and so his very appearance in the film is a kind of resurrection, and the movie was explicitly advertised with that feature. The ability of film as a medium is clearly shown here, for the movie began a final scene in which Dom and the resurrection of Walker drive off together, looking at each other with brotherly love—but the images of Walker are created by digital manipulation of Walker's actual biological brother to create the illusion.

We must note that Dom and his crew are acting as mercenaries, not legally constituted authorities. They are aided by what seems to be a shadowy government agency, but our heroes do all the work. Any time the police or any other conventional government forces appear, attempt to intervene in mayhem, to restore order, they are utterly defeated. This follows the pattern of the Bad Resurrection being beyond the control of conventional authority.

The terrorists, Deckard and his allies, are the personification of evil and threat. The most prominent terrorist is African and so activates any audience dread of the foreign Other. This fellow has a hard, implacable look, as terror might were it to take on a human face. References to previous, famous acts of terror abound. In one improbable but exciting scene, our heroes steal a flashy sports car being kept high in a skyscraper. They drive the car out of the skyscraper, and it zooms through the air into the skyscraper just like it that is right next door. In other words, we have an airborne machine crashing into the Twin Towers. Where have we seen that before? Note that the high-tech ability of film to portray such an improbability is key to the effect of the text. This and other references to 9/11 are a kind of resurrection, a recycling, of that pivotal event in American history.

The film builds to a final climax with a terrific fight on top of a building between Dom and Deckard. Dom's crew manages to destroy the building with explosives, and although Dom escapes, we see Deckard sliding down with the wreckage of the building into its foundations below. It is clearly a kind of burial. But lo and behold, in following scenes we see that Deckard has been resurrected, seeming none the worse for wear, and is being locked away in a super-maximum-security prison and kept way underground (burial again). Smart money is on Deckard's resurrection from this grave in a future installment.

HALLOWEEN AND *FRIDAY THE 13TH* MOVIES

Two of the most successful and oft-repeated film franchises in American culture are those related to some variation on the titles *Halloween* and *Friday the 13th*. The films themselves are thus a kind of resurrection; whether it is bad or not depends on one's tastes. I find them remarkably similar in form and remarkably consistent with the pattern of the Bad Resurrection. The Wikipedia page for the *Halloween* franchise lists ten films between 1978 and 2009 ("*Halloween* (Franchise)"). Twelve iterations of *Friday the 13th* between 1980 and 2009 are noted ("Friday the 13th (Franchise)"). The *Friday the 13th* page also suggests that the film was inspired by the slightly earlier *Halloween*, so any formal resemblance between them should not be surprising.

The general idea behind *Friday the 13th*, founded with the original 1980 version, is that a child named Jason was drowned in a lake at summer camp in 1958. This death is morally weighted, as the two counselors assigned to watch him were engaged in a sexual escapade at the time. Some people attempt to reopen the camp in 1979 after previous attempts thwarted by fires and bad water. But as a small group of counselors work in the camp, a killer stalks the grounds. There is suspicion that this is Jason, returned.

The luckless counselors trying to open the camp are killed one after another. Then a strange woman arrives, who reveals that she is the mother of the boy who drowned and is seeking revenge on the tribe of counselors. The counselors attempt to kill her but, after seeming to have died, she rises up and must be decapitated before she stays down. At the end of the film, the decomposing body of Jason emerges from the lake to finish off the luckless crew. The police finally arrive to a scene of carnage and one surviving counselor.

This basic story is of course full of the elements of the Bad Resurrection. There is a resurrection of the bad luck at the camp, more than once, as disaster besets every attempt to open it. The tragedy that was Jason's death returns in the slayings of the counselors. Jason's mother is a kind of resurrection or return of Jason. And then, most horribly, the animated corpse of Jason resurrects to attack the remaining counselors. The ineffectuality of officialdom is also present in the arrival of the police only at the very end. To the extent that they can protect themselves at all, the counselors must become the only authorities in the isolated camp.

Other iterations of the film show the same patterns of Bad Resurrections, with changing contents. *Friday the 13th: A New Beginning* begins with a young boy walking through a graveyard and seeing two grave robbers digging up the corpse of Jason Voorhees (of course, he was floating about in the lake in the first film). The corpse comes to life (so it is an actual resurrection) and kills the grave robbers. The sight of this so shatters the boy that he spends years in an asylum before being released to a halfway house, another kind of resurrection. The halfway house is a regular den of sexual activity among some of its residents, which moralizes the murders, and moralization of evil is a component of the Bad Resurrection. Soon townspeople are being murdered. The chief of police in this small town tells the mayor he believes the culprit is Jason, resurrected, but the mayor discounts the story and does not support the chief—another case in which conventional authority is ineffectual.

In the end, it appears as if one of the residents of the house has been impersonating Jason. He is killed. But Tommy is shown putting on a mask and assuming the persona of Jason at the end—yet another resurrection, and a setup for a sequel.

As noted, the original *Halloween*, from 1978, emerged only two years before the first *Friday the 13th*, and some argue was the inspiration for it. *Halloween* became the theme of several films, each one formally similar to the first. The original film begins with a masked figure stalking a teenage couple as they (here's your moralization again) have sex in a house. The figure stabs the couple. The owners of the house arrive, and it is revealed that the murderous figure is Michael Myers, the six-year-old brother of the stabbed girl, who appears to have become catatonic and empty from the experience.

The boy is put into a mental asylum, a kind of burial away from the world. Fifteen years later, he escapes, and for what seems like an eternity he leads the little town a merry chase, killing and murdering as he goes. His rampage is intertwined with more moralization in the form of teenagers making out and smoking pot shortly before they get it in the neck. All this time, the town's chief physician, Doctor Loomis, and the police seem totally unable to find or restrain Michael. It is civilians who eventually (if temporarily) kill him. But in the final scene, Michael is resurrected and rises up ominously from the ground, promising more murder and sequels. And indeed, in all of those sequels, Michael Myers comes and goes, is put down and then resurrected, in an ongoing cycle of Bad Resurrections. Throughout the film, the ability of the camera to play with light and dark, with scenes partially in focus and partially out, makes good and scary use of the mechanism of film.

CONCLUSION

When a homology crosses texts and experiences, we might look for ways in which the texts advises people as to how to confront those lived situations. All of us experience Bad Resurrections beyond those described here in one way or another,. Some of these Bad Resurrections are major, some minor, but they are a recurring part of life. Perhaps you or a friend has the Bad Resurrection of recurring cycles of addiction and cure. Maybe there is a love interest who cycles in and out and in and out of your life, with disastrous consequences. Maybe there is some crushing and burdensome task at work that you think you have finished and put away for good, but no, it reappears in some form. We may not all face cancer and terrorism, but the Bad Resurrection is in ways large or small a recurring fact for most if not all of us.

Texts can offer at the very least the consolation of learning that Bad Resurrections are inevitable. Even terrible experiences may become more bearable if we can place them through art and culture, if we can see our suffering articulated at least on a formal level in films, television, literature, and art. Just as there are experiences of Bad Resurrections beyond cancer and terrorism, so there are these cultural forms beyond the two movie series described here that may advise audiences as to how to confront Bad Resurrections. As rhetorical critics, we can study those texts to learn what advice they may have for our own resurrections. As for the two film series here, we must conclude that they instill in audiences a mistrust of authority and conventional wisdom. Police, sheriffs, doctors, and community leaders are at a loss as to what to do. At the same time, the films reinforce authoritarian and conventional moral precepts, for it seems as if the most mundane moral failings lead in short order to a violent end. These films, if not every text involving Bad Resurrections, therefore seem to cut across American culture on the angle of rugged self-reliance coupled with repressive morality. They augment a *Little House on the Prairie* morality, a morality of the doomsday preppers who lay plans to go it alone in times of peril while often articulating the most stringent ethical principles. It can be through exploring texts and experiences in American culture that we find these interesting connections among seemingly unrelated artifacts.

WORKS CITED

Aden, R. C. *Popular Stories and Promised Lands: Fan Cultures and Symbolic Pilgrimages.* U of Alabama P, 1999.

Adorno, T. W. *The Jargon of Authenticity.* Northwestern UP, 1973.

Ahlgren, P. "Mother of Fire Victims Always Wanted Many Children, Relative Says." *Milwaukee Journal*, 15 Nov. 1987, p. A16.

Ahmed, S. *Queer Phenomenology: Orientations, Objects, and Others.* Duke UP, 2006.

Alford, C. F. *Levinas, the Frankfurt School, and Psychoanalysis.* Wesleyan UP, 2003.

Altheide, D. L. *Media Power.* Sage, 1985.

Altheide, D. L., and R. P. Snow. *Media Logic.* Sage, 1979.

Althusser, L. *Lenin and Philosophy and Other Essays.* Translated by B. Brewster, Monthly Review Press, 1971.

Aristotle. *Rhetoric.* Translated by W. Rhys Roberts, Modern Library, 1954.

Asante, M. K. *The Afrocentric Idea.* Rev. ed., Temple UP, 1998.

Atiyah, M. "100 Years of Mathematics." *Normat*, vol. 48, 2000, pp. 123–26.

Augustine. *On Christian Doctrine.* Translated by D. W. Robertson, Jr., Library of Liberal Arts, 1958.

Bargren, P. "Drawn Together: Spaulding, Carr Long Crossed Paths." *Milwaukee Journal*, 15 Oct. 1987, pp. B1–2.

Barillier, E. *Steampunk!* Les Moutons Mecaniques, 2010.

Barnard, M. *Fashion as Communication.* 2nd ed., Routledge, 2002.

Barnhurst, K. G., M. Vari, and I. Rodriguez. "Mapping Visual Studies in Communication." *Journal of Communication*, vol. 54, 2004, pp. 616–44.

Bednarek, D. I. "Education of Minorities Emerges as Top Priority." *Milwaukee Journal*, 25 Oct. 1987, pp. B1–2.

_____. "Integration Lawsuit Settled." *Milwaukee Journal*, 22 Oct. 1987, p. A1.

Benjamin, W. *Illuminations.* Translated by H. Zohn, edited by H. Arendt, Schocken Books, 1968.

Boggs, C. *The End of Politics: Corporate Power and the Decline of the Public Sphere.* Guilford, 2001.

Breyfogle, W. "The Good Servant: St. Mark's AME Church Is a Bastion of Concern." *Milwaukee Journal*, 22 Oct. 1987, pp. D19–20.

Brummett, B. "Burke's Representative Anecdote as a Method in Media Criticism." *Critical Studies in Mass Communication*, vol. 1, 1984, pp. 161–76.

_____. *Clockwork Rhetoric: The Language and Style of Steampunk.* U of Mississippi P, 2014.

_____. *Rhetorical Homologies: Form, Culture, Experience.* U of Alabama P, 2004.

_____. *Rhetoric of Machine Aesthetics.* Praeger, 1999.

_____. *The World and How We Describe It: Rhetorics of Reality, Representation, Simulation.* Praeger, 2003.

Brummett, B., and D. L. Bowers. "Subject Positions as a Site of Rhetorical Struggle: Representing African Americans." *At the Intersection: Cultural Studies and Rhetorical Studies*, edited by T. Rosteck, Guilford, 1999.

Brummett, B., J. Gunn, J. Hoffman, and A. Young. "NSFW: Experiencing Immanentism or Transcendence upon Hearing Gilbert Gottfried's Rendition of Fifty Shades of Grey in the Postmodern Workplace, or Liberatory Criminology." *Science Journal of Sociology and Anthropology*, vol. 2014, Article ID sjsa-235, 4 pp., 2014, doi: 10.7237/sjsa/235.

Bryant, D. C. "Rhetoric: Its Function and Its Scope." *Quarterly Journal of Speech*, vol. 39, 1953, pp. 401–24.

Buhle, P. *Popular Culture in America.* U of Minnesota P, 1987.

Burke, K. *Attitudes toward History.* New Republic, 1937.

_____. *A Grammar of Motives.* Reprint, U of California P, 1969. Originally published in 1945.

_____. *Language as Symbolic Action.* U of California P, 1966.

_____. *Permanence and Change.* Reprint, Bobbs-Merrill, 1965. Originally published in 1935.

_____. *The Philosophy of Literacy Form.* 3rd ed., U of California P, 1973.

_____. *A Rhetoric of Motives.* Reprint, U of California P, 1969. Originally published in 1950.

Butler, J. *Bodies That Matter: On the Discursive Limits of "Sex."* Routledge, 1993.

_____. *Gender Trouble: Feminism and the Subversion of Identity.* Routledge, 2006.

Cancer Research Awareness. www.cancer-research-awareness.com. Accessed 2 June 2017.

Cha, T. H. K., editor. *Apparatus.* Tanam, 1980.

Chambers, I. *Popular Culture: The Metropolitan Experience.* Methuen, 1986.

Christopulos, M. "Loss of Grandson Brought Back a Painful Memory." *Milwaukee Sentinel*, 1 Oct. 1987, part 1, p. 12.

Cicero, M. T. *De Oratore.* Translated by E. W. Sutton and H. Rackham, Harvard UP, 1976.

Cole, J. "Study Details Barriers to Minority Gains." *Milwaukee Sentinel*, 5 Nov. 1987, part 1, p. 1.

Collins, P. H. *Black Feminist Thought: Knowledge, Consciousness, and the Politics of Empowerment.* Routledge, 1990.

Conrad, K. "Direct Payments Might Help" [Letter]. *Milwaukee Journal*, 25 Oct. 1987, p. J20.

"Culture." *The Oxford English Dictionary.* Compact ed., 1971.

"Culture." *The Oxford English Dictionary.* Compact ed., supp. 1987.

Cunibert, B. "Quiet Death to Freedom." *Milwaukee Journal*, 11 Oct. 1987, pp. J1–2.

Cuprisin, T., and M. Lisheron. "Stabbing Victim Dies; Had Gone to Clinic First." *Milwaukee Journal*, 25 Oct. 1987, pp. B1–2.

Daniel, J. L., and G. Smitherman. "How I Got Over: Communication Dynamics in the Black Community." *Quarterly Journal of Speech*, vol. 62, 1976, pp. 26–39.

De Atley, R. "The Musical Genius Is an Eccentric Man-Child." *Milwaukee Journal*, 6 Oct. 1987, XTRA, p. 10.

Deger, R. "Shaw Defends Free Tuition Plan as Youth Incentive." *UWM Post*, 12 Nov. 1987, p. 1.

De Palma, B., director. *Scarface.* Universal Pictures, 1983.

Deshotels, M. M. "Aid Cuts Hit Families Hard" [Letter]. *Milwaukee Journal*, 25 Oct. 1987, p. J20.

Dlugi, J. "Letters to the Editor." *Milwaukee Journal*, 15 Nov. 1987, p. J13.

Donovan, A. *The Art of Steampunk.* Fox Chapel, 2011.

Ellison, R. *Invisible Man.* Random House, 1952.

Esposito, K. "300 Protest Racism, Response on UW-Madison Campus." *Milwaukee Journal*, 16 Oct. 1987, p. A12.

_____. "2 Stories of Pain, Prejudice." *Milwaukee Journal*, 9 Nov. 1987, p. A1.

Faust, P. "Brewers' Sheffield Is Arrested Again." *Milwaukee Journal*, 15 Oct. 1987, p. C2.

Finnegan, C. A. *Picturing Poverty: Print Culture and FSA Photographs.* Smithsonian, 2003.

Fisher, W. K. "Narration as a Human Communication Paradigm: The Case of Public Moral Argument." *Communication Monographs*, vol. 51, 1984, pp. 1–22.

_____. "The Narrative Paradigm: An Elaboration." *Communication Monographs*, vol. 52, 1985, pp. 347–67.

Fiske, J. *Reading the Popular.* Unwin Hyman, 1989.

_____. *Understanding Popular Culture.* Unwin Hyman, 1989.

Foss, K. A., and S. K. Foss. *Women Speak: The Eloquence of Women's Lives.* Waveland, 1991.

Foss, S. K. *Rhetorical Criticism: Exploration and Practice.* Waveland, 2004.

"Friday the 13th (Franchise)." *Wikipedia*, https://en.wikipedia.org/wiki/Friday_the_13th_(franchise). Accessed 24 Mar. 2017.

Frye, N. *The Educated Imagination.* Indiana UP, 1964.

"Funeral Set for Woman Slain in Northwest Side Apartment." *Milwaukee Journal*, 11 Nov. 1987, p. B11.

Gates, H. L., Jr. *The Signifying Monkey: A Theory of African-American Literary Criticism.* Oxford UP, 1988.

Gerbner, G., L. Gross, M. Morgan, and N. Signorielli. "The 'Mainstreaming' of America: Violence Profile No. 11." *Journal of Communication*, vol. 30, 1980, pp. 10–29.

Gilbert, C. "Blacks Count the Reasons for Long Bus Ride." *Milwaukee Journal*, 9 Nov. 1987, pp. B1–2.

_____. "Fire Victims at Rest at Last." *Milwaukee Journal*, 11 Oct. 1987, p. B1.

Gill, B., and R. Romell. "Diverse Social Bills Had Role in Tragedy." *Milwaukee Sentinel*, 5 Nov. 1987, part 1, p. 1.

Gilliam, T., director. *Brazil.* Universal Studios, 1985.

Goldmann, L. "Introduction to the Problems of a Sociology of the Novel." *Telos*, vol. 18, 1973/1974, pp. 122–35.

Gramsci, A. *Selections from the Prison Notebooks*. Translated by Q. Hoare and G. N. Smith, International Publishers, 1971.

Gribble, J. "2nd of 3 Charged with Killing Vendor Arrested in Arkansas." *Milwaukee Journal*, 15 Oct. 1987, pp. B1–2.

Guensburg, C. "Who's That Man in the Mirror, Michael?" *Milwaukee Journal*, 6 Oct. 1987, XTRA, p. 10.

Hajewski, D. "Poverty Forces Families to Double Up." *Milwaukee Journal*, 16 Oct. 1987, pp. B1–6.

Halberstam, J. *In a Queer Time and Place: Transgender Bodies, Subcultural Lives*. New York UP, 2005. Sexual Cultures.

Hall, S. "Signification, Representation, Ideology: Althusser and the Post-Structuralist Debates." *Critical Studies in Mass Communication*, vol. 2, 1985, pp. 91–114.

"Halloween (Franchise)." *Wikipedia*, https://en.wikipedia.org/wiki/Halloween_(franchise). Accessed 24 Mar. 2017.

Hariman, R. *Political Style: The Artistry of Power*. U of Chicago P, 1995.

Hariman, R., and J. L. Lucaites. "Performing Civic Identity: The Iconic Photograph of the Flag Raising on Iwo Jima." *Quarterly Journal of Speech*, vol. 88, 2002, pp. 363–92.

Hartsock, N. *The Feminist Standpoint Revisited and Other Essays*. Westview, 1998.

Heath, S., and G. Skirrow. "An Interview with Raymond Williams." *Studies in Entertainment: Critical Approaches to Mass Culture*, edited by T. Modleski. Indiana UP, 1986.

Hoft, J. "Confirmed: 117 Gitmo Detainees Returned to Terrorism So Far or 18% of Released Detainees." *Gateway Pundit*, 23 Feb. 2016, www.thegatewaypundit.com/2016/02/confirmed-117-gitmo-detainees-returned-terrorism-far-18-released-detainees/. Accessed 2 Jun 2017.

hooks, b. *Where We Stand: Class Matters*. Routledge, 2000.

Hopkins, S., director. *The Ghost and the Darkness*. Constellation Entertainment, 1996.

Jackson, D. "An American Place." *Milwaukee Journal*, 22 Oct. 1987, p. D11.

Jameson, F. *The Political Unconscious: Narrative as a Socially Symbolic Act*. Cornell UP, 1981.

Jankowski, M. E. "Reporters Showed Sensitivity" [Letter]. *Milwaukee Journal*, 25 Oct. 1987, p. J20.

Jones, R. P. "Dean Defends UW Action in Cases of Racism." *Milwaukee Journal*, 1 Nov. 1987, p. A1.

_____. "Racist Incident Hurt UW Recruiting Efforts." *Milwaukee Journal*, 1 Nov. 1987, p. A1.

_____. "2 Stories of Pain, Prejudice." *Milwaukee Journal*, 9 Nov. 1987, p. A1.

_____. "UW Dean Stays Calm in Storm over Racism." *Milwaukee Journal*, 9 Nov. 1987, p. A6.

Kasten, R. W., Jr. "Heat Assistance Vital" [Letter]. *Milwaukee Journal*, 25 Oct. 1987, p. J20.

Kenney, S. J., and H. Kinsella, editors. *Politics and Feminist Standpoint Theories*. Haworth, 1997.

Kinneavy, James L. *A Theory of Discourse*. Prentice Hall, 1971.

Kissinger, M. "Blueprint for Tragedy." *Milwaukee Journal*, 16 Oct. 1987, p. A1.

Kissinger, M., and G. C. Rummler. "Once Again, 5 Firemen Feel Helpless." *Milwaukee Journal*, 15 Oct. 1987, pp. B1–2.

Klotz, R. J. *The Politics of Internet Communication*. Rowman & Littlefield, 2003.

Knapp, M. L., and A. L. Vangelisti. *Interpersonal Communication and Human Relationships*. 5th ed., Allyn & Bacon, 2005.

Knoche, E. "Mother in Filthy Home Didn't Know How to Flush Toilet." *Milwaukee Sentinel*, 5 Nov. 1987, part 1, p. 5.

Kramer, C. "Women's Speech: Separate but Unequal?" *Quarterly Journal of Speech*, vol. 60, 1974, pp. 14–24.

Kren, M. "Suffering Called Heart, Soul of King, Malcolm X." *Milwaukee Journal*, 15 Oct. 1987, p. D2.

Lacan, J. *Écrits*. Translated by A. Sheridan, W. W. Norton, 1977.

Leach, E. "Structuralism in Social Anthropology." *Structuralism: An Introduction*, edited by David Robey, Oxford UP, 1973, pp. 37–56.

Leff, M. C., and F. J. Kauffeld, editors. *Texts in Context: Critical Dialogues on Significant Episodes in American Political Rhetoric*. Hermagoras, 1989.

Lévi-Strauss, C. *The Raw and the Cooked*. Harper & Row, 1969.

Lorenz, K. Z. "Analogy as a Source of Knowledge." *Science*, vol. 185, 1974, pp. 229–34.

Lynch, K. A. "A New Cornerstone." *Milwaukee Journal*, 22 Oct. 1987, p. D4.

McCallister, M. "Milwaukee Urban League Study." *UWM Post*, 12 Nov. 1987, p. 1.

Meyrowitz, J. *No Sense of Place: The Impact of Electronic Media on Social Behavior.* Oxford UP, 1985.

Mitchard, J. "Grief Will Come, but Not Just Yet." *Milwaukee Journal*, 15 Oct. 1987, p. A1.

_____. "Rise Up: Family Privately Recalls 5 Lives." *Milwaukee Journal*, 23 Oct. 1987, p. B1.

Modleski, T., editor. *Studies in Entertainment: Critical Approaches to Mass Culture.* Indiana UP, 1986.

Morvay, J. E. "Grandmother Didn't Get Last Goodbye." *Milwaukee Sentinel*, 1 Oct. 1987, part 1, p. 1.

Mukerji, C., and M. Schudson. "Popular Culture." *Annual Review of Sociology*, vol. 12, 1986, pp. 47–66.

Mulvey, M. "Peer Pressure Called Main Obstacle for Black Students." *Milwaukee Sentinel*, 5 Nov. 1987, part 1, p. 5.

Nakayama, T. K., and J. N. Martin. *Whiteness: The Communication of Social Identity.* Sage, 1998.

News 4. WTMJ-TV, Milwaukee. 15 Oct. 1987. Television.

News at 6. WITI-TV, Milwaukee. 15 Oct. 1987. Television.

Norris, T. "Taking a Chance on Love." *Milwaukee Journal*, 8 Oct. 1987, pp. D1–2.

Paracelsus Clinic. "Cancer—Disease of Civilization in the 21st Century." www.paracelsus.com/biological-medicine/cancer?gclid=CLK7gd6379ICFUa2wAod_REP6A. Accessed 24 Mar. 2017.

Plato. *Gorgias.* Translated by Walter Hamilton, Penguin, 1960.

_____. *Phaedrus.* Translated by W. C. Helmbold and W. G. Rabinowitz, Library of Liberal Arts, 1956.

_____. *Republic.* Translated by B. Jowett, Easton Press, 1980.

Postman, N. *Amusing Ourselves to Death: Public Discourse in the Age of Show Business.* Penguin, 1985.

Quintilian, M. F. *Institutio Oratoria.* Translated by H. E. Butler, Harvard UP, 1969.

Rakow, L. F., and L. A. Wackwitz. *Feminist Communication Theory: Selections in Context.* Sage, 2004.

Ramis, H., director. *Groundhog Day.* Columbia/Tristar, 1993.

Richards, I. A. *The Philosophy of Rhetoric.* Oxford UP, 1936.

Richfield, I. "High Birth Rates Unhealthy" [Letter]. *Milwaukee Journal*, 25 Oct. 1987, p. J20.

Romell, R. "Loss of Life Is Worst in 104 Years." *Milwaukee Sentinel*, 1 Oct. 1987, part 1, p. 1.

Romell, R., and B. Gill. "Fatal Fire Wasn't the First Tragedy for Family Plagued by Poverty." *Milwaukee Sentinel*, 5 Nov. 1987, part 1, p. 1.

Salwitz, J. C. "Terrorism Is a Cancer." Nov. 2015, www.kevinmd.com/blog/2015/11/terrorism-is-a-cancer.html. Accessed 24 Mar. 2017.

Schultze, S. "Learnfare May Mean Turmoil for Schools." *Milwaukee Journal*, 25 Oct. 1987, p. 1A.

Sedgwick, E. K. *Epistemology of the Closet.* 2nd ed., U of California P, 2008.

Sellers, S. *The Hélène Cixous Reader.* Routledge, 1994.

Sharira, I. "Why the Fight against Terrorism Is Like the Fight against Cancer." *Psychology Today*, 2 Oct. 2011, www.psychologytoday.com/blog/the-narcissus-in-all-us/201110/why-the-fight-against-terrorism-is-the-fight-against-cancer. Accessed 24 Mar. 2017.

Short, C. R. "Colleges Should Show Intolerance of Racism" [Letter]. *Milwaukee Journal,* 15 Nov. 1987, p. J13.

"Six Children Killed in House Fire." *Milwaukee Journal*, 15 Oct. 1987, p. A1.

Smith. S. P. "Death of a Fisherman." *The Sun*, March 2017, pp. 19–23.

Snow, R. P. "Interaction with Mass Media: The Importance of Rhythm and Tempo." *Communication Quarterly*, vol. 35, 1987, pp. 225–37.

Sontag, S. *Illness as Metaphor.* Farrar, Strauss and Giroux, 1978.

Storey, J. *Cultural Studies and the Study of Popular Culture: Theories and Methods.* U of Georgia P, 2003.

Strongman, J. *Steampunk: The Art of Victorian Futurism.* Korero Books, 2011.

Sullivan, K. R., director. *Guess Who.* Columbia Pictures, 2005.

"Survivor Goes Home." *Milwaukee Journal*, 7 Oct. 1987, p. A1.

Sykes, L., Jr. "Things Had Been Looking Up before Slaying, Husband Says." *Milwaukee Journal*, 17 Nov. 1987, p. B1.

Takano, J. "The Truth of Cancer Diseases and Evil Spirits." www.pyroenergen.com/articles12/cancer-diseases.htm. Accessed 10 Apr. 2017.

Ten O'Clock Channel 12 News. WISN-TV, Milwaukee. 15 Oct. 1987. Television.

Tessler, R. "Fathers Shirk Responsibility" [Letter]. *Milwaukee Journal*, 25 Oct. 1987, p. J20.

Thomas, J. C. "Landlords Too Often Blamed" [Letter]. *Milwaukee Journal*, 25 Oct. 1987, p. J20.

"A Time to Weep." *Milwaukee Journal*, 22 Oct. 1987, p. A8.

Toulmin, S. *The Uses of Argument.* Cambridge UP, 1958.

Treichler, P. A., and C. Kramarae. "Women's Talk in the Ivory Tower." *Communication Quarterly*, vol. 31, 1983, pp. 118–32.

VanderMeer, Jeff, and S. J. Chambers, editors. *The Steampunk Bible: An Illustrated Guide to the World of Imaginary Airships, Corsets and Goggles, Mad Scientists, and Strange Literature.* Abrams Image, 2011.

Walsh, F. "Defeating Cancer, the 'Evil Genius.'" *BBC News*, 11 Feb. 2015, www.bbc.com/news/health-31365272. Accessed 10 Apr. 2017.

Wan, J., director. *Furious 7.* Universal Pictures, 2015.

Ward, M. "Grim Echoes." *Milwaukee Journal, Milwaukee Magazine*, 15 Nov. 1987, p. 6.

WebMD. "Remission: What Does It Mean?" www.webmd.com/cancer/remission-what-does-it-mean. Accessed 24 Mar. 2017.

Westphal, C. "Treating Terrorism Like Cancer." *Boston Globe*, 2 Apr. 2016, www.bostonglobe.com/opinion/2016/04/01/treating-terrorism-like-cancer/6mSHClNC9U1fdvZOAj90PM/story.html. Accessed 24 Mar. 2017.

Wilkerson, L. "Child and Fire Experts Sort through the Flames." *Milwaukee Journal*, 25 Oct. 1987, p. G5.

Willard, M. N. "Séance, Tricknowlogy, Skateboarding, and the Space of Youth." *Popular Culture: A Reader*, edited by R. Guins and O. Zaragoza Cruz, Sage, 2005, pp. 462–78.

Williams, R. *Keywords: A Vocabulary of Culture and Society.* Oxford UP, 1976.

_____. *Marxism and Literature.* Oxford UP, 1977.

SUGGESTED READINGS

Culture-Centered Criticism

Asante, M. K. *Kemet, Afrocentricity, and Knowledge*. Africa World Press, 1990.

Atwater, D. F. *African American Women's Rhetoric: The Search for Dignity, Personhood, and Honor*. Lexington, 2010.

Baca, D., and V. Villanueva. *Rhetorics of the Americas 3114 B.C.E. to 2012 C.E.* Palgrave Macmillan, 2014.

Baldwin, D. L. "Black Empires, White Desires: The Spatial Politics of Identity in the Age of Hip-Hop." *That's the Joint: The Hip Hop Studies Reader*, edited by M. Forman and M. A. Neal. Routledge, 2004, pp. 159–176.

Banks, A. J. *Digital Griots: African American Rhetoric in a Multimedia Age*. Southern Illinois UP, 2011.

Basso, K. *Western Apache Language and Culture*. U of Arizona P, 1990.

Carbaugh, D., editor. *Cultural Communication and Intercultural Contact*. Lawrence Erlbaum, 1990.

Dundes, A., editor. *Mother Wit from the Laughing Barrel: Readings in the Interpretation of Afro-American Folklore*. Prentice Hall, 1984.

Fong, M., and R. Chuang, editors. *Communicating Ethnic and Cultural Identity*. Rowman & Littlefield, 2004.

Gates, H. L., Jr. *Figures in Black: Words, Signs, and the "Racial" Self*. Oxford UP, 1986.

Geertz, C. *The Interpretation of Cultures*. Basic Books, 1973.

Griefat, Y., and T. Katriel. "Life Demands *Musayara*: Communication and Culture among Arabs in Israel." *Language, Communication and Culture*, edited by S. Ting-Toomey and F. Korzenny. Sage, 1989, pp. 121–138.

hooks, b. *Black Looks: Race and Representation*. South End, 1992.

Jackson, R. L., and E. B. Richardson, editors. *Understanding African American Rhetoric: Classical Origins to Contemporary Innovations*. Routledge, 2003.

Kincaid, D. L., editor. *Communication Theory: Eastern and Western Perspectives*. Academic Press, 1987.

Kirkpatrick, A., and Z. Xu. *Chinese Rhetoric and Writing: An Introduction for Language Teachers*. Parlor Press, 2012.

Kitwana, B. *The Hip Hop Generation: Young Blacks and the Crisis in African-American Culture*. Perseus Books, 2002.

Lemert, C. *Dark Thoughts: Race and the Eclipse of Society*. Routledge, 2002.

Luyaluka, K. L. *Afrocentric Spirituality*. Kinshasa, 2014.

Mao, L. *Reading Chinese Fortune Cookie: The Making of Chinese American Rhetoric*. Utah State UP, 2006.

Mao, L., and M. Young. *Representations: Doing Asian American Rhetoric*. Utah State UP, 2008.

Mullen, R. W. *Black Communication*. UP of America, 1982.

Perryman-Clark, S. *Afrocentric Teacher-Research: Rethinking Appropriateness and Inclusion*. Peter Lang, 2012. Studies in Composition and Rhetoric.

Smitherman, G. *Talkin' and Testifyin': The Language of Black America*. Houghton Mifflin, 1977.

Vanderwert, W. C., editor. *Indian Oratory*. U of Oklahoma P, 1971.

Walker, F. R., and D. M. Greene. "Exploring Afrocentricity: An Analysis of the Discourse of Jesse Jackson." *Journal of African American Studies*, vol. 9, no. 4, 2006, pp. 62–71.

Wallace, M., and G. Dent, editors. *Black Popular Culture*. Bay Press, 1992.

Xing, L. *Rhetoric in Ancient China, Fifth to Third Century B.C.E: A Comparison with Classical Greek Rhetoric*. U of South Carolina P, 2011.

Marxist Criticism

Allor, M. "Relocating the Site of the Audience." *Critical Studies in Mass Communication*, vol. 5, 1988, pp. 217–33.

Aune, J. A. *Rhetoric and Marxism*. Westview, 1994.

Baudrillard, J. *For a Critique of the Political Economy of the Sign*. Telos, 1981.

Becker, S. L. "Marxist Approaches to Media Studies: The British Experience." *Critical Studies in Mass Communication*, vol. 1, 1984, pp. 66–81.

Cantor, P. A. *Gilligan Unbound: Pop Culture in the Age of Globalization*. Rowman & Littlefield, 2001.

Centre for Contemporary Cultural Studies. *Culture, Media, Language.* Hutchinson, 1980.

Cloud, D. L. *We Are the Union: Democratic Unionism and Dissent at Boeing.* U of Illinois P, 2011.

Collins, R., et al. *Media, Culture, and Society.* Sage, 2013.

Corcoran, F. "Television as Ideological Apparatus: The Power and the Pleasure." *Critical Studies in Mass Communication*, vol. 1, 1984, pp. 131–45.

D'Amato, P. *The Meaning of Marxism.* Haymarket Books, 2006.

Deleuze, G., and F. Guattari. *What Is Philosophy?* Translated by H. Tomlinson and D. Burchell, Columbia UP, 1994.

Eagleton, T. *Literary Theory.* 2nd ed., U of Minnesota P, 1996.

_____. *Marxism and Literary Criticism.* U of California P, 1976.

Fiske, J. "The Discourses of TV Quiz Shows or, School + Luck = Success + Success + Sex." *Central States Speech Journal*, vol. 34, 1983, pp. 139–50.

_____. "Meaningful Moments." *Critical Studies in Mass Communication*, vol. 5, 1988, pp. 246–51.

_____. "Television and Popular Culture: Reflections on British and Australian Critical Practice." *Critical Studies in Mass Communication*, vol. 3, 1986, pp. 200–16.

_____. "Television: Polysemy and Popularity." *Critical Studies in Mass Communication*, vol. 3, 1986, pp. 391–408.

Frow, J. *Marxism and Literary History.* Harvard UP, 1986.

Gramsci, A. *Selections from the Prison Notebooks.* Translated by Q. Hoare and G. N. Smith, International, 1971.

Grossberg, L. "Strategies of Marxist Cultural Interpretation." *Critical Studies in Mass Communication*, vol. 1, 1984, pp. 392–421.

Gurevitch M., et al. *Culture, Society and the Media.* Methuen, 1982.

Hebdige, D. *Subculture: The Meaning of Style.* Methuen, 1979.

Lentricchia, F. *Criticism and Social Change.* U of Chicago P, 1983.

McGee, M. C. "A Materialist's Conception of Rhetoric." *Explorations in Rhetoric: Studies in Honor of Douglas Ehninger*, edited by R. E. McKerrow. Scott, Foresman, 1982, pp. 23–48.

_____. "Power to the ←people→." *Critical Studies in Mass Communication*, vol. 4, 1987, pp. 432–37.

Morley, D. *The "Nationwide" Audience: Structure and Decoding.* British Film Institute, 1980.

Nelson, C., and L. Grossberg, editors. *Marxism and the Interpretation of Culture.* U of Illinois P, 1988.

Riedner, R.C. *Writing Neoliberal Values: Rhetorical Connectivities and Global Capitalism.* Palgrave MacMillan, 2015.

Ritzer, G. *The McDonaldization of Society.* Pine Forge, 2000.

Seabrook, J. *Nobrow: The Culture of Marketing and the Marketing of Culture.* Vintage, 2001.

Williamson, J. *Consuming Passions: The Dynamics of Popular Culture.* Marion Boyars, 1988.

Feminist Rhetorical Criticism

Beauvoir, de, S. *The Second Sex.* Alfred A. Knopf, 1953.

Chavez, K. R. *Queer Migration Politics: Activist Rhetoric and Coalitional Possibilities.* U of Illinois P, 2013.

Cloud, D. L. "Foiling the Intellectuals: Gender, Identity Framing, and the Rhetoric of the Kill in Conservative Hate Mail." *Communication, Culture, and Critique*, vol. 2, 2009, pp. 457–79.

Connell, R. W. *Gender and Power.* Stanford UP, 1987.

Foss, K. A., and S. K. Foss. *Women Speak: The Eloquence of Women's Lives.* Waveland Press, 1991.

Foss, K. A., S. K. Foss, and C. Griffin. *Feminist Rhetorical Theories.* Sage, 1999.

K. A. Foss, S. K. Foss, and C. L. Griffin, editors. *Readings in Feminist Rhetorical Theory.* Sage, 2004.

Freeman, E. *Time Binds: Queer Temporalities, Queer Histories.* Duke UP, 2010. Perverse Modernities.

Gilligan, C. *In a Different Voice.* Harvard UP, 1982.

Irigaray, L. *This Sex Which Is Not One.* Cornell UP, 1985.

Jagose, A. *Queer Theory: An Introduction.* New York UP, 1997.

Keohane, N. L., M. Z. Rosaldo, and B. C. Gelpi, editors. *Feminist Theory: A Critique of Ideology.* U of Chicago P, 1981.

Kuhn, A. *Women's Pictures.* Routledge and Kegan Paul, 1982.

Lockford, L. *Performing Femininity: Rewriting Gender Identity.* AltaMira, 2004.

Pomerance, M., editor. *Ladies and Gentlemen, Boys and Girls: Gender in Film at the End of the Twentieth Century.* State U of New York P, 2001.

Probyn, E. *Outside Belongings.* Routledge, 1996.

Rand, E. J. *Reclaiming Queer: Activist and Academic Rhetorics of Resistance.* U of Alabama P, 2014.

Ryan, K., and N. Meyers. *Rethinking Ethos: A Feminist Ecological Approach to Rhetoric.* Southern Illinois UP, 2016.

Young, I. M. *Throwing Like a Girl and Other Essays in Feminist Philosophy and Social Theory.* Indiana UP, 1990.

Psychoanalytic Criticism

Davis, D. "Identification: Burke and Freud on Who You Are." *Rhetoric Society Quarterly*, vol. 38, no. 2, 2008, pp. 123–47.

Deleuze, F., F. Guattari, R. Hurley, and M. Seem. *Anti-Oedipus: Capitalism and Schizophrenia.* Penguin, 2009.

Freud, S. *New Introductory Lectures on Psychoanalysis.* W. W. Norton, 1990.

Gunn, J. *Modern Occult Rhetoric: Mass Media and the Drama of Secrecy in the Twentieth Century.* U of Alabama P, 2005.

_____. "For the Love of Rhetoric, with Continual Reference to Kenny and Dolly." *Quarterly Journal of Speech*, vol. 94, 2008, pp. 131–55.

Hall, C. S. *A Primer of Freudian Psychology.* Mentor, 1954.

Johnson, K. A., and J. J. Asenas. "The Lacanian Real as a Productive Supplement to Rhetorical Critique." *Rhetoric Society Quarterly*, vol. 43, 2013, pp. 155–76.

Lacan, J. *Écrits.* Translated by A. Sheridan, W. W. Norton, 1977.

Lundbergh, C. *Lacan in Public: Psychoanalysis and the Science of Rhetoric.* U of Alabama P, 2012.

Nichols, B. *Ideology and the Image.* Indiana UP, 1981.

White, M. *Tele-Advising: Therapeutic Discourse in American Television.* U of North Carolina P, 1992.

Zizek, S. *The Essential Zizek: The Complete Set.* Verso, 2009.

_____. *How to Read Lacan.* W. W. Norton, 2007.

Visual Rhetorical Criticism

Atzmon, L. *Visual Rhetoric and the Eloquence of Design.* Parlor Press, 2011.

Benson, T. W. *Posters for Peace: A Reader in Communication and American Culture.* Penn State UP, 2015.

Brennan, T., and M. Jay, editors. *Vision in Context: Historical and Contemporary Perspectives on Sight.* Routledge, 1996.

Evans, J., and S. Hall, editors. *Visual Culture: The Reader.* Sage, 1999.

Finnegan, C. A. *Picturing Poverty: Print Culture and FSA Photographs.* Smithsonian, 2003.

Gries, L. *Still Life with Rhetoric: A New Materialist Approach for Visual Rhetorics.* Utah State UP, 2015.

Handa, C. *Visual Rhetoric in a Digital World: A Critical Sourcebook.* Bedford/St. Martin's, 2004.

Hariman, R., and J. L. Lucaites. *No Caption Needed: Icon Photography, Public Culture, and Liberal Democracy.* U of Chicago P, 2007.

Hartley, J. *The Politics of Pictures: The Creation of the Public in the Age of Popular Media.* Routledge, 1992.

Hill, C. A., and M. Helmers. *Defining Visual Rhetorics.* Routledge, 2004.

Kuhn, A. *The Power of the Image.* Routledge and Kegan Paul, 1985.

Olson, L. C., C. A. Finnegan, and D. S. Hope, editors. *Visual Rhetoric: A Reader in Communication and Visual Culture.* Sage, 2008.

Prelli, L. J. *Rhetorics of Display.* U of South Carolina P, 2006.

Rybczynski, W. *The Look of Architecture.* Oxford UP, 2001.

Dramatistic/Narrative Criticism

Aden, R. C. *Popular Stories and Promised Lands: Fan Cultures and Symbolic Pilgrimages.* U of Alabama P, 1999.

Biesecker, B. A. *Addressing Postmodernity: Kenneth Burke, Rhetoric, and a Theory of Social Change.* U of Alabama P, 1997.

Blakesley, D., editor. *The Terministic Screen: Rhetorical Perspectives on Film.* Southern Illinois UP, 2003.

Brown, R. H. *Society as Text: Essays on Rhetoric, Reason, and Reality.* U of Chicago P, 1987.

Brummett, B. "Burkean Scapegoating, Mortification, and Transcendence in Presidential Campaign Rhetoric." *Central States Speech Journal*, vol. 32, 1981, pp. 254–64.

_____. "Burkean Transcendence and Ultimate Terms in Rhetoric by and About James Watt." *Central States Speech Journal*, vol. 33, 1982, pp. 547–56.

_____. "Electric Literature as Equipment for Living: Haunted House Films." *Critical Studies in Mass Communication*, vol. 2, 1985, pp. 247–61.

_____. "Symbolic Form, Burkean Scapegoating, and Rhetorical Exigency in Alioto's Response to the 'Zebra' Murders." *Western Journal of Speech Communication*, vol. 44, 1980, pp. 64–73.

Burke, K. *Counter-statement*. Reprint, U of California P, 1968. Originally published in 1931.

_____. *The Rhetoric of Religion*. U of California P, 1961.

Campbell, K. K., and K. H. Jamieson. *Form and Genre: Shaping Rhetorical Action*. Speech Communication Association, 1978.

Cawelti, J. *The Six-Gun Mystique*. Popular Press, 1973.

Chesebro, J. W., editor. *Extensions of the Burkeian System*. Tuscaloosa: U of Alabama P, 1993.

Coupe, L. *Kenneth Burke: From Myth to Ecology*. Parlor Press, 2013.

Derrida, J. *Writing and Difference*. Translated by A. Bass, U of Chicago P, 1978.

Goffman, E. *Frame Analysis*. Harper Colophon, 1974.

_____. *Strategic Interaction*. Ballantine Books, 1972.

Hawhee, D. *Moving Bodies: Kenneth Burke on the Edges of Language*. U of South Carolina Press, 2012.

Rogin, M. P. *Ronald Reagan, the Movie: And Other Episodes in Political Demonology*. U of California P, 1987.

Warnick, B. "The Narrative Paradigm: Another Story." *Quarterly Journal of Speech*, vol. 73, 1987, pp. 172–82.

Wolin, R. *The Rhetorical Imagination of Kenneth Burke*. U of South Carolina P, 2001.

Worthen, W. B. *Drama: Between Poetry and Performance*. Wiley-Blackwell, 2010.

Media-Centered Criticism

Bennett, W. L. *News: The Politics of Illusion*. 2nd ed., Longman, 1988.

Blumler, J. G., and E. Katz, editors. *The Uses of Mass Communications: Current Perspectives on Gratifications Research*. Sage, 1975.

Braudy, L., and M. Cohen. *Film Theory and Criticism*. Oxford UP, 2009.

Brooks, C. G. *Lingua Fracta: Toward a Rhetoric of New Media*. Hampton Press, 2009.

Brummett, B. "The Homology Hypothesis: Pornography on the VCR." *Critical Studies in Mass Communication*, vol. 5, 1988, pp. 202–16.

Chesebro, J. W. "The Media Reality: Epistemological Functions of Media in Cultural Systems." *Critical Studies in Mass Communication*, vol. 1, 1984, pp. 111–30.

Gumpert, G., and R. Cathcart. *Inter/Media*. Oxford UP, 1982.

_____. "Media Grammars, Generations, and Media Gaps." *Critical Studies in Mass Communication*, vol. 2, 1985, pp. 23–35.

Handa, C. *The Multimediated Rhetoric of the Internet*. Routledge, 2013.

Hartley, J. *The Uses of Television*. Routledge, 1999.

Haynes, W. L. "Of That Which We Cannot Write: Some Notes on the Phenomenology of Media." *Quarterly Journal of Speech*, vol. 74, 1988, pp. 71–101.

Kaczmarcyk, L. C. *Computers and Sc Computing for Good*. CRC Press, 201

Levy, M. R. "VCR Use and the Concept of Audience Activity." *Communication Quarterly*, vol. 35, 1987, pp. 267–75.

Mander, J. *Four Arguments for the Elimination of Television*. William Morrow, 1978.

McGonigal, J. *Reality Is Broken: Why Games Make Us Better and How They Can Change the World*. Penguin, 2011.

McLuhan, M. *Understanding Media: The Extensions of Man*. McGraw-Hill, 1964.

Morley, D. *Understanding Computers in a Changing Society*. Cengage Learning, 2012.

Newcomb, H. *Television: The Critical View*. 3rd ed., Oxford UP, 1982.

O'Donnell, V. J. *Television Criticism*. 3rd ed., Sage, 2016.

Piccirillo, M. S. "On the Authenticity of Televisual Experience: A Critical Exploration of Para-social Closure." *Critical Studies in Mass Communication*, vol. 3, 1986, pp. 337–55.

Rosengren, K. E., L. A. Wenner, and P. Palmgreen, editors. *Media Gratifications Research*. Sage, 1985.

Slayden, D., and R. K. Whillock, editors. *Soundbite Culture: The Death of Discourse in a Wired World*. Sage, 1999.

Vande Berg, L., L. A. Wenner, and B. Gronbeck, editors. *Critical Approaches to Television*. Houghton Mifflin, 1998.

Warnick, B., and Heineman, D. S. *Rhetoric Online: The Politics of New Media*. 2nd ed., Peter Lang, 2012.

White, S. A., editor. *Participatory Video: Images That Transform and Empower*. Sage, 2003.

INDEX

Pages followed by e indicate exercises, t indicate tables, and f indicate images or figures

ABOUT THE AUTHOR

Barry Brummett is the Charles Sapp Centennial Professor in Communication and chair of the Department of Communication Studies at the University of Texas, Austin. He received his PhD from the University of Minnesota in 1978 and taught at Purdue University and the University of Wisconsin before coming to the University of Texas at Austin in 2001. Brummett has authored, coauthored, or edited numerous articles, scholarly essays, and books, including *Rhetoric of Style, Clockwork Rhetoric: The Language and Style of Steampunk, Contemporary Apocalyptic Rhetoric, Techniques of Close Reading, Rhetoric of Machine Aesthetics,* and *The Politics of Style and the Style of Politics.* His research pursuits include the rhetoric of popular culture, epistemology, and the theories of Kenneth Burke.